# People *of the* Wind River

# People *of the* Wind River

~

## *The Eastern Shoshones*
### 1825–1900

## Henry E. Stamm, IV

UNIVERSITY OF OKLAHOMA PRESS : NORMAN

Portions of this work were previously published in Henry E. Stamm, IV, "The Peace Policy Experiment at Wind River: The James Irwin Years, 1870–1877," *Montana The Magazine of Western History*, vol. 41 (1991), 56–69, and "Range Wars: Cowboys and Indians at Wind River, 1880–1890," *Journal of the West* (January 1999), and are used with permission.

Library of Congress Cataloging-in-Publication Data

Stamm, Henry E. (Henry Edwin), 1948–
    People of the Wind River : the Eastern Shoshones, 1825–1900 / Henry E. Stamm, IV.
        p.     cm.
    Includes bibliographical references and index.
    ISBN 0–8061–3175–6 (cloth  :  alk. paper)
    1. Shoshoni Indians—History.    2. Wind River Indian Reservation (Wyo.)—History.
I. Title.
E99.S4S73    1999
978.7'63—dc21                                                                                            99–33978
                                                                                                                    CIP

Text design by Gail Carter.

The paper in this book meets the guidelines for permanence and durability of the Committee on Production Guidelines for Book Longevity of the Council on Library Resources, Inc. ∞

# Contents

# Illustrations

## PHOTOGRAPHS

## MAPS

## CHARTS

## TABLES

# Preface

Friday, July 3, 1868, was a day like many others during that year in the western lands of the United States. Another new treaty was forged; this time at Fort Bridger, Utah Territory, between the United States and two American Indian tribes, the Bannocks and Eastern Shoshones. This document established the Shoshone and Bannock Indian Agency and reservation in the Wind River Basin in what would become west-central Wyoming, approximately 150 miles northeast of Fort Bridger.[1] In many respects, the Fort Bridger Treaty was unremarkable—it represented the ongoing efforts by the United States to protect white overland emigrants and future railroad routes from attacks by various American Indian tribes. It also contained language aimed at transforming Indian peoples into white-defined versions of upstanding citizens. Similar agreements were reached with other Indians throughout the late 1860s under the impetus of the United States Indian Peace Commission.[2]

The Shoshone negotiations did contain one notable characteristic. The reservation would impose federal structure and bureaucracy on a distinctive human community already in development in the valleys of the Big Wind River and its tributaries. The members of this community, American Indians and whites, frequently interacted with each other in friendly relationships based on marriage, trading partnerships, and military alliance against common enemies. Underneath this veneer of mutual goodwill, however, lay radically different understandings of the world.

In general terms, white residents and officials of Wind River Basin believed in the American system of government and economy, rooted in the Jeffersonian ideal of the yeoman republican farmer. They believed they had the right to occupy the lands and direct the lives of "less fortunate" human beings, such as foreigners, African-Americans, and American Indians. Land was at the center of the belief because it represented the basic resource for market-oriented farms and ranches or was the source of valuable minerals to fuel industrial expansion. At the very least, individual plots of ground were necessary to sustain individual families.[3]

Whites also carried with them a religious legacy that made little sense to their Indian neighbors. Received Christianity, regardless of denomination, contained an inescapable tension concerning an individual's spiritual status. Simply put, one could never be sure about God's mercy—eternal life was a faith assumption. Christian spiritual focus rested on a blessed afterlife. One might engage in a regimen of charity, good works, and righteous living as a response to God's presumed graciousness, but salvation was still available to the most flagrant scoundrels if they repented their "sinful" ways on their deathbed.[4]

By contrast, these white concepts of property and piety had no meaning for Shoshones or Bannocks. Their religious beliefs and practices were not separate components of existence, but permeated all aspects of living. Spiritual gifts benefited the band or even the whole tribe, enabling the people to harvest the animal and vegetable bounty of the land and defend themselves against enemies. The land and its resources represented collective sustenance, with no specific boundary markers owned by any one individual or family. Moreover, the economic cycles were grounded in spiritual beliefs. Thus spirituality had a physical reality; prayers and rituals had temporal consequences. Shoshones believed in an afterlife, but the white concepts of "heaven" and "hell" had no parallels in Shoshonean wisdom. For Shoshones and Bannocks, specific spiritual power or "medicine" was necessary to achieve success in hunting, warfare, trading, and in healing illnesses.

So the Wind River world, populated by the three human tribes—one white and two American Indian—contained different sets of assumptions and beliefs. For years these systems coexisted in wary tolerance despite white attempts to limit native autonomy. In 1885, however, in the aftermath of the great buffalo slaughter on the Plains, the Indians lost their means of economic independence. The death of the buffalo precipitated a radical shift in native religion and economy. The Indian peoples of Wind

River began a long period of poverty and population decline that transformed their spirituality. Meanwhile, white residents increased in both numbers and financial status.

For many historians, ethnologists, and anthropologists, especially those who have published works on Indian culture since the 1970s, the history of the Eastern Shoshones strikes familiar chords. Like the White Earth Anishinaabeg of Melissa L. Meyer's *White Earth Tragedy,* Eastern Shoshones represented the coming together of a number of different bands within one reservation complex. Moreover, the Shoshones and Anishinaabeg maintained long-standing subsistence patterns well after establishment of their respective reservations. Both peoples practiced ancestral religious beliefs regardless of the presence of Episcopal and Catholic missionaries; in the case of the Shoshones, conversions or surface adaptations to Christianity were much less in evidence. Both the Anishinaabeg and Shoshones faced severe challenges from off-reservation industries: timber companies in the case of Anishinaabeg; cattle and sheep ranching at Wind River. In essence, the Anishinaabeg and Shoshones exhibited remarkable similarities as multicultural communities in contact.[5]

Parallels can also be drawn to Richard White's groundbreaking assessment of environmental and subsistence alterations among Choctaws, Pawnees, and Navajos after contact with Euroamericans. White suggests that, although each of these three peoples followed different paths to economic dependency, the link between environmental disruption, subsistence economies, and global markets cannot be ignored. Where Choctaws hunted deer and cultivated corn for their living, Pawnees pursued buffalo and planted corn, and Navajos herded goats, sheep, and horses and practiced small-scale horticulture. These Indian groups demonstrated apt incorporation of trade with emigrants, farmers, and merchants into their subsistence rounds. Yet, long-term contact with whites eventually disrupted the balance of the subsistence cycles. In each case, market forces overwhelmed subsistence practices. To some extent, the remoteness of Shoshone country protected that tribe's reliance on buffalo hunting and gathering wild herbs and berries. The persistence of buffalo in the Wind River, Powder River, and Big Horn River Basins, in fact, granted Shoshones an extension of their buffalo-based economy a decade longer than other Plains peoples. Nevertheless, even Shoshonean economic stability succumbed to the Wyoming stock industry. In the face of economic decline, many Shoshones did not necessarily equate such incursions by outside forces with loss of culture or with dependency. Loretta Fowler discovered similar imperturbability among the Gros Ventres and Assiniboine people of Fort Belknap Reservation in Montana, as well as in her study of Northern Arapahoes.[6]

Part of the resiliency of Shoshones and other Indian tribes lay in the strength of their leaders, who sometimes fought with whites, but more often served as cultural brokers and mediators of the needs of their people. As shown by Fowler, Catherine Price (*The Oglala People, 1841–1879*), and Thomas Kavanagh (*Comanche Political History*), head-men of the Northern Arapahoes, Oglala Sioux, and Comanches were cultural brokers more often than war leaders. So it was with Eastern Shoshone band headmen who trod the thin line between representing the consensus of their people and placating U.S. officialdom. Adaptation to reservation life took place within Shoshone cultural norms, even as those very norms underwent transformation in response to changing environmental and economic circumstances. Moreover, the Wind River metamorphosis uncannily resembles the world of the Northern Utes described in David Rich Lewis's *Neither Wolf nor Dog*. At Uintah Reservation, Utes tried to combine hunting with farming, a familiar pattern that characterized Wind River Shoshones.[7] Shoshones added one more dimension to the hunter-farmer dichotomy, however, by scouting for the U.S. Army.

This work goes beyond recognizing the similarities to other historical and ethnographic works. First and foremost, I aim to tell the story of the peopling of the Wind River. The beginning and ending dates are arbitrary. The year 1825 marks the start of a permanent white presence in Shoshone country and the death of Chief Washakie in 1900 provides a symbolic as well as actual break with the nineteenth century. However, any number of beginning or ending dates could do. Lewis and Clark's contact with Northern Shoshones in 1805 comes to mind, as does the dawning of Washakie's role as head chief of the Shoshones, in whites' eyes, in 1851. The two Fort Bridger treaties, in 1863 and 1868, nicely serve as other points of departure. The 1872 Brunot cession was the first reduction of the size of the Wind River reserve. The Northern Arapahoes entered the picture in 1878; the last buffalo hunt occurred in 1885; in 1896, the government purchased the Hot Springs. Permanent allotments under the terms of the Dawes Act of 1887 were parceled out after 1906, when half the reservation was opened to non-Indians. Other significant events or dates offer interpretative possibilities far into the twentieth century.

I chose, instead, to focus on a narrower period. The heart of discussion follows the few brief years from 1868 to 1885—the years of Shoshonean strength before it became utterly clear which vision for Wind River would prevail. I seek, moreover, no overarching theme and follow no specific mode of analytical inquiry. Instead, I try to narrate the intricacies of the Wind River community from its origins to 1900. This entails conveying some sense of what it meant to be Shoshone before the reservation years. I also point to the reasons for transformations in the settled post-buffalo years. Yet, the primary story lies in the microscopic view of seventeen years. It affords more detailed observations of the interactions among the various members of the Wind River community. The minutiae of day-to-day living illustrates the degree to which Shoshones shaped their experience in myriad ways and maintained their sense of identity in the face of unrelenting attempts to alter their existence.

The Introduction traces Shoshone ethnography and history from their origins in the Great Basin to their resurgence on the Wyoming plains in 1825. Shoshones owned the primary historical claim to Wind River, dating to approximately 1500. In the mid-1700s through the early 1800s, other Indian peoples, including Arapahoes, Blackfeet, Cheyennes, Crows, and Lakotas, challenged their dominance. By the early 1800s, white tribes— explorers and fur trappers—also invaded the area. The appearance of these white newcomers coincided with a renewal of Shoshone spiritual and economic life and greater military vitality.

Part One tells the story of the movement of peoples in, through, and to the Wind River region. Chapter One examines the Shoshone expansion and increased interaction with Mormons, merchants, farmers, ranchers, and government officials. This chapter also chronicles the rise to leadership of Washakie, to whom whites ascribed the role of head chief from 1851 until his death in 1900. It concludes with the signing of the first Shoshone treaty in 1863, which established "Shoshone country" in the Basin areas of Idaho and western Wyoming, but ignored Eastern Shoshone claims on Wind River.

Chapter Two, which covers 1863 to 1870, follows the transitional movements of both whites and the Eastern Shoshones toward the Wind River region and relates the creation of the Shoshone and Bannock Indian Agency in 1868. During this period, Fort Bridger housed the agency headquarters and few Shoshones made any permanent attempt to occupy their reservation at Wind River. Still, a heterogeneous mixture of individuals and groups competed and cooperated for the lands and resources of the reservation area.

By 1871, however, the agency buildings were on-site and the trials of the first administration were underway. Chapter Three considers the changes in the community as a result of the implementation of the reservation and the Peace Policy system. This period brought early conflicts between the Indian agent and local whites, ongoing intertribal warfare on the Plains, and a decided resistance by Shoshones to white attempts at assimilation. Chapter Four considers this same time period, 1871 to 1873, from a native perspective. Specifically, it examines the intertribal relations between the Eastern Shoshones and the Bannocks and the 1872 removal of the latter to Fort Hall. Furthermore, the chapter discusses the Brunot Treaty agreement of 1872, the first major territorial cession made from Wind River lands.

Part Two discusses agency and reservation history from 1872 to 1885. It opens with Chapter Five, which examines white attempts to "civilize" Shoshones—that is, to make them into farmers—and analyzes Shoshonean economy from 1871 to 1877. Chapter Six covers two disparate topics: the early missionary and educational policies mandated under the Peace Policy, and the migration of Northern Arapahoes to the reservation in 1878. The Arapahoes and Shoshones were historical enemies, so this stressful addition to the Wind River community signaled a major realignment in the future human relations of the area.

The two concluding chapters of Part Two detail the activities and policies of Wind River Indian agents between 1877 and 1885. Incompetence, malfeasance, and bureaucratic bumbling by agents and employees marked the Shoshone Agency during this time. All of this ineptness corresponded to the federal government's reduction of support for its Indian "wards." The combination of local and national policies, therefore, adversely affected native inhabitants of the reservation.

Part Three, which contains Chapters Nine, Ten, and Eleven, diverges from the strict chronology of the first eight chapters and takes a topical approach to the period from 1878 to 1885. Chapter Nine delves into the transformations that occurred beyond the reservation boundaries. The continuing expansion of white settlers into the region, the formation of Fremont County and the town of Lander, and the rise of the cattle industry in the Wind River region severely circumscribed the ability of Shoshones and Arapahoes to maintain traditional subsistence patterns.

Chapter Ten covers the first well-organized religious and educational thrusts of Mormons, Episcopalians, and Roman Catholics into the heart of native culture. Chapter Eleven concentrates on the relationships between the Arapahoes and the Shoshones and on their general responses to increasing white encroachments on their autonomy. Separate tribal goals often thwarted native consensus and weakened their efforts to remain independent in the face of agency corruption.

Finally, the Epilogue traces the economic and spiritual transformations of the Shoshones in the years after the extinction of the buffalo. This was a time of upheaval and alienation in all areas of native life. Wind River native peoples, weakened by hunger and poverty, suffered wave after wave of influenza epidemics. The reservation became a vast holding area for tremendous herds of white-owned cattle. The federal government accelerated the process of forced acculturation by using the Wind River Boarding School to divorce its students from their native traditions. By the time of Washakie's death, the Shoshones' traditional economic and political life was in disarray, and their tribal spiritual underpinnings were still evolving to meet the new, twentieth-century demands of a rapidly changing world.

This work began as a seminar paper nine years ago under the direction of Colin Calloway. I thank him for all the years of encouragement, guidance, and examples of good writing. I also extend thanks to Linda Marston for her map-making skills. To my friends at the Wind River Reservation, thank you for the many of hours of patiently leading me through family genealogies, for revealing meanings of ceremonies, and above all, for your friendship and trust in my work. Mark Agnew deserves credit for reading through some of the revisions of the early chapters and helping me to clarify my thoughts. To my wife, Beth Hudnall Stamm, I owe the credit for making sure I stayed on task and finished what I set out to do, for allowing me long absences from home for research trips, and providing the love, support, and a goodly portion of the spirit so necessary to make a book like this come to life.

# People *of the* Wind River

# Introduction

## *Shoshone History To 1825*

Many anthropologists, ethnologists, and historians—including Robert Lowie, Demitri B. Shimkin, Åke Hultkrantz, and Robert and Yolanda Murphy—have attempted explanations of Shoshone origins. According to most of these writers, Shoshonean-speaking peoples originally inhabited the southwestern Nevada region of the Great Basin.[1] Over the course of several millennia, these groups migrated northward and northeastward throughout the Basin. No consensus exists about the precise dates of Basin occupation and expansion, but at least one researcher, Richard Holmer, claims that Shoshone people lived in the upper Snake River Valley near present-day Fort Hall, Idaho, as early as 3500 B.P. His reading of the archaeological evidence suggests that clusters of family bands hunted deer, antelope, and buffalo; fished for salmon and trout in the Snake River and its tributaries; and supplemented their diet with seasonal wild vegetables, herbs, and nuts.[2] Another archeologist, Julie E. Francis, believes that as early as two thousand years ago Shoshonean people migrated even farther eastward and crossed the Wind River Mountains, inscribing rock art near the Dinwoody Lakes in Wyoming as their legacy.[3]

Despite this evidence of long-term residency and movement to the periphery of the Great Plains, the transformation of these ancient Shoshonean peoples into the Eastern Shoshones of the late nineteenth century required massive demographic shifts. Climates and ecosystems, as well as knowledge, ceremonies, and language changed over time and contributed to ongoing cultural renewal. European-borne epidemics also stimulated tribal changes. Thus, the process of becoming "Eastern Shoshones" involved extensive relocations and transformations over several centuries.

## SHOSHONE ORIGINS TO 1800

The first steps toward Eastern Shoshone identity began in A.D. 1350 when climatological changes inaugurated Plains-based economies. The "Little Ice Age" brought lingering drought conditions to the Great Basin and areas of increased precipitation in the Great Plains, augmenting shifts in animal populations. For the next two centuries, herds of large game decreased in the Basin and Columbia River Plateau while those in the Plains flourished. Beginning circa A.D. 1500, significant numbers of Shoshone people followed the game to the western reaches of the Plains. Perhaps as early as A.D. 1600, some bands, generally referred to as Shoshones or Snakes, headed in a northeastward direction. Others, who became known as the Comanches, traveled southeast.

During their early occupation of the Plains, the Shoshone-Comanche groups organized themselves into four integrated social systems that reflected both their Basin origins and the demands of the Plains ecosystem. In practical terms, their spiritual beliefs, economic activities, and band social structure all followed from this dual heritage. The two smallest groups, the nuclear family and the extended family bands, exemplified the typical social organization of Basin Shoshones that depended on individual or family pursuits such as elk hunting in the mountains or gathering wild vegetables. The other two groups, local residential bands and political divisions, included larger populations that required corporate, collective, massed tribal action (as in buffalo hunts). Local bands comprised several family bands, and political divisions combined one or more local bands.[4]

The nuclear family represented the smallest unit, but more commonly, nuclear families joined with their closest relations (representing two to four generations) to operate in extended family bands.[5] The members of a family band, working together, gathered herbs and grass seeds and hunted small game animals or larger ones such as elk and moose, whose grazing patterns were better suited to individual than to organized hunters. Shoshone-Comanche children learned about themselves and their community within the context of these nuclear families and family bands.

Storytellers evoked images of mythological heroes like Coyote and Wolf in folk tales and legends, and explained the realities of the Shoshone-Comanche cosmology.[6]

At the next level, groups of family bands (often but not necessarily related) typically traveled together under the leadership of a headman. The local bands formed the primary buffalo-hunting organization and provided the main defensive or offensive unit against Plains enemies. The largest social organization, the political division, consisted of one or more of the local bands. European observers frequently confused local bands and divisions; they sometimes accorded band names and leadership to what surely were large divisional gatherings. Political divisions came together infrequently and perhaps only for large-scale buffalo hunts, warfare, or annual collective ceremonies.[7]

The men who led the local bands and the divisions possessed *puha*, or "medicine" power. According to Hultkrantz, Lowie, and other ethnologists, puha enabled individuals to achieve military or economic success and probably represented an older, Basin-oriented religion.[8] Kavanagh points out that "the conjunction of medicine power and war honors created the authority to influence the direction of social and political actions."[9] Whatever gifts of power a person might obtain were used for the benefit of the family, band, or collective tribe. The exercise of power in war, hunting, or healing contributed to the overall welfare and health of the larger community, not just the one endowed with puha.[10]

Puha acquisition generally required individual effort. Hultkrantz notes that "except for certain great medicine men especially chosen by the spirits, all who desire puha must themselves seek the spirits."[11] This distinction, between actively seeking spiritual power or simply being chosen or identified, demonstrates the Basin/Plains duality. Basin Shoshones often received puha via dreams, which did not require special preparations, while Plains peoples used vision quests. However, the distinction between passive versus active acquisition of power vastly overstates the reality. Unbidden and unsought visions certainly informed the lives of Plains peoples and a vision quest was not the only protocol for puha acquisition. Yet for an intentional seeker of puha among the Plains Shoshones, enduring a quest ordeal at the rock art sites of ancestors in the Wind River Mountains was perhaps a more normative route. By fasting and prayer, the individual seeker might receive the gifts of a particular spirit (*puhagan*, or power-giver), often delivered through dreams or trancelike consciousness. The spirit(s) also instructed the recipients in the nourishment of the puha, as well as in the construction of "medicine bundles" and the uses of the puha. Not every seeker won spiritual power; some men failed the endurance part of the quest, while in other cases the puhagan proved elusive.[12]

Armed with puha, the local band and division leaders directed their people to follow the immense herds of buffalo on the Great Plains. Between 1500 and 1700, the Shoshone-Comanche bands and divisions became a powerful presence. Sometime during the latter part of this era, the two peoples gradually separated into distinctive northern and southern communities. The exact date and the nature of this process remains unknown, but acquisition of horses probably accelerated the split. Horses were taken in raids, beginning in the 1690s, when allied Ute and Comanche forces raided Spanish and Pueblo settlements in New Mexico. Two political divisions, the Yamparikas (Root-Eaters, or Yampa Root Eaters) and the Kotsoteka or Kutsindüka (Buffalo-Eaters), became identified with both Comanches and Shoshones. Spanish observers in the 1700s noted that the Yamparikas were the most northerly of the Comanche peoples (occupying the plains of present-day northern Colorado), while American fur trappers in the early 1800s gave the same name to a Shoshone (or Snake) band in present-day southern Wyoming.[13] Evidently, the Yamparika connection funneled horses from the Spanish settlements to the northern Rockies and perhaps acted as the mediator between the northern Plains Shoshones and southern Plains Comanches.

Horse ownership gave the Shoshones and Comanches of the early eighteenth century a clear advantage over other Plains tribes. Obviously, horses enhanced the pursuit of migratory buffalo herds that became the primary socioeconomic activity of their lives. In short, the Shoshone-Comanche Indians were among the earliest nomadic, mounted, buffalo-hunting Plains peoples. Moreover, since Shoshone-Comanches did not adopt seasonal farming like their rivals the Apaches, Caddos, Crees, and Pawnees, they increasingly used their mounts in warfare to limit access to the buffalo herds by these tribes. In fact, as their horse herds increased, Shoshones and Comanches extended their hunting on the western Plains from the Saskatchewan River in Canada to the Red River along the Oklahoma-Texas border and to Taos and Santa Fe in New Mexico between 1720 and 1750. In a goodly portion of this vast territory, they perhaps were the dominant peoples.[14]

However, they were not the only Indians competing for the resources of the northern Plains. During the same period that Shoshone-Comanche bands migrated eastward to the Plains, Mountain Crow Indians split from their upper Missouri River origins among the Hidatsas and moved westward to the Big Horn and Absaroka Mountains along the Montana and Wyoming border.[15] Farther west, Flatheads, Nez Perces, and Cayuses occupied the game-rich lands of western Montana and northern Idaho, but also made occasional hunting forays into the Plains. All of these groups, including the Shoshones, may have had tense relationships with one another, but they all had one common enemy in the Blackfeet. The Blackfeet, a northern Plains people whose hunting territory extended well into Canada, ended the horse-based superiority of the northernmost Plains Shoshone bands. About 1750, the Blackfeet gained both horses and fire-arms, the latter from Cree and Assiniboine Indians by way of the Hudson Bay fur trade. The Shoshones, still without guns, were driven by the Blackfeet from the Canadian and Montana plains. A smallpox epidemic in 1781 and another in 1800 further reduced Shoshonean tribal populations and power.[16]

In the south, Spanish soldiers, who possessed guns in abundance, eventually forced Comanches to peace negotiations in 1785. Unlike their northern cousins, the Comanches actually benefited from the geo-political realignments in the south. A twenty-year period of relatively stable relations between the Spanish and the Comanches in New Mexico led to fruitful trading partnerships, which enabled Comanches to maintain their hegemony over other southern Plains Indians far into the 1800s.[17]

No such peace came to the Shoshones: well-armed Blackfeet raiders made numerous forays west of the Rockies against their Shoshone foes. The Shoshones' retreat from the Plains between 1750 and 1780 probably decreased the frequency of their interactions with the Comanches.[18] The smallpox outbreak in 1781 thus deepened the woes of people who in one generation could remember their conquest of the northern Plains. In fact, by 1806 their presence east of the Big Horns was represented by hunting parties or solitary traders, not by permanent occupation.[19]

## EASTERN SHOSHONES, CIRCA 1800

The creation of the Eastern Shoshones as a distinct political division or tribe took place against the backdrop of a rapidly evolving geopolitical landscape. The Mountain Crows lived in the Yellowstone, Absaroka, and Big Horn regions of Montana and claimed control of the eastern slopes of the Big Horn Mountains. At the same time, they contested the Shoshones for hunting rights in the Big Horn Basin of northern Wyoming. Nez Perce and Cayuse tribes, who lived in the border areas of the Basin and the Columbia Plateau, engaged in occasional warfare against the Shoshones and impeded their movements to the northwest. On the north-central plains of Wyoming, Montana, and the Dakotas, enemies such as the Arapahoes, Teton Sioux, and Cheyennes gained power and strength, raiding as far as the Green River Valley (just west of the Wind River range). The net result of these encroachments was that at the time of Lewis and Clark's historic contact with "Snake" Indians in 1805, most of the Plains-oriented, horse-owning, buffalo-hunting Shoshones lived on the western slopes of the Rockies in Montana, Wyoming, Idaho, and Utah.[20] The only nominal allies of the Shoshones to the north were the Flatheads of western Montana. Flatheads may have once fought with Shoshones in the 1700s, but apparently they entered trading alliances and marriage partnerships with their southern neighbors around the turn of the nineteenth century. For example, the famous Shoshone leader, Washakie, had a Flathead father, and another Flathead, the long-lived John Enos, eventually dwelt with the Shoshones.

The decline of the Shoshone empire in the eighteenth century makes identification of specific tribal divisions and their zones of occupation difficult. However, the Shoshones encountered by Lewis and Clark lived at the northern end of Shoshone country and probably came from the Agaidüka, or Salmon-Eaters division. They generally resided in large villages in the Lemhi River Valley, a major tributary of the Salmon River in present-day north-central Idaho. Although they still sought buffalo, by 1800 their primary diet depended on salmon. The two Americans reported that the Agaidüka name for themselves was Cho-sho-né, which offers one origin for the Shoshone name.[21] Another group, known as the Tukudüka or Sheep-Eaters, lived in smaller villages in the Sawtooth and Bitterroot Mountains and as far east as Yellowstone. Although the Sheep-Eaters were

Shoshone-speaking people, they may have preceded the general Shoshone-Comanche movement from the Basin by a millennium or more. Archaeological evidence suggests they had adapted to the mountains for several thousand years and were not part of the main eastward migration in the A.D. 1500–1700 period.[22] Eventually both of these Northern Shoshone divisions became known by whites as Lemhi Shoshones.[23]

The core group of Eastern Shoshones stemmed from people called the Kutsindüka (Buffalo-Eaters) by other Shoshone groups. Like the Salmon-Eaters and Sheep-Eaters, the Buffalo-Eaters were generally referred to as Snakes by the first American explorers in the Rocky Mountain region. In fact, the generic term *Snake* was applied to all Shoshones in the early nineteenth century. The Buffalo-Eaters also acquired other names—Plains Shoshones, Washakie Shoshones, Wind River Shoshones—but these sobriquets came from mid-nineteenth-century white observers, as did the title of Eastern Shoshone. In the 1790s they lived along the eastern edges of the Basin. Their territory spanned the corridor of the upper Green River Valley of western Wyoming and extended southwestward to Bear Lake and Salt Lake (presently southeastern Idaho and northern Utah). Of all Shoshone divisions, the Buffalo-Eaters possessed the largest horse herds and represented the direct descendants of the earlier rulers of the northern Plains. They continually battled old enemies like the Blackfeet and new foes from the east and northeast like Arapahoes, Cheyennes, Gros Ventres, and Sioux for the rich buffalo grounds of present-day Wyoming and Montana. Despite their retreat from year-round occupancy of the Plains, they retained Plains-style social structure—most European observers described large local bands under the leadership of dominant chiefs or headmen.[24]

Other local and family bands, drawn from the mixed Bannock and Shoshone groups of the Fort Hall region of Idaho and the Northwestern Shoshones of Utah and southern Idaho, frequently joined the Buffalo-Eaters on Plains journeys. Comanche and Shoshone Yamparika bands formed part of this eastern contingent. The people who eventually inhabited the Wind River reservation counted members of each of these branches and included Salmon-Eaters, Sheep-Eaters, Bannocks, Paiutes, and Western Shoshones.[25]

The people who became Eastern Shoshones thus comprised an amalgamation of numerous cultural backgrounds that spanned the breadth of

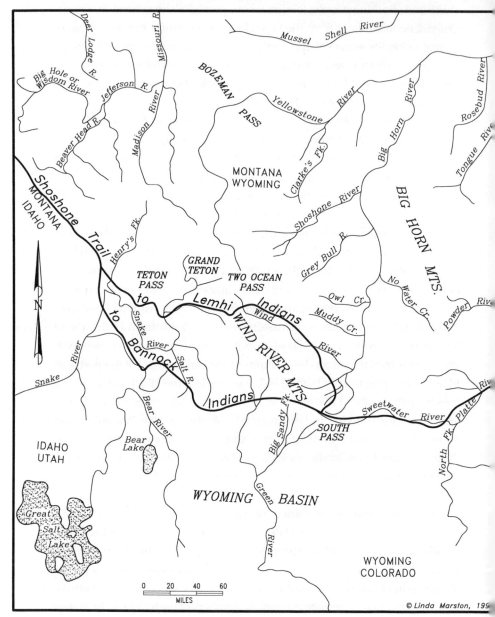

Map 1. Shoshone Country, 1750–1825

Shoshonean traditions, yet coalesced around the Plains-oriented buffalo-hunting legacy of the Plains Shoshone–Comanche traditions. As committed buffalo hunters throughout the ebb and flow of their collective tribal history, they nevertheless understood life in terms of both Basin and Plains structures. Moreover, the tremendous upheavals in the Shoshone world between 1780 and 1840 forced adaptations in many aspects of cultural knowledge. Nothing demonstrates this more clearly than the story of Ohamagwaya, or Yellow Hand, who brought the Sun Dance to the Shoshones.

## OHAMAGWAYA, THE SUN DANCE, AND EASTERN SHOSHONE IDENTITY

According to various Shoshone oral histories, the Shoshone Sun Dance originated in the early 1800s through a vision given to Ohamagwaya, or Yellow Hand.[26] The unifying theme of these stories is that a dream visitor told Yellow Hand to arrange willow poles around a centrally placed forked cottonwood pole, which was adorned with a buffalo skull and an eagle. The center pole represented Tam Apö (Father Sun, or the supreme deity); the surrounding poles, his helpers. The dance itself, "the dry-standing dance," lasted three days and nights during which the participants fasted and abstained from water. Ohamagwaya's dream visitor (an old man, or a white man, or a white-haired man, or a buffalo, depending on the source of the tradition) told him that the prayers of the faithful and the visions given to the dancers would ensure long life, good luck, success in war, and healing for both the whole community and individuals.[27]

The Shoshone Sun Dance, as well as Ohamagwaya's own story, unfolded during the critical transitions between 1780 and 1840 and at least two generations after the split between Plains Shoshones and Comanches. During this time Plains Shoshones fell back from Blackfeet attacks, suffered terribly during the smallpox epidemic of 1781, and gradually regained their strength after 1820, when American fur trappers traded them guns for buffalo robes and beaver pelts. In many ways, the transformation of Plains Shoshones into Eastern Shoshones begins with Ohamagwaya. He is the first human culture hero of the people and is honored for his role in the Sun Dance. Indeed, contemporary Sun Dance leaders still trace their lineage (familial or spiritual) through Ohamagwaya.

Ohamagwaya (Oxamaguea or Ohamaquea in Spanish) was born circa 1760–65. His father, Ecueracapa, was a Kotsotecka (Buffalo-Eater in the Comanche language) Comanche leader. In February 1786, Ecueracapa began peace negotiations with Spanish officials, with final revisions made in July. Ohamagwaya attended some of these meetings and was chosen, along with several other Comanche representatives, to accompany the Spanish emissaries taking the signed agreement to Mexico. Later, he led a joint Comanche-Spanish war party against Apache villages. Despite his growing leadership abilities as evidenced by his emissary and raiding party experiences, he did not inherit the leadership of his band. When his father suffered a fatal wound in 1793 during an attack on the Pawnees, the Spanish learned that another man, Encanguane, was elected the new "general" of the Kotsotekas. In fact, Spanish records do not show anything concerning Ohamagwaya after 1787.[28]

Ohamagwaya remained hidden from white sources for nearly thirty years. He surfaced following a protracted period of both peace and turbulence in the southern Plains. During these years, 1786 to 1820, Comanche fortunes rose tremendously, but warfare also escalated as some Comanche bands engaged Pawnees, Osages, Arapahoes, Kiowas, Cheyennes, and Navajos. Just as significantly, other Comanche bands sought more peaceful coexistence with their Plains neighbors. The anthropologist Thomas Kavanagh estimates that beginning as early as 1790, but more likely in 1806, Kiowas and Comanches gradually set aside their differences. One result of their interactions was Comanche assimilation of several Kiowa ceremonies, perhaps including the Kiowa Sun Dance. The Comanche word for Sun Dance, for example, is an adaptation of the Kiowa word for the same ceremony.[29] In addition to warfare and religious innovation, other transformational processes swept across the Plains. Disease, primarily smallpox, marched through many different tribes, with outbreaks noted in 1800–1801 and in 1816. At some point during this turbulent time, Ohamagwaya shifted his geographical locale northward and spoke his vision to the Shoshones.

American fur traders recorded his movements, although a variety of phonetic renderings of his name makes clear identification tenuous. For example, between 1818 and 1819 trapper Andrew Ross tried to quell tensions among several Shoshone factions in Idaho. He noted that two chiefs, the brothers Amaquiem (a possible phonetic version of Ohamagwaya) and Pee-eye-em, led a large contingent of mounted buffalo-hunting Snakes. Their presence intimidated the other Shoshone bands. A few years later, in 1825, James Beckwourth observed the wonders of an old Shoshone prophet-chief named Omogua (Ohamagwaya), who could reveal the future and bring hidden things to light. In Shoshone terms, Omogua clearly exercised power and influence derived from "medicine," or puha, which attests to the authority one would expect from a visionary leader. Ross's depictions of the two leaders in Idaho also indicate their possession of puha—in that other local band leaders acquiesced to their commands. Both Ross and Beckwourth described the Snake leaders as middle-aged or older, which certainly could apply to an individual born in the 1760s.

Much clearer linkages between Ohamagwaya and the Sun Dance emerge in Shoshone oral history. In tribal accounts, Ohamagwaya receives credit for giving the first Shoshone Sun Dance. Washakie, the primary intermediary and leader of the Eastern Shoshones between 1850 and 1900, and the informants for Shimkin and Hultkrantz in the 1930s and 1960s all ascribe the Shoshone Sun Dance traditions to Ohamagwaya's vision. Washakie may have had contact with Ohamagwaya. He told Captain Patrick Henry Ray (during an interview in the 1890s) that Ohamagwaya was the "chief medicine man" who introduced the Sun Dance and led a band of Shoshones along the Bear, Snake, and Green Rivers. According to Washakie, Ohamagwaya and most of his followers died from smallpox, but the dates of their deaths are unknown. They possibly occurred during the late 1820s or in the 1837 pandemic. By the early 1840s, two other leaders headed the Eastern Shoshones.[30]

Although the facts of Ohamagwaya's life rest on fragmentary reports by whites and the sometimes conflicting accounts in Shoshone oral testimonies, certain truths nevertheless stand out. First, Ohamagwaya migrated from his Comanche homelands. What follows is conjecture, but offers a feasible path that Ohamagwaya may have taken into Shoshone country. From 1750 until well into the 1800s, Blackfeet, Arapahoe, and Cheyenne peoples attacked Shoshone bands to gain horses and human captives for exchange in the burgeoning trade on the northern Plains. Shoshones still acquired many of their ponies through their Comanche contacts, most probably the Yamparika bands. One can easily imagine that Ohamagwaya, after successfully leading Kotsotecka war parties against Apaches and taking part in diplomatic missions to Mexico, left his family band to join Yamparikas heading to Shoshone country on a horse-trading venture. To speculate still further: he may have won war honors during some long-forgotten encounter with Blackfeet raiders. Perhaps puha enabled him to heal sicknesses, or as Beckwourth noted, to make known things that were hidden or to dream the future. His contemporaries, both white and Indian, clearly saw Ohamagwaya/Amaquiem/Omogua as an extraordinary individual with powerful and special gifts.

Shoshones revere him as the originator of the Sun Dance. More importantly, the adoption of this ceremony by the buffalo-hunting Shoshone bands corresponded with the renewal of their strength and the formation of the Shoshone political division that evolved into the Eastern Shoshones. It is important to understand what the Sun Dance meant in the social and religious orientation of the people, and particularly, in relationship to puha.

In both Basin and Plains traditions, either dreams or visions (those that came unbidden or those actively sought in vision quests) can impart puha to individual healers, hunters, or warriors.[31] Ohamagwaya's life demonstrates the reception of this kind of power. Even more importantly, however, his vision gave an entirely new ceremony to the people, one that reoriented their understanding of their cosmology and their temporal place in the world. The Sun Dance provided the spiritual link between the world of Plains buffalo hunters and that of Basin dwellers who celebrated Tam Apö as the supreme deity. In Basin thought, Tam Apö resided in the sun. It was the Sun Dance, however, the quintessential ceremony of the Plains, that unleashed the puha of Tam Apö. Furthermore, puha from Tam Apö not only blessed or empowered individuals with Basin-style "medicine," but also insured the very existence of the tribe or band, which is a Plains-oriented concept. As Hultkrantz writes: "The Sun Dance presupposes tribal organization and a camp circle. It also fulfills extremely important religious needs in an extensive, militarily organized group of buffalo hunters, since it guarantees the existence of the tribe, its solidarity, its ability to resist enemies, its supply of food. Now, the main emphasis was placed on the collective unit and not on the individual."[32]

The ceremony usually took place annually during the summer, frequently in June, before the tribe split into its component bands. This was not a rule set in stone. Sometimes the location was in the Wind River Valley, at other times in the Green River region near present-day Fontenelle

Reservoir. There are also some indications the event may have occurred during the winter, not the summer. Furthermore, the dance did not take place every year. For instance, in the mid-1850s the whole tribe congregated in August in the Deer Lodge Valley of Montana. Elija Wilson, a white boy who lived several years with the Eastern Shoshones, observed what surely must have been the peripheral warriors' dances, gambling, and horseracing that generally characterized the Sun Dance gathering of the Shoshone bands. Wilson stated that this grand assembly took place every three years.[33]

Whatever the frequency, season, or site of its practice, the Sun Dance innovation occurred shortly before the arrival of American mountain men. These newcomers, unlike other Plains Indian invaders, were welcomed in Shoshone camps. Although the Shoshones had bartered for European trade goods for over a century through the Comanches, the tribe participated in such trade second-hand. Few Shoshones made direct contacts with white traders between 1700 and 1820 because very few whites, if any, penetrated the Rocky Mountains before 1800. And, despite advances well into the Plains during the middle part of the 1700s, most Shoshones did not travel far enough east to make direct contact with the trading centers established by British, French, and Spanish companies. The northern fur trade in the 1700s, for example, concentrated on the Mandan and Hidatsa villages of the upper Missouri River, where traders from the British North West Company and Hudson's Bay Company descended southward from the Canadian prairies. French and Spanish traders rarely ventured from their posts along the lower Missouri or from Santa Fe.[34] Lewis and Clark's explorations of the early 1800s, however, enticed a flow of adventurers into the Indian trade. Still, regular interactions between Shoshones and the trappers and fur traders did not begin until 1825. Then, from 1825 to 1840, the "rendezvous" system of collecting furs and exchanging trade items rapidly enveloped the Shoshones and exposed them first-hand to white customs, culture, and religion.

This direct access to guns, ammunition, woolens, flour, glass beads, and metal goods rejuvenated the Shoshones and helped them once more achieve parity in warfare and buffalo hunting on the Plains.[35] Thus the aftermath of Ohamagwaya's vision provided an efficacious and creative solution—in the arrival of white friends with desperately needed weapons—to the social disruptions in Shoshone lives caused by disease and the advance of Arapahoes, Blackfeet, Cheyennes, and Crows. As noted by Howard L. Harrod, a scholar of Plains Indian spirituality, this religious transformation "played an essential role in determining the direction and shape of social change. If individual and social identity was threatened, religious experiences and practices were central to any social reconstruction."[36] Following the adoption of the Sun Dance, the buffalo-hunting Shoshone bands reformed themselves into the Eastern Shoshones, a political division that increasingly found its future influenced by the machinations of the Americans. For the remainder of the century, the power of visions and the puha granted by Tam Apö through the Sun Dance led the Eastern Shoshones on a course that ultimately returned them, permanently, to the lands of the Wind River Basin.

# PART ONE

~

# *Claiming Wind River*

## 1825–1873

*Chapter One*

# Shoshone Country

## 1825–1863

## SHOSHONE AND WHITE INTERACTIONS, 1825–1840

The influx of American fur trappers into the heart of Eastern Shoshone country began as a trickle during the late 1810s, but increased to a steady stream by the mid-1820s. Although worldwide demand for beaver pelts sparked these initial explorations, their success depended on establishing amicable relationships with the Indians. Eastern Shoshone band leaders welcomed the newcomers and the potential for trade for European goods, especially guns and ammunition. This resulted in two distinct cultural adaptations by the Shoshones. First, Shoshonean desires for white-produced goods gradually enmeshed the tribe in European-style market economies between 1825 and 1840. Second, the development of trading relationships with whites led to interracial marriages, mixed-blood offspring, and the need for leaders who were as skilled in diplomacy as they were in hunting or war.

These market forces changed the indigenous hunting and gathering subsistence economy that had sustained the Shoshones throughout the 1700s and early 1800s. Hunting activities broadened in scope so that collecting beaver pelts and (later) buffalo hides, took on commercial dimensions. Despite setbacks associated with several generations of warfare, the Shoshones were not a poverty-stricken people at the time the first fur traders encountered them. But, with abundant buffalo on the plains, as well as smaller herds in the Green River and Snake River Valleys during the 1700s, the Shoshonean nomadic life cycle meant moving to the "harvest," not simply avoiding famine. Plains warfare limited, but did not prevent, access to the easiest hunting. Moreover, the high desert and mountain environment of the Shoshones' range yielded elk, deer, fish, and a large variety of roots, berries, and other vegetable matter.[1] Market hunting, however, gradually modified the focus from subsistence harvests to accumulating beaver pelts, and, after 1840, buffalo robes. Commercial trade and the "rendezvous" became an important part of the yearly travels of many Shoshone bands.

The rendezvous system itself altered the Shoshones' environment. Swarms of mountain men, often traveling in groups of sixty or more, linked up with Shoshone (or other Indian) family bands. They scoured the drainages of the Green River, upper Snake River, and lower reaches of the Big Wind River for beaver and other marketable skins. During the height of the system, from 1825 to 1840, trappers, Nez Perces, Flatheads, Crows, Bannocks, Utes, and Shoshones met once or twice every summer at designated sites in the Green River, Bear River, Snake River, or Wind River drainages. These rendezvous provided venues for bartering and entertainment: the participants exchanged their goods, gambled on horse or foot races (or at cards or hand games), and bought and sold wives. Occasionally, Blackfeet raiders livened up the festivities, attacking either Shoshones or trappers going to or from the rendezvous meetings.[2]

This orientation toward market hunting had several corollaries. First, since the rendezvous brought trappers and traders into Shoshone country, Shoshones were less likely to risk perilous trading ventures to the old centers of trade at the Mandan and Hidatsa villages on the upper Missouri River, or to the mecca of Santa Fe to the south. Second, the sheer numbers of hunters and trappers, whites and Indians alike, placed great demands on the wildlife populations in the heart of Shoshone country. As beaver dwindled in both popularity and numbers during the latter stages of the rendezvous, the Shoshones increasingly relied on buffalo robes as the medium of exchange. This made access to the Plains even more crucial, especially after white emigration along the Oregon Trail in the 1840s further reduced the numbers of buffalo in the Green and Snake River basins.[3] Third, the net result was increased competition for the resources of the Plains. Conflicts and confrontations on the Plains magnified as the Arapahoes, Cheyennes, Gros Ventres, Blackfeet, and Sioux fought for living and hunting space against the Crows, Shoshones, and eventually, white settlers.[4] Faced with a need for arms and ammunition, many Eastern Shoshone bands continued to cultivate friendships among whites who sojourned in their lands, from mountain men to Mormons, and eventually included farmers, ranchers, missionaries, and soldiers.

Friendly trade associations between trappers and Shoshones were not the only legacy of the fur trade era. Eastern Shoshones welcomed the trappers into the core of their marriage and kinship systems. Many of the mountain men married Shoshone women; this facilitated the fur collection process and increased their safety. Traveling with small family bands whose leaders were knowledgeable of both terrain and hunting opportunities opened more avenues for exploiting regional resources. At the same time, the trappers gained defensive strength against tribes who were either hostile to the trappers' presence or hostile to allowing Shoshones to have direct access to the traders' wares. Osborne Russell, for example, wintered in 1840 with a Shoshone encampment (probably a small local or family band) that included a polyglot assortment of French traders and Iroquois, Creek, and Seminole Indians married to Shoshone women.[5] The children of such unions often became influential tribal leaders, mediators, and intermediaries in the 1860s and later, or in some cases, opportunistic allotment holders on the reservation.[6]

Following the demise of the rendezvous system, a community of trappers and their Indian wives and children coalesced around Jim Bridger's trading operations on Black's Fork of the Green River in southwestern Wyoming. Bridger had remained in this region following the 1839 rendezvous and conducted business from various temporary sites, operating from hide dwellings. By 1842 a few rudimentary log buildings were in place, but the formal opening of Fort Bridger, as it became known, occurred during the white migrations of 1843. Its location established the facility as an important link on the Oregon Trail, functioning as a collection and distribution center for Indian and white goods.[7]

Perhaps in partial response to this growing white presence in Shoshone country, new leaders emerged in the tribe. Although such men still needed fighting and hunting successes in order to win tribal acclaim, they also learned to mediate for the Shoshones with the white newcomers. Tracing the leaders of specific Eastern Shoshone bands, however, is a difficult task. Generally speaking, most American fur traders and trappers did not record their thoughts about Shoshone life or leadership and the extant Shoshone oral history contains little information about the pre-reservation period. Nevertheless, at least two headmen and several local or family band leaders acquired some measure of prominence between 1825 and 1840 and continued the traditions of a powerful chieftainship established by the example of Ohamagwaya.

Very likely, Ohamagwaya died in the late 1820s—all clear references to him ceased after 1825, when Beckwourth described Omogua's powers and authority. One of his apparent successors was a band leader called Little Chief by Euroamericans, but known as Mohwoomhah or Mawoma to his people. Spaniards may have noticed Mohwoomhah as early as 1829, when a Yamparika (either Comanche or Shoshone) named "Namaya" visited Santa Fe on a diplomatic mission. The first clear identification of Little Chief occurred in 1831 when trapper William A. Ferris visited the Shoshone region and named its four principal leaders: Horn Chief, Iron Wristband, Little Chief and Cut Nose. Ferris reported that Blackfeet killed Horn Chief in 1832.[8] Of the remaining men, Little Chief and Iron Wristband grace the pages of trapper Osborne Russell's memoirs, while Ferris kept track of Cut Nose. Russell, who first met Iron Wristband in 1834, said that Mohwoomhah and Iron Wristband were brothers, with the latter called Pahdahewakunda by the Shoshones. The painter Alfred Jacob Miller depicted Little Chief at least twice in 1837 (recording his Shoshone name, Mawoma), once in portrait and again in a landscape scene with Mohwoomhah heading a large body of Shoshones.[9] Throughout most of the 1830s, then, Mohwoomhah clearly functioned as an important headman and interacted with whites. If the Spanish "Namaya" also refers to Mohwoomhah or Mawoma, then this individual may have indeed been a claimant of Ohamagwaya's mantle.[10]

What emerges from these descriptions is that the Eastern Shoshones seemed to follow three strong chiefs (Pahdahewakunda, Mohwoomhah, and Cut Nose), men who probably functioned as local band leaders, from 1832 into the 1840s. Both Russell and Ferris indicate that Pahdahewakunda was the principal leader during this time. This suggests that Pahdahewakunda served as the head chief during the important fall buffalo hunt on the Plains, which was the only large divisional gathering of Shoshones where he might have had the chance to exercise an overarching authority. The Green River band of Shoshones, for example, followed Cut Nose. According to Ferris, Cut Nose adopted white-style dress and lived in a mixed Indian-white community. In 1843, Matthew C. Field, another voyager to the West, also mentioned Cut Nose's leadership among the Green River Shoshones.[11] Moreover, in 1840 Russell had learned that Mohwoomhah (and his three hundred lodges of followers—approximately eighteen hundred people) was disgruntled with Pahdahewakunda's leadership.[12] By 1843 both Mohwoomhah and Pahdahewakunda had died of natural causes. For the remainder of the decade, whatever large-scale political coalition might have existed among the Eastern Shoshones fractured into the component family bands and smaller-sized local bands.[13]

Russell, who was intensely interested in the state of Shoshone affairs, identified three of the younger warriors/leaders in 1840, calling them "the pillars of the nation and [men] at whose names the Blackfeet quaked with fear."[14] The three were Inkatoshapop, Fibebountowatsee, and Whoshakik. Russell's reference to Whoshakik (better known as Washakie) is the earliest mention of the man whose name became synonymous in whites' eyes with the Eastern Shoshones. Of the other two leaders, Miller painted Inkatoshapop (referred to as Incatashapa) in 1837, while Fibebountowatsee surfaces again in 1852 as Tibebutowats. (Interestingly, an additional spelling of Fibebountowatsee occurs in 1855 when Indian Agent George W. Armstrong noted that Tababooindowestay meant "white man's son.")[15] Matthew Field named more Shoshone chiefs in 1843, stating that Wakska and Ungatushapa were the "principal Snake chiefs."[16] Ungatushapa clearly is a variant spelling of Inkatoshapop and it is likely that Wakska (Field recorded the name phonetically as *Waks-ka*) refers to Wiskin (also called Cut Hair), a band leader identified by Indian Agent John Wilson in 1849.[17] According to Field, these two leaders were hunting in Crow territory (the Big Horn Basin) in 1843 while Cut Nose remained in the Green River area around Bridger's trading post.[18] Field's Wakska might refer to Washakie if William Hamilton's memoirs are considered. Hamilton, a young trapper who worked the streams of the Green, Wind, and Big Horn Rivers in the mid-1840s, spent part of 1843 in the camp of Washakie. At the time, Washakie led buffalo hunts in the Big Horn drainage (which was considered Crow territory—indeed, Hamilton reports that Washakie's band and a Crow band met and exchanged goods).[19] Thus, perhaps as many as five different men headed Shoshone bands during the 1840s, with two of them, Cut Nose and Washakie, clearly known for their friendship to trappers and traders.

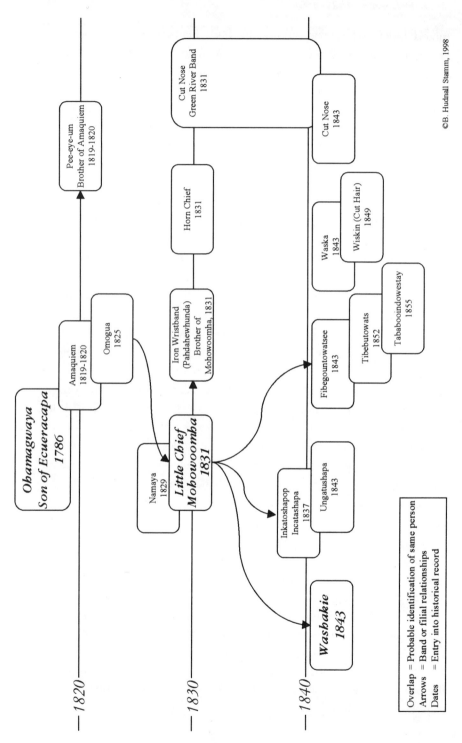

SHOSHONE LEADERS, 1818–1855

Overlap = Probable identification of same person
Arrows = Band or filial relationships
Dates = Entry into historical record

©B. Hudnall Stamm, 1998

Regardless of the intricacies of Shoshone leadership, in the minds of white observers Washakie eventually became the designated leader for all Eastern Shoshones. Very little documentary evidence exists concerning his early life, but his story, like that of Ohamagwaya, illustrates the transitions and adaptations of Shoshones to the permanent presence of white settlers in Shoshone country.

## WASHAKIE AND THE EASTERN SHOSHONES

The facts of Washakie's birth and childhood are probably destined to remain part of Shoshone lore, but are worth exploring. By several traditions, Washakie's birth date is either 1798 or 1804. John Roberts, the Episcopal missionary who came to the Shoshone and Bannock Agency in 1883, recorded the former date in his records. Washakie's gravestone, however, was inscribed with the latter at the insistence of J. K. Moore, the agency trader.[20] Both dates are probably too early. On the other hand, the birth year—1825—implied by Richard H. Wilson, Shoshone Indian Agent from 1895 to 1897, is too late. (He thought Washakie died at age seventy-five.)[21] A more likely birth date is circa 1808–10 (explained below).

Additionally, there is some question about Washakie's association with the Shoshones, or at least the Plains or Eastern Shoshones. According to one of his biographers, Grace Raymond Hebard (who gathered most of her material from one of Washakie's sons in 1926), Washakie was born in Montana of mixed Shoshone-Flathead heritage. Hebard believes that following a Blackfeet raid on his village, Washakie, his surviving siblings, and his mother joined a band of Lemhi Shoshones. Supposedly, Washakie's mother and some of his siblings returned to the Flatheads later, while Washakie remained with the Lemhis. During his adolescence, Hebard thinks that Washakie joined a passing band of Bannocks and finally, between 1826 and 1832, merged with a Shoshone band in the Green River region.[22]

In contradiction, Washakie told Captain Patrick Henry Ray, the agent at the Shoshone Agency from 1893 to 1895, that he had joined the Shoshones when he was sixteen and had met Jim Bridger at the same time.[23] According to Washakie, Bridger was slightly older than Washakie. Since Bridger was born in 1804 and first entered Shoshone country in 1824, logically the two young men either met that year or perhaps during a later rendezvous.[24] If Washakie remembered his age correctly, then he, the Eastern Shoshones, and Bridger crossed paths between 1824 and 1826; hence he was probably born between 1808 and 1810.

Other evidence points to this conclusion. Washakie and Bridger became lasting friends, trapping together for a number of years on the Green and Snake Rivers.[25] This activity was important for Washakie's passage into adulthood. Shoshone males had to prove themselves either in hunting or war in order to secure mates, a process that could take as long as ten years after the voice change. Marriage signaled the entrance into adulthood.[26] Thus Washakie's adventures with Bridger provided the requisite experience in hunting, while participation in raiding parties against the Blackfeet and Gros Ventres proved his warrior abilities.[27]

Washakie's stories about Shoshone raids on Blackfeet camps when he was still a "boy" reveal the vastness of Shoshone territory. He considered Bear River his home country, yet Shoshone raiders would travel well north of the Yellowstone River to attack the Blackfeet in their camps near the Crazy Mountains (approximately fifty miles northeast of present-day Bozeman) or in the canyon of the Upper Missouri. Other battles occurred when Blackfeet warriors invaded Shoshone camps. The raiders sought horses, weapons, and scalps; territorial gains or total destruction of enemies were not their ultimate motives.[28]

Washakie probably began his long association with whites during his adolescence and grew into adulthood leading a dual role, one with white trappers, and one with the Shoshones. This interval—ca. 1825 to 1833— fits well with Shoshonean life cycles and matches his family's oral tradition, which places Washakie's first marriage in 1833 or 1834. One other fact corroborates this analysis of Washakie's birth and early life: Bridger's third wife, Mary, was one of Washakie's daughters. Bridger and Mary Washakie married in 1850, suggesting that Mary was born circa 1833 to 1835. (Adolescence was brief for Shoshone females. It began at menarche—midteens during pre-reservation years—and ended a short time later with marriage.) If Washakie was born earlier than 1808, he waited an unusually long time before marrying and beginning his family.[29]

Washakie's close association with Bridger continued until familial and band responsibilities claimed more of his attention. Following the birth of his fourth child, Washakie apparently assumed greater duties as a Shoshone war chief. He told General Ray that he began leading and organizing the raids, not just accompanying them. This rise in status occurred about the same time that Bridger expanded his business on Black's Fork. As Russell noted in 1840, Washakie was a young warrior feared by the Blackfeet.[30]

At this point Washakie acknowledged that he was not yet a "chief," but the deaths of Pahdahewakunda and Mohwoomhah in 1843 edged him toward that role. Although Russell claimed that the Shoshonean leadership system broke down after the untimely deaths of these two primary leaders, Washakie noted near the end of the decade that Gahnacumah was the acknowledged chief of the Shoshones.[31] For most of the intervening years, however, the larger groups of buffalo-hunting Shoshones divided into numerous bands. Younger warriors like Washakie generally headed these bands, which concentrated in the Green River Valley and Cache Valley corridor (southwestern Wyoming to northeastern Utah). Yet, by 1849, John Wilson, newly appointed agent for the Salt Lake Indian Agency, placed Washakie among the four important chiefs of the buffalo-hunting, horse-owning Shoshones. The others were Mono, the aforementioned Wiskin, and Oapich (Big Man). Wilson derived his information from Jim Bridger and Louis Vasquez (Bridger's business partner at Fort Bridger), which leads to the speculation that the two traders probably pointed out the Indian leaders with whom they had had favorable dealings.[32]

Nevertheless, between 1849 and 1851, events unfolded in such a way that Washakie was perceived by whites as the titular chief of the Eastern Shoshones. His rise to prominence was one of three processes that affected the evolution and creation of the Wind River community. The other two occurred as a result of the ongoing influx of white emigrants through Shoshone country.

The new settlers altered the existing underpinnings of Indian-white relationships and forced political realignments and changes within all peoples who lived in the Wind River–Green River–Salt Lake geographical area. The first series of alterations began in 1851 as Mormons in Utah Territory sought to diminish the economic and political control of tformer fur trappers and mixed-blood Indians. Concurrently, Washakie and the Shoshones engaged in a "play-off system" between these two regional powers. The U.S. seizure of Fort Bridger in 1857 during the short-lived Mormon War inaugurated the next set of events. Washakie and the Eastern Shoshones moved eastward across the Rockies, shifting their economic stronghold to the Wind River Valley. This allowed Washakie the freedom to maintain peaceful relations with all whites—Mormons, mountain men, and soldiers. Unfortunately for the Bannocks and Basin Shoshones in Idaho and Utah, there was no escape from expanding white settlements. Consequently, they increasingly resisted wayfaring whites as well as settlers and communities. This transitional period ended in the Bear River Massacre of 1863, bringing on the pre-reservation treaty period of 1863 to 1868.

## EASTERN SHOSHONES, 1850–1863

Washakie's rising star partially reflected new federal policies for the emigration routes of the trans-Mississippi West. In order to protect the overlanders, whose numbers rapidly multiplied with the 1847 Mormon migration and the Forty-niners, Indian agents and commissioners bargained for peace with and among the various tribes whose hunting grounds were violated by the travelers.[33] The federal government made its first overtures to Washakie in 1849, when Agent Wilson contacted him about resolving differences concerning thefts of Ute and Paiute horses by Washakie's Shoshones.[34]

Although this council between the Shoshones, Utes, and Paiutes was delayed until 1852, a more important recognition of Washakie's leadership abilities occurred at the famous 1851 Treaty of Fort Laramie. In order to safeguard the overland trails, representatives of the Central Superintendency of the Office of Indian Affairs arranged to meet ten thousand Plains peoples (Sioux, Cheyenne, Crows, Arapahoes, Arikaras, etc.) at the famous trading post. They were forced to move the assembly to Horse Creek, a tributary of the North Platte River, when delays in the delivery of presents for the Indian leaders and the appetites of horses and people exhausted supplies of fodder and food.[35] The council intended to establish tribal boundaries and promote peaceful intertribal relationships. More importantly to the federal government, the Indian attendees were supposed to leave white emigrants alone. Thinking that other Indians whose territories were bisected by the trails also needed to sign the Fort Laramie Treaty, Jacob H. Holeman, Indian Agent for the new Utah Superintendency, hired Jim Bridger to gather various Shoshone bands to attend the council. (The Utah Superintendency was established at the same time as Utah Territory, with Brigham Young serving as ex-officio superintendent and governor, as well as the head of the Church of Latter-day Saints.) However, the council negotiations were set for late August—the time of the Shoshones' primary buffalo hunt.[36]

Contacting all the Eastern Shoshones proved a difficult task. Holeman and Bridger met some of the bands on August 22, 1851, at their camp near the old St. Mary's Stage Station on the Sweetwater River. Once there, they discovered that Gahnacumah, the acknowledged head chief, and his followers were hunting buffalo and did not respond to the request for a council. Moreover, the day after the two whites met with the camp leaders, Cheyenne raiders killed two Shoshones. In the absence of Gahnacumah, the remaining band leaders questioned the veracity of the "peace" negotiations and argued for three days about accompanying Holeman to Fort Laramie. Bridger then turned the Shoshone deliberations into an opportunity to elevate the status of his friend, Washakie. The trader persuaded Washakie to gather the warriors about him, take charge, and lead the procession to Fort Laramie. Washakie, in his own words, as recorded by an interviewer, "called in all the young men who had been to war with him and told him [them] he was going to stay with the white men and they must make up their minds to go or stay, and they all said they would stay. There were a good many of them. They selected Washakie as their war chief."[37]

This "election" began Washakie's chieftainship (although Washakie clearly stated that at this point he was "war chief," not "head chief"). Some sixty to eighty warriors followed him to Fort Laramie. His authority among the Shoshones, however, was never absolute and depended on circumstances that reflected the new world of post-1850 Shoshone country—the ability to win concessions from whites and to continue to succeed in the more traditional leadership roles of finding buffalo and defeating enemies.

Whites continued to enhance Washakie's image in the 1850s. For example, Washakie and four other Shoshone headmen agreed to a truce with four Ute leaders on September 3, 1852 (the same council that had been delayed since 1849). Agent Holeman inspired this meeting; a year earlier he had urged the federal government to make treaties with the Utah Superintendency tribes, similar to the one concluded at Fort Laramie.[38] Following Holeman's lead, Brigham Young mediated the Shoshone-Ute pact, sealing the peace with gifts of clothes, ammunition, beef, and flour. The Mormon leader noted that the Indians left Salt Lake "in apparently high spirits and good and friendly feelings towards each other as well as the whites."[39]

At that same meeting, Young attempted to gain permission from both tribes for Mormon colonization on Indian lands. Washakie and the other Shoshone leaders, who represented twenty-six lodges only (about 150 people), readily agreed. According to Young, "I then asked the Shoshones how they would like to have us settle upon their land at Green river; they replied that the land at Green river did not belong to them, but that they lived and inhabited in the vicinity of the Wind river chain of mountains, and the Sweetwater but that if we would make a settlement on Green river, they would be glad to come and trade with us."[40]

Apparently, Washakie's band had moved from the Bear River–Green River–Fort Bridger hunting grounds (present-day southwestern Wyoming and northeastern Utah) to the western edges of the Wind River Mountain range and the lands of the upper Green River. Therefore, Washakie had no objection to permitting access to the contested land (Green River to Salt Lake) still occupied by other Shoshone, Bannock, and Ute groups. Holeman wrote that these latter bands, however, "were equally opposed, and expressed their disapprobation to Mormons settling on their lands, in the strongest terms."[41]

Furthermore, Mormon towns along the lower Green River to Salt Lake corridor were welcome additions to the trading posts that former trappers (including Jim Baker and John Robertson, who were both married to Shoshone women) rapidly developed near the ferry crossings of the Oregon-California-Mormon Trails. The proposed towns, together with the trading posts and Fort Bridger, meant more competition and therefore better prices for the Indian robe and hide trade.[42] However, the diversity of peoples in this region doomed the 1852 peace as Utes, Mormons, mountain men, and Shoshones vied for economic and political viability over the next five years.

The Mormon-dominated Utah legislature fomented some of the problems. Beginning in 1850, Utah required permits to construct bridges or operate ferries on the rivers and streams along the Utah portions of the Oregon Trail. The trapper/Indian community resisted these legal impediments, preferring instead to maintain their unregulated enterprises. This led to confrontations between legal permit holders and the mountain men in 1852.[43] By 1854, the Shoshones were voicing their concerns about the new political state of affairs. John M. Hockaday wrote to George Many-penny, the Commissioner of Indian Affairs, that "Shoshones are displeased with . . . 'white men' not married into their nation or tribe" being granted charters to operate ferries, bridges, or cut timber.[44] The Shoshones claimed they were the only ones who could grant these privileges, not the government.

Meanwhile, the Utah legislature increasingly believed that Jim Bridger was inciting Indians to attack Mormon colonies throughout the region. At the very least, Utah officials thought he provided guns and ammunition during the Walker (Ute) War of 1853. (Chief Walker was the primary leader of the Ute delegation to the 1852 Ute-Shoshone peace talks in Salt Lake City.) Regardless of the truth of these accusations, an attempt was made to arrest Bridger. He escaped, but Mormon entrepreneurs soon took charge of Fort Bridger. In 1855, Bridger's partner, Louis Vasquez, officially sold his interest in the post to Lewis Robinson, the quartermaster general of the Utah Militia. Bridger, however, never yielded his claim to the store.[45]

Officially, Washakie and his band took no part in either the ferry squabbles or the Fort Bridger takeover. In fact, he tolerated an even stronger Mormon presence in 1853 when Fort Supply, a missionary station, was founded twelve miles to the south of Fort Bridger on Smith's Fork (a feeder stream to Black's Fork). However, his good will extended only to boost trading opportunities, not to encourage Mormon infiltration of his band. In response to a request for permission for the missionaries to take Shoshone wives, Washakie may have conveyed a humorous and subtly contemptuous alternative to one of the missionaries, James S. Brown. According to Brown, whose veracity cannot stand exacting scrutiny, Washakie said:

> We cannot afford to give our daughters to the white men, but we are willing to give him an Indian girl for a white girl. I cannot see why a white man wants an Indian girl. They are dirty, ugly, stubborn, and cross, and it is a strange idea for white men to want such wives. The white men may look around though and if any of you could find a girl that would go with him, it would be alright, but the Indian must have the same privileges among the white man.[46]

By mid-1854, however, Washakie apparently regretted his previous invitation to the Mormons and for the next few years waffled in his dealings with them. During a drunken rage in 1854, he railed against Mormon encroachments on Shoshone lands, bemoaning loss of game and timber and complaining about ejection of Shoshone peoples from Mormon towns. Further, he threatened to kill whites who ventured east of the Green River and north of Big Sandy River. This incident took place at the Mormon ferry on the Green River, near present-day La Barge and over sixty miles north of Green River, Wyoming. According to Hosea Stout, a Mormon missionary, Washakie consorted with a group of ex-trappers, about whom Stout recorded: "the Mountaineers as usual throng in here to day drinking swearing & gambling." One these "mountaineers," Elisha Ryan, forcibly took over the ferry operation during a drunken spree. Apparently returned to sobriety, Washakie quickly retracted his threat the next day and perhaps gave some thought to negative consequences that might have stemmed from his harsh words.[47]

In 1856, Washakie again reversed his behavior toward Mormons. Early in the summer, he accepted Brigham Young's overtures regarding Shoshone farms (made palatable, of course, by Young's "gifts"). Young reported that "the Shoshones have expressed a desire to commence farming operations next spring, and have solicited me to make a location for them."[48] Later that year, on behalf of Mormon evangelizers, Washakie chastised his fellow Shoshones for rejecting *The Book of Mormon*:

> You [Shoshones] are all fools; you are blind, you cannot see; you have no ears, for you do not hear, you are fools for you do not understand. These men are our friends. The great Mormon captain (Brigham Young) has talked with our father above the clouds, and he told the Mormon captain to send these good men here to tell us the truth not a lie.[49]

Many of the other Shoshones at this meeting wanted Mormon tools, clothing, and food, not the Mormon bible. Washakie, on the other hand, recognized that tacit accommodation was necessary to acquire these items. Perhaps his recent experiences helped him realize that confrontational demands carried little weight and thwarted Shoshone goals.[50]

Washakie was not the sole arbiter of Shoshone-Mormon relationships during this time. In fact, he did not attend the second round of peace talks with the Utes held in 1855. Tibaboendwartsa was the primary negotiator for the three hundred Shoshones present at this meeting in Salt Lake City.[51] Washakie's absence did not necessarily mean any lessening of his status. In fact, his absence may have indicated his ongoing success in procuring food and "presents" for his band from the Mormons or by hunting, while Tibaboendwartsa's people suffered in comparison.

Differential treatment of these two leaders at the hands of whites helped to sustain a rivalry, if not outright antagonism, between Washakie and Tibaboendwartsa. Tibaboendwartsa resented Washakie's prominence and sought to gain similar status for himself. The fact that Washakie and Tibaboendwartsa generally did not attend the same meetings with white agents and representatives exacerbated the tensions between the two leaders. For example, in 1852 U.S. agents at Fort Laramie proclaimed Tibaboendwartsa chief of the Shoshones, ignoring Washakie's leadership the previous year at the Treaty of Fort Laramie. Tibaboendwartsa's band apparently did not benefit from his favorable status. In 1855 Tibaboendwartsa's people still needed supplies and Brigham Young needed the leader's cooperation for widespread peace between Shoshones and Utes. Washakie, having previously reached a peace accord, had no pressing need to attend this meeting.[52] Following the 1855 negotiations, Tibaboendwartsa believed the Mormons promised him aid-on-demand. In October 1855 and again in December, his band, which included one hundred warriors, threatened the residents of Fort Supply for failing to fulfill promises of food.[53]

Regardless of Tibaboendwartsa's stance toward the Mormons, Washakie clearly revealed his own policy vis-à-vis the church in 1856. J. Robert Brown, who was traveling through Shoshone country that year, met the Shoshone leader, along with a subchief, Brazil, at Echo Canyon to the southwest of Bear River. (If Brown was accurate about the status of Brazil, then this individual was probably Bazil, who indeed was a subchief and important band leader.) Brown wrote, "Wassakee [sic] wanted us to tell Brigham Young and the Mormons that he was mad at them."[54] He was appeased a few days later in a meeting at Fort Bridger with three Mormon representatives, who lavished presents on the band (forty lodges, three hundred people).[55] Without a doubt, Washakie had pursued political and economic goals toward the Mormons that focused on maximum gain for minimum commitment. He wanted Mormon settlements in order to increase trading opportunities, and he was willing to entice Brigham Young and other Utah officials with vague promises about farming or settling down in order to keep the "presents" flowing. Covertly, he opposed any attempt by the Mormons to control or limit the "mountaineer" establishments—which for years had been outlets for the Shoshone fur and robe trade and whose proprietors were married into the tribe.

His feelings toward Mormons hardened in 1857. When President Buchanan sent 2500 troops from Fort Leavenworth to quell the "Mormon War," Washakie offered 1200 warriors to the U.S. cause and against the Mormons.[56] Although the army refused his offer, he nevertheless bolstered his reputation for allegiance to the federal government. His friendship with whites caused him much trouble from 1857 to 1863.

In the late 1850s up to the mid-1860s, Washakie's band of Shoshones underwent a radical shift in geographical locales, one that was more severe than the earlier change from Bear River to the Sweetwater River. From 1854 through 1858, Washakie apparently traveled into southwestern Montana for the fall buffalo hunt, generally traversing the territory drained by the Big Hole and upper Madison Rivers and camping in winter near Henry's Lake on the Idaho-Montana border. In the spring the band reversed directions, eventually making its way to trade horses and hides in Salt Lake.[57] The Montana excursions, of course, covered lands where Washakie, as a boy, raided the Blackfeet. They presented other dangers. Both the trip north of the Snake River and the return to the Snake River put the Shoshones on the borders of Crow country.

Although the Crows and Shoshones were allies during much of the rendezvous period and into the 1840s, peaceful relationships often depended more on avoiding conflict than on rendezvous friendships. Furthermore, the Fort Laramie Treaty of 1851 gave the Crows rights to the upper Wind River Basin, the Big Horn Basin, and the Yellowstone region. More specifically, Crow land in what is now Wyoming extended southward up the South Fork of Powder River to the crest of the Rattlesnake Mountains, then followed the upper portions of the Sweetwater River, and finally headed north along the crest of the Wind River Mountains and into Yellowstone Park. This huge territory encompassed all of what would become the Shoshone and Bannock Indian Agency (Wind River Reservation), as well as vast amounts of rangeland in central Wyoming.[58]

Washakie generally respected the terms of the Fort Laramie document and the Shoshones' journeys to the Montana buffalo grounds usually skirted Crow territory by staying west of the Tetons and Yellowstone. Yet, this route did not guarantee safe passage and violent confrontations remained a possibility. For example, Washakie's movements beginning in the fall of 1855 led to a major battle (possibly the famous "Battle of Crowheart Butte") between the two tribes in midsummer of 1856. The fight stemmed from the Shoshones' migrations into Montana and reflected the dangers of traversing border areas. Events began innocently enough. Following the fall trading season in Salt Lake in 1855, Washakie spurned the offer of Agent Armstrong to meet at Fort Supply and instead headed north to hunt buffalo. Over the course of the winter, his Shoshone band camped near present-day Dillon, Montana. In the early spring they headed north and hunted and fished near the confluence of the Big Hole and Beaverhead Rivers. From there, the group moved eastward to the Madison River, then upstream (south) to the Continental Divide, and finally to the southeast and Henry's Lake. Still traveling in a southeastward direction, but in Crow territory, Washakie's band encountered a large Crow group. According to Elijah Wilson, a white boy who spent two years with the Shoshones, nearly fifty Shoshones and over one hundred Crow warriors were killed. The legend of Crowheart Butte says that Washakie met the Crow leader in solitary combat in order to end the bloodshed. Washakie supposedly emerged with the Crow's heart as a symbol of victory. Wilson believes Washakie was willing to risk the fight in order to get to prime hunting grounds.[59]

The disputes with the Crows continued over the next two years, possibly to the detriment of the Shoshones. F. W. Lander, the Superintendent of the U.S. Overland Wagon Road (and special agent to the tribes along the route), and B. F. Miller, his assistant, noted in 1858 that the Shoshones were in bad condition.[60] More than likely, the Crow encounters interfered with the spring hunt and forced an early retreat from the buffalo fields, which hampered trading opportunities and led to summertime starvation.

Perhaps because of these conflicts, Washakie entertained the idea of creating Shoshone "farms" or a reservation at the southern end of the hunting territory. In 1858 he informed agent Jacob Forney that he wanted land on Henry's Fork (a feeder stream to the Green River on the Wyoming-Utah border). A year later he told Lander that the Elk Mountain territory (probably part of the Uinta Mountains of northeastern Utah) would be satisfactory. Forney and Lander wanted Washakie's reservation to be devoted to agriculture and not hunting. Washakie promised Forney he was agreeable to farming if the agent provided proper instruction, but he turned down Lander's offer of seeds and implements. He hinted to Lander that he might accept cattle herding as an alternative to farming. In both cases his implied cooperation netted his band food and clothing.[61]

Intertribal politics provided other inducements for Washakie to enter treaty negotiations with the United States. Basin Shoshones, as well as Bannocks, Utes, and Paiutes began to step up the pace of their raids on white homesteaders and emigrants. Elijah Wilson wrote that when Pocatello's Northwestern Shoshones and Bannocks joined Washakie's followers at the "great encampment" near Deer Lodge in the summer of 1855, the Bannocks possessed clothes and supplies taken from an emigrant train.[62] The frequency of the attacks increased after 1859, and Washakie began to lose followers to the warring bands. More than likely, his young warriors saw no chance for personal advancement under his policies of peace toward whites. In fact, Lander recognized this situation and sought to strengthen Washakie's waning hold over the Eastern Shoshones. He urged that "any steps which could be taken to augment the power of Washakie[,] who is perfectly safe in his attachment to the Americans and Northern Mountaineers, would also prove beneficial."[63]

Washakie's peace policy also suffered erosions closer to home. The Eastern Shoshones, like their Basin cousins, experienced a gold-inspired period of white migration. As early as 1842, the Sweetwater River area to the south of the Wind River Valley had yielded gold to the hands of a trapper from the American Fur Company. However, unidentified Indians killed him before news of his find could spark a gold rush.[64] In 1855, forty men prospected the length of the Sweetwater Valley, found a few specks of the precious metal and mined off and on until 1861, when most of them abandoned the digs for better pay cutting hay and erecting telegraph poles for the Overland Stage Company.[65]

For those who remained, the South Pass Stage Station served as a base for mining efforts during 1861 and 1862. In 1862, however, a Shoshone party, undoubtedly belonging to one of the Plains bands, drove the miners from their claims. Farther east, a small party of Shoshones killed a laborer who worked at the Sweetwater Stage Station; he had not understood their demands for food.[66] It is unlikely these actions came from Washakie's band, but they reveal that his urgings for peace toward whites went unheeded among all the Plains-going Shoshones.

In 1859, Washakie supposedly headed twelve hundred Eastern Shoshones assisted by four to six subchiefs.[67] By 1861,however, agent William H. Rogers reported that "his [Washakie's] tribe have deserted him, or as they say they have thrown him away. . . . He told me last summer [probably via a runner, since Rogers indicated he had not met the chief at the time of this letter] that his Indians lost Confidence in him that he had made them promises of goods on the word of the Superintendent to him; . . . they seem to think that the bad Indians who kill & steal get presents while they get only promises."[68] Rogers then went on to suggest spending $8,000 to $10,000 in goods to soothe Washakie's feelings and to help restore his authority.[69] At least some presents reached the band, but a new agent/superintendent, Benjamin Davies, delivered them. Davies also recommended a reserve for the Eastern Shoshones on Green River.[70]

Davies, like Rogers before him, enjoyed a short tenure in what was becoming an increasingly difficult job. His replacement, Henry Martin, pushed even harder for treaties to settle tribal disputes along the Overland Stage route and the emigrant trails. Following a meeting in 1861 with Washakie and several of his subchiefs, as well as with a few Ute leaders, Martin declared that both tribes wanted formal agreements with the United States: "They express their willingness to cede to the United States all the lands they claim in this Territory, with the exception of reservations necessary for their homes; and ask, in return, that the United States shall make them annual presents of blankets, beads, paint, calico, ammunition, &c, with occasional supplies of beef and flour sufficient to make them comfortable."[71]

This statement bears analysis. From Washakie's point of view, it amplified his earlier offers to Brigham Young in 1852 and 1855 to allow settlement on Green River and to accept a designated reserve.[72] He made it clear, however, that his people required annual gifts, beef, and flour to seal the concession. In other words, Washakie wanted to secure his tribe's presents (and such gifts had not been automatically forthcoming over the past twelve years) and he wanted to make sure food was available when the tribe needed it.

The proposed territorial cession was not clearly identified at this meeting, but likely included lands in the Green River, Bear River, and Salt Lake region. Washakie's band had vacated this area as a summer residence a decade earlier. Nevertheless, this concession still could penalize the Shoshones. If the Shoshones denied themselves easy access to the Green River Valley, then hunting grounds north of the Snake River would become harder to reach. It is likely that in Washakie's mind this might be a worthwhile sacrifice if it limited his band's contamination by the warring Shoshones on the west side of the Rockies. At the same time, the land concessions would gain material support from whites, and thus make the increased likelihood of war with other Plains tribes in the Wind River and Big Horn Valleys more tolerable.

Congress acted on Martin's report. On July 22, 1862, Indian Commissioner William Dole authorized Martin (designated a Special Agent), Superintendent James D. Doty, and Agent Luther Mann (appointed in late December 1861) to negotiate a treaty with the Shoshones to protect the overland routes. Luther Mann was the agent in charge of the Fort Bridger subagency, created in 1861 for the Shoshones. However, Congress made no distinctions between the various Shoshonean bands—the appropriation of $20,000 was intended to be divided equally among all Shoshones, not just the Eastern groups led by Washakie.[73]

Before serious negotiations got underway, warfare erupted in the Basin. Luther Mann, the new Shoshone agent, was powerless to stop the conflicts. He realized the root of the problem was the depletion of game and habitat west of the Rockies, but he lacked the financial wherewithal to compensate native peoples for their losses. He was, however, quick to recommend the Wind River valley as a future reservation for the Eastern Shoshones in order to isolate them from the fray.[74] Mann was the first official to suggest that the Shoshones should live permanently at Wind River.

The raids abated with the onset of winter, but Doty doubted that a treaty could be arranged with the Shoshones without offending other tribes like Bannocks and Paiutes (the appropriation called for negotiations with only the Shoshonean bands along the emigrant trail). Therefore, he did not plan to meet with any Indians until Congress had time to reconsider the matter.[75]

Congress, however, had no time for debate. Colonel Patrick Connor's forces destroyed a winter camp of Shoshone warriors, women, and children on January 30, 1863, on the Bear River in Idaho near the northern Utah border. Approximately 240 Indians died. Connor's attack, the "Bear River Massacre," sparked intermittent retaliation by various Shoshone and Bannock bands over the next several months. This resistance, however, was short-lived. By June 1863, Mann and Doty reported that the Basin tribes were ready to talk.[76]

On July 2, 1863, Doty and Mann negotiated a treaty that included all Shoshone groups except four bands. Washakie and Wanapitz served as the principal chiefs, although this designation probably reflected white sympathies and not necessarily the preferences of the Shoshones. The other Shoshone signers of the treaty were Toopsapowit, Pantoshiga, Ninabutz, Norkok, Tahvonshea, Weerango, Tootsahp, and Weeahyukee. Bazil, whose arrival was delayed, signed later. Some of these leaders appear on reservation census rolls, but with the exception of Bazil, Norkok, and Tahvonshea, most of them are not found in extant documentary sources. Nevertheless, they represented the diversity of leadership among the Plains-going Shoshones.

Bazil, for example, headed a band of mixed-blood Shoshones and trappers that generally resided near Fort Bridger. He may have had strong Sun Dance connections—his sons led the Sun Dance during the 1870s and 1880s. Norkok also symbolizes the trapper influence on the Shoshones. He was born circa 1825–30, the son of a French trapper and a Ute mother (the latter captured and reared by the Shoshones). His father, Battise, operated a ferry on the Green River as late as 1858. Norkok became the main Shoshone interpreter during the early reservation years, but tended to remain highly independent of Washakie. Moreover, Norkok and another treaty signer, Tahvonshea (also known as Tawunasia), Tobeshe, Tavonshea, Taboonsheya, and Tabonsheya), may have been sullen participants at the treaty council. Both were reputedly present at the Bear River slaughter.[77] As to Tahvonshea/Tawunasia, most references to him are generally negative—he led his followers along different paths than those advocated by Washakie and desired by white officials. According to reports by Indian agents in the 1870s and 1880s, Tawunasia (who was born in 1830) was a full-blood Shoshone who resented Washakie's leadership.[78]

The treaty council, therefore, brought together disparate Shoshone bands, some of them still reeling from the aftermath of the winter and spring fighting. After three days of hard bargaining, the signers agreed to the following articles: (1) peace existed between the Shoshone peoples and the United States; (2) all travel routes through Shoshonean territory would be open and safe, including ferries and settlements along the trails, with any Indian offenders to be handed over to federal officers; (3) telegraph lines, mail and stage routes, and a future railroad would remain unhampered; (4) the Shoshone country was defined as the Snake River to the north, the Wind River Mountains and the North Platte River to the east, and the Yampa River and Uinta Mountains to the south, with the western boundaries left open; (5) in compensation for the "inconveniences" of articles two and three, the Shoshones would receive $10,000 in annuities for a period of twenty years; and (6) at the conclusion of the treaty, the participating bands would receive six thousand dollars in goods and presents.[79]

The treaty provisions focused almost entirely on U.S. goals, not on the desires of the various Shoshone bands. The annuities, for example, did not include food nor did the articles take into account the problems of hunters-gatherers in an arid region. Whites gained rights to passage through the Basin, but this could only mean increased pressure on scarce animal and plant resources as Shoshones and whites vied for sustenance and settlements. This competition had been the primary motivation behind the "Shoshone uprising" in the first place. The only food-rich lands (buffalo habitat) included in "Shoshone country" lay in the southeast corner at the confluence of the Sweetwater and the North Platte—and this bordered Arapahoe territory. Finally, Washakie was unable to bargain for a reservation in the Wind River Valley. It seems that the U.S. was unwilling to violate the boundaries set by the 1851 Fort Laramie Treaty—Wind River to Big Horn River was still Crow land.[80]

These and other problems continued to plague both white and Shoshone leaders over the next five years. In the meantime, the Wind River region lured many whites, Crows, Shoshones, Cheyennes, Arapahoes, and Sioux to its rivers, hills, and plains. At the creation of the Shoshone and Bannock Agency in 1868, a flourishing yet conflicted community was already in place.

*Chapter Two*

# Shoshone Country

## 1863–1872

EASTERN SHOSHONES AND WIND RIVER, 1863–1870

The human focus on Wind River increased in intensity between 1863 and 1868. For the Eastern Shoshones, the area became extremely important because the Wind River region still offered access to plentiful buffalo herds on Wyoming's eastern plains. White settlers and immigrants had disrupted most of the buffalo habitat west of the Rocky Mountains. Thus, the Shoshones concentrated their hunting efforts as well as their winter camps within striking distance of the remaining herds.[1] This meant that conflicts with Mountain Crows over the Big Horn Basin and Yellowstone continued unabated. At the same time, new enemies—Lakotas, Cheyennes, and Arapahoes—also hunted these same lands.[2] Finally, gold seekers prospected and eventually staked claims to the headwaters and tributaries of the Sweetwater River near the southern borders of the Wind River. These three human streams rapidly flowed toward the Wind River after 1863.

Washakie's initial, pre-1863 desire for a reservation in the valley probably represented the need for hunting rights, not permanent residence. Residential permanence never concerned most Plains-going Shoshones, including Washakie. For years his winter camps reflected tremendous variety: Bear Lake on the Utah-Idaho border; Fort Bridger, Wyoming; the Bitterroot Mountains of Montana and Idaho, and the broad valleys of the Shoshone and Wind Rivers.[3] His hunting ranged over even wider locales: from the Bitterroots to the Montana plains in the north and northeast, to southern Wyoming, farther south to the Uinta Mountains of Utah, and as far west as the south-central Idaho desert of the Snake River Valley.[4] The specific identification with Wind River, therefore, more than likely reflected Washakie's understanding of the changed human and animal geography within the mountains spanning southern Montana to northern Utah.

In the aftermath of the 1863 treaty negotiations, many disparate groups became more closely linked with Washakie. In part, this was due to government design; larger shares of the annuities were distributed from Fort Bridger than from either of the Idaho sites of Fort Hall or Soda Springs. Luther Mann noted in his annual report for 1865 that "deserters" and others had been "attracted by Wasakee's rising home" and the tribe now totaled eighteen hundred people, up from fourteen hundred the year before.[5] In fact, four distinct local bands (and component family bands) occasionally merged under Washakie's leadership, especially for buffalo hunts on the Plains.

This contingent included the Bannocks of the Fort Hall region of the Snake River, whose language, although different from Shoshone-Comanche, shared similar roots. Others were Idaho-based Shoshones who lived in the same region and who frequently traveled with the Bannocks.[6] These mixed Bannock-Shoshone bands were among those that attacked emigrants and white settlements during the troubles of the late 1850s and early 1860s.

Nevertheless, from the mid-1860s until 1872, they often joined the Eastern Shoshones on hunts in Wind River. In September 1866, for example, Bart Henderson, a white prospector, nearly collided with Bannock hunters under Taghee's leadership while both the Bannocks and Henderson's party chased the same buffalo herd along the Wind River. Taghee escorted Henderson to a large Indian camp (about eleven hundred Shoshones, Bannocks, and Utes), where Washakie exercised his rights as the hunting-camp leader to entertain the guests. Henderson recalled that Washakie's hospitality included a meal served on plates, with teacups and saucers. Washakie wore gifts received from F. W. Lander—a long white duster, a Colt sidearm, and a saber—as symbols of his standing among whites.[7]

Other Eastern Shoshone allies included two major Shoshone family bands in Idaho and one in northern Utah. Pocatello led the Idaho band that headquartered between Bannock Creek and Salt Lake. As Elijah Wilson pointed out, Pocatello and Washakie were not always on friendly terms because Pocatello advocated war against the emigrants.[8] The second Idaho band, probably led by Sanpitch and Black Beard, tended to stay in the Bear Creek, Salt Lake, and Fort Bridger triangle. The third group (in Northern Utah) was the Fish Eaters, who remained in the Bear River–Logan River region. This latter band, led by Bear Hunter, suffered serious casualties at the Bear River Massacre, as did the Shoshones under Sanpitch.[9]

A fourth band, one usually counted as part of Washakie's band, generally resided on Henry's Fork or Black's Fork of the Green River. This group existed primarily as the mediators or negotiators of the Indian-white trade around Fort Bridger. Like many other Shoshones who made Fort Bridger their home, the leader of this group, Bazil, was the son of a trapper (French) and a Shoshone mother.[10]

Other factors besides government intervention also aided Washakie's ascending reputation. Many Northern Shoshone and Bannock bands, forced to leave the dwindling resources of the Basin to more lucrative sites in Wyoming's mountains and plains, joined Washakie's forces and generally deferred to his leadership. With more warriors under his command, Washakie could afford to take more risks and hunt buffalo on Wyoming's plains. The risks, of course, came from increased exposure to traditional enemies who were also seeking subsistence with greater frequency in Wyoming. The larger tribal population reduced this threat somewhat and certainly added to the probability of success for both Washakie and his followers in buffalo hunting, which required a collective effort.[11]

Typically, the various bands gathered in the fall (late August to early September) to the east of South Pass near the headwaters of the Sweetwater River. Following one large hunt in that area, or farther north into the Wind River Valley, the bands usually split to go to their winter camps. For the Idaho Shoshone and Bannock groups, this might mean traveling back to Green River or other areas west of the Wind River Mountains, but the main body of Eastern Shoshones divided into four main bands. According to Shimkin,

> The band led by Ta'wunasia would go down the Sweetwater to the upper North Platte. That led by Dï'kanïp [not identified in other sources] went straight east to the Powder River Valley; that led by No'oki [Norkok] skirted the base of the Big Horn Mountains, passing through Crow territory, then swung south again to the Powder River

Valley. Washakie ascended Big Wind River, and then crossed the divide to winter near the headwaters of the Greybull.[12]

Although Shimkin's names for the leaders contrasts to some extent with the work done by Hultkrantz, both researchers generally agree on the bands' basic geographical locales. Moreover, three of the four chiefs named by Shimkin agree with the reports made in 1869 by the Indian Agent at Fort Bridger, Lieutenant J. H. Patterson. Patterson identified the Eastern Shoshone leaders as Norkok, Washakie, Tabonsheya [Tawunasia], and Bazil.[13]

In the early spring, most groups hunted and fished, if possible, near their winter camps, waiting for their horses to regain strength after surviving winter's storms and reduced food sources. Then the bands joined Washakie in the Wind River Valley for another buffalo hunt, leaving as summer approached to hold a Sun Dance near Fort Bridger. Following this important ceremony, the people dispersed in smaller band or family units until the fall hunt.

Some traveled to Salt Lake to trade with the Mormons, while others spent the summer in the mountains to hunt deer, elk, and small game and to collect important roots and berries. Still others, perhaps belonging to Bazil's or Norkok's bands, remained at Bridger to sell their accumulations of robes and furs. For example, both Utah Superintendency head O. H. Irish (in 1865) and agent Luther Mann commented on the importance of the Salt Lake City and Fort Bridger robe and fur trade. In 1866, Shoshones sold over a thousand buffalo robes.[14] In total, about fifteen hundred people took part in this annual cycle (although this number might vary by five hundred persons either way, depending on circumstances such as the participation of Bannocks or Utes, or the decisions of Shoshone band leaders). Then in late summer the cycle would begin again, with one major addition. The bands usually congregated around Fort Bridger during this time and waited for the annual distribution of their treaty goods. This practice continued into the early 1870s.[15]

The importance of Fort Bridger to the Eastern Shoshones during the 1860s was not new; clearly the post had been a major component of Shoshone nomadic cycles since the early 1840s. Just as the tribe gathered in the Wind River Valley for the spring and fall hunts, Fort Bridger became

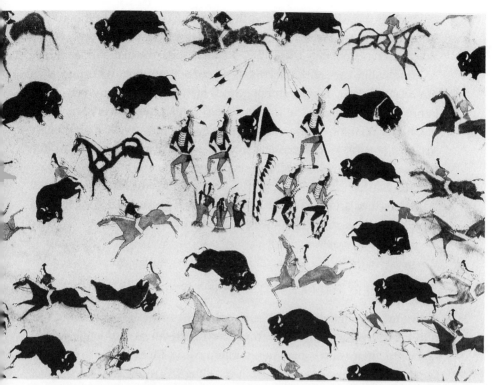

Elk hide painting by Cadzi Cody (or Codsiogo) depicting Sun Dance and buffalo hunt. Note the buffalo head in the forked center pole, and the drum group. Courtesy American Heritage Center, University of Wyoming.

the base for summer activities. Yet the inclusion of "annuity time" into the yearly travels required a new adjustment by the tribe—waiting for their "presents" sometimes upset the fall transition to Wind River.

In 1864, for example, most of the tribe tarried near Fort Bridger until October, anticipating the annuity distribution. While they waited, early snows closed the mountain passes to the Wind River Valley. This meteorological setback paralleled human problems: new incursions of white prospectors to the Sweetwater area scared game from the valley. Washakie was bitterly unhappy about the situation and insisted that the government provide food to his people and forgo the other gifts.[16] Agents Mann and Irish scrambled for funds, doled out some food rations, and appeased Washakie to some extent with promises to deliver the rest of the annuities as soon as they arrived in the spring. For the remainder of the 1860s, Washakie's Shoshones continued to receive their annuities at Fort Bridger, although they generally made their winter camps east of the mountains.

The fact that the Shoshone bands waited for the annuities suggests two observations. First, the government goods held value for the Indians, either intrinsically or as items for further trade. Therefore, they were willing to put off the fall hunt. A corollary is that the summer hunting-fishing-trading season was reasonably successful—it is unlikely that hungry people would have neglected their stomachs in order to obtain cloth and metal goods. Second, Washakie's leadership in part depended on the fact that he could act as intermediary for the tribe and obtain such goods for "free." His rage reflected both a sense of betrayal by the agents as well as loss of status in the eyes of his people.

## MINERS, MERCHANTS, AND TOWNS, 1866–1868

White miners, merchants, townspeople, and farmers also entered the quest for Wind River lands. Like their Shoshone counterparts, white bands launched their forays into the southern Wind River region from Fort Bridger. The furtive prospecting efforts of the 1850s and early 1860s paid off in 1867, when a large vein, the Cariso Lode, came to light. In the wake of the discovery, and despite the obvious presence of "hostile" Sioux (who chased the Cariso prospectors from their claims in 1867), the miners organized the Sweetwater Mining District, with a western boundary set approximately twelve miles east of South Pass. Three towns sprouted quickly: South Pass City, Atlantic City, and Hamilton City (better known as Miner's Delight). By the summer of 1868, the oldest of the three, South Pass City, had a thousand people, complete with two stores, saloons, and perhaps as many as a hundred log houses and buildings.[17]

Merchants marched in lockstep with the miners from Fort Bridger into the disputed lands. In 1866, Major Noyes Baldwin, a former commander of the fort, tried to start a trading station in the Popo Agie River Valley (located between the southern edge of the Wind River Valley and the Sweetwater River Valley). Although he hoped to capitalize on the Shoshone trade, his establishment attracted Sioux bullets and arrows instead, forcing his retreat.[18] By 1867, however, the early gold successes prompted William A. Carter, the sutler at Fort Bridger, to make an exploratory journey to the mining camps, with an eye to opening a store at South Pass City. Carter had a decade of experience trading with the Shoshones at Fort Bridger. By 1866, perhaps as much as 10 percent of Carter's yearly take of $100,000 came from Shoshones, either directly or indirectly. Although his business with Indians is hard to document, the Shoshones reportedly sold $10,000 in furs in 1866–67. He used an in-house token system to barter with Indians and therefore had no need to keep ledgers for this trade. Individual Indians were given brass tokens in payment for robes, dried meat, or hides. The tokens then became legal tender for purchasing supplies in the store. (James K. Moore, the long-time Indian Trader for the Shoshone and Bannock Indian Agency and a former Carter employee, used this method at his reservation store.)[19]

Carter never established a retail outlet in the mining towns, but Baldwin eventually opened a store in South Pass City in 1869 and one in Lander in 1874.[20] Another merchant who became involved in both white and Indian business, Worden P. Noble, founded a general store in Atlantic City in 1868, then within a year started a successful freighting operation for both army and Indian supplies. In the 1870s he filled beef contracts for the reservation and was a partner in the second Indian Trader store.[21]

Perhaps as many as three thousand people flocked to the mining towns during the 1867–70 period; not all of them to dig holes in the ground. Some, like Baldwin and Noble, opened retail businesses. Others found profit in supplying vegetables and other produce to the miners. The best source of farm-grown food lay in the Wind River Valley, "the only arable land within 100 miles of the mines."[22] By 1868, therefore, a number of farmers, three towns, as well as numerous mining claims were in full-scale development on the southern edges of the Wind River region.

## RESERVATION CREATION, 1868

The Eastern Shoshones' rivals—Lakotas, Cheyennes, and Arapahoes—also entered the competition for Wind River during the 1860s. Their histories lie beyond the present study, but it is important to understand the impetus for their actions. White migrations to Colorado, spurred by gold discoveries in 1858, hastened permanent splits in both Cheyenne and Arapahoe peoples, with northern bands moving from the Colorado Front Range to the eastern plains of Wyoming north of the North Platte River.

Atlantic City, ca. 1870. Courtesy American Heritage Center, University of Wyoming.

Meanwhile, several divisions of the Teton Lakota—primarily Oglalas, Miniconjous, and Sans Arcs—possessed rights to the eastern edges of the Powder River Basin. By the mid-1860s, Arapahoes under Medicine Man took over the North Platte to Sweetwater ranges, while Black Bear's people intermarried with Lakotas and traveled from the North Platte to the Black Hills. The Cheyennes moved back into their old hunting lands of the pre-1851 treaty era—the northern and eastern sides of the Big Horn Mountains. In so doing, they forced the Crows to retreat to the west side of the Big Horns.[23]

In 1866, the government sought to win new concessions from the Lakotas in order to construct forts along a new road (the Bozeman Trail) from Fort Laramie to the Montana goldfields (thereby bisecting the prime buffalo-hunting grounds of the Powder River). Red Cloud and Man-Afraid-of-His-Horse, two prominent Oglala Lakota leaders, refused to sign, although Spotted Tail of the Brule Lakota did (as did some of the "Laramie Loafers"—Sioux who congregated about Fort Laramie). The

South Pass City, ca. 1870. Courtesy American Heritage Center, University of Wyoming.

Brule, however, hunted south of the Platte River, so the army did not gain the permission of the Lakota most affected by the Bozeman Trail. When Forts Kearny, Reno, and Smith were constructed anyway, the Lakotas, Arapahoes, and Cheyennes began concerted efforts to repel whites from the lands guaranteed to Indians by the 1851 agreement.[24] They also surged westward from the North Platte–Powder River lands into the heart of the Wind River, a distance of no more than 150 miles, to attack both Shoshone hunters and the Sweetwater miners. Thus white intrusions through the middle of Oglala lands to the east of Wind River and southeast into Arapahoe-Cheyenne territory in Colorado contributed to the convergence of peoples on Wyoming's plains. This resulted in increased intertribal warfare over dwindling buffalo herds.

The Plains-going Shoshones took on new importance in white eyes in the changed realities of the mid-1860s. Luther Mann baldly stated the case in 1867: "Their [Shoshone] occupancy of the valley, with suitable protection from the government, would prevent the raiding war parties of Sioux from interfering with the development of the mines just discovered and being opened in the vicinity of South Pass, where, within a few days, a large party of miners were driven away by a small band of hostile Indians, after three or more of their number had been inhumanely murdered."[25] In other words, a reservation for the Shoshones at Wind River could shield whites from Sioux attacks. This fact, as much as anything, explained the willingness of Wind River whites to tolerate a nearby Indian reservation.

At the national level, other concerns sparked plans for creating a Shoshone reserve. In mid-1867 crews of the Union Pacific Railroad hammered in the tracks of the "iron horse" in Nebraska; by January 1868 passenger trains steamed into the new boomtown of Cheyenne. Completion of the transcontinental line inevitably meant more emigrants and white settlers on Indian lands, which meant increased destruction of game and ongoing warfare with Plains Indians. Furthermore, the land grants given to the railroad builders were not valid until Indians relinquished their own claims first. In other words, numerous factors coalesced to bring about calls for new treaties with all the affected tribes.

The United States Congress began the new treaty process in 1867 by creating the Indian Peace Commission.[26] The Commission, comprised of army officers and civilians, dealt at first with only the Plains tribes along the Missouri, Arkansas, and Platte Rivers. Their main objective was to make peace with "hostile" Indians, but their vision extended westward as well to those bands still at peace with the government. In their report of January 7, 1868, the Commission stated that "in the course of a short time the Union Pacific railroad will have reached the country claimed by the Snakes, Bannocks, and other tribes, and in order to preserve peace with them the commission should be required to see them and make them satisfactory arrangements."[27]

Congress agreed with the recommendations. The Peace Commission met with the Bannocks and the Eastern Shoshones in early July, 1868, at Fort Bridger. On July 3, 1868, the council attendees signed a new treaty of peace between the Shoshones, Bannocks, and the United States. The cornerstone of the thirteen articles was the creation of a reservation in the Wind River Valley for the exclusive use of the Shoshones.

The new treaty contained several important elements. First, the Shoshones were not required to make a permanent relocation to Wind River until the agency building, residences, and shops were constructed. More significantly for the Shoshones, the same clause granted them the right to hunt off-reservation on the "unoccupied lands of the United States." Other articles provided for education of Indian children "in order to insure the civilization of the tribes entering into this Treaty," and for allotments of land, seeds, and farm implements to heads of households. The treaty further specified in exact detail the clothing and other goods the Shoshones would receive each September for the next thirty years. Another clause gave the Bannocks future rights to their own separate reservation. Although the Indians gained certain rights and privileges, the United States treaty commissioners clearly stated federal policy in the treaty—the Indians were supposed to become farmers.[28]

Despite the broad sweep of the treaty's provisions, it ignored one potential problem. The new reservation's southern borders included two of the towns in the Sweetwater Mining District. This may have been a mapping oversight, but the treaty language specifically stated that only authorized personnel had the right to reside within the reservation boundaries or even to cross its lands. Miners and settlers were not "authorized personnel." In other words, complications attended the reservation's birth, precluding simple and painless delivery. Moreover, while the treaty writers may have had visions of a neat and orderly future history for the Shoshones and their new home, the complex amalgam of peoples, cultures, and economies of the Wind River community insured a far different outcome, one in which the various peoples spoke their own stories.

## FORGING A RESERVATION COMMUNITY, 1868–1870

In July 1868, the Shoshone and Bannock Indian Agency in the Wind River Valley existed only as a geographical place. However, it encompassed a vast diversity of plant and animal life, climate, and geological structures. Essentially a basin cut through by the Wind River–Big Horn drainages, the three-million- acre reservation included high mountains, arid sagebrush hills, relatively flat plateaus, and conifer forests. Elevations range from five thousand to twelve thousand feet and higher along the crest of the Wind River Mountains. Temperatures drop to –50 degrees Fahrenheit or lower in winter and rise over 100 degrees in summer. Rainfall measures less than twelve inches annually in most of the lower elevations, while snowfall

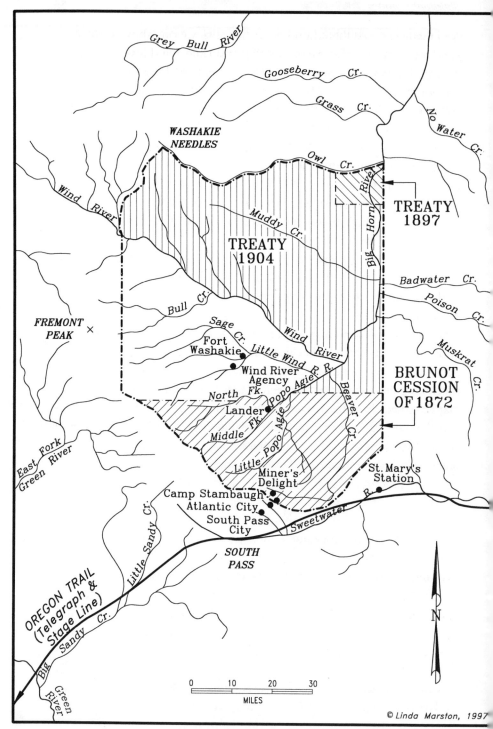

Map 2. Shoshone and Bannock Indian Agency, 1868–1872

frequently exceeds three hundred inches at elevations above eight thousand feet. The major streams—the Big and Little Wind Rivers, the Popo Agie and its branches, and the Big Horn River (which for the most part is the northward-flowing and lower portion of the Big Wind River)—typically bulge to overflowing during the spring thaws, often cutting ribbonlike channels through gravel beds. By late summer, however, especially in drought years, even the largest rivers recede to easily forded trickles.

The more mountainous areas supported elk, mule and white-tail deer, and mountain sheep, while the plains and arid plateaus abounded with antelope, sage hens, and jackrabbits. The most important food source for the Shoshones, buffalo, mainly ranged north and east of the reservation in the Big Horn River and Powder River Basins. Edible wild berries (currants, gooseberries, hawthorns, and rose berries), greens (honey plants, gilia, cinque-foil), wild roots (tobacco root, biscuit root, Indian turnips, sego lilies, and onions), and grass seeds also grew in various locations throughout the reservation area.[29]

At the time of the creation of the reservation, the Eastern Shoshones were accustomed to methodical and cyclical harvests of the bounty of Wind River environment. In the late winter months (February to April), the whole tribe generally gathered in the Wind River Valley to go to the buffalo grounds of the Big Horn Basin. They also supplemented fresh buffalo meat diets with fish, rabbits and early greens. Summer meant dispersal into bands and family groups; travel to Fort Bridger for trading; hunting mountain sheep, elk, and deer; and collecting seeds, berries, and roots. In autumn (August to October), the bands slowly filtered back to Wind River, gathering en masse for the important fall buffalo hunt when the animals were at their heaviest weights. During the winter months, Shoshones resided in small family bands. Some remained in the Wind River area; others camped along the Sweetwater or the foothills of the Absaroka Mountains (in present-day Montana). Pemmican diets and the occasional elk or beaver sustained the families until they again gathered for the spring hunt.[30]

Thus, while the agency existed on paper, the reservation served as the Shoshones' pantry and their part-time home. There were no agency buildings, storerooms, houses, or offices on-site at Wind River in 1868. Luther Mann, Jr., the first agent, continued to work from his office inside the military post of Fort Bridger, as he had done since his appointment in

1861 as the agent-in-charge of the Fort Bridger subagency within the Utah Superintendency. Meanwhile, the Shoshones (and Bannocks) adhered to their traditional nomadic cycles of periodic occupancy of Wind River. Nevertheless, a heterogeneous community slowly evolved in the valley as its members forged common bonds.

The Sweetwater gold rush had lured miners to a region that was both Indian battleground and Indian hunting territory. Shoshones knew Wind River's perils from long experience; their nomadic life partially reflected the dangers of summering east of the mountains. White miners paid no heed to Shoshonean experience, but neither their ignorance nor their bravado protected them from intertribal conflicts—they were drawn into the thick of Plains warfare.

Intensified fighting formed a backdrop to the formation of the Wind River community. In the summer of 1867, for instance, skirmishes scared the miners to such a degree that Agent Mann feared they would retaliate against any Indian group that wandered in their direction, including Washakie's band. In order to prevent bloodshed, but more importantly to instruct the whites about the benefits of having a "friendly" tribe live among them, the agent visited the mining camps and towns in the fall of 1867. Mann timed his trip so that his arrival preceded that of the Sho-shones, who were on their way to the fall hunt east of the Wind River Mountains. Mann informed F. G. Head, Superintendent of Indian Affairs for the Utah Superintendency, that he assured "the miners that the best feeling existed between these Indians and the whites, and that their presence in the valley would be protection against any more raids by the Sioux, which proved true, all hostilities having ceased against the miners until after the Shoshones had returned to this agency."[31]

Mann hedged his report; it is quite likely he knew that seasonal peace generally halted Indian warfare during the winter months. The Oglala Sioux quickly took up their weapons in the following spring with a raid on the Shoshones. Sporadic attacks continued on the mining towns throughout the treaty summer of 1868.[32] Nevertheless, Mann's efforts marked the beginning of wary cooperation between the Eastern Shoshone bands and the whites who occupied Shoshone lands. For the next few years, Wind River whites recognized the defensive value of their nomadic neighbors. In this case, self-preservation outweighed resentment against the fact that the new agency interfered with homesteads and mining claims. On their part, the Shoshones valued the additional firearms held by the miners and the increased trading opportunities. These factors generally overcame grumbling directed toward whites who drove away game or whose settlements were unwelcome fixtures on the reserve.

Wind River whites and Shoshones quickly acknowledged their common plight in spring 1869, when Red Cloud's Oglala warriors stepped up the pace of their attacks. The Sioux killed eight settlers and miners and twenty-five Shoshones in April and May. Mining town residents pleaded with Governor John A. Campbell to send in troops and weapons for protection; Washakie wanted even more—a permanent barracks. Campbell, Wyoming's first territorial governor as well as the ex-officio Superintendent of Indian Affairs for the new territory, urged General Christopher C. Augur to send out support from Fort Bridger.[33] In particular, the governor hoped that the army's backing would convince Washakie to remain at Wind River and function as a barrier to the Sioux: "It is very desirable that these Indians be induced to settle on their Reservation, not only in order that they may be prepared to carry out their part of the Treaty, but also because the presence of these Indians will serve to assist in protecting the Wind River Valley and the miners in the Sweetwater from the Sioux."[34]

In June 1869, Campbell reported that Luther Mann was on his way to the reservation to establish an agency, with General Augur sending infantry in support. By the end of the month Washakie had his army post; Camp Augur was built on the Big Popo Agie River.[35] Mann, however, only scouted the valley and did not move his headquarters to the new post. Instead, he continued his operations from Fort Bridger and used Camp Augur as a subpost for the Shoshone and Bannock Agency.

The increased defenses did not deter Sioux raiders. In mid-September, 1869, nearly 150 warriors engaged the soldiers and retreated only after a two-hour battle. Still more attacks occurred during the rest of the month, with four people killed very near Camp Augur.[36] The conflicts continued well into 1870, with various reports stating that the attacking warriors were Sioux, Cheyennes, and Arapahoes.[37]

While Red Cloud and the Oglala Sioux clearly resented white and Shoshone penetration into Wind River, the Northern Arapahoes perhaps were unfortunate or unwilling participants in these struggles. Their tribal elders had been working to untangle themselves from involvement in the Plains warfare ever since the Sand Creek Massacre in 1864. Arapahoe

Governor John A. Campbell. Courtesy American Heritage Center, University of Wyoming.

leaders Black Bear, Medicine Man, Little Wolf, Littleshield, and Sorrel Horse had met with the Peace Commissioners in 1868, initially hoping to secure their own reservation in Wyoming, but tribal disunity weakened their bargaining position. At the conclusion of the council, they agreed to move in 1869 to one of three places: near the Missouri River with the

Sioux; in Indian Territory with the Southern Arapahoes; or near Yellowstone with the Crows.[38]

None of these options pleased the tribe. Instead, they wanted to stay in Wyoming and avoid absorption into larger Plains groups. Medicine Man and Black Bear continued their efforts to gain a Wyoming location, hoping to reach some sort of accommodation with the Shoshones and share their reservation. General Augur and Governor Campbell arranged an October meeting in 1869 between Washakie and Medicine Man, Sorrel Horse, Friday (who knew Washakie personally), and others, but the Shoshone chief warily avoided all contact with his rivals and went hunting in the Big Horns.[39]

The two tribes finally met in February 1870 and the Arapahoes received permission to occupy Shoshone country. This was, however, a short-lived peace. Seven more miners lost their lives in an Indian attack on March 31, 1870, and the Arapahoes were blamed (along with the Sioux and Cheyennes). A combined white and Shoshone party, 250 strong, responded by killing eight to fourteen Arapahoes, including Black Bear, on April 8. This escalated hostilities on all sides and strained Shoshone-Arapahoe relationships. The Arapahoes left the area shortly thereafter, but managed to convince Governor Campbell that they were innocent of the attacks on the mining camps. But Washakie remained suspicious of the Arapahoes, despite the peaceable gestures. Furthermore, the Shoshones had just renewed friendly relationships with the Crows, an alliance that opposed the Arapahoe, Cheyenne, and Sioux combination.[40]

The Sioux remained a serious threat to the Wind River community. The mining towns lost nearly half their populations, evacuated largely due to fear of warfare. Consequently, the army established Fort Stambaugh in August 1870 to protect the miners. Fort Stambaugh, located within a few miles of the three towns, lay thirty miles from Camp Augur (renamed Camp Brown in March 1870).[41] Thus, before even a single agency building rose from the valley floor, the Wind River reservation contained one mining town and fort, with two other towns and another fort nearby. More whites than Shoshones lived there year round.

## FROM FORT BRIDGER TO WIND RIVER, 1869–1871

Despite the addition of two military posts to the Wind River region, Fort Bridger remained the Shoshone and Bannock headquarters. Several factors dictated this situation. First, Indian attacks were too numerous to allow business during the summer months in Wind River (neither post carried sufficient troop strength to provide complete protection). Second, the Shoshones refused to abandon their normal routines. Finally, a change in administration at the national level interfered with agency operations.

President Ulysses S. Grant's inauguration in March 1869 heralded a new direction in U.S. Indian policy, although reforms of the "Indian system" had been advocated throughout the Civil War era by religious crusaders such as John Beason of Oregon and the Episcopal Bishop of Minnesota, the Right Reverend Henry B. Whipple.[42] Moreover, in 1865 Congress authorized the Doolittle Committee to examine the condition of Indian tribes and to suggest reforms in the way the United States approached its Indian "wards." After touring the West and visiting various tribes, the Doolittle Committee issued a report of its findings in January 1867. The release of the report came on the heels of attacks by Oglala Sioux on military establishments on the northern Plains between 1865 and 1867, including the famous Fetterman Massacre of December 1867.[43] Galvanized into action by the Doolittle report and the violence, members of the Society of Friends (Quakers), Whipple's Episcopal contacts, and other Christian reformers convinced Grant to "civilize" Native Americans by exposing them to the influence of good Christian Indian agents and teachers, and, at the same time, abandon the "morally corrupt" practices of previous administrations. Grant began by removing agency appointments from congressional patronage and naming army officers and Quakers to the positions. Thus, Captain J. H. Patterson replaced Luther Mann in July 1869, with Lieutenant G. M. Fleming taking charge in November 1869. Another officer, J. W. Wham, took over in August 1870.[44]

Grant's actions put him at odds with congressional members because of his bold attack on their patronage perquisites. In retribution, the Congress refused to confirm the military appointments. A compromise was reached during the summer of 1870 when the president and his Secretary of the Interior, Jacob D. Cox, asked other denominations to join with the Quakers and the government to reform the Office of Indian Affairs. In essence, the "Quaker Policy" of 1869 evolved into the "Peace Policy" a year later.[45] The president, upon the recommendation of the United States Board of Indian Commissioners, approved final appointments to the agencies. This board, a group of successful businessmen named by President Grant to oversee Indian affairs, possessed quasi-legal governmental powers and operated somewhat independently of both Congress and the Department of the Interior. It was hoped by both the administration's Peace Policy proponents and by the churches involved that this peculiar church-state combination would hasten the domestication and integration of Indian tribes into the general fabric of American life (i.e., into "civilized and Christian" American life).

The pace of national Peace Policy reforms proceeded at a normal bureaucratic tempo. The Quakers, as authors of the original plan, had begun their work in mid-1869 in Nebraska and Kansas. Other reservations, such as the Shoshone and Bannock Agency, received their Christian appointees much more slowly. Thus, the first Peace Policy agent for the Wind River peoples, Dr. James Irwin, did not assume control until May 7, 1871.[46]

Before the Peace Policy filtered into Wyoming, the rapid turnover in agents prevented implementation of treaty requirements. Therefore, the military and civilian agents who held office between 1869 and 1871 accomplished little more than disbursing annuity goods and dispensing food; this they did from Fort Bridger. Furthermore, beginning with Luther Mann's departure and continuing until Irwin's arrival, a complex set of relationships characterized the reservation administrations.

The intricacies of reservation politics began in the governor's office. Governor Campbell wanted the Shoshones to settle down. He also wanted them to sell the southern portion of the reservation in order to dispel the problem of trespassing whites on Wind River lands. A pragmatist, Campbell clearly favored his white constituency, especially the South Pass area miners and the mine owners. On February 21, 1870, Campbell wrote to the Secretary of the Interior, noting that only the unpalatable use of military force could expel the miners. As an alternative, he believed that the Shoshones would be willing to "permit the residence of bona fide settlers and farmers on certain designated portions of their reservation," which might mean that these "parties of whites and friendly Indians would form a mutual protection against the hostile Indians."[47]

Campbell knew that in order to obtain a land cession from the Shoshones, he had to fulfill the government's treaty obligations first. That is, he needed appropriations for buildings, irrigating ditches, and agricultural supplies. In late May, 1870, he wrote that he was "anxious to get the

Shoshoni. I.

Washakie's camp at South Pass, ca. 1870. Courtesy American Heritage Center,
University of Wyoming.

buildings up . . . this summer, in order to convince the Indians we are in
earnest, and [to] be ready to put in crops next spring."[48] In the same letter
he gave further evidence of appeasing the Shoshones: he reported that
he had instructed Agent Fleming to give the Shoshones "provisions if
necessary and report their condition and wishes as soon as possible."[49]

Fleming was caught between pleasing Campbell and pleasing Washakie.
The Shoshone leader complained that the government violated the treaty
(no buildings erected, for example) and he insisted on receiving annuities
at Fort Bridger. Washakie also used impeccable logic, arguing that the
government would save time and money by shipping goods only as far as
Bridger and forgoing the expense of freighting goods an additional 150
miles to Wind River.[50]

In other words, Washakie forestalled a permanent relocation to Wind
River. It appears that he hoped to manipulate the government into
adopting a Shoshonean vision of reservation existence—with a Wind

Close-up of Washakie's camp. Note Washakie with the saw, working on a teepee pole. The white man standing right of Washakie is Lieutenant Young. Left of Washakie is Dick Washakie, his son. To the right of Lt. Young is Tegotie. George Washakie, another son, is standing in back. Second from the right end is one of Washakie's daughters. The first man seated on the ground to the right of Washakie is Matavish. The rest of people, unidentified, are presumably Washakie's wives, children, and other relatives. Courtesy American Heritage Center, University of Wyoming.

River agency to provide aid and sustenance during winter's harsh climate, and a Fort Bridger base from which to continue traditional Basin excursions in the summer. For the next few years, Washakie's vision prevailed, much to the consternation of agents, the governor, and Wind River whites.

Washakie's negotiations probably gained strength from the confused state of the Fort Bridger subagency. Governor Campbell called for Fleming's replacement in July 1870 because the agent "insolently" answered Campbell's questions about the June distribution of food and annuities.[51] The veracity of Campbell's accusations is doubtful, but it is clear that Fleming had not spent much time organizing his office affairs. When J. W. Wham, Lieutenant Fleming's successor, arrived in August 1870, he reported:

The Agent had no office nor office furniture, and the only papers that I received was one map of the Reservation and one copy of the Treaty of 1868, and one circular relative to the appointment of Traders. I found no funds on hand, and the only property that I found was Two Wall Tents. I have rented an office until such time as work is commenced on the Agency building, when I would recommend that the Agency be transferred to that point. There is no Indians here and the Agent dont know where they are.[52]

Wham immediately began to prepare for the task that lay before him. The day after his arrival, the new agent proposed an agency budget (totaling $96,000), sought permission to purchase a horse and a wagon for his transportation, and urged that the government advertise for bids for the erection of agency buildings.[53] With Campbell's backing, Wham made quick progress. By November, he was located on the reservation at Camp Brown and the Shoshones received their annuity goods in the Wind River Valley for the first time.

Despite his apparent success, Wham endured his share of bureaucratic tribulations: he was called to account for an exorbitant salary ($1,400 annually) paid to his agency carpenter and to explain why he exhausted the $10,000 allotted to his incidental fund. Wham defended himself, saying that he wanted discretion to pay his employees what he thought they were worth, as long as he did not exceed his total employee budget ($6,800). He was able to hire an agency farmer for $900 yearly, and Norkok accepted $500 to interpret. A physician agreed to $1,200. His heavy drain on the incidental fund was blamed on building repairs, purchases of a heating and cook stove and grain for the horses, and a salary for a courier to send messages to the Indians. In addition to the budgetary problems, the Shoshones faced starvation—Sioux and Cheyenne attacks prevented subsistence hunting. As Wham put it, either "the cheyennes & sioux must be driven away or the shoshones and Bannocks must be fed."[54]

No one, including the troops from Fort Stambaugh and Camp Brown, vanquished the "cheyennes & sioux." Forced to choose the second route, Wham obtained permission to issue temporary rations, but impending winter snows and communication delays hampered his efforts. He also feared that the provisions would not last beyond the middle of December. Washakie, however, circumnavigated the bureaucratic channels by more traditional means—his tribe of hunters-gatherers discovered thirteen hundred pounds of potatoes at Tilford Kutch's truck farm. Tilford Kutch was one of the settlers who homesteaded in the Wind River Valley before the 1868 treaty. Wham asked Commissioner Parker to reimburse Kutch $192.00 for the stolen potatoes.[55]

Other complications arose. Wham signed a contract for erecting the agency buildings with the firm of Swingle and Williams on November 14, 1870, but two months passed before the contract received approval and work started. Purchases of seeds, farming implements, machinery, and other necessary equipment also required authorization. So did an official survey of the reservation, which never had been drawn. These delays frustrated Wham but characterized interactions between all Indian agencies and the Office of Indian Affairs.[56]

Nevertheless, Wham's attempts to forge an agency yielded interesting consequences for the fledgling community in the Wind River Valley. Most contacts between the Shoshones and their white neighbors had been limited to trading, especially in the mining areas; a few marriages; and joint defense. Wham facilitated even more interactions between the heterogeneous cultures inhabiting the region. He hired local men in agency positions, drew from the pool of mining-town workers to build the agency's infrastructure, mediated disputes, and encouraged farming efforts by whites in the Wind River Valley. In fact, during Wham's tenure, whites increased their share of the economic life of the reservation. For example, Swingle and William, builders of several structures in the mining towns and dabblers in other businesses, successfully bid on the agency office building contract. Merchant J. V. A. Carter of Fort Bridger served as the first agency physician. John Felter, who once leased his buildings in South Pass City as court and jury rooms, became a subcontractor for the agency's masonry work.[57]

To some extent, then, the prosperity of Wind River whites paralleled the amount of government spending for the reservation. As the gold mines played out in late 1870 and into 1871, the reservation's potential for fiscal salvation to area whites loomed even larger. Prospective employees, building contractors, and food and/or supply vendors all saw the reservation as an integral part of their futures. In some sense, the Wind River whites assumed an "ownership" aura concerning the reservation. When official policies interfered or otherwise planted obstacles to fulfilling future visions, conflicts emerged.

The first and, to some extent, the longest-lasting problem faced by Wham and subsequent agents concerned the status of white settlers on reservation lands, especially those who homesteaded before the treaty. Wham posted at least one notice in the *South Pass News* ordering whites from the reservation, but this notice affected only those who settled after November 3, 1870, not those who were Wind River Valley residents before that date.[58] For these pioneers he probably favored, as did Governor Campbell, the "movement on foot to detach the Popoagie Valley [the disputed area] from this Reservation and [have it] thrown open for settlement."[59] In other matters, Wham used the army to chase white buffalo hunters from the reservation—Washakie bitterly complained about these hunters because they drove the animals east toward the Sioux and added to the dangers of subsistence hunting.[60]

Wham did not stay long enough at the agency to reap any fruit from his policies. On December 24, 1870, he requested a leave of absence, putting the agency affairs in the hands of J. E. Hodges, his highly paid carpenter and right-hand man.[61] Although Wham returned to the reservation in March 1871, he did so only to pack his belongings. In the spring of 1871 he was reassigned as agent to the Oglala Sioux, assuming charge of the Red Cloud Agency in Nebraska. Dr. James Irwin, formerly of Cheyenne, Wyoming, and most recently a resident of Atlantic City, Wyoming, replaced Wham. This change in agency management corresponded to the implementation of the Peace Policy at Wind River. It also severed the reservation's official ties to Fort Bridger, despite the meager facilities of the agency in the Wind River Valley. Hodges reported that the agency building was a three-room affair that served as both office and residence. All other treaty-required features were missing: no employee houses, no fenced or cultivated fields, no tools, and no school.[62] Yet, because Irwin already lived in the area, his immersion into his tasks began within the confines of the reservation. Unlike his predecessors, Irwin learned to know the Shoshones as fellow Wind River peoples, not from the farther view offered by Fort Bridger.

*Chapter Three*

# James Irwin vs.
# Wind River Whites

## 1871–1873

### THE PEACE POLICY COMES TO WIND RIVER, 1871

Dr. James Irwin's appointment as Shoshone and Bannock Indian Agent changed the composition of the Wind River community of peoples. Specifically, his presence at the agency interjected a new layer of bureaucracy. Under previous agents, U.S. government policies and regulations did little to hamper the freedom of exchange between area whites and Indians. J. W. Wham, for example, actually aided such interactions. Robert Hughes, a Sweetwater County representative in the second territorial legislature, said Wham invited people "to come on and improve the Reservation, and make it more valuable, and the Indians had asked them to stay and settle there, as they were a protection against hostile Indians."[1] Irwin's appointment, however, ushered in different rules by which community life had to be conducted. As the first administrator of these regulations, Irwin attracted widespread attention from area merchants, townspeople, and farmers. Likewise, the actions of whites precipitated further responses from Irwin.

Problems in the Wind River Valley began with the implementation of the new federal Peace Policy. Irwin intended his administration to reflect the tenets of President Grant's directives, that is, to "civilize" and "Christianize" Native Americans according to white definitions. However, there were at least two flaws in these ideals. First, the policy's authors neglected (or intentionally disregarded) incorporation of Native American voices in charting future paths. This meant that adherence to Peace Policy goals by Indians was not guaranteed: most Native Americans had their own interpretations of treaty obligations and generally acted to fulfill the tribal visions, not those of federal policymakers.

Secondly, besides ignoring Indians, the eastern orientation of many of the Peace Policy writers did not reflect the views of their western constituents. Irwin marched into this trap. Many Wind River merchants, miners, and settlers eventually opposed his understanding of the Peace Policy. They had recommended the doctor's appointment believing that his administration would reflect the needs and concerns of the local white community and only secondarily those of the Indians. Therefore, the tensions inherent in this heterogeneous community of Wind River whites and Wind River Indians served notice that forging any semblance of common life goals was nearly impossible.

The initial questions in Irwin's tenure, however, did not involve local tensions. Instead, they began at the national level and illustrated cracks in the management of the Peace Policy. Irwin was a non-Episcopalian assigned to an Episcopal agency and, contrary to Peace Policy expectations, as well as those of the church's missionary board, patronage politics tainted his appointment.

The Episcopal Church's participation in the Peace Policy began with the formation of its own Indian Commission in December 1871. An arm of the Domestic Committee of the Board of Missions, the Indian Commission had an initial $50,000 budget that hardly covered the costs of missionaries, teachers, and church or school buildings at its seven assigned agencies. The church had not requested the supervision of the Shoshones and Bannocks—the Indian outreach work in Dakota Territory agencies among the Sioux, Cheyenne, and Ponca tribes severely taxed its fiscal resources.[2] Indeed, the Reverend Henry Dyer, Secretary of the American Church Missionary Society of the Episcopal Church, revealed his surprise about the Shoshone "acquisition." He wrote to Secretary of the Interior Columbus Delano on February 23, 1871: "A note just received from Col. Colyer informs me that you have placed the Shoshone and Bannock Agency in Wyoming Territory under the care of our Society. As this is the first intimation we have had of the disposition of this Agency, I beg to ask whether the assigning of this Agency to our Society is in accordance with any previous understanding, or is it something new?"[3]

The assignment was "something new" and not entirely welcomed. Church officials discovered that there were limits to the federal cooperation with the religious organizations invited to Peace Policy parleys. The Commissioner of Indian Affairs, Francis A. Walker, informed Dyer that the Society could not dispense $5000 authorized by Congress for school buildings nor spend federal funds to hire teachers until after the schools were constructed. This instruction countered Dyer's hopes that the church could use federal monies to defray church-related expenses regarding schools and teachers. Moreover, the Episcopal Church in Wyoming Territory was poverty-stricken and lacked adequate clergy for white parishes and missions. Wyoming parishioners contributed only four dollars in 1869 and seventeen dollars in 1870 to Indian mission work.[4]

There were other weaknesses in the church's role among the Shoshones. Simply put, the church submitted to political pressure when it took on the Shoshone and Bannock Agency. President Grant's second Secretary of the Interior, Columbus Delano, traded the Wind River reserve to the church in exchange for a patronage favor. Delano wanted the church to name J. W. Wham as agent in charge of the Red Cloud Agency in what is now western Nebraska. This agency, designated for the Oglala Sioux, was another addition to the existing Episcopalian network of Peace Policy reservations, but Wham, like Irwin, was not an Episcopalian. There was no rule that required Peace Policy agents to adhere strictly to sponsoring denominations, but the practice was customary. Wham may have had some ties to the church, but he was deemed "heretical" by 1872 and his administrative troubles led to his removal that year.[5] Since Wham had been the pre-Peace Policy agent for the Shoshones, Delano's maneuvering violated the tenets of Peace Policy principles. At the same time, the Episcopal Church gained two more agencies (adding prestige and influence, despite the financial pitfalls), but had to accept less control because of the non-Episcopal background of Wham and Irwin. Thus at the federal level, Peace Policy ideals suffered grievous wounds at the hands of Grant's highest administrator and by church leaders who bowed to political pressures. Adding irony to injury, Delano himself was an Episcopalian.[6]

Nevertheless, the Episcopal Church eventually had some cause for rejoicing in Irwin's appointment and was able to repair some of the "cracks" in its connection with the Peace Policy. Although he began his agency position as a nominal Quaker, Irwin became a steadfast communicant in the Episcopal fold. Furthermore, Irwin possessed some Episcopal connections—he attended services at St. Mark's Episcopal Church in Cheyenne, Wyoming, in 1868 and 1869 and had strong recommendations from its members as well as from the Right Reverend George M. Randall, Bishop of the Missionary District of Colorado, New Mexico, and Wyoming.[7]

Irwin brought other credentials with him that kept church leaders from experiencing embarrassment about their decision to support his application.[8] Unlike many new Indian agents, Irwin had both administrative experience and some knowledge of Indians. Born in Pennsylvania on July 23, 1817, trained as a physician in Iowa, Irwin had his first official contact with Indians during the Civil War, when he served as a surgeon with the Eighth Iowa Infantry. Irwin treated the captured and injured Sioux who were banished to Davenport, Iowa, in 1862 in the aftermath of their revolt at Spirit Lake, Minnesota.[9]

Following his service in the Union Army, Irwin traveled west. In 1868 he moved to Cheyenne, where he operated the city hospital and coroner's office and during this time worshipped at St. Mark's. He relocated a year later to Atlantic City, opened a medical practice, and was appointed a county justice of the peace.[10] Undoubtedly these positions afforded Irwin the opportunity to encounter influential white members of the Wind River community. When the gold mines started to play out, resulting in a declining population and subsequent loss of paying clientele, Irwin touted his experiences and connections to obtain the agency position.[11]

## JAMES IRWIN VERSUS WIND RIVER SETTLERS, 1871–1873

Irwin's relationship with the Episcopal Church thus may have had tenuous beginnings, but it did not interfere with his initial administration. On the other hand, his relationship with area whites, begun under relatively favorable circumstances, degenerated rapidly and definitely affected his leadership. His problems began innocuously enough, but by the end of his first year in office, Irwin's tenure as agent was in doubt.

The first difficulty that tested the doctor's capabilities lay in the agency's physical condition. The contract for the erection of the agency buildings and residences had been awarded to local builders Swingle and Williams in November 1870.[12] They began their work in January 1871 during agent J. W. Wham's absence and before Irwin's arrival. When Irwin moved to the reservation in May, the buildings stood unfinished and exhibited numerous examples of slipshod construction: the roof leaked, uneven floors revealed the ground beneath, and chimneys cracked. Irwin's complaints to the contractors about the situation garnered a slow response—they did not return to work until August 17. Two weeks later they completed the task to Irwin's satisfaction.[13]

This relatively benign action, however, set the tone for some far-reaching consequences. At first glance, Irwin merely demanded what was right and held the contractors accountable for their performance. From another perspective, Irwin's action meant that the agency was not going to be the proverbial "gravy train" for local whites. To some extent, Irwin, and the bureaucracy for which he stood, required an "honest day's work for an honest day's pay." At the very least, Irwin's presence meant that Wind River whites no longer had free access to the reservation. Unlike Wham, Irwin erected an administrative barrier between Indians and settlers in the Wind River community.

Wham also contributed directly to Irwin's troubles. Whereas Columbus Delano played patronage politics at the national level, Wham had tried to do the same at Wind River. He wanted J. E. Hodges, his highly paid assistant, to succeed him. He attempted to aid Hodges's appointment by suggesting that the Shoshones objected to Irwin. Just before Irwin's arrival at the agency, the Shoshones left the reservation (in violation of their treaty agreement) to go to the Basin regions. Although this was part of normal Shoshonean routine, Wham used the Indians' absence to impugn Irwin's reputation. Wham concocted a story that the Indians feared that Irwin would poison them in revenge for the killing of his teenage son in 1870. Seventeen-year-old Frank Irwin had been a victim of a Sioux attack on the mining camps and his father knew the Shoshones were not involved.[14]

Irwin's predecessor placed other impediments to the smooth transition of agency management. He refused to release agency funds to Irwin's account for over four months, preventing Irwin from making necessary purchases for the Indians.[15] Wham may have engaged in a local swindle as well, although only circumstantial evidence suggests this. Before Irwin's arrival, Wham arranged several business contracts with R. L. Smith (referred to as Captain Smith by the editors of the *South Pass News*), concerning deliveries of beef and flour and the erection of an agency blockhouse.[16] The Treasury Department found irregularities in some of the vouchers issued by Wham to Smith, including the absence of delivery dates and of formal contracts. On at least one occasion, treasury auditors denied payments.[17]

Perhaps as a result of these errors (or violations), either Irwin or the Indian Affairs Office switched vendors for the flour and beef contracts for the remainder of the year.[18] This action seemingly provoked Smith into making Irwin's job more difficult than it already was. Irwin noted in a December letter to acting Commissioner Henry Clum that "there is a class of men hanging around this agency with whom I am not popular. As soon as my name was mentioned, these men headed by a certain Captain Smith and others attached to J. W. Wham's party have not failed to throw every obstacle my way."[19]

Irwin also had confrontations with other men who were Wham's associates. One of these, Benjamin F. Lowe, had a long history in the Wind River area. He had worked as a freighter on the Oregon Trail, as a trader for the South Pass Overland Stage Station, and for the Pony Express. He later played a part in the founding of Lander in 1884. Believing that Lowe was reliable, Irwin hired him in 1871 as a messenger and interpreter to the Indians. Irwin hoped that Lowe would help to downplay the rumors spread by Wham and Captain Smith. He did not realize, however, that Lowe and Wham might have colluded on falsifying the Shoshone Agency payroll, with Lowe orchestrating a theft of Indian annuities. Irwin's appeal to Clum in December described his disillusionment with Lowe:

> When the Indians arrived Lowe came with them and proposed that we would divide up their (Shoshone) annuites [sic] and said I was d——md Green, that he could show me how to make money, that it was customary, etc. He then grew angry and demanded that I pay him one thousand dollars a year as Bannock interpreter, and carry some other name on the roll, and employ him under his real name as messenger, and give him plenty to do on paper and permit him to be Sole Trader for the Bannocks, and threatened that through his influence with the Indians and other parties give me trouble. That he did not care a G——d d——m for the Indians, but that he had followed the matter up for three years, and that if he could not make a stake here he would take the Bannocks where he could.[20]

Benjamin Franklin Lowe.
Courtesy Pioneer Museum,
Lander, Wyoming.

Lowe's illegal propositions illuminate other means by which whites sought to profit from the Shoshones. Before Irwin arrived at the agency, Wind River area whites had enjoyed lucrative trade and gambling opportunities with Indians involving buffalo hides and annuity or treaty goods.[21] Irwin observed that the Indians did not wear or value annuity items such as coats or pants, with the result that area whites could outfit themselves at little cost: "white men are on the lookout and get them [annuity clothing] for a little Paint, Powder or Fish Hooks."[22] As evidence, Irwin told Felix Brunot during the latter's investigation of agency affairs that "I have received several notes from white persons asking when the annuity goods would be issued; saying that they wished to be on hand, and get a lot of them."[23] In order to solve this perceived problem, Irwin recommended that the Indian Office spend more on blankets and less on clothes, high-crowned hats, or shoes, since the Shoshones discarded those items or quickly traded them. Irwin noted that "the amount paid for these articles is lost."[24] Curiously, Irwin's suggestion to spend more money on blankets illustrates his pragmatic acceptance of the Indians' rejection of "civilized" white clothing and, to some extent, his own reluctance to insist on strict adherence by the Indians to the Peace Policy. In this case, Irwin's advocacy of Indian culture subtly thwarted assimilationist demands.

Furthermore, Irwin worked diligently to end this free association and save government funds by limiting the Indian trade to government-sanctioned merchants. These restrictions supposedly protected Indians from unscrupulous dealers (and gamblers), but also bound native peoples more closely to their reservations, thereby giving agents tighter control over Indian movements and economies. Shoshones continually battled Irwin and all other agents who sought to impose these kinds of policies throughout the remainder of the century.

Although Irwin hoped to stem the off-reservation trade and put the government's annuity appropriations to more "civilized" use, his main agenda focused on controlling fraud. This lay at the root of his fight with Lowe and it also provoked a clash with John W. Anthony, a prominent Atlantic City resident. In 1870 Anthony owned $18,000 in real and personal property, including a lumber mill. He had served as a Sweetwater County commissioner from December 1869 to fall 1870 and had been Irwin's business partner.[25]

Like so many others, Anthony had profited from agency contracts. Anthony's mill supplied the logs to Swingle and Williams for the first agency buildings, and in 1870 Wham hired Anthony to plow the agency farm. Irwin followed suit the following summer, paying Anthony up to six dollars per acre for his services. Irwin also purchased oxen and harnesses from Anthony (for $870) on behalf of the agency.[26]

Although Anthony had been a strong supporter of Irwin, relationships between the two men soured in fall 1871 as Anthony tried to influence agency policies and attempted to convince Irwin to cheat the Indians and the government. Irwin noted that "I have discovered that Mr A expected large contracts and big pay when Mr A- would do a job just as low and well as any body else[.] I was disposed to farm him, but no farther."[27]

James I. Patten, hired in October 1871 as the agency's schoolteacher and lay missionary, said that Anthony tried to drive a wedge between Irwin and himself. Allegedly, Anthony claimed that Irwin kept Patten from performing his duties by refusing to build a school. Patten refuted the accusations.[28] Irwin ordered Anthony from the reservation, charging him with "interfering with the affairs of this Agency, disturbing or trying to disturb the minds of the Indians and white men to the prejudice of the interest of the Indians, the Government, and good order."[29]

Anthony's dismissal illustrates an even larger problem for the agency's relationship with Wind River whites. The ongoing presence of white trespassers on the reservation, of whom Anthony was one, threatened treaty agreements and disrupted the general community of Wind River peoples. Moreover, if the May 1871 editorial in the *South Pass News* can be believed, white sympathies probably favored the illegal settling of towns and farms, not Indian rights. In the midst of the controversy and rumors concerning Irwin's "poison plot" (and fully six months before Irwin posted eviction notices to anyone) the newspaper's editor wrote the following:

> We received a communication from Dr. James Irwin last week, which we refrain from publishing because of its belligerent attitude. The Doctor labors under the misapprehensions that the NEWS charged the departure of Washakie to the appointment of himself as Indian Agent. Our "false informant," as the Docter styles him, said that Washakie would very likely have migrated had any one else been appointed. At any rate, Doctor, our people want that valley for agricultural purposes, and Washakie might as well look elsewhere for summer quarters. Wind River valley answers his purpose to winter in, but it is entirely too hot for him in summer. He don't mind "taking in" ten or twenty Cheyennes, but when it comes to doing the hospitable to the Arrapahoes, Cheyenne and Sioux, he ain't a mouthful for them. There are 1,400 ponies in his tribe—enough to start several livery stables, but if they should be patronized only once by the Sioux, Old Washakie would be as bad off as Richard the 1st. These considerations had greater influence in deterring him from opening a hotel and livery stable in the valley than any dereliction on the part of the predecessor of Mr. Irwin, as claimed in the letter above.[30]

In this instance, it seems that the editor clearly understood the nomadic patterns of the Shoshones as well as the ongoing possibilities of tribal warfare in the valley. At the same time, the paper also suggests that at least a few white settlers had designs on the fertile bottomlands of the Wind River drainage system, regardless of any official treaty stipulation. In his nominal attempt to enforce the treaty regulations, J. W. Wham had ignored or been unwilling to remove trespassing settlers if they had homesteaded before November 3, 1870.[31] This fact partially explains the confident and sarcastic tone of the editorial in the *South Pass News*—Wham and the settlers were counting on the government buying the southern portions of the reservation.[32] Irwin, however, did not base his actions on the possibilities of future governmental negotiations. Instead, he made a strict assessment of the treaty language, which stated that only authorized whites (i.e., agency employees) could remain on reservation lands, and assumed the task of forcing relocations of people whose land claims were negated by the terms of the Fort Bridger Treaty. Irwin began his campaign in late fall 1871.

In November Irwin asked Captain Robert A. Torrey, commander at Camp Brown, to remove one Ted Ivens, "who has been a squatter on this reservation near old Camp Brown, and who has been in the habit of prostituting squaws."[33] Irwin also warned store proprietors in the mining towns—Henry J. Johnson, John Curry, and James Kime, all of them licensed liquor dealers at Miners Delight—that severe consequences would befall them if they continued selling liquor to the Indians.[34] Taking further steps, the agent and soldiers from Camp Brown burned ramshackle and empty cabins that allegedly were used for prostituting Indian women, and tried to prevent non-governmental cattle from grazing on reservation lands. However, while Irwin ordered stockmen to drive their cattle from the reservation, he did not enforce this decree because the winter of 1871–72 was quite severe. He did have one Frank Bethune removed because Bethune "defiantly" violated Irwin's warning not to take his cattle on the reservation. Bethune received the warning before he moved his stock from Green River to Wind River.[35]

Lowe and Anthony led the counterattack against Irwin, with Lowe leveling charges against the agent in late November 1871. Lowe claimed that Irwin owed him money, that the agent employed former Confederate soldiers, that he hired an incompetent drunk as the Bannock interpreter, and that he used the agency threshing machine to mow and thresh non-agency wheat. Irwin refuted Lowe's claims and charged Lowe with conspiring to cheat the government.[36]

When Irwin traveled to Washington in early February 1872 to discuss the agency's conditions with Commissioner Walker, Anthony apparently used the time to foment further complaints against the agent. Upon his return to Wind River, Irwin found that during his "absence a party of dissatisfied speculators, writing with gamblers, drunkards, and squaw men with whom I am in bad repute, have reported me to the Indian Department and have tampered with the Indians in an outrageous manner, but I am happy to say without effect."[37] The agent wasted little time in removing the irritating "thorns" in his side; on April 6, 1872, he ordered Anthony, John Conoway, John Felter, Fred Johnson, U. P. Davison, and Tilford Kutch from the reservation. When they paid no heed, he issued second notices five weeks later.[38]

The lives of these men offer interesting glimpses into the relationships between the Indian and white residents of Wind River. Felter, who had been the subcontractor on the masonry work for the agency blockhouse, lived on the reservation in a house built for reservation employees. However, he operated a gambling parlor in the house and Conoway was a partner. Conoway and Felter's friendship began when Conoway boarded with Felter and his family in Atlantic City in 1870. Anthony provided the wagons to haul away their gambling booty of Indian annuity goods. Johnson had been the Bannock interpreter for Irwin, but the agent discovered the young man was a drunk who gave whiskey to the Indians. Kutch and Davison were two of the early Wind River settlers, but they cohabited with Indian women, changing partners with enough frequency to suggest that prostitution occurred.[39]

More charges ensued against Irwin following the April battle, and the attacks broadened. Anthony and the others submitted a petition to Wyoming Supreme Court Associate Justice W. T. Jones in late April. Jones responded by suggesting an investigation.[40] According to the new reports, Irwin wrongfully deprived government contractors of housing. They also accused Irwin of nepotism, of enriching himself and forming his own "ring" of favorite vendors, freighters, and illegal employees.[41]

There was some truth in the claims against Irwin. His son-in-law, William Stephenson, was hired as the agency engineer, although the 1870 census listed his occupation as carpenter. Fincelius G. Burnett, the agency farmer, had been a close neighbor of both Irwin and Stephenson when the three lived in Atlantic City. Charles H. Oldham, one of the agency's two carpenters, was another former Atlantic City resident. He and his brother, James, together with Stephenson and Burnett, had been partners in mining ventures before accepting reservation jobs. The other carpenter, Leander C. Bliss, also came from Atlantic City. Darius Williams, the blacksmith, was another early settler, but one who supported Irwin and was tolerated by the Shoshones.[42]

## THE BRUNOT INVESTIGATION, 1872

The heart of Irwin's disputes with Wind River whites, however, really stemmed from the southern boundary problems. The inclusion of white towns and homesteads within the reservation sparked continual criticism and conflict, generally directed at Irwin. In response, on May 4, 1872, the Office of Indian Affairs directed Felix R. Brunot, the head of the Board of Indian Commissioners, to investigate the charges against Irwin. (Brunot also was an evangelical Episcopalian and an author of the Peace Policy.) A month later, on June 1, Congress authorized Brunot to negotiate with the Shoshones for their southern reservation lands.[43]

He began his examination of the Shoshone agency in September 1872. Taking great pains to interview Indians, military officers, unhappy townsmen, and numerous settlers, Brunot ultimately concluded that "the course of Agent Irwin in endeavoring to put an end to the demoralizing parties which have in times past followed the Indians to the reservation, and even have been tolerated in the Agency buildings, and in banishing from the reservation men who were the promoters of such practices and were obstacles in the way of good government is entitled to the highest commendation."[44]

Captain Torrey perhaps made the best assessment of the agent's activities:

> Dr. Irwin has quite faithfully executed his duties as Agent in this reserve, looking carefully after the interests of the Indians in his charge, and being as liberal and lenient in his dealings with white men on this reservation as his sense of duty would permit. . . . If he had acted otherwise much of the opposition he has met with would have been avoided. . . . No Agent who discharged his whole duty . . . could possibly avoid trouble, vexations, and opposition when brought into conflict with the white element. . . . Some of this embittered feeling against the Agent arises not as much from what he has done,

as the way he has done it, as perhaps some orders have been issued inopportunely, and expressed in a manner not calculated to dismiss opposition.[45]

In a similar vein, Brunot noted that Irwin's policies were not directed toward "orderly" settlers in the valley, many of whom had been tolerated or encouraged to settle in the Popo Agie and Wind River Valleys by previous agents, but only toward "bad men." He expressed hope that the agreement recently signed by the Shoshones, in which they sold the southern third of their reservation, would put an end to the complaints by opening up the agricultural lands coveted by the mining-town citizens.[46]

Despite the exoneration, Irwin's early administration was marked by questionable decisions that would come back to haunt (or enrich) future agents. In all of the testimony, it is clear that government vendors could graze their stock on the reservation's ranges without paying compensation either to the government or to the Indians. For example, James K. Moore, the post trader at Camp Brown (licensed November 28, 1870) as well as the official Shoshone and Bannock Agency Trader (licensed January 12, 1871), kept both his draft animals and a beef herd on the reservation free of charge.[47] Agency employees, including Irwin, also expected similar privileges for any horses, pigs, or milk cows they kept for personal use. This practice set a dangerous precedent for future agency-white relationships. Wind River farmers and ranchers became too accustomed to using reservation property for personal use. In the 1880s and 1890s, bitter feuds ignited when various agents attempted to curtail this early form of government subsidy.

Irwin also practiced nepotism and favoritism, which encouraged fraud, incompetence, and mismanagement. It was a popular practice, however; nearly every Shoshone agent between 1868 and 1900 hired either relatives or friends, or both. The Office of Indian Affairs tolerated nepotism to some extent, but no agent escaped from claims of favoritism in vendors or employees. Additionally, political party affiliation became grounds for personal attacks (local Democrats, for instance, complained in 1893 that the Shoshone agent hired only Republicans when the Democrats controlled the White House).[48]

The tinder that would ignite these future battles thus lay smoldering following Irwin's actions. Because the reservation represented a vital link

to the economic success of Wind River whites, his monetary decisions—
concerning employees, bids, contracts, freighting, building, etc.—sparked
intense interest among the valley's white citizens. The fact that investigations of the agency could be brought by citizen (and later by Indian)
complaints insured that no agent, beginning with Irwin, was immune to
the interconnectedness of all the Wind River peoples.

*Chapter Four*

# Shoshones, Bannocks, and the Brunot Treaty

## 1871–1872

### SHOSHONES AND BANNOCKS, 1871–1872

Squabbles between the Shoshone and Bannock Indian Agent and his white neighbors at first rarely involved either of the reservation's two tribes. In fact, during the summers of 1871 and 1872, few Indians resided permanently at Wind River, and less that half of the tribal peoples remained during the winters. Ultimately, the Indians became embroiled intimately in the debates, and suffered the greatest loss—Irwin's respite from white criticism came at the severance of over seven hundred thousand acres from the reservation in September 1872.

Until that time, however, both tribes parlayed the slow development and construction of reservation buildings and farms into a protracted period of noncompliance with the Fort Bridger treaty stipulations. In fact, many aspects of the treaty requirements were of little concern either to the Shoshones or the Bannocks. Intertribal political events had far greater significance for them than did adherence to words recorded by white men.

In May 1871, the Wind River Shoshones and their Bannock neighbors vacated the valley, not to escape a possible poison attempt at the hands of Agent Irwin, as former Agent Wham alleged, but to escape the possibilities of inopportune meetings with enemy tribes.[1] Their absence was soon justified; in late June, white citizens lost several horses to a raiding party of a hundred Northern Cheyennes and Sioux. The outsiders evidently planned a raid on Shoshone mounts, but took the substitute opportunities upon discovery their Indian targets had vanished.[2]

Perhaps unknown to the Wind River tribes, their agent worked throughout the summer of 1871 to prevent such attacks and raids and to make the
transition to reservation life more palatable. Irwin continually sought
blankets, arms, ammunition, and food supplies for the Shoshones and
Bannocks in preparation for their return in the fall. He recognized that
the probability of full-time residency remained quite slim unless the
government provided increased defense (or the means thereof), enough
food and clothing to make hunting for subsistence unnecessary, and
ongoing support until farming efforts had a chance to prove successful.
Most of his appeals, however, were ignored or vetoed. Lieutenant General
Philip H. Sheridan, for example, said that the army could spare no more
troops for either Camp Brown or Fort Stambaugh because Sioux warfare
on the eastern plains threatened white settlements and the Union Pacific
Railroad. When Irwin read this reply, he tersely asked for "plenty of
ammunition."[3]

The food crisis that Irwin had anticipated throughout the summer surfaced in September. A few Indians from both tribes returned to Wind River
on September 4, earlier than expected, and "starved out." Five days later
the bulk of the Shoshones appeared "in a suffering condition." Without
authorization, Irwin "met them in Popoagie Valley and purchased four fat
. . . cattle estimated at 2700 lbs. nett for $300, and nothing was left but
Bones and Hooves in less than two hours. . . . I have furnished 4000 lbs
of potatoes and will distribute a portion of their goods which has arrived
tomorrow."[4]

On the surface, Irwin's decision reflected a humanitarian response to
genuine need, but the act of feeding hungry people contained a variety of
symbols and interpretations for both the agent and for the Indians. For
Irwin, no other option seemed viable. He explained his emergency purchases to acting Commissioner Clum: "Some twelve hundred hungry
Indians suddenly arrived at the Agency expecting relief. They have fed on
cured berries until many were sick. To give them some subsistence was
an absolute necessity."[5] At this stage of his administration, it seems clear
that Irwin was not intent on fostering Indian dependency on the government, a condition that occurred in the late 1880s. If anything, the Indians
manipulated Irwin. With immediate hunger assuaged, Shoshone and
Bannock warriors could delay early fall hunts and thereby avoid potential
battles with enemy tribes. Late October forays were preferable; they

included the safety factor of snowfalls in the Laramie and Big Horn ranges, which blocked easy access into the Wind River region from the east. On the other hand, fall snowstorms could also inflict havoc on deliveries. A three-day storm in October, for example, held up cattle and flour shipments.[6]

The Indians also had reason to assign other meanings to Irwin's efforts. For them, the government lived up to its obligation to meet their needs. Historian Richard White calls this the Indian peoples' understanding of the "Great Father"—the responsible parent who provides his children what they need. (Conversely, of course, whites also used the "Great Father" analogy, but assigned to it the meaning that children should obey without question the words of the parent.)[7] At the same time, the Bannocks began to see a different side of the "Great Father"; their access to the federal larder depended on their cooperation with Washakie and the Wind River peoples. As will be seen, the Bannocks refused to stay in this subservient status.

Irwin's communications about the tribes' return indicated the Bannocks' growing dissatisfaction, as well as Washakie's slim hold over the Shoshone bands. Irwin wrote Clum on September 11, saying that "the Bannocks are under the influence of traders I fear and are scattered."[8] Two days later Irwin reported that most of the Shoshones arrived at the agency on September 9, although Washakie indicated that some of his tribe refused to return from Utah. Supposedly, they were under the influence of whiskey dealers.[9] Both of Irwin's letters, taken in the context of general Shoshone history, give glimpses of the fragile coalition headed by Washakie and of the Bannocks' independence.

On the one hand, Washakie demonstrated his leadership by bringing in the large majority of his followers and satisfied their faith in him by obtaining provisions from Irwin. On the other hand, splinter groups of Bannocks and Shoshones, loosely attached to Washakie, chose their own roads. Washakie appealed to Irwin to bring in these recalcitrant groups, especially the Shoshones, ostensibly to keep them from getting into trouble.[10] In this matter, Washakie acted very much the intermediary for his followers. He served as an advocate for the Eastern Shoshones, defended their actions (or distanced himself from those he thought harmful to the larger group), and generally voiced the consensus of the people. Therefore, Washakie's plea to Irwin contained at least three levels of meaning, none of which probably occurred to Irwin. (Washakie revealed his opinion of Irwin in September 1872 when he confided to Felix Brunot that Irwin "was slow about things, and I like him for that.")[11]

First, by asking Irwin to help him, Washakie kept in the agent's good graces. Second, the Shoshone leader had learned from extensive experience how to use whites to bolster his tribal control. Finally, he probably had a real fear that if the errant bands joined other Basin tribes in "hostile" actions against whites, his own reputation for peacekeeping would be sullied (which might result in a real loss of power or influence with whites and therefore within his own tribe).

The Bannocks, in the meantime, were making a concerted effort to distance themselves from Washakie's domination. Their leaders strove to make that point clear to federal officials during the treaty negotiations of the 1860s, despite a long history of trading and hunting partnerships with the Wind River Shoshones. In 1868, for example, Chief Taghee (who became head chief in 1867) acknowledged the friendship with Washakie's people, but insisted that the Bannocks have their own lands.[12]

The Bannock presence at Wind River had followed a typically convoluted route. In pre-contact times, they probably were a Northern Paiute tribe that migrated from southeastern Oregon and associated themselves with a group of Shoshones who generally wintered near Fort Hall. Both groups adopted the horse culture and with it some aspects of the buffalo economy. Although buffalo had been plentiful in the upper Snake River Valley before 1840, increasing pressure by white emigrants and settlers depleted the herds in Idaho and forced the Bannocks and the Fort Hall Shoshones to move their fall hunts to Montana, near the headwaters of the Missouri and Yellowstone Rivers. Often the hunts involved Flatheads, Nez Perce, or Lemhi and Wind River Shoshones. During summers, hunting big game basically ceased; the Bannocks fished for salmon in the Snake River, sometimes as far west as the Boise, Payette, and Weiser Rivers.[13]

The Bannocks did not entertain kindly the white intrusion into the Basin region. Emigrant and settlers' stock were inviting targets, and occasionally the Bannocks drew their neighbors into raids or battles against whites.[14] Calmer relationships eventually ensued in the years following the Bear River Massacre in January 1863. This was especially true when Taghee rose to prominence among the Bannocks. Taghee's reputation among whites for peacemaking and wise council rivaled that of Washakie, so much that during the late 1860s most of the Bannocks remained on generally friendly terms with emigrants, settlers, and soldiers. The Bannock chief used his standing and the tribal professions of peace to press for a distinct Bannock homeland.[15]

The 1868 Fort Bridger Treaty granted the Bannocks' wish, but the treaty required annuity distribution at the Wind River agency, not at Fort Hall. For the next several years, Bannock annuities came to Wind River, despite the protests of Taghee. To some extent, Washakie blocked the Bannocks' efforts to reside at Fort Hall—the Shoshone leader probably wanted the extra protection afforded by the combined mass of the two tribes against potential Sioux, Cheyenne, or Arapahoe invaders.[16]

Washakie also may have wanted to control the distribution of government goods. For example, Irwin handed out annuity blankets to both tribes in April 1872. Twelve hundred blankets had been designated for the Bannocks and 900 for the Shoshones, yet Irwin gave 384 Bannock blankets to the Shoshones. He argued that "the number of Bannocks was five to sixteen Shoshones, that the Bannocks had but a short time before received the remaining portion of their annuities for 1871 and they had also drawn some annuities at Fort Hall a short time before."[17]

Irwin's just action must have struck the Bannocks as overt favoritism for the Shoshones. Washakie probably had a voice in Irwin's decision in this matter, although the evidence is speculative. However, considering the difficulty that Irwin faced with Wind River whites at this time, it is likely that the agent was doing everything possible to court Washakie's favor and avoid being attacked from within as well as without.

As a result of the forced distributions at Wind River, and of the diminished resources in Idaho, Taghee's Bannocks (and Pocatello's Shoshones, another band that eventually settled at Fort Hall) hunted buffalo with the Eastern Shoshones from 1867 to 1871. Theoretically, each chief had equal authority, but Washakie probably assumed the primary leadership—the hunts took place in his domain. Besides enduring a loss of prestige and a partial merger with Washakie's people, the Bannocks suffered other blows at Wind River. During the 1868–69 hunting seasons the Wind River Valley was not a safe haven—attacks by Sioux warriors left twenty-nine Bannocks dead.[18]

Thus, in the winter of 1870–71, Taghee and his Bannocks, together with the Fort Hall Shoshones, tended to avoid Wind River altogether and resisted the submergence of their own tribal identities within the Wind River Shoshones. Maintaining their separateness came at a heavy price—by casting their lot west of the Rocky Mountains, the Bannocks faced stiff competition for land and food resources with white settlers. Furthermore, while Fort Hall Agency was functioning in late 1868, available rations and annuities were intended for the Boise and Bruneau Shoshone bands, not the Bannocks or mixed Bannock-Shoshones. Even then, the government frequently ignored its obligations to the Fort Hall Indians and food stocks were rarely adequate. Thus, the several bands of Shoshone and Bannock peoples who migrated toward Fort Hall tended to leave when food ran out. The government continued to ship supplies and food intended for Taghee's and Pocatello's bands to Wind River until 1873, so the mixed Bannock-Shoshone peoples had only occasional access to annuities and rations. For the most part, they eked out a living by sporadic hunting and depended on Mormon generosity. Pocatello's solution to the food problem lay in casting his lot with the Eastern Shoshones—he continued to risk hunts in Wyoming as late as 1874–75. Pocatello did not decide to settle permanently at Fort Hall until 1876.[19]

Taghee's death in March 1871 ended the amicable feelings between the Wind River Shoshones and the Bannocks. Without Taghee's moderating influence, the Bannock-Shoshone coalition fractured, with some of the Bannock bands assuming more aggressive postures toward Basin whites. A few of these groups chose their own way before Taghee died. In December 1870, Agent Wham reported that several Bannocks traveled to Montana and bartered furs for guns and food at Fort Ellis, frightening white settlers along the way. It was these Bannocks that Washakie deemed "bad," although more than likely he recognized that a few members of his own tribe (perhaps Tawunasia or Norkok) joined the Bannocks' ventures, welcoming the opportunity to counter his authority.[20]

Several of the Bannock peoples who remained at Wind River were no less active in determining their future. In February 1872, Irwin informed Commissioner Walker that the Bannock bands had met in council at the agency (on January 14, 1872) and requested that the 1868 treaty promise be honored. They insisted on going to their reservation at Fort Hall. Walker took up the matter with Secretary of the Interior Columbus Delano, but the Secretary's consent was predicated on the Shoshones refusing to allow the Bannocks at Wind River. Most of the Wind River Shoshone bands, however, were hunting off the reservation during the early spring months, so they delayed their answer to Delano until May. According to Irwin, the Shoshones were disgusted by the Bannocks and no longer tolerated their presence. Irwin quoted Washakie's thoughts on this matter in late May 1872: "Before Tie-gee died the Bannocks had ears, now they have a great many Chiefs, and they dont hear, any of them, and they will not hear us. They have got no ears. They go off to the Crows and steal horses, and we are afraid they will get us all into trouble."[21]

The members of the Shoshone council went on to say that only "some good Bannocks" could stay. Given the Shoshones' complaints about the other tribe, "good Bannocks" could only be those who had "ears," and heeded Wind River Shoshone wisdom. Irwin added his opinion, noting that the Bannocks were "a superior Indian physically and mentally to the Shoshone," but were too unsettled at the moment to benefit from government assistance.[22] Their nomadism prevented him from performing his duty to them. However, he did believe that they would abide in the Portneuf River Valley or at Fort Hall. Although Irwin may have appreciated the Bannocks' physical appearance, clearly their independence bothered him. Like most whites of the era, he saw their actions in negative terms only, not as indications of their attempts to determine their own future. He was no wiser in his dealings with the Shoshones.

The final separation of the two tribes took place following the various council meetings of spring 1872. The Bannocks moved without waiting for government approval, while the Shoshone tribal members split into their smaller divisions and headed into the Basin. Irwin concerned himself once more about their ultimate destination and the potential lack of food at Wind River, but he need not have bothered. The U.S. officially acknowledged the Bannock claims to Fort Hall in September 1872.[23] The majority of the Bannocks remained in the Basin regions after this time, although Eastern Shoshones continued to trade with and visit Bannock relatives and friends on a regular basis.

## THE BRUNOT TREATY, 1872

Thus in fall 1872, the Bannocks stayed at Fort Hall. Meanwhile, Washakie's Shoshones returned to Wind River to face a new challenge, one far more serious than the tensions with the Bannocks. Simply put, the status of the

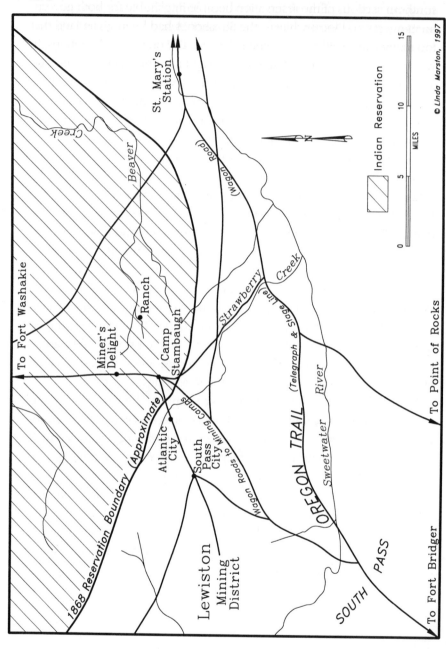

Map 3. Detailed view of southern reservation boundary, 1868–1872

Inside the map:

To Fort Washakie

Creek

Beaver

St. Mary's Station

1868 Reservation Boundary (Approximate)

Miner's Delight

Ranch

Camp Stambaugh

(Wagon Road)

Strawberry

Creek

Atlantic City

South Pass City

Wagon Roads to Mining Camps

Lewiston Mining District

OREGON TRAIL (Telegraph & Stage Line)

Sweetwater River

SOUTH PASS

To Point of Rocks

To Fort Bridger

N

Indian Reservation

0   5   10   15
MILES

© Linda Marston, 1997

southern sections of the reservation became intolerable for both government agents and local whites—the Shoshones had been given land that
too many white settlers and miners desired. The only feasible options, in
whites' eyes, were to negotiate a land swap or to purchase the contested
acreage. The Shoshone plan, to force "undesirable" interlopers from the
reservation, generally went unheeded except for the efforts of Agent Irwin.

One of the problems with the Shoshonean idea was that it placed
reservation employees in an untenable position. Shoshones accepted many
whites into their midst, such as fur trappers, merchants, or farmers who
were willing to share their bounty with the Indians. They probably tolerated the whiskey sellers and gamblers as well. They did not want white
hunters or stockgrowers—the practices of both groups made subsistence
hunting less feasible. Agency officials, however, could not be selective
about whom they allowed on the reservation—the cries of favoritism, or
illegal "rings," or political scandals rang too loudly in the white community.

The problems of white trespassers on Indian land began with the 1868
treaty, but did not end there. Essentially, the government acted too slowly
to rectify the situation or prevent it from worsening. For example, thirteen
months after the treaty signing, Governor Campbell noted the ongoing
influx of whites into the reservation area and astutely observed the
government's failings: "The fact that nothing had been done towards
carrying out the treaty has led to the suspicion that the Government did
not intend to strictly observe it, and that settlers would be permitted to
occupy the land."[24] Campbell's words referred to erecting agency buildings, starting agency farms, and surveying boundaries, none of which had
been done by 1870. In February 1870, the governor realized military action
was the only means of removing the whites. Furthermore, he mentioned
the Shoshonean option as a possibility—he believed they might actually
desire "bona fide" farmers for mutual defense purposes. Yet, by the end
of the year Wind River whites clearly had a different solution in mind.
Agent Wham articulated their plans: "to detach the Popagie Valley from
this reservation and [have it] thrown open for settlement."[25] Thus, when
Agent Irwin began to root out the "undesirables a year later," that is, those
whose activities he deemed harmful or as impeding Indian progress
toward "civilization," he reaped his whirlwind of protest and retribution.

In very real ways, Irwin's decisions ran counter to the majority opinions
in the Wind River community, both Indian and white. For example, the

Shoshones may have tolerated gamblers, liquor dealers, or even procurers of Indian women for prostitution. Whites such as J. W. Anthony may indeed have obtained annuity items by gambling, but gambling was an inherent part of Shoshonean culture and was no "sin" in Indian eyes. At this point, neither was intoxication. No Peace Policy agent, however, could permit such blatant violations of government ideals or tolerate such "corruption" of Indian "wards." Irwin's intervention in the nature of Indian-white relationships at Wind River therefore proscribed previous patterns of interactions.

Moreover, Irwin represented a national reform impetus that went beyond Indian policy. During much of the nineteenth century, various proponents of moral reform sought to curb drinking, gambling, prostitution, and a host of other perceived ills that supposedly infested various segments of the American population. Indians were not the only targets of the reformers, or even the primary ones. The thrust of the reform effort, wherever the battles took place, was that the reformers themselves assumed that they knew what was best for society; the voices of the "reformees" were never considered.[26] In the same vein, Indians like the Shoshones lost whatever rights to free association they had held in pre-reservation days and were forced to submit, at least publicly, to Peace Policy definitions of proper behavior (and these definitions somewhat mirrored reform ideals). Privately, of course, many individual Shoshones rejected this layer of control and took responsibility for their own lives. Their actions continued to bedevil their agents; gambling, drinking, and going AWOL continued unabated.

The government finally acted to end the conflicts on June 1, 1872, when Congress authorized negotiations with the Shoshones to "relinquish a part of their reservation."[27] Felix R. Brunot headed to Wyoming in September 1872 to accomplish this task, as well as to investigate the complaints against Irwin. Commissioner Brunot wore several other hats during the summer of 1872. In addition to the hearings on Irwin's conduct and the Shoshone council, he also was supposed to "pacify" the Indians along the path of the Northern Pacific Railway, which was under construction, and to meet with other tribes for additional land cessions. Accordingly, he visited Crow Agency in Montana in July, then traveled to Colorado to see the Utes, and finally to the Shoshone and Bannock Agency. Brunot made it clear from the beginning that the Shoshone council deliberations would be on his terms, not those of the Indians. The commissioner soon experienced, however, the inherent strength of Shoshone leaders. What follows is a detailed look at the Brunot-Shoshone council meetings, for they reveal many facets of the Shoshones' decision-making process, as well as their expectations for their life on the reservation.[28]

A day before his arrival in the Sweetwater mining district, Brunot got an inkling of the hazards of living in disputed territory—an unidentified party of Indians had killed two white men and had stolen four horses. As a safety measure, Colonel Williams, fifteen soldiers from Fort Stambaugh, and the agency farmer, Finn Burnett, escorted the commissioner to the agency. All the excitement, however, elevated jittery feelings and a squad of infantry and a group of miners fired shots at each other for two hours, each believing the other group to be the "hostile" Indians. Luckily, someone discovered the error before either side inflicted injuries.[29] Once at Wind River, Brunot discovered that the Shoshones were still camped at Green River and immediately directed Irwin to send a runner to bring them in. He also asked Colonel Brisbin, the commander at Camp Brown, to speed the tribe through the mining towns. Normally, the Shoshones took time to trade and "pow-wow" with the townspeople on their trips to and from the valley. Washakie, in turn, requested through Brisbin that the meetings be held at Fort Stambaugh, which meant local whites could also attend the proceedings. Brunot refused because he wanted to discuss terms with the Shoshones only, and thus prevent any non-governmental influence or pressures on the tribal leaders.[30]

When the council began, however, the Shoshones did all they could to control the tempo of the discussions. The talks began on September 26, 1872. Brunot opened with prayer, then digressed on various topics in attempts to learn more about the Indians' feelings toward the reservation and to get them to agree about the necessity of sending their children to school. He closed his preamble by saying that he did not want to talk about such subjects at the moment, but "to hear what Washakie and the others wish to say." He told them: "I want you to speak whatever is in your hearts."[31] Washakie refused the gambit, instead replying: "I have nothing to say. We want you to tell us what you came here to say."[32] Brunot acknowledged that there were land issues to consider, but that he would discuss them later. He tried to return to his original course, once more asking Washakie: "I came to hear your words and to carry them to the great father. . . . Have you nothing you wish to say about the Agency, the buildings or the farms[?]"[33]

Washakie answered, but with words that must have surprised Brunot. "I would like to have houses here. I do not like to live in lodges. I am afraid of the Sioux. They come here and hunt for scalps in this valley. I would like to have houses. We would like to talk about the land."[34] The chief's reply conveyed several meanings, some more obvious than others. On the surface, Washakie recognized the defensive value of white houses against possible attacks. In fact, he informed Irwin in May 1872 that the tribe would start building houses in the coming fall because they feared being shot while sleeping in their tents.[35] He also may have misunderstood the terms of the 1868 treaty; Washakie evidently believed that the government was obligated to build houses for Indians as well as erect agency buildings. This became a sticking point in the talks with Brunot.[36] Without question, of course, Washakie wanted to talk about the land issues.

What he did not say, however, reveals as much as what he did. Fears about Sioux raids, for example, contained the silent accusation that the government was not doing its part to prevent the intertribal wars. Furthermore, he made no comments concerning the state of the agency nor of the Indians' farms. Nor did he mention schooling for the Shoshone children despite the fact that James I. Patten, the agency teacher, had been working since the previous fall. Brunot wanted information on these topics, yet Washakie pointedly ignored the issues. Although one can only speculate as to Washakie's intentions, it seems likely that the Shoshones still viewed reservation life on their own terms, not the government's. At this point, education and farming were low priorities. They would remain so as long as the Shoshonean political and economic institutions offered viable alternatives to white cultural mandates.

For his part, Brunot disregarded the housing discussion and the silent testimony to his leading questions, and launched into the heart of the negotiations over the proposed land exchange. He recounted the short history of the problems along the southern borders, whereby the 1868 treaty made white settlers illegal trespassers. Then he informed the Shoshone council (virtually all the men of the tribe) that Congress wanted to swap land to the north of the reservation for the Popo Agie River Valley on the south, and thereby at one stroke grant illegal settlers legal homestead rights. One of the Shoshone leaders, Toop-so-po-not, however, recalled a slightly larger historical perspective and astutely remarked, "I did not know there were any whites here when the Buffalo were here."[37]

Brunot evidently brushed this reminder aside and proceeded to outline the exchange. Washakie refused the deal and countered with a surprising offer that engendered a lively debate.

> *Washakie.* In that valley (proposed to be ceded) there is plenty of grass, berries, Prairie Squirrels and fish; plenty of everything. It is good land. I do not know what to do about it. I have two hearts about it. This land is good, that in the north is poor, and I think it belongs to the Crows. When you were at the Crows, did the Crow Chief tell you to trade this land off?
>
> *Mr. Brunot.* I did not say anything to the Crows about it, it was none of their business. The land does not belong to them.
>
> *Washakie.* The Shoshones think it belongs to the Crows.
>
> *Mr. Brunot.* I will show Washakie by the map that it does not belong to the Crows.
>
> *Washakie.* That land belongs to the Crows, the Sioux and everybody. If we went there, the Sioux might come in and scalp us. I do not want that land. If the whites want to buy this land, it is all right, but I do not want to trade it for land anywhere.[38]

Brunot had not anticipated this turn of events. Washakie's offer to sell the disputed land was not what Brunot expected or what he had been empowered to accept. Moreover, his response indicates that the commissioner did not comprehend Indian intertribal relationships. For Brunot, map boundary markings transferred legal titles. From his perspective, the land to the north of the Wind River reservation belonged to no one. Washakie and the Shoshones, however, based their negotiations on decades of participating in the Plains economy. For them, the government offer merely invited trouble with neighboring tribes. Moreover, the 1868 treaty gave the Shoshones the right to hunt in the north. There was no reason to bargain for rights they already possessed.

Brunot was so unsettled by Washakie's response that he questioned the chief's authority, asking the other headmen to speak up. Washakie insisted that he spoke for all, but Brunot persisted. Toop-so-po-not answered for the others, reiterating Washakie's original proposition.[39] By the end of the first day, the Shoshones agreed to sell the land for twenty-five thousand dollars, to be paid in five yearly installments of cattle. In making this bargain, the tribe again acted from Shoshonean, not white, visions for the tribal future, as seen in the following discussions:

> *Mr. Brunot.*   Suppose we were to make a bargain about cattle, what would you do with the cattle[?]
> *Wisha.*   We would corrall [*sic*] them and milk them.
> *Washakie.*   If we got cattle, we would keep them here and herd them, like we do our horses.
> *Mr. Brunot.*   If you had cattle would some of you stay here all the time and herd them[?]
> *Washakie.*   Whenever we move up Wind River we would have to take them along. We would like to have cattle. The Utes and all the other Indians have cattle. We are poor and have none.[40]

From the Shoshones' perspectives, no deviation from normal routines would be necessary. They could herd cattle, so they believed, as easily as their horses, and required no commitment to permanent residence.

The negotiations concerning the prospective cattle payments reveal other aspects of Shoshonean life. Brunot asked if the Indians' penchant for gambling might result in the loss of their cattle, so that one Indian might obtain more than his fellows, or if whites might win Indian cattle. No Indian answered the first question; it was irrelevant—nothing in the recorded conversations indicates that the Shoshones expected private ownership of the cattle—food sources were shared (and unlike their horses, the cattle were viewed as potential food). As to the second question, Degonda scornfully noted: "We would take the same care of them that we do of our horses. The whites do not beat us out of them."[41] The implication was, of course, that whites could not take Indian cattle by gambling.

A further implication in this statement is that the goods that whites did "beat out" of the Shoshones were those that ultimately did not matter or were not worth much within the Shoshone economy. James Irwin unknowingly hinted this in a letter to the Indian Office written over a year before Brunot's council. He stated that the Shoshones "will not ware [*sic*] coats & pants" and that whites obtained them easily in trade.[42] James Patten indicated as much when he testified that John Felter and John Conoway won annuity goods by gambling.[43] The arts of trading or wagering depend in part on offering what one values little in return for the chance to gain what one values highly; the Shoshones were well aware of these principles.

The headmen also used the cattle talks to reiterate their fears of invading tribes—Arapahoes, Cheyennes, and Sioux offered greater threats to a cattle herd than did white gamblers. Brunot understood this conversational direction and assured the Shoshones that the U.S. army would hunt down any "bad" Indians who did not remain at peace with the Shoshones.[44]

Throughout the remainder of the council session, the Shoshones continued to respond and to negotiate from their own perspectives. In doing so, however, they ultimately gained less compensation for the land they ceded than Brunot was willing to pay. Brunot expected to bargain with the Indians over the price, but they accepted his initial offer. The commissioner retired at the end of the first meeting needing only to draw up the official papers.[45]

The talks resumed in the afternoon of the next day, September 27. Brunot explained the full extent of the new boundary lines and warned the Shoshones that in the future they would have to respect fences and use roads rather than travel through private fields. The Shoshones responded by affirming friendship for any future white settlers in the ceded lands and promising to stay on the roads.[46]

Brunot finally broached the subject of housing, suggesting that perhaps the Indians might want part of their payments in houses, rather than in cattle. After discussing this with his tribesmen, Washakie said that they desired five thousand dollars in houses. At this point, however, confusion took over—Washakie insisted that the first treaty guaranteed houses for the Indians. Brunot agreed that the Shoshones should have houses, but that the 1868 treaty made no provisions for them. Therefore, if the tribe took houses, they would receive only four years of cattle payments. Washakie demanded five years. Unwilling, perhaps, to pursue the discussion further, Brunot then asked Washakie for tribal confirmation that Washakie should receive five hundred dollars per year for five years (Brunot stated "it was right he should have it").[47] The other men approved; Brunot tried to bring closure by describing the process of treaty ratification in Washington.[48]

Before the Shoshones signed the agreement, however, Agent Irwin evidently sensed lingering dissatisfaction about the Indian houses and attempted to pacify Washakie:

> *Dr. Irwin.*   The Shoshones have always said they wanted houses before they could settle down and go to farming.
> *Washakie.*   I told you long ago that we wanted houses, and the treaty promised them.
> *Dr. Irwin.*   I want to make houses, but I cannot unless I have money to do so, and the Great Father has not given me any money for that purpose. The Treaty does not promise any.
> *Washakie.*   Let us sign the Treaty now as it is getting late.[49]

Irwin perhaps accomplished his goal, but Washakie's closing words imply resignation, not agreement. The Shoshone leader masked his true feelings about the 1868 treaty: did he really feel that the treaty provided for Indian housing, or was he trying to interject a post facto article into the older document? Whatever his motive, his repeated declarations eventually prompted action. Brunot recommended that Secretary Delano appropriate an additional ten thousand dollars for Shoshone houses.[50]

The council reconvened for the final talks on September 28. Brunot opened with a long recitation of the history and state of affairs between the U.S. and the Wind River Shoshones following the 1868 Fort Bridger Treaty. The commissioner pointed out that both the government and the Indians had lived up to the treaty requirements in some areas, and that both had failed to do so in others. In true storytelling fashion, he urged everyone involved to forget the past mistakes and begin again:

> When the snow melts on the Mountains, it is all gone, when the leaves are gone in the fall you never see the same leaves anymore. So it is with these things that we have not done. They are all gone. They are away behind us. Let us leave them there and forget about them. But we want to begin again right here, and all that is before us, we can see and do.[51]

From this point Brunot explained that Agent Irwin was there to serve the Indians and listen to their needs. One of their needs, as seen by

Brunot, was learning to farm. He referred to the Agency farm which Irwin had had plowed and fenced during the summer, noting that the agent would show the Indians how to farm and produce food for themselves. Next, Brunot addressed education, saying that if the Indian children were educated (including industrial education), then they would not need to have an agent, or farmer, or blacksmith to do things for them. He urged the men to send their sons and daughters to school, just as Washakie was doing with his sons.[52]

Finally, Brunot turned to the issue of the remaining white settlers on the reservation. He stated that they would leave next year, but that the Indians should leave them alone (including their crops and fences), because these whites had the right to the fruits of their labor. To this Washakie replied, "That is good talk." At the same time, he hinted at his lack of absolute authority: "Sometimes an old woman pulls down a pole from a fence and we cannot help it."[53] Brunot countered: "You will show that you think it good talk, by doing what you can to protect them."[54]

Brunot concluded the meeting by once more referring to Indian housing. He re-read the 1868 treaty, noting that housing was required for the agent and employees, but not for the Indians. Washakie then suggested the current agreement superseded the old treaty, evidently pushing one more time for houses for his people. Brunot negated Washakie's statement, however, saying that the 1868 treaty was still valid. After that, he made his final offer to listen to what the Indians wanted to say, but Washakie silenced the proceedings: "It is very little we Indians know to talk about."[55]

The scathing contempt and rebuke contained in this message probably escaped Brunot. For three days, the Shoshones had articulated as clearly as they could what they wanted in terms of living on the reservation: cattle, housing, and protection from their enemies. In return, they were willing to give up 700,000 acres of their reservation. They also were receptive to the prospects of farming and to educating their children in white schools, but these issues probably reflected an accommodation to agency administrative plans; they were not priorities for the Indians themselves.

For three days, Felix Brunot brushed aside most of these concerns and did not truly hear what the Shoshones were telling him. He discounted the real threats of Plains warfare, despite his own proximity to Indian hostilities at South Pass. He also doubted their methods of herding cattle. From his perspective, the most important thing was to settle the border disputes and prod the Shoshones to a sedentary, agricultural existence. Only the housing issue really gained his attention, but to some extent his recommendation to provide additional funding was a weak gesture. Brunot, for whatever reason, refused to renegotiate the treaty terms and include an additional item for housing, thereby belying his stance that he was willing to offer a higher price for the ceded land. The government, therefore, was not obligated to appropriate the necessary funds for Indian houses.

Still, the Brunot agreement contained several desired elements. The Shoshones were promised a cattle herd, Wind River whites gained access to fertile land, and the government deflected criticism, at least for the moment. The only problem was that Congress did not ratify the agreement until June 1874. This meant new boundaries remained unsurveyed until 1875 and the Shoshones suffered sporadic deliveries of their stock cattle.[56] Furthermore, intertribal warfare continued unabated for the next several years. The overall effect of the Brunot agreement on the Wind River community of peoples varied according to the particular group. Whites literally gained ground as new settlers rushed into the ceded parts of the reservation in advance of congressional approval. The local white economy expanded from mining-based operations to farming and ranching. The Bannocks, of course, were excluded from the Brunot council and no longer had official rights to Wind River, but many bands continued to participate in joint Shoshone-Bannock buffalo hunts. In the place of the Bannocks, agency employees became permanent additions to the community mix, with some of them serving dual roles as agency vendors. Other newcomers included a band of Sheep Eater Shoshones under the leadership of Togwotee, who were moved from their mountain homes in 1872 to Wind River. Togwotee, in fact, may have been a signer of the Brunot Agreement; the clerk of the proceeding recorded the name of Toquata, who possibly was the Sheep Eater leader.[57] As for the rest of the Shoshones, perhaps Brunot's admonition to them to learn to farm fell on receptive ears. In 1873, for example, Washakie and others made relatively serious attempts at agriculture. More powerful factors, however—governmental budgetary crises, enemy attacks, weather, and grasshoppers—prevented any wholehearted commitment to permanent Shoshone residence at Wind River. In other words, the Wind River community at the end of 1872 had altered only slightly in its composition from pre-reservation days.

# PART TWO

~

# *Agency Affairs*

## 1872–1885

# Chapter Five

# To Farm or Not to Farm?

## Shoshone Economy
### 1872–1877

FARMING, FIGHTING, AND HUNTING, 1872–1874

From the earliest days of the Utah Superintendency, white agents attempted to convince the Shoshones to quit hunting and take up agriculture.[1] The emphasis on making farmers out of Shoshone and Bannock hunters intensified with the creation of the reservation. The brunt of the federal pressure to plow the Wind River prairie lands, however, at first fell on white shoulders. Specifically, James Irwin, and not the Shoshones, was responsible for inaugurating the Indian farms. Irwin found his job a tough row to hoe, so to speak. He wrote to Ely Parker, the Commissioner of Indian Affairs, on June 3, 1871, that he could not till the tough prairie sod without oxen, since the Indian ponies were too small to pull the plows. Two days later he explained further that his lack of progress in agricultural development stemmed from having to meet more pressing needs first; incidental expenditures went toward completing the employees' houses instead of purchasing necessary farm equipment. In fact, the newly hired employees finished their own houses, six in all, before beginning their agency duties. The fact that J. W. Wham had not yet transferred agency accounts also hampered Irwin.[2]

Nevertheless, by late summer three hundred acres had been fenced and plowed; Irwin's former partner and future nemesis, John W. Anthony, had been hired at six dollars per acre to do the plowing. Burnett and the rest of the agency employees set about completing an irrigation canal that Wham had begun the previous summer.[3] The agency field was not

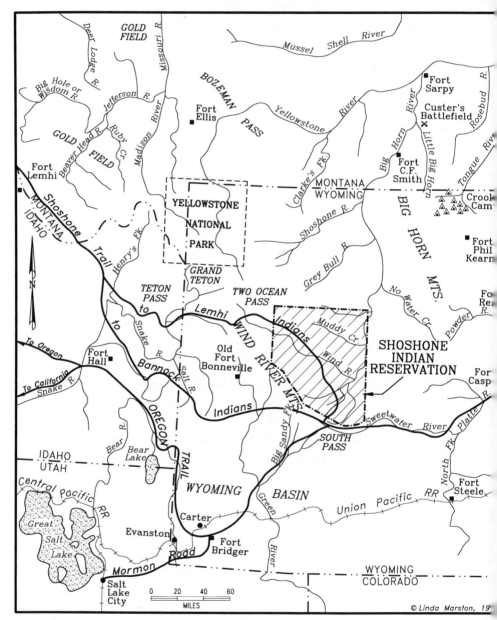

Map 4. Shoshone Country, 1872–1885

planted in 1871, however, because seeds, harnesses, and other necessary farm equipment arrived too late to put in a crop. Nevertheless, the ground had been broken and Irwin expected the Shoshones to commence farming in the spring.

Irwin's expectations suffered a few setbacks during the winter of 1871–72. In February 1872, the agent noted that the Indians wanted permission to go on their trading journey to Utah, despite the fact that the agency had its own in-house trader, James K. Moore. Irwin commented that "Salt Lake is indeed a bad place for them to visit, as they are neither taught good habits, or respect for the government."[4] If denied permission, Irwin felt he might induce the Shoshones to farm, but the government also would have to feed and protect them.

Then, in March, eighteen "lodges" of Bannocks and Shoshones went hunting, but ran into trouble. Arapahoe hunting parties had scared off the buffalo and heavy snowfalls kept the Wind River tribes trapped. Seventeen other lodges remained close to the agency, afraid to go hunting because of the nearness of Sioux and Arapahoes. Irwin was forced to feed both groups. This situation reveals several interesting aspects of the new reservation life. First, the government implicitly expected the Indians to hunt in order to provide for themselves (and thereby lower government costs). Such an expectation flatly contradicted stated policy. Second, they also were expected to stay on the reservation, not hunt, and turn to farming for food (and reduce government costs). This meant that Indians had to risk starvation while learning to farm because they had to put a great deal of trust in the agent's ability to scavenge food—or resort to stealing food for themselves from area whites. Third, only a small number of Shoshone and Bannock bands actually wintered in Wind River during 1871–72. Irwin's lodge count indicates only thirty-five tepees—approximately 175 to 210 people—remained in the hunting camps or near the agency. Either Irwin was unaware of other bands or lodges on the reservation, or many of the "twelve hundred hungry Indians" whom he fed in October 1871 had left the area. In any case, the reality of the situation suggests that for the majority of Wind River Indian peoples, farming was not a truly viable option at the time.[5]

Despite the threats of Arapahoe attacks on Shoshone hunters, the heavy spring snows, and the reliance on hastily acquired rations, Irwin reported some initial "progress." By mid-May, the Indian farmers had planted fifty to sixty acres in wheat, twenty-six more in potatoes, and six in turnips.[6] Thus, approximately one-fourth of the agency farm finally was in production. The plowing and planting process, however, was far from routine. Robert B. David wrote the following about that initial experience, based on an anecdotal memory of the agency farmer, Fincelius G. Burnett:

> The long-awaited plows and harness arrived for the use of those on the reservation. On an appointed day, the Shoshoni began to arrive at the office of the agent to learn the white man's methods of plowing. The entire proceeding was amusing to the Indians. Helped by the white men, they finally had the horses harnessed to the plows, and all drove to the field where they formed a long line. . . . Finally, all was ready. Each unit was informed that at a given signal it must cut a furrow straight ahead across the field. Every Indian grasped his handles and his muscles tensed.
>
> There was a yell, and all started at the sound. There was pandemonium everywhere. Here, a pony balked; there, a plow bit too deeply. In another place, three teams came together in a crashing mess of flying straps and whirling handles, while beyond the mix-up could be seen a dozen pairs of horses running away with broken harness flying, and plows leaping behind them. Clouds of dust rose on all sides. The Shoshoni were treating the spectacle with great amusement. Laughing uproariously, they were betting which team of runaways would be leading at the farthest limits of the field. . . .
>
> When this [planting seeds] had been accomplished, the Shoshoni packed up their belongings, hitched their travois behind their ponies and departed in a body to pursue their annual summer hunting.[7]

Burnett told his granddaughter, Esther Burnett Horne, a slightly different version of the story: "you Should have Seen those indians after we got them Started; all of them wore blankets. can you imagine an indian driving a green team; holding on to a plow; and trying to keep track of his blanket at the same time?"[8]

Both accounts, besides conjuring images of high comedy, imply much about the Shoshones' commitment to agriculture during the spring of 1872. The Indians turned spring planting into a gambling event, then left the bulk of the chores to their white supervisors while they resumed their normal lives. It seems clear that farming was merely a peripheral activity, perhaps even a subterfuge to appease white demands in order to get on with the real business of living as an Indian. Irwin unknowingly accommodated Shoshonean culture at this point, yet indicated satisfaction with farming "progress." He also informed Commissioner Walker that the Indians left the reservation because of lack of game in the immediate area and fear of warfare.[9] Put within the context of traditional Shoshone spring activities, the anecdotal stories suggest that this attempt at agriculture represented a clear case of Indian adaptation of white culture to fit native norms.

Subsequent events of 1872, however, altered the norms, so that farming became much more attractive to the Indians the next spring. When word reached Irwin about the impending Brunot negotiations, the agent interrupted the Shoshones' summer. He traveled toward Salt Lake in late July in order to intercept the tribe during their summer migrations and to make sure they returned to Wind River in time for the council talks. Irwin found most of the tribe gathered around Fort Bridger in early August, "entirely destitute of food of any description."[10] He obtained rations for them, sent them hunting for several weeks in the upper Green River Valley, and then arranged for plenty of provisions to greet them back at the agency.

In the aftermath of the Brunot meetings, Irwin enjoyed a steady stream of administrative accomplishments that pointed to a change in Indian habits for the coming year. For example, in early November 1872 he requested additional farm implements, evidently convinced that more Shoshones were willing to farm. In January 1873, he reported that Washakie and many of the headmen intended to stay during the summer on the reservation, farm, and send their children to school. Only a few bands planned to journey from Fort Bridger to Utah.[11]

Undergirding Irwin's accomplishments, however, was the fact that he encountered few problems in maintaining a steady supply of beef and flour rations. At this time each person received about three and one-half to four pounds of beef per week (or eight to ten ounces per day) and about four pounds of flour per week. In addition, each family received bacon, rice, beans, and baking powder.[12]

The emphasis on keeping the Shoshones well fed produced several results; one was enticing them to remain close to the agency for the winter. Nearly eight hundred Shoshones stayed on the reservation, and Irwin expected that four hundred more would appear as news of the Shoshones' newly found prosperity spread. Washakie actually sent runners to scattered bands to tell the good news, and, no doubt, to bolster his own reputation.[13] More importantly, as far as Irwin was concerned, the tribe put far greater effort into farming during the spring of 1873. He almost gloated about the transformation: "This spring the Shoshones for the first time have tried farming, and have gone at it with zeal and energy. They have planted about 200 Acres of land—and I believe next year, if the way is open they will cultivate successfully Six Hundred Acres."[14] Two weeks after this initial burst of enthusiasm, the agent added further prognostications: "The Shoshone Indians will henceforth successfully till the earth, and raise stock, and the time is not distant when the Shoshone mixed-bloods that are scattered more or less among five of the surrounding tribes will be attracted to the rich valley on this reservation, on seeing the improved condition of the parent stock."[15]

Irwin maintained his happy frame of mind in his annual report of September 17, 1873, with special attention paid to the fulfillment of his prophecy:

> Neighboring tribes of Indians have sent runners to the agency to see if it was true that the Shoshones had settled quietly down on their reservation and commenced farming. . . . Shoshones who left the tribe long ago, and other Shoshones, mixed bloods, numbering 46 lodges and 216 souls, have lately come into the agency, and ask that they may be permitted to stay and learn to farm; and it is reported among the Indians that many more desire to come, and I have no doubt will be here in due time.[16]

Irwin's jubilant assessment of Shoshonean compliance with the Fort Bridger Treaty stipulations overlooked some important aspects of the tribe's apparent reversal of attitude toward agriculture. First, Washakie relied on the abundance of food and the agent's support to expand his reputation and consolidate his power over dissident bands. He had done the same only a few years earlier, in 1866 and 1867, to gain Pocatello's and Taghee's cooperation in buffalo hunting. Second, the companies of cavalry and infantry stationed at Camp Brown strengthened Washakie's status and calmed some of the fears about potential summer warfare. Third, Washakie still wanted houses built for the tribe and bartered farm work for housing. He gauged Irwin correctly in this respect, for the agent assured the Indian Office that the Shoshones were serious about farming and raising stock and therefore deserved permanent houses.[17] Finally, farm produce added to the traditional sources of the Shoshonean wealth, but was not enough to replace them. Besides the annual annuity payments (worth $10,000) and subsistence rations (beef, flour, and other foods totaled over $20,000), in 1873 the tribe owned 2400 horses valued at $48,000 and sold $8,000 in furs. By comparison, the farm yielded 1100 bushels of wheat, 2500 bushels of potatoes, 30 tons of hay, and 30 bushels each of peas, beans, and beets. This produce was worth approximately $8,000.[18]

One final observation should be offered. Plowing and planting the Shoshone farm was a collective effort and a few families maintained small, private vegetable gardens. However, forcing ongoing communal labor throughout the summer proved elusive. The tribe farmed like it hunted: working as a massed unit for a few weeks, then dividing into the lodge groupings. Irwin perhaps grasped some of these truths about this tribal activity, but did not understand them fully. By 1874, he complained that the Shoshones refused to work "together in a common community," that only "several lodges of immediate relatives" would work a plot of land.[19] Farm work did not alter or transform the basic Shoshonean culture—tribal income, whether by hunting or by farming, reflected the primacy of the band or lodge unit in 1873.

## JAMES K. MOORE, POST TRADER

There were other ramifications to Irwin's policies in the winter and spring of 1873 besides inducing a flurry of Shoshone agricultural activity. In order to keep the tribe well fed, Irwin made repeated emergency purchases of beef and flour from James K. Moore, the official Indian Trader at the agency.[20] This expanded Moore's already substantial fiscal ties to the reservation. Actually, Moore's involvement in Wind River affairs exemplifies an aspect in the development of Shoshone-white interactions.

Moore was born in Georgia in 1843, but his aunt reared him in Washington, D.C. As a ten-year-old boy, he served as a congressional page, then later as a Supreme Court bailiff. In 1864 he traveled west, armed with letters of recommendation. He joined Ben Holladay's Stage and Express

Company, then in 1868 clerked for Judge William A. Carter at Fort Bridger. A short time later he managed the Bridger-Carter warehouse at Carter Station, under the supervision of Richard Carter, the brother of Judge Carter. Undoubtedly, Moore used his experiences and connections to win the Post Trader license at Camp Augur (later Camp Brown) in July 1870. Furthermore, a $4,000 loan from Judge Carter underwrote this initial business venture. A few months later, in November 1870, Moore obtained the Indian Trader license for the Shoshone and Bannock Agency.[21] Since the Shoshone's annuities were channeled through Fort Bridger from 1868 to 1870, Moore established contact with Washakie and the Shoshone tribe at that time. As the manager of the warehouse, Moore participated in the distribution of the goods to the Indians. According to Moore's son and namesake, James K. Moore Jr., the trader and the Indian chief became fast friends.[22]

Moore's store became an integral part of the Shoshones' life—he purchased their furs and robes and offered for sale such items as canned goods, dried fruit, cloth, tent canvas, matches, ammunition, tobacco, coffee, flour, and many other staples. He copied the Bridger trading system, which used in-house brass tokens as the basis for exchange.[23] This version of "script" limited the trading options of the Indians. In later years, Moore paid wages in tokens for hauling wood, or for sales of hay, wheat, or other farm products. The Shoshones made other uses of the brass pieces, or "yellow money," by wagering them in their games of chance.[24]

Agent Irwin facilitated Moore's success. As early as April 1872, Irwin relied on Moore's beef herd to supplement the Shoshone diet. In October, Irwin purchased emergency flour rations from Moore; the 1873 purchases represented continuation of past policies.[25] Further, Irwin allowed Moore's herd grazing privileges on reservation lands without exacting any payments, fees, or taxes from the trader. In other words, the U.S. subsidized the very beef that Moore sold to Camp Brown and the Shoshone agency. As time went on, Moore also purchased wheat from either the Indians or the surrounding white farmers, had it ground at the agency mill at little or no cost, then sold the flour back to the agency or the post.[26]

Irwin was not the first agent to grant these dubious privileges. J. W. Wham set the precedent. Part of the hue and cry raised about Irwin's actions toward local whites in 1872 was the fact that he changed the "players" in this "game," but did not alter the game. The concessions allowed government contractors, vendors, and employees to raise stock, grow gardens, or otherwise use reservation property for personal ends, without paying appropriate rent or fees, and were common practice at Wind River into the twentieth century. In some ways, the distinction between "honest" or "corrupt" agency administrations was quite blurred; only the degree of abuse defined the labels.

## WARFARE AT WIND RIVER

The happy collaboration of the Shoshones and Irwin, Burnett, and Moore during the first half of 1873 was shattered during the summer. A Bad Face Oglala Sioux band led by the son-in-law of Oglala war leader Red Cloud reminded the entire Wind River community of the dangers inherent in summering in the valley. On July 24, two women, Mrs. Richards (about sixty), and her niece, Miss Hattie Hall (about forty-five) were killed and some of their stock were driven off in a particularly gruesome event. The two women were homesteading and using some of the buildings or cabins of the original Camp Augur/Brown on the banks of the Popo Agie River, where Lander was eventually raised. The new Camp Brown had been moved about fifteen miles north to the junction of the North and South Forks of the Little Wind River in 1871 to site it closer to the Shoshone Agency. The killings were gruesome—the attackers mutilated the women's bodies (Irwin described numerous arrow and spear wounds and noted that medicine poles had been thrust into their vaginas). On August 17 the invading Indians launched three more attacks in various parts of the reservation. Irwin also heard reports that two large bands of the "hostiles" were massed within a day's ride of the reservation, poised for an assault.[27]

In fact, a fortuitous turn of events may have averted a full-scale battle. The Right Reverend George M. Randall, Episcopal Bishop for the Missionary Diocese of Colorado, New Mexico, and Wyoming, made his last visit to the reservation during the summer of 1873 (he died shortly after this trip). Randall, as was customary, preached to agency employees and to any Shoshones who cared to listen. Farmer Burnett recalled that the assembled congregation met in the log school building, stacked their firearms in the corner, and that "this wonderfull man would hold servis [sic] and he would hold us spellbound with his wonderful elagent [sic] sermons. Just as grand and inspiring as if he had been preaching to a great audience in some Grand Cathedral."[28] Apparently, unknown to the enthralled listeners, a Sioux war party had the building surrounded and was prepared to attack. They were dissuaded, according to Burnett, when they "heard a small man with a big voice making a great talk, which they could not understand; but they knew that he was a great medicine man and they were afraid to attack us."[29]

Fear permeated the valley to such a degree that the agency employees sent their wives and families to Salt Lake City in order to protect them. The families stayed away for at least a year, returning either in the fall of 1874 or 1875.[30] The Shoshones, in the meantime, besieged Irwin with requests for arms and ammunition and Irwin added his own pleas to send for additional troops to Camp Brown. He also redoubled his efforts to obtain appropriations for Indian housing and submitted plans and estimates for simple log structures, all in hopes of convincing the Shoshones to remain in the valley and continue their farming efforts.[31]

Irwin may have alleviated Shoshonean doubts, or perhaps the threats of enemy incursions abated with the onset of fall. At any rate, the agent reported that almost all the Shoshones were on the reservation in September and that 150 families intended to farm during the next year. In the same communication, he suggested that the department settle the claims of the remaining white farmers who owned property within the reservation, so that the Indians might put the buildings and plowed fields to use. Irwin said the whites were willing to give up their claims and that the vegetables and cereals already in cultivation would go a long way toward making the Indians self-supporting.[32] Unfortunately, bureaucratic processes moved slowly. The white farms remained in operation and the claims stayed in litigation for decades.

Although the Indian Office rejected reclamation of white farms, Irwin's main program, emphasizing plentiful food rations and building Indian houses, had better luck. The office accepted Irwin's justifications for emergency beef purchases throughout 1873 and, despite the onset of the "Panic," granted him permission to let bids for the houses. He assured the home office that the Shoshones truly intended to settle down and farm, noting "there is every reason to believe that the whole Shoshone Tribe with three or four exceptions, will go to work the coming Spring, if provision can be made for so many."[33] Irwin's decisions, however, reflected several sets of realities. He bought twenty thousand pounds of beef from

Moore between July 1 to October 1, primarily because the official government contractor, General Grenville M. Dodge, did not deliver the four-hundred-head herd until late September. Some of the Shoshones of whom Irwin spoke in glowing terms actually were mixed-bloods and employed by the agency. For example, Irwin had hired Mathias McAdams, whose wife was the daughter of the Shoshone subchief, Bazil, to herd and slaughter the cattle. McAdams's yearly salary of $1,000 came from the sale of the beef hides (worth three to four dollars each). His marriage stemmed from the trapper era of Fort Bridger. His sons continued the trapper connection by marrying the daughters of Jack Robertson and his Shoshone wife. They formed part of the mixed-blood families attracted to the increasing wealth of the Shoshones. McAdams's father-in-law, Bazil, was one of the band leaders who insisted on yearly trading journeys to Fort Bridger, despite the presence of Moore's store at the agency.[34]

Irwin's buoyant mood and the Shoshones' farming successes dissipated rather rapidly in 1874. At the end of January, the Indian office informed the agent that he had already exhausted his funds for the fiscal year. Irwin was instructed to delay the housing and the stock-cattle contracts until the summer, when Congress could appropriate more money for the next fiscal year.[35] Dutifully following orders, Irwin carried on negotiations over the next several months with the department and with Samuel Fairchild, a former mining-town merchant turned building contractor. Fairchild submitted the winning housing bid ($5000 for ten houses). Irwin persuaded Fairchild to finish the housing, then wait until summer to receive his money. The Indian Office agreed to those terms.[36]

## CATTLE DELIVERIES AND OTHER TREATY VIOLATIONS

Delivery of the first stock cattle under the terms of the Brunot agreement raised other concerns. Irwin still feared that not enough Shoshones could be found during the summer months to provide herders. Once again, Sioux warriors in the valley threatened the peace, upset the Shoshones, and made more difficult the tasks of herding both the beef and potential stock herds.[37]

Irwin had just cause to worry about the prospective stock cattle—not about problems with Sioux raiders but with Congress. The Brunot cattle were included in the general congressional appropriations in June 1874 for the Indian Department, although the *Act of Confirmation* did not pass until December.[38] In other words, it was impossible to arrange a timely delivery of a cattle herd. When Irwin realized the ramifications of this fact, he asked that two payments of cattle be made in the spring or early summer of 1875 instead of a first installment late in the fall of 1874. Irwin wished to avoid problems inherent in receiving shipments of cattle that were already stressed from the trail drive and that had to face the almost immediate onset of harsh weather. However, the Indian Office ignored his wishes and the first cattle delivery came in late September.[39]

Unlike their agent, the Shoshones began 1874 on a good note. They had had a successful winter hunting season, and when combined with the provisions obtained for them by Irwin, they actually had food surpluses to carry them into the spring and early summer.[40] Moreover, Irwin had devised a new plan that figured to keep the Shoshones in beef. In order to offset the weight loss in the beef herd that always took place during the winter, Irwin forwarded a proposal from Moore to provide beef on an as-needed basis, at the slaughter weight. The meat would come from cattle already in the valley and thus conditioned to the winter weather. Moore's idea cost more per net pound, but saved money overall because contracts normally paid on the gross weight of fall deliveries and did not factor in winter shrinkage. Under the existing arrangement, lower springtime weights required higher slaughter rates to meet ration requirements, resulting in depleted supplies before the fiscal year's end. In previous years, this forced Irwin to ask Indians to hunt for subsistence at the very time fields were supposed to be planted, or, as in 1873, to seek approval for his emergency purchases. Irwin's request for the new plan was granted in July and Moore got the 1874–75 beef contract.[41]

Irwin's efforts and their own hunting prowess kept the tribe in good fortune until July. Although the Shoshones sold $10,000 in furs during 1874, a summer grasshopper infestation nearly destroyed their crops. Irwin reported that the wheat and oats were ruined, while the potatoes and vegetables suffered severe damage. A second omen of change also emerged in July. The Shoshones and the troops from Camp Brown, responding to reports of "hostiles" in the region, encountered a large camp of Arapahoes on No Water Creek, a tributary of the Big Horn River located northeast of the reservation. The resulting battle on July 4, known as Bates' Battle (after the Camp Brown leader), was a solid victory for the Shoshones, but still left them reluctant to pursue farming as a full-time occupation. By their reasoning, as long as enemies could threaten their safety, summer living in Wind River was not "easy."[42]

Third, the tardy implementation of the Brunot agreement encouraged violations of the still valid 1868 Fort Bridger Treaty by both whites and Indians. For example, numerous white settlers swarmed into the ceded but unsurveyed lands, convinced that the government would not act against them. Settlers were soon followed by merchants, over whom Irwin had little control and with whom a few Indians gladly traded. In July or August 1874, for example, Noyes Baldwin opened a store on the Popo Agie River near the site of old Camp Brown (present-day Lander).

At first, Irwin tolerated the presence of Baldwin and the settlers. But Baldwin's clerk, Frank E. Coffey (or Ecoffey), soon attached a liquor store to Baldwin's establishment, which quickly earned a reputation as a violent haven of gamblers and drunkards. Irwin interceded on behalf of the tribe and gained an arrest and conviction for illegal alcohol sales, but his actions immediately drew the ire of Wyoming territorial officials.[43] Wyoming Supreme Court Justice Joseph M. Carey questioned the agent's authority over the ceded lands, while W. R. Steele, a delegate to Congress, told Commissioner Smith that he considered Irwin's behavior "under all the circumstances . . . an unjustifiable exercise of arbitrary power."[44]

Whites were not the only treaty violators. Irwin discovered that several bands of Shoshones made a new trail over the Wind River Mountains during the summer to obtain whiskey from traders located on the headwaters of the Green River. Irwin again took decisive action, using troops from Camp Brown to arrest the two dealers. This resulted in a case dismissed for lack of evidence and a suit of false arrest lodged against Irwin, Captain Robert Torrey, Sweetwater County Commissioner Blanchard, and James Patten, all of whom took part in the raid. (This case dragged on for some time. Hearings were held in June 1875, then postponed until January 1876.)[45]

More importantly, the problems with illegal whiskey sales demonstrated the ongoing lack of control by the agent over "his Indians." The fact that the government was either unable or unwilling to act against white interlopers made matters worse: because the government did not abide by its words, many Shoshones felt no obligation to abide by theirs. To put it another way, many bands simply disregarded treaty requirements and laws and continued to live their lives according to their own precepts. Regardless of the pressures put on them by Irwin or by Washakie, various band leaders still made traditional, independent decisions about the directions their own followers should travel.

One final incident in 1874 undermined the Shoshones' move toward agriculture. The first payment of stock cattle under the terms of the Brunot agreement arrived very late in the year, too late, in fact, for milking. According to Irwin, this disappointed the Indians.[46] It may have added to their lack of faith in the government as well. Furthermore, the annuity goods and flour deliveries also arrived late in the season, probably due to the contract problems caused by the appropriations delay. Heavy November snowstorms interfered with freighting the supplies to the agency, so that only one-half of the goods and flour could be retrieved from the railhead. Ultimately, the harsh and snowy weather thwarted Irwin's attempts to keep the tribe well fed and clothed over the winter. Once more, he had to ask the tribe to hunt in the spring of 1875 until freighting could start up again.[47]

With the apparent dwindling of government support, whether due to untimely weather or spending decreases, Shoshonean motivation to plow and plant more land faded rapidly. In 1875 the tribe quickly reverted to more traditional economic practices and cyclical nomadism. Irwin wrote that while on the spring hunt "a number of them were induced to visit Utah, and were baptized in the Mormon Church, and advised to leave their reservation, and drive the Gentiles out of Utah."[48] Enemy Indian attacks in April and again in June reminded those who were foolish enough to remain in the valley why Shoshones generally headed into the Basin during the spring and summer months.[49] Furthermore, government spending cuts hampered Irwin's ability to instruct or motivate the Indians to farm. Fiscal year 1874–75 reduced Shoshone appropriations by one-sixth and labor costs by nearly 40 percent. (For 1873–74, the Shoshone Agency received $30,000 in articles intended to subsist them, and the agent was allotted $6,800 in labor costs. This decreased to $25,000 and $4,000, respectively.)[50] Irwin lost employees, and the Indians either could not or would not perform farm chores without white supervision. Irwin observed that few Shoshones

> are able or have the ingenuity to plow the soil, fence, and build, without more assistance than can be furnished them under the last act of Congress. It would be a fair comparison to say that under such

circumstances they would be equal to good stout white boys, twelve to fourteen years old, and unused to labor. . . . A Shoshone goes to work with a will, or perhaps a sense of duty; he is impatient of delay; and if there is no one to show him, he does as he thinks best, and fails; under the discouragement he returns to his old companions—his horse and gun.[51]

Although at one level Irwin used this description to bolster his request for more funds (he wanted $9,300 in wages for the 1875–76 fiscal year, but the ongoing national depression meant continued level appropriations),[52] at another he clearly stated what the tribe was really doing—hunting. Furthermore, another locust/grasshopper invasion reaped its own brand of harvest on the agency's crops, adding further to the Shoshones' distaste for farming.[53] The net result was a drastic decrease in farm production, while fur sales remained high. Whereas in 1873 the Shoshones gathered over 3600 bushels of oats, potatoes, and other vegetables, the 1875 haul amounted to only slightly over 2300 bushels. Fur sales gained ground, from $8,000 to $10,000. This market held up the following year. In 1876, Irwin estimated that the tribe harvested only 1050 total bushels, but earned $10,000 from furs.[54]

## OFF-RESERVATION WARFARE

In fact, 1876 represented a pivotal year in Shoshonean life and moved the tribe even further from farming. The stepped-up hostilities between the U.S. Army and various Cheyennes and Hunkpapa, Oglala, and Teton Sioux, which eventually led to the famous Battle of the Little Big Horn in late June, offered something of a bonanza to Shoshone warriors. On June 14, about 120 Shoshones led by Wisha, Nawkee (a variation of Naakie), and Luishaw (or Luisant, a French-Shoshone mixed-blood), joined General Crook's campaign on the Rosebud against the Sioux. Not only did they receive soldier's rations while on the trail, the army arranged for their wives and children to be fed from Camp Brown's storehouses, because Irwin again ran short on supplies. On top of all this good fortune—being paid to fight and having their families supported at the same time—the Shoshones experienced the thrill of victory, or at least a well-earned stalemate against their old enemies.[55]

Following the Rosebud encounter, the warriors returned to Wind River on June 21, perhaps to spread the news of the army's largess. During their absence from the front lines of battle, of course, the Shoshone warriors missed the stunning defeat meted out by Hunkpapa medicine man Sitting Bull and Oglala war leader Crazy Horse on Custer's vaunted Seventh Cavalry. Perhaps in response to the news of Custer's debacle, the Shoshones absented themselves from the reservation in even greater numbers on July 11; Washakie led two hundred men to the army camp located on the northeastern slopes of the Big Horn Mountains. For the next month, the Shoshones impressed Captain John Bourke with their military precision and appearance as both army troops and Indian scouts enjoyed the bivouac in the abundance of the Powder River region. Their pleasure was short-lived. When the army marched downstream and entered the Yellowstone River Valley, supplies grew scarce, both from delays in the mule trains and from lack of game and fish. Consequently, Washakie took his followers back to the Wind River on August 20.[56]

Nevertheless, the summertime adventures effectively separated the warriors from agency plows and scythes. Fighting for a living also left them little time for herding cattle. While the Shoshone men enjoyed their military sojourn, Irwin arranged for Mathias McAdams to monitor the tribe's cattle, soon to be doubled with the arrival of Hampton Denman's new stock. Essentially, then, the agency or the army provided the means that allowed the Shoshones to escape agricultural responsibility.[57]

In fact, Irwin generally acted as the "good father," in the Shoshone sense of the term, by meeting their needs or coming to their rescue. For example, in October 1876 the buffalo hunt in the Big Horn Valley northeast of the reservation turned into a surprise battle with a group of Cheyennes and the Shoshones suffered casualties. Following their typical patterns, the tribe split into two groups; the larger village stayed with Washakie near the mouth of Owl Creek and Big Horn River. A smaller band, under the leadership of Naakie and Tagundum, were farther downstream (that is, north of Washakie's camp), near the confluence of the Greybull and Big Horn Rivers. The Cheyenne band, led by Dull Knife, killed six Shoshones from the smaller group and captured most of their horses and clothing on October 30. Irwin replaced their lost blankets and shirts from his incidental fund.[58]

In the aftermath, ninety-five Shoshone men left their winter camps and again joined General Crook, this time seeking retribution against Dull Knife. They succeeded in late November 1876, as fifteen hundred soldiers and four hundred Indian scouts (not all Shoshones) destroyed the Cheyennes' two hundred lodges and provisions. The Shoshone scouts collected numerous Cheyenne scalps.[59] More than likely, Irwin gave his blessing to this retribution—army rations certainly helped to conserve agency beef. Furthermore, he clearly identified with Shoshones in seeing Cheyennes as the "enemy." Thus, by the end of 1876 most Shoshones had returned to their traditional ways, with slight adaptations. Many warriors, for example, found military service to their liking and regularly served as scouts throughout the rest of the decade. In addition to the battles with the Sioux and Cheyennes, several of them took part in the army campaigns against the Bannocks and Nez Perce, in 1878 and 1879.[60]

Those who were not fighting were hunting or trading. Not only were traditional activities welcomed, they also were the only stable source of income for the tribe as ongoing problems in governmental food and annuity deliveries generally resulted in distribution delays. Bureaucratic corruption also disrupted the agency's management. A scandal involving the government freight contractor, D. J. McCann, resulted in Shoshone goods languishing over the winter of 1876–77 in the Union Pacific Railroad warehouse at Bryan, while the beef supply again ran out in April 1877.[61]

Almost all thoughts of farming during the next summer vanished and the tribe's movements clearly reflected the return to familiar patterns. In July 1877, only thirty-five lodges remained under Washakie's direct control while the rest of the Shoshones hunted or traded in Utah, or visited Fort Hall.[62] Agent Patten's annual report for 1877 (James Patten replaced Irwin in 1877) tried to gloss over the agricultural debacle, stating that "the Shoshones are rapidly drifting toward a useful and industrious life," and that they had planted one hundred acres in the face of serious disillusionment from the locust plagues.[63] Without a doubt, however, few Shoshones had been convinced of the wisdom of farming. Nearly every experience during the first decade of reservation life indicated otherwise.

James Patten's assumption of the agency post in June 1877 may have contributed to the Shoshone's general rejection of summer affairs at Wind River. Patten took over for Irwin when the latter was appointed to take charge of the Oglala Sioux at Red Cloud Agency. The tribe was not happy to see Irwin leave; in fact, Washakie, Toopsepoowot, Eotah [Oatah], and Norkok wrote that

> we have heard with sorrowing hearts, that our good Agent, Dr. Irwin, is about to be called away from us, to assume other duties. We fear that our Great Father intends to send some stranger here for our Agent. He might not like Indians. We might not like him. He might be quick to get angry with us. The Shoshones all know James I. Patten our former teacher. He taught our children for a long while. They all know him. He talks good Shoshone. He knows all our people. He has never lied to us. We believe he will give us all the goods the Great Father sends to the Shoshones. We want Mr. Patten for our Agent. He was with our old Agent and knows how he treated us, how he managed our affairs. Because he has been with us a long time he knows our wants better than any stranger could, and will be able to let the Great Father know what is best for us. He can induce our men to continue to farm and to improve themselves better that one whom we do not know and in whom we would have no confidence. He is our friend.[64]

The soon-to-be ex-Shoshone agent reiterated the chiefs' feelings a week later. Irwin wrote that "my Indians are not well pleased about my going away," although they were mollified somewhat when he informed them he was going to take charge of Red Cloud Agency and "bring the Sioux under subjection."[65] Irwin had done his best to meet Shoshone demands, that is, he truly attempted to give the Shoshones all the goods sent to them by the "Great Father," and he had the confidence of the tribe. Breaking in a new agent, despite the candidate's familiarity with the tribe, would prove a troublesome task.

The chiefs plainly indicated that they expected Patten, who met their character test, to continue strong intercessions on behalf of the tribe. That was the implicit bargain in order for them to accept any "inducement" to farm. Thus, in 1877 the Shoshones still offered essentially the same argument to the government as they had to Felix Brunot four and a half years earlier. If the U.S., through its agent, fed, clothed, and housed the tribe in a timely and acceptable manner, and protected them from their enemies, then they would farm. If not, then their actions between 1872 and 1877 stated just as plainly that they were prepared to employ themselves in traditional pursuits. Few white officials, if any, understood the Shoshones' offer. Fewer still would have approved the manner in which Shoshones were willing to farm (or herd cattle). Nevertheless, for most members of the tribe, agriculture was an addition to their nomadic economic base, not a replacement of it.

*Chapter Six*

# Preachers, Teachers, and Northern Arapahoes

## 1870–1878

### RELIGION AND THE EARLY RESERVATION EXPERIENCE

In addition to proclaiming that buffalo hunters must become farmers, the government pursued a second policy on Indian reservations during the 1870s. In the eyes of whites, it was not enough to see nomadic peoples confined to reservations and settled on individual plots of land; Indians needed to convert from their "heathen" religions to Christianity. Missionaries, not government officials, prosecuted this part of the Peace Policy.

The missionary arm of the Episcopal Church acted slowly to staff its various reservation assignments with clergy, teachers, and agents. In many cases, the missionary committee's tardiness meant that the initial recommendations for Peace Policy appointments came from diocesan bishops and not the committee. Other nominations came from sources outside the church entirely, as was the case in James Irwin's nomination process.[1]

Although the church's entrance into Wind River affairs was confusing, at least the diocesan bishop, the Right Reverend George M. Randall, possessed some familiarity with the area. In spring 1870, he had assigned the Reverend John C. Fitman to South Pass City. For a brief time Fitman held services at the Chapel of the Good Samaritan for the town's miners and merchants, but retreated, along with many of his parishioners, in the wake of Sioux attacks on the mining camps. The next year Randall visited the region himself, reporting that he conducted services at South Pass City and Atlantic City, and that James Irwin and James I. Patten served as the church's agent and missionary teacher-lay reader, respectively.[2]

The mere presence of Episcopal representatives on site, however, did not insure wholesale conversions to Christianity among the Shoshones, nor were the Indians enthusiastic about enrolling their children in Patten's school. Instead, they wanted their youngsters to remain with them throughout the year. Randall's report of 1872 observed that "the Indians, thus far, have not been inclined to send their children to school. It was hoped that when they returned to the Reservation, they would be disposed to remain, and might allow their children to receive instruction."[3] Considering that few Shoshones permanently resided on the reservation, few children received "instruction."

Evangelism, as opposed to formal schooling, had slightly greater success: Randall baptized two adults and their children during the 1872 visit, confirmed the parents, and married an Indian woman to a white man.[4] By 1873, Patten's work gained a few more converts and eleven children received baptism, although he added the following caveat: "It must not be supposed that these wild children were made to fully realize the benefits from this sacred rite, not wholly."[5]

Both Patten and Bishop Randall clearly saw their tasks as bringing white religion and "civilization" to the Shoshones. Patten described his duties as "visiting the Indians . . . , making their acquaintance, studying their dialect . . . , and endeavoring to lead them on to the adoption of the civilized life and ways of the white man."[6] His schooling efforts concentrated at first on the Shoshone girls, but later included boys, while his church services relied on Morning Prayer and hymn singing to redirect Shoshonean spirituality toward Christian tenets. Singing hymns evidently appealed to the Shoshonean musical tastes, for Patten believed "they learned our songs and hymns and the older ones in the Camps learned them from the children, when going on their annual buffalo hunt."[7]

Randall focused his preaching even more directly on combining Christianity with white civilization, that is, on farming as a way of life. In 1873, on his last visit to the reservation, the bishop delivered the following sermon (the one that warded off Oglala raiders):

> I am pleased to see, that you [the Shoshones] have begun to plant the land, and that so many of you have crops, which are looking well, and which you will soon reap. Dr. Irwin, the Agent, is you best friend. He wishes to do you good. He will give you good advice. He

will teach you to do what will make you happy. I want you to do what he says. The Great Father, at Washington will send you food and clothing, and seed, and ploughs and carts, so that you may raise wheat and potatoes, and keep cows, and be like the whites, who live on farms, and have good clothing and plenty to eat.

I want you to be good Indians, and take care of your children, and send them to school, that they may learn to read and write, and speak good words, and do good actions. The Great Father, in Washington, has sent Mr. Patten here, to teach your boys and girls. Let them go to school every day.

The GREAT SPIRIT sees all you do, and hears all you say. He will love you, if you do right. He will punish you, if you do wrong. If you are good Indians, you will be happy, as long as you live, and when you die, you will be happy. . . .

May the GREAT SPIRIT take care of you always, and may you always be good, and He will love you and your children.[8]

Randall's use of the "Great Father" and "Great Spirit" images probably was not lost on his Shoshone listeners, but the bishop and the Shoshones almost certainly attributed different meanings to the words. Randall, of course, used both terms to mean that if the Shoshones farmed, behaved themselves, and submitted to white authority and religion, then both God and Washington would bless the tribe. Randall's interpretation clearly posited a one-way correlation between behavior and blessings with a future-time orientation. Behaving well—becoming Christian farmers—had to come first, then gifts and spiritual favors would follow. The Shoshones heard the same promises, but probably understood them in light of their current situation, that is, in present-time orientation. The year 1873 was a bountiful one for the tribe, with plentiful food, gifts, and "blessings" coming to them from Washington. More than likely they deduced that they already were doing "right" by both the "Great Father" and the "Great Spirit."

Further, the term "Great Spirit" had no meaning in Shoshonean spirituality. They knew the supreme divinity as Tam Apö—"Our Father"—and viewed him as the creator of the world.[9] Of course, many and diverse spirits which inhabited the Shoshonean world, but none was named "Great Spirit" or had the overarching power that Randall inferred. The only other claimant to the Great Spirit title might have been the "medicine doll"

of Tam Apö, whose presence only had meaning in the context of the Sun
Dance. The medicine doll was the symbolic representative of the Sun
Dance, and the vision leader specifically commissioned it for the ceremony.[10] In Shoshone terms, therefore, Randall's use of "Great Spirit" was
nonsensical, unless his translator compensated with meaningful language.
This action, however, would have negated Randall's intentions. It is highly
unlikely that he would have approved his understanding of the "Great
Spirit"—the "Lord God Almighty" in his terms—as equated with Tam Apö
or spirits of Shoshonean cosmology.

The translation difficulties reveal far deeper theological impasses
between Randall and his Indian listeners than mere problematical word
selections. Randall's sermon germinated from ideas totally alien to Shoshone ears. As a bishop in apostolic succession, Randall had inherited
centuries of received wisdom held dear by members of the "holy catholic
church," that is, the church universal. His theological patrimony embraced
doctrines such as original sin, Augustinian ideas of the unworthiness of
humanity, the need for repentance, the trinitarian nature of God, and the
Johannine prescription that Jesus was "the way, the truth, and the life."[11]

His theological underpinnings were yoked to another set of ideals,
inherited from specific American understandings of the Enlightenment.
Randall clearly understood the notions of "manifest destiny" and American
republicanism, both of which carried the "burden" of forwarding the
inevitable progress of humankind and civilization to ever-greater heights.
These, too, were foreign to Shoshone ears, but his sermon explicitly
expressed this ideal: to "be like the whites." In other words, he admonished
them to give up a spiritually based hunting-gathering existence, to turn to
agriculture, and to embrace the mythological republicanism of the white
American yeoman farmer. To state the obvious, Randall and the white
world he represented expected Shoshones to denounce their own cultural
and psychological heritage and convert to an entirely new worldview.

Both Randall's sermon and Patten's recollections of his missionary
experiences indicate some of the obstacles in carrying out this assignment.
Patten attempted to conduct academic and religious instruction among
people who insisted on maintaining their nomadic lives. Randall's linkage
of Christianity with white society imbued his sermon with spiritual power
that had differential applications—at least for the Sioux warriors who over-
heard him and refrained from launching their planned attack.

Patten lived on the reservation long enough to learn the Shoshones' language, but Randall spoke through an interpreter. It is unlikely, therefore, that gospel stories made much impact on the Shoshones. Throughout the 1870s, no evidence suggests that Christianity replaced native religious beliefs or even superimposed Christian doctrines over existing spiritual practices.

In fact, Patten may have inadvertently weakened his Christian witness because of his ignorance of the linkage in Shoshonean wisdom between hunting, health, and the spirit world. Patten's venture into the Shoshonean spiritual realm began innocently enough, as a response to a change in federal policy. Financial uncertainties following the Panic of 1873 resulted in employee wages at the agency falling from $6,800 for the 1873–74 fiscal year to only $4,000 for the 1874–75 year.[12] Further, employees had to justify their work even to keep their reduced pay. Patten tried to combat this threat to his livelihood with an unusual strategy. When the tribe left the reservation on the 1874 fall buffalo hunt, Patten accompanied them and operated a traveling day school, essentially maintaining year-round classes.[13]

This was the first time Patten observed Shoshone life away from the influence of the agency. He was startled to see "mild-mannered" Indians transform themselves into "grotesque" figures in the ceremonial evening dances preceding the hunting.[14] His ethnocentrism demonstrated his lack of knowledge about Shoshone spirituality and its infusion into every aspect of life. Dancing, in this instance, was the spiritual aspect of the hunting event. His uninformed comprehension of the religious dimension of Shoshonean life became even more apparent two weeks later. During the hunt, the tribal diet of fresh buffalo meat wreaked havoc on Patten's digestive system. When his own medicines failed to bring relief, Comanche, a Shoshone medicine man, concocted a potion that corrected the malady.[15] On the surface, this incident reflected the compassion the Shoshones may have felt for the welfare of their white "teacher." Beyond this display of common humanity, however, lay a concern to make sure Patten returned safely to the agency at the conclusion of the hunt. This would deflect any negative sanctions against them that might have resulted if Patten had remained incapacitated from the hunting journey. At an even deeper level, Patten's "cure" at the hands of Comanche represented a triumph of native medicine and spirituality over Christianity and "white man's medicine." In

Shoshonean culture, the healing arts intertwined with religious belief.[16] The Christian faith must have carried little weight in Shoshone minds if one of its own believers could not obtain relief from the pain of diarrhea and excess gas! Patten quit his job after this trip, suffering from both the salary cut and persistent Shoshone skepticism of Christian teachings. Although Patten returned to the reservation as its second Peace Policy agent in 1877, the position of teacher and missionary remained open until 1878.

Patten's problems, as well of those of the Episcopal bishops and missionaries who succeeded him at Wind River, lay in ignoring the complex nature and power of Shoshonean religion. In essence, the Shoshones' continued reliance on their own economy during the early reservation period guaranteed the continuity of their religious beliefs and practices as well. Unlike white religion and economy, which generally were separate entities in the nineteenth century, Shoshone religion intertwined with Shoshone economy and the entire nomadic cycle. As long as the traditional economy remained sound, no compelling reason existed to abandon traditional religion. The structure of their spirituality, therefore, largely shielded them from Christian impositions. According to Albert Brackett, a visitor to the reservation in the late 1870s, Shoshonean belief in Tam Apö, the Sun Dance, Coyote, Wolf, and other cosmological beings and ceremonies remained unwavering.[17] Thus, as possessors of a successful economy, a lifelong educational milieu that trained tribal members in their common life together, and a spirituality that infused and knitted together the aspects of their everyday existence, Shoshones had little inclination to convert to Christianity.

Randall, Irwin, and Patten all faced this unified Shoshonean belief system during a time when the Peace Policy spiritual initiatives were especially weak at the Shoshone and Bannock Agency. They did little to change this situation. Randall made only three visits to the reservation (1871–73); Patten served only three years as the lay missionary and teacher (1871–74); and the Indian Commission of the national Episcopal Church absolutely reneged on its responsibilities to the Shoshones under the Peace Policy format. In 1875, Irwin was quite blunt about the dearth of the Episcopal presence:

> The Shoshone Indians of this Agency have been totally overlooked by the P.E. Church. Since the death of Bishop Randall there has never

been a representative of the Church at this Agency. The Church has never spent one dollar for any purpose. This Agency is not even mentioned in its reports. We have neither Church, School, nor Missionary. The Golden opportunity is passing away. The next administration may change the whole policy; and while I am a church man, I would advise, that if steps are not taken early to open a School, and the way for Christian training provided; that the jurisdiction be tendered to some other Christian denomination, who will nominate their Agent, and with hope and courage and Gods blessing try to Christianize my Indians. I know the P.E. Church at large is benevolent, and in earnest in missionary work, and I do not believe that it is aware of this oversight.[18]

The church was aware of the "oversight," but lacked money to do anything about it. The aftermath of the national depression of 1873 severely curtailed donations to missionary enterprises. The new bishop of Colorado and Wyoming, the Right Reverend John Franklin Spalding, spent the first two years of his episcopate worrying about the state of affairs among his white parishioners, especially in Colorado.[19] He noted in his sermon at the 1875 convocation of his diocese: "The monetary panic which began soon after the death of my lamented predecessor, has in no measure abated."[20] His lament about diocesan financial difficulties was echoed in the report of the national Episcopal Indian Commission: "The Commission has not ventured to undertake Mission work, during the past year, among the Shoshones in Wyoming, or in the Indian Territory. There has been no lack of willingness on its part to do, in these cases, what ought to be done; but the means at its command have not been such as to warrant any going beyond the large field in which Mission Work at many points was already in operation, for whose support it had to make provision."[21]

By 1876 the financial crisis peaked, moderating somewhat the following year. In 1877, at least, Rev. Spalding could turn his attention to the lack of spiritual direction among Wind River inhabitants:

[We need] services at the Shoshonie Indian Agency, Lander City, Miners' Delight, Atlantic City, &c. A school should at once be established for the Indian children, who were, several years since, placed by the Government under our care. If a clergyman were in charge, and could conduct the school, by the aid of members of his family or a "sister," he would be able to supply religious privileges to hundreds of people on the stage line between South Pass and Camp Brown, a distance of fifty miles—people who have long been utterly neglected by all religious organizations.[22]

Spalding had not ignored the reservation totally between 1874 and 1877. He had visited in September 1875 (possibly Irwin's springtime complaint sparked a response) and observed the ration distribution. At that time he commented favorably on the Shoshones' agricultural attempts, offered them encouragement, and agreed with them that the federal government needed to provide the tribe more aid and supervisors: "The one farmer of the Agency could not possibly give the help and instruction needed."[23]

He also consulted the headmen about a reservation boarding school, telling them he would lobby both Washington and the church—to whom he referred as "the Great Father and the Council of the Church"—for such an institution. Interestingly, Spalding understood the children who had attended Patten's day school were "laughed at." Therefore, he pitched the boarding school as a place to lodge "orphans and uncared for children" and assure them "good living." Spalding's comments about orphans are curious. No evidence suggests the tribe had unwanted children. This may have been a spurious remark of Spalding's, or perhaps white men had sired and subsequently abandoned their fatherly responsibilities. True orphans existed, but given Shoshone kinship terms—father's brother was called "father," mother's sister was "mother"—and the presence of grandparents in family constellations, Shoshone children generally had sufficient relatives to insure ongoing care.[24]

On the other hand, the bishop's reference to the "Great Father's" desire to provide housing and food for the tribe's unwanted children reinforced the Shoshonean image of "father." Finding food for their children and teaching them the accumulated tribal lore certainly fit with Shoshonean understandings of male roles. Further, Spalding's advocacy for their needs seemed to place few restrictions on the parents' own behavior. Again, this apparent freedom mirrored native practices. Like Randall and Patten before him, Spalding unwittingly articulated the Indian image of "father," not that of the white authoritarian who commanded obedience from his children and limited their autonomy.

Spalding also viewed agency mission work in terms of fulfilling obligations to white residents. His 1877 diocesan convention report, for example, strongly emphasized the need to provide clergy for the increasing numbers of white inhabitants in the Wind River area and suggested that Indian missionary staff could act in this capacity. No doubt this seemed expedient, given the financial burdens of his widespread diocese. The accent of this message, however, was on the "neglected" white populace, not on serving the Shoshones.[25]

Finally, Spalding reveals the chasm that separated Shoshone spirituality from typical Western religion. For whites, Christianity focused on the ministrations and preaching of the clergy within restricted notions of time and space (Sunday meetings, weddings, burials, pastoral visits, etc.). Shoshones, however, understood that "the tribal group itself is the total religious community that receives, modifies, and transmits the religious tradition to the next generation"[26] and that neither time nor space fettered that transmission. Both concepts of religion collided in the early reservation community; both remained intact and unmodified for each group. By 1877, Irwin, Spalding, and white members of the Wind River community had made few inroads into Shoshonean traditions. The native culture remained opaque and unintelligible to white observers, but continued to sustain the native peoples of that same community.

## NORTHERN ARAPAHOES AND WIND RIVER, 1870–1878

Whereas Shoshones held off white ideas of farming and religion throughout most of the 1870s, late in the decade radical changes occurred on the reservation that forever altered their status in the larger Wind River community. In 1878, the Northern Arapahoes joined the Shoshones as "temporary" residents of the Shoshone and Bannock Indian Agency.[27] The initial push for this change dated to 1869–70, but the actual relocation of former enemies onto Shoshone land was made possible by a variety of factors following the 1874 encounter—Bates' Battle—between the two tribes on No Water Creek. Although Shoshones and the soldiers from Camp Brown counted this battle as a victory, it set into motion processes that ultimately limited Shoshone hegemony over their own lives and land.

Unlike the Eastern Shoshones, Northern Arapahoe bands faced an uneasy future at the beginning of the 1870s. Following the abortive attempts to win peace with Washakie and the Shoshones in 1869 and 1870, the Arapahoes led by Medicine Man, Sorrel Horse, Little Wolf, Black Coal, Friday, and others tried to arrange settlements for themselves near Fort Caspar. Federal agents denied their request, suggesting that the tribe seek accommodations with either the Gros Ventres near the Milk River, or at the Siouan Red Cloud Agency.[28] Smallpox outbreaks among the Gros Ventres, as well as Arapahoe desires to stay in the Powder River region, thwarted the first option. The second alternative increasingly became a necessity as white incursions into Powder River lands interrupted hunts and provoked fighting between the whites and Arapahoes. Between 1872 and 1874, Arapahoes frequently asked for subsistence from Red Cloud Agency officials and military personnel. At the same time, leaders such as Black Coal cultivated friendships with army officers in hopes of obtaining their own reservation.[29]

The tenuous nature of Northern Arapahoe existence took a turn for the worse in the summer of 1874 when the tribe suffered a devastating defeat in Bates' Battle (discussed in the previous chapter). The combined Shoshone–U.S. Army attack on a large Arapahoe hunting camp located on the southwestern flank of the Big Horn Mountains destroyed the Arapahoes' independence. For the next two years, the tribe struggled for survival, both culturally and physically. Meager agency rations never quite satisfied hungry stomachs and tribal political power waned in the wake of the economic dependency. Intermediary chiefs lacked bargaining strength for their requests for a separate agency. Consequently, some of the bands broke away to join their relatives, the Southern Arapahoes, in Indian Territory.[30]

Nevertheless, Black Coal continually sought help from his army officer friends. He emerged from these talks as the chief representative for the Northern Arapahoe bands who remained at Red Cloud Agency during the 1874–75 period. To bolster his pleas, Black Coal and the other Arapahoe leaders tried to convince whites that the tribe was peaceful and did not intend to join "hostile" Sioux and Cheyenne bands. Thus they, as well as the more dependent Sioux and Cheyenne groups, signed an 1876 agreement by which the three tribes relinquished claims to the Black Hills and agreed to go to reservations in either Indian Territory or near Fort Randall and the Missouri River. In return, the Indians were promised subsistence rations, schools, and agency employees to aid attempts at farming.[31]

Despite their signatures, Black Coal, Little Wolf, Sharp Nose, Crazy Bull, Six Feathers, and White Horse still objected to joining their southern kinsmen and continued to press for a Wyoming reserve for the northern bands. They backed up their words with conciliatory actions: many Arapahoe warriors enlisted as scouts for General Crook's campaigns against "hostile" Sioux and Cheyenne bands. In return for this display of loyalty and courage, the "scout chiefs" hoped to secure influence with the army officers. Ultimately, they were successful. They also restored tribal confidence in their leadership. Fowler writes that in addition to winning a Wyoming home, "the scout chiefs revitalized intermediary authority . . . and improved their position in intertribal relations."[32] The respect accorded them eventually benefited all the northern bands after the Arapahoes moved to Wind River—their political power was strong enough to resist Shoshonean attempts to oust them from the reservation.

The actual migration to Wind River began after a council held in September 1877 in Washington between Sioux and Arapahoe leaders, President Rutherford B. Hayes, and Secretary of the Interior Carl Schurz. Black Coal led the Arapahoe delegation and argued against the tribe's placement in either of the two reserves designated by the 1876 agreement. Instead, he suggested another option, apparently made by tribal consensus:

> Our tribe held three councils before I came away and we all agreed that if you would give us good land—we are a small tribe—we will be happy. We want a good place in which to live. We are a small tribe; our village is 170 lodges; we would like to join the Snakes. The Snakes are a small tribe. The old people of the two tribes are dying off. A long time ago we used to travel together and were at peace; and I guess now the young people around me would like the Snakes. I think we will get along all right. I am good and I guess they are good. The way Dr. Irwin told me. He used to be agent for the Snakes. The Dr. knows all about it.[33]

Black Coal's words fell on receptive ears. The Arapahoes were author-ized to travel to the Sweetwater country for the winter and President Hayes promised them guns, pistols, ammunition, and annuity goods. In the meantime, James Irwin, the Shoshones' former agent, was ordered from his post at Red Cloud Agency to proceed to Wind River to get the

Shoshones' approval for the move.[34] Irwin met with several of the Shoshone leaders in October 1877 to discuss the Arapahoe situation. According to F. G. Burnett, the ex-farmer for the Shoshone and Bannock Agency, Washakie, Norkok, Wahwannabiddie, Moonhabe, and Wesaw all agreed to terms of peace with the Arapahoes and to a temporary residence on the reservation.[35] Irwin wrote Indian Commissioner Ezra Hayt on October 27 that both tribes "understand that the Arapahoes are to hunt this winter and be located on or near the Sweetwater in the spring."[36]

The Shoshones agreed to this plan, although they knew that their present agent, James Patten, would also serve a dual role as the Arapahoes' agent. They were quite disturbed several months later when they discovered the government's duplicity concerning the exact location of the Arapahoes' new home. Patten wrote:

> There is a large majority of the tribe, including Washakie the Chief, and nearly all the leading men, who strongly object to their [the Arapahoes] coming, and, of dividing their reservation with any other tribe. The Shoshones did agree, and are still willing to make peace with the Arapahoes. They have nothing to say against their agent, having the charge over the former tribe also, but want them placed on a reservation apart from the Shoshones, and, they give as a reason, that the reservation as it is at present, is none too large for the use of the Shoshones, and furthermore, the Shoshones are afraid that the two tribes will not agree well together.[37]

Patten went on to report that the Shoshones believed the council with Irwin in October 1877 simply was a negotiation to agree to peace terms, not to share the land.[38] Irwin apparently thought the same; he revealed his disgust at government's intentions in a letter to Patten on December 6, 1877: "The Arapahoes should have a reservation but the government has no right to filch it off the Shoshones."[39]

The Arapahoes started their trek toward Wind River on October 31, 1877, perhaps oblivious to the political whirlwind stirring up the dust on the path ahead of them. Lieutenant H. R. Lemly accompanied them from their camps on the White River near Red Cloud Agency, reaching Fort Fetterman on November 13. By November 18 the tribe, still at Fetterman, had slaughtered the last of the 155 cattle issued to them, eaten or jerked the meat, and traded the hides for other goods. They eventually settled in for the winter fifty miles west of Fort Caspar, but within reach of a buffalo herd.[40]

The annuities and rations promised by President Hayes were late getting to Fort Fetterman, which is one reason the tribe pushed on to their winter camp with its nearby buffalo herd. As usual, government communications accounted for some of the problems. Patten was put in charge of the annuity distribution, but he did not even receive notice of this duty until December 4. Transportation conflicts at Green River and at Cheyenne delayed his arrival at Fort Fetterman until December 20. Neither annuity goods nor Arapahoes awaited him.[41]

Patten caught up with the tribe on December 26 and immediately held an informal council with the headmen. As Friday interpreted, Patten reiterated the ideas that the Arapahoes should live on a reservation, learn to farm, raise stock, and build houses. Black Coal, displaying peaceful and cooperative intentions, responded by saying that "they wanted peace, and the Sioux would not let them have it," and that they were glad the president wanted them to have their own agent.[42] With that opening gambit, Black Coal pressed the tribes' more critical needs. He said he still feared reprisals from the Sioux, as well as confrontations with nearby Utes. Patten wired this concern to the Indian Office on the same day, stating that "several hundred Utes [are] within a short distance of the Arapahoes" and that the Arapahoes lacked ammunition and felt defenseless. More importantly, without bullets, buffalo hunting was difficult.[43]

Black Coal and the other elders impressed Patten: "Black Coal, Sharp Nose, and Six Feathers, Chiefs, are good types of Mountain Indians, and I have great faith that an attempt to civilize this tribe, will be attended with a good measure of success."[44] He asked for ammunition on their behalf, distributed the goods which had finally arrived, and returned to Shoshone Agency in early January.[45]

The first band of Arapahoes, under Black Coal's leadership, made their appearance at Wind River on March 13, 1878. Ten other headmen and Black Coal drew rations from Camp Brown on March 18 and conferred with Patten about their future. He reported that interpretation with them was difficult, which suggests Friday was not among them, but that the men wanted instructions and were "anxious" to settle down. This first meeting set off a slight panic; a group of Shoshones near the post thought the

James Irwin and Arapahoe headmen. Standing (left to right): Iron, Irwin, Sharp
Nose; seated (left to right): White Horse, Black Coal, Little Wolf. Courtesy Pioneer
Museum, Lander, Wyoming.

Arapahoes were raiders, not their new neighbors. Cooler heads prevailed, however, and prevented trouble. At that time, the main body of the Arapahoes was still hunting in the Powder River region.[46]

On March 22, the majority of the Shoshones returned from their winter hunt. Two weeks later, the leaders of the two tribes met informally in a joint council to discuss the situation on the reservation.[47] Patten reported that the Shoshones still objected to the Arapahoes, but would consent to the wishes of the government. Both tribes, he said, wanted a formal meeting chaired by General Crook to discuss the final destination of the Arapahoes. At this point, both tribes probably expected that the Arapahoes would receive lands near Shoshone territory, but not within the existing reservation boundaries. Patten believed, however, that "it is a foregone conclusion that the Arapahoes will be located on the Shoshone reservation."[48] He expected to take charge of the Arapahoes, but he thought that the Shoshones should be compensated a "just sum" for the loss of their land. He also felt the Arapahoes should receive a "separate and distinct" agency.[49]

As for the Arapahoes, Patten exhibited mixed feelings about their presence, first offering the following compassionate view of the condition of the tribe and their willingness to become "good Indians":

> A good many of the children in the Arapahoe Camp have the measles. The adult portion of the band, are terribly afflicted with syphilitic and other diseases, and it will be readily observed how deplorable a condition is theirs, and of the necessity of the immediate settlement of the tribe, providing them with medical attention, and all other civilizing influences thrown around them. There is every reason to believe that the Arapahoes have fully determined upon changing their mode of life.[50]

Acting on the side of charity, he arranged for F. G. Burnett to deliver extra beef supplies. Then Patten reversed his posture, possibly reflecting subtle hostility to the new responsibilities imposed on him by the increased native population at the agency. He suggested that the tribe be given a full year's supply of annuities in order for them to prove the worthiness of their "determination" to act "civilized." Concerns for the plight of the Arapahoes vanished. Instead, he expected them to accept their goods, go off to their part of the world, wherever that might be, and return for re-supplies only after they presented evidence that their actions mirrored their words. At the same time, however, he wanted to name new candidates for agency positions, claiming that he needed more employees to meet the larger workloads.[51]

Patten's ambivalence continued as the remainder of the Arapahoes journeyed into the valley. On April 24, he reported that seven hundred members were within three miles of the agency, with two hundred to three hundred more still "straggling" in. He sent emergency rations to the latter bands, but still requested instructions about his next course of action. He did not want them settling close to the agency buildings.[52] Patten's concerns were not just his own. Many Shoshones camped close to the agency headquarters. More than likely, they, too, did not want nearby Arapahoe camps.

Despite the resistance offered by Patten and the Shoshones, the Arapahoes quickly took steps to ingratiate themselves at the agency and at Camp Brown. In midsummer, White Horse, Six Feathers, Washington, Buffalo Wallows, and Eagle Head (all were bandleaders or noted warriors) joined the agency police force. Other men enlisted as army scouts, repeating the process they had followed in the 1876 and 1877 campaigns against the Sioux and the Cheyennes.[53] Significantly, Arapahoe responses to formation of the Indian Police force at Wind River directly contrasted with Shoshonean recalcitrance. Patten said that "[none of the Shoshones] have responded as yet, they wish to see the Uniforms and accouterments, and want extra pay for their horses—Washakie does not favor the movement, and the Shoshones generally think it will interfere too much with the freedom of their movements, to have a police watch their motions."[54] Arapahoes, on the other hand, possessed a well-defined, stratified social structure that eased warriors' transitions to scout or police service. Furthermore, tribal elders and headmen exerted control over the selections to these agency positions, acting so that the entire tribe benefited from participation and cooperation with the agency. The tribe expected their wage earners to share their incomes, not selfishly keep the proceeds of their jobs for the sole benefit of their immediate families.[55]

The leaders of both tribes, of course, acted in the interests of their constituents. Black Coal, Sharp Nose, and Friday, the accepted heads of the three main Arapahoe settlements, sought to make their residence at Wind

River legitimate; therefore, they appeared to cooperate with Indian Office mandates. On the other hand, Washakie tried to maintain the Shoshones' more advantageous standing. Heretofore their movements on and off the reservation had been unrestricted; they had been able to manipulate their agent into meeting tribal demands; and Washakie had enjoyed unencumbered freedom as the only spokesperson and authority figure recognized by whites for the entire Eastern Shoshone conglomerate.

The Arapahoes' behavior, however, threatened Washakie's preeminence. The conciliatory face of the Arapahoes put the old chief's behavior in a new light as seen by interested white observers. Washakie's reputation, as well as that of most Eastern Shoshone peoples, suffered some damage in the comparison. For a few more years (until 1885), the tarnish did not matter because the buffalo economy sustained Shoshonean traditions. Nevertheless, the Arapahoes' arrival at Wind River signaled a change in the composition of the human community of the valley. In the place of political and economic parity with their white neighbors, Wind River's Native Americans gradually slid into second-class citizenship. Although the Arapahoes were not the cause of this transformation, their arrival marked the beginning of the new era.

*Chapter Seven*

# Administrations of James Irving Patten and Charles Hatton

## 1877–1882

During the seven years after the Arapahoes' relocation to Wind River, they and the Shoshones withstood a succession of four inept or ineffective agents. Two of these men, James Patten and James Irwin, owned good reputations earned from previous associations with the Shoshone and Bannock Agency, but proved unfit during the 1877 to 1885 period. The other two agents, Charles Hatton and Sanderson Martin, were patronage players who tried to take advantage of the reservation system for their personal benefit. Yet a common thread linked the efforts of all four men: each witnessed and participated in a seesaw battle for authority over reservation affairs between themselves, area whites, the Arapahoes, and the Shoshones.

### THE PEACE POLICY IN RETREAT

James I. Patten started his new tenure at Wind River on June 1, 1877, by succeeding James Irwin, who had been transferred to Red Cloud Agency.[1] On the surface, Patten seemed an ideal replacement for Irwin. He had worked between 1871 and 1874 as the first lay missionary and teacher at the agency and knew the Shoshones' language. After he resigned this first position, Patten had settled in the area, probably on the Big Popo Agie River just south of the reservation border.[2]

At the time of his appointment, Patten was thirty-seven years old. Like other Wind River settlers, Patten had followed wandering paths to the region. He was born in Ohio in 1840, served in an Illinois regiment in

1863, and moved to Central City, Colorado, after his discharge. By 1870 he was living in Laramie, married to the former Clara Anzey Gamble White, and attending St. Matthew's Episcopal Church. Their first daughter, Stella, was born in 1869 in Laramie, while the second, Fanchon, was born in 1871, near the time of the family's relocation to Wind River. When Patten accepted the agency position, the household also included Clara's twenty-year-old stepson, William (Willie) F. White, the child of a former husband.[3]

Ostensibly, Patten, like other Indian agents during the late 1870s, still operated under Peace Policy guidelines. In reality, President Grant's departure and the subsequent inauguration of Rutherford Hayes resulted in a steady reversal of Grant's church-state cooperative policies. The Office of Indian Affairs and its Board of Indian Commissioners continued oversight of agencies and reservations, but the new Interior secretary, Carl Schurz, centralized his control and reduced religious influence. He hoped that his direct management style might prevent agency corruption, which had persisted despite the moral undertones of the Peace Policy.[4] Ultimately this meant that churches and their agents had less discretionary power to advocate for, or to abuse, their Indian clients. These restrictions forced Patten to seek departmental approval before deciding a course of action. This represented real change from James Irwin's first administration—Irwin had made decisions first, then sought permission.

Schurz's plan had far-reaching consequences. One was the gradual abandonment of the Department of the Interior's association with religious denominations. This set the stage for a return to more overt patronage politics.[5] As this policy change filtered down to local arenas such as the Wind River Valley, local economic and political pressures created more interference in agency affairs. James Irwin had weathered such storms in 1872 and successfully served five more years, but James Patten had fewer political resources at his disposal. As a result, his foes, both Indian and white, achieved his ouster in two and one-half years.

## CRIMES AND MISDEMEANORS FROM WITHOUT

Patten's woes started early—conflicts surfaced three weeks into his administration. First, new gold discoveries in Montana sent prospectors streaming northward with no hesitancy about trespassing on the reservation. After consulting with Captain J. Mix, the commanding officer at Camp Brown,

Patten allowed passage, as long as the miners caused no other trouble.[6] This expedient decision on the part of Mix and Patten ran counter to Irwin's example from 1871 to 1877. Irwin generally restricted unauthorized travel through reservation lands.

Another problem appeared in June. This one involved criminal activities beyond the agency's borders and had been ongoing since the previous fall. Specifically, the Union Pacific Railroad confiscated the 1876 annuity shipment because the government's freight contractor, D. J. McCann, failed to pay the freight charges. The supplies languished in the Bryan depot warehouse throughout the winter and into the following summer. By June 18, 1877, Patten had finally arranged for local freighter Worden P. Noble to deliver the goods and rations, but further delays in authorization ensued.

In the meantime, McCann's indictment for fraud did not appease the Shoshones; they needed their supplies in order to supplement their hunting and hide-trading economies. Unwilling to abide the delays, a number of Shoshones left the reservation in 1876, disgusted with the government's failure to distribute the annuities. Others departed in mid-June 1877. By July 25, only Washakie and thirty-five lodges remained near the agency—the rest were in Utah or at Fort Hall.[7] (Most returned, however, in time to witness the arrival of the Arapahoes.) Thus Patten's first summer on duty started with an inherited fiasco, but one that was made worse because he could not solve it on his own authority.

Before two months were out, Patten suffered further tests. Because Patten refused to hire Charles Walker (in reality an alias for John W. Anthony), he endured a barrage of charges similar to the ones launched against Irwin during the Brunot investigation in 1872. Anthony initially claimed that (1) non-employees lived in agency housing, (2) whites lived on the reservation who were neither agency nor military employees, (3) whites illegally lived with Indian women, and (4) employees illegally kept private stock herds on the reservation.[8] When these charges brought no official response, Anthony tried again. In early 1878, he formally complained that "the free use of Liquor at the agency by the agent Patten and employees . . . would lead one to believe that the agency was a Common Liquor Saloon."[9] Like Irwin before him, Patten was absolved of personal culpability by an official investigation (which took place during fall 1878).[10]

From Patten's perspective, Walker/Anthony's actions represented ongoing persecution by area whites against the agency. For instance, in October

1877 Patten informed Commissioner John Q. Smith that "the largest majority of the people, living on the southern border of this reservation (there are a few honorable exceptions) are in favor of almost anything to bring the government and the agent into disrepute with the Indians who belong to this reservation."[11]

To some extent, Patten's conflicts with the both Shoshone and white members of the Wind River community illustrated events beyond his control. Such situations mounted throughout his agency rule, but Patten did not handle them gracefully. For example, the Sioux wars prompted President Hayes, in August 1876, to ban the sale of weapons and ammunition to Indians by the licensed traders.[12] This order only temporarily halted arms sales in the valley. Homer S. Davis, Noyes Baldwin, and Eugene Amoretti, all Lander merchants, took up the slack over the course of the next year. Patten noted that Amoretti also sold alcohol to the Shoshones, especially those who "are not susceptible of moral influences."[13] In order to combat these temptations, Patten posted warnings that unauthorized whites should leave the reservation immediately and that he would arrest "disobedient" Shoshones. He noted, somewhat smugly, that his orders "created quite a furore among the settlers on the southern border."[14]

Patten's actions had several important consequences in the Shoshone community at Wind River. The Shoshones who ignored Washakie's leadership (presumably those who were "not susceptible of moral influences") and left the reservation gained access to unsupervised trade. This meant they not only avoided Patten's control, they also escaped Washakie's domination. Perhaps in partial response to this situation, Washakie repeatedly demanded that Patten get the ammunition ban lifted. The chief knew the absentee Shoshones would return to Wind River for the fall hunt in 1877 and, more than likely, wanted to reassert his ability to wring desired goods from the agency and Washington.[15]

Unknown to either Washakie or Patten, the ban was lifted in October, but by then it was too late to do much good. When the news arrived at Wind River, the Shoshones had already gone hunting; a large buffalo herd wandered too near the reservation to be ignored and Washakie vowed to hunt it with bows and arrows.[16] Thus by the end of 1877, few Shoshones were satisfied with Agent Patten—he represented the failure of the government to provide them with timely deliveries of rations and goods. Moreover, he hindered their attempts to provide for themselves by trying to stop their "illegal" trade and by taking too long to resolve the ammunition dilemma.

White residents perhaps had their own doubts about the new agent. More than likely, the fracas with Anthony demonstrated that at least some of the white citizens along the southern border of the reservation resented Patten's operations. It is likely that Patten's neighbors expected a greater laissez-faire attitude from him than he had exhibited. These series of events, coupled with the arrival of the Arapahoes in early 1878, signaled a disastrous start to Patten's administration. His job did not get any easier.

## THE DOWNWARD SPIRAL

Three issues emerged in 1878 to challenge his leadership and ingenuity. First, he had problems with the Episcopal Church over hiring teachers for the reservation's native children. Second, management of "his Indians" did not go smoothly—intertribal difficulties arose over unwanted appearances by Utes and Cheyennes; the government cut rations; and the government required Indians to "work" in order to obtain rations. Finally, his employees, contractors, agency traders, and even his own family undermined what little authority he possessed.

Inadequate financial support stymied the teacher-hiring process. Although the Fort Bridger Treaty required the government to provide schoolteachers for the reservation, few candidates could be enticed to ply their trade so far removed from "civilization" without better-than-average compensation. Even Patten's original departure from reservation employment in 1874 had been motivated by a salary cut and conditions had improved little during the interim. Moreover, the Episcopal Church still exercised some supervision of the educational services. Eventually, Joseph W. Coombs, a relative of Bishop Spalding, won the appointment as the agency teacher, but he came at a price. Coombs wanted $1,000 yearly and the Indian Office only offered $700. A compromise was reached when Spalding's diocese and the church's mission board agreed to make up the difference. Whether he was worth it never figured in the negotiations. Coombs was a forty-eight-year-old math and English teacher from Camden, Maine, with no experience either in the West or in teaching Indian children. Yet no one cast doubts on his qualifications. On the other hand, his appointment marked a milestone of sorts: this was the first time the church made a substantial monetary contribution to affairs at Wind River.[17]

Despite Coombs's successful candidacy, Secretary Schurz's tighter rein over Indian agency employment practices was quite visible. Spalding broached this subject to Commissioner Ezra A. Hayt in March 1878: "A report has reached me that the policy of giving the nominations of officers of Indian Agencies to the authorities of different religious denominations is to some extent being given up. I hope it is not so. May I ask you whether there be any truth in such rumours?"[18]

There was more than some truth to the "rumours." In July 1878, the Arapahoes complained to Wyoming's governor, John W. Hoyt, about insufficient aid offered to them by the agency.[19] Three new positions were added in response, but the Episcopal Church had no voice in nominating any of the candidates. In September, Commissioner Hayt filled one of those positions by appointing Ellis Ballou, a Baptist, as the Arapahoes' teacher. Ballou's appointment, in fact, represented blatant patronage—his cousin was General James Garfield, who later won the presidential election of 1880.[20]

Patten's intertribal difficulties began in spring 1878. Twenty to thirty lodges of White River Utes under "Captain Jack" invaded Wind River in early May, seeking trade in horses and buffalo robes. Patten wanted them back on their own reservation because they interfered with the spring planting and they consumed Shoshone rations.[21] At the same time, several lodges of Northern Cheyennes from Tongue River area moved into the camps of the Arapahoes, sharing the latter tribe's food. Later in the month, still more Utes, this time from the Uinta Valley, headed toward Patten's agency.[22] Patten persuaded the White River Ute bands to leave, but several Shoshone groups took the Ute departure as a means of "escaping" the Wind River area themselves. In fact, Governor Hoyt reported that roving bands of Shoshones upset white settlers in Uintah County and that the Utes near Rawlins (White River territory lay to the southwest of Rawlins) were angry at delays in receiving their annuities.[23] The Cheyennes, with one exception, gained all necessary approvals and stayed on the reservation. The exception was a small Cheyenne band, labeled "hostile" by Patten, which also made an "escape" from the reservation.[24]

Patten had two major objections to the visiting bands. First, they usually demanded rations, although he refused these requests. More importantly, the "wandering" tribes enticed "his Indians" from more "civilized pursuits." He wanted intertribal visits stopped and requested congressional action on the matter:

> I would recommend, for the purpose of preventing Indians from a distance from those living within the buffalo countries, especially during the planting and harvesting seasons, that Congress pass a law prohibiting all persons, including Indians, from hunting and killing buffalo during the months of March, April, May, June, July, August, September, and October. There would be no difficulty in enforcing such a law, but the Indians must be provided with abundance of subsistence during the period named.[25]

The matter of "subsistence" was crucial to his argument. Rations had been in short supply ever since the Arapahoes' arrival. The fact that the Shoshones and Arapahoes shared their provisions with their visitors, as any good hosts would, exacerbated the meagerness of their foodstuffs. The existing amounts of rations, except for a 20 percent increase in beef and flour deliveries, had been prorated between the two tribes. That is, the Arapahoes' presence did not lead to an automatic increase in food allowances. In fact, Congress had cut the total funding for the Shoshone and Bannock Agency from fiscal year 1877 to fiscal year 1878. As a result, Patten had to plead for every morsel he could wring from the Indian Office.[26]

The government compounded the supply problems with other regulations. Beginning March 1, 1878, all Indians had to work either for themselves or for an agency in order to obtain rations. Work, or course, meant "civilized" endeavors, not hunting, trading, trapping, fishing, or gathering wild roots and berries.[27] Many of the Shoshones responded by farming a two-hundred-acre common plot, but Patten constantly worried that insufficient food would cause them to throw down their hoes and resort to "the chase." His fears came true in the incident with the Utes and again when Tawunasia (Taboonsheya) and 150 Shoshones left the reservation without Patten's permission.[28] By October, nothing Patten could say deterred either Shoshones or Arapahoes from hunting buffalo. The Shoshones left for the Big Horn Basin, while the Arapahoes headed east to Powder River.[29]

In many of these situations, Patten was powerless to solve the problems. He was not, however, entirely blameless, especially concerning the
conduct of his agency employees. Frankly, he did little to stop graft and
corruption on the part of his employees and vendors. For example, many
whites still illegally pastured their stock on Indian lands. They included J.
K. Moore, the agency trader; James Irwin, the former agent; S. G. Davis
and his son-in-law, George Wroe, who provided dairy goods to Camp
Brown; William Evans, William Jones, James Rogers, and Stephen Giri, all
of whom homesteaded claims made before the 1868 treaty. Others were
Worden Noble, Angus McDonald, and Henry DeWolf, local freight contractors; and F. G. Burnett, the former agency farmer and 1878–79 beef
contractor.[30] The Indian Office did not act on this usurpation of the reservation until December 1878, then it directed the agent to collect taxes from
the stockowners. Patten responded by suggesting the department buy him
a horse and saddle so that he could inspect the herds. He also accepted
and forwarded excuses from Moore and Irwin as to why they should be
excluded from paying the tax.[31] No evidence suggests that Patten ever
collected the fees from any of the stockgrowers.

## INDIAN IRE

In other matters, Patten answered charges originally raised by J. W. Anthony
concerning thefts of Indian goods by agency employees. He noted that the
thefts from the warehouse were a regular occurrence, but he blamed losses
on Indians, not employees. He then requested extra building material to
construct more secure facilities.[32] Both Washakie and Black Coal, however,
refuted Patten's accusations. Both of them told Governor Hoyt in July that
they believed Patten cheated them. Black Coal bluntly stated, "He may be
a good man, but Washakie does not quite think so, and I feel the same way.
He may be a good man, but he talks crooked and does not understand the
Indian business. We fear he keeps for himself what belongs to us."[33]

The Arapahoe leader went on to accuse the agent of withholding food
from his people and making the Shoshones share their rations. Hoyt
dismissed most of these claims, observing that "Agent Patten appears to
be a conscientious and faithful officer, and is said to be improving in practical efficiency; but it is clear that he has not been able to impress himself
as a man thoroughly competent and fit for the position he holds."[34]

Hoyt's July visit, sparked by complaints from the Indians, revealed other distressing features of Patten's administration. First, the Shoshones disliked hauling timber (used for fencing, firewood, or constructing buildings) for agency business without being paid—they did not accept Patten's argument that rations were payment enough. Second, the Arapahoes were especially unhappy with J. K. Moore because he offered low prices for their furs. To some extent, Hoyt exonerated the trader by finding that the "cash system" rule for trading and market declines accounted for the lower prices. The cash system originated from the Indian Office on November 19, 1877, but was not in use at Wind River until February 1878, about the time of the Arapahoes' arrival. The change outlawed Moore's token business. Patten thought the Arapahoe complaints stemmed from the fact that Moore no longer offered "extra" gifts or presents, which the Arapahoes had received in their dealings with Red Cloud Agency and Fort Laramie traders. On the other hand, Hoyt wrote that Moore "is getting rich, and might possibly do well if his profits were less."[35]

One other government rule provoked the Arapahoes. The Indian Office banned the sale of beads and paint by Indian traders on May 4, 1878. This undermined the ability of women to earn money from selling traditionally crafted decorative garments and items. It also made it more difficult to sustain life by native practices, which surely must have been the intent of federal policies.[36]

Governor Hoyt's unofficial investigation in July was followed by a federal inspection in November. The government's inspector, Erwin C. Watkins, generally concurred with Hoyt's assessment of Patten: "Agent Patten is not a man of much force of character; but is beyond a doubt—a thoroughly good man."[37] Watkins found much greater fault with Patten's employees. James Kelly, the agency police chief and farmer; James Edwards, the blacksmith; and Edward Blanchard, clerk and agent-in-charge whenever Patten was off-reservation, were all found guilty of drinking liquor on the reservation and in the agency buildings whenever Patten was not around. Watkins fired Kelly on the spot and instructed Patten to dismiss the other two when replacements could be hired. Watkins went on to record that some residents, soldiers, and laundresses traded for Indian annuities, "but in none of these cases, has the trade been large."[38]

Watkins also looked into J. K. Moore's various business enterprises: the Indian trading post, Camp Brown's store, and the military saloon. He concluded that Moore conducted a legal trading post, but the line of demarcation between the three businesses was not clear enough. In other matters, Watkins faulted agency freighting contracts. Camp Brown generally paid from five to fifty cents less per hundredweight for deliveries than did the agency.[39] Although Patten escaped censure for these discrepancies, they probably represented what Watkins termed the agent's shortcomings in his "force of character."

Patten's troubles, including those of his own making as well as those fomented by others, continued into 1879. For example, Washakie's diehard opposition to an Indian police force at Wind River eventually inspired the Arapahoes to follow suit. Patten wrote Commissioner Hayt in July 1879 "that it is impossible to organize the force among the Shoshone because Washakie positively refuses to have anything to do with it, or allow any of his people to engage in it, and the Arapahoes have caught the infection, and will furnish no more men for the force, at least at present."[40]

Washakie flexed his authority against Patten on other issues as well. In May 1879, he sent a messenger to his old friend from Fort Bridger, James Van Allen Carter. Carter duly wrote to Secretary Schurz, registering Washakie's complaint that the Shoshones suffered from "scant supplies, absolutely insufficient; irregular issues of what little they can get; and general lack of regard for the comfort and health of the tribe at the hands of Mr. Patton."[41] Patten was aware of the dissatisfaction—on May 6, he noted that the beef and flour issue was nearly exhausted and that the Indians would not stay around to see if he corrected the deficiency.[42]

The government's tight purse strings caused other storms at Patten's expense. One cost-cutting measure implemented during the summer required Indians to haul their own freight from railroad depots. The Indian Office purchased over forty wagons and paid the Shoshones and Arapahoes for the use of their ponies as well as for time and labor.[43] Although the men of both tribes appreciated the chance to work for cash, they agreed to do so only within the framework of their traditions. That is, the Arapahoe council chiefs distributed jobs among their various bands, while Washakie assigned the Shoshones to freighting duty.[44] However, Washakie violently objected to freighting at the time of the fall hunt. He claimed that Shoshones still needed to hunt for their winter supply of dried meat and to have trading goods. Further, hauling supplies wore out their horses, making them unfit for buffalo hunting. Washakie had his way.[45]

These and other flaws in his management made it clear that Patten's days as an Indian agent were waning. The first push to remove him may have come from Washakie. According to Seth F. Cole, who had been licensed as an Indian Trader to replace Moore in 1879 (but who never ousted Moore from the position in reality), Washakie accepted Patten as the agent with the proviso that the agent's "stepson should not be alowed on the reservation and he says that in less that three months Patton made him boss farmer."[46]

## THE SINS OF THE WIFE?

Bishop Spalding, who was quite upset with Clara Patten's and Willie White's interference in agency affairs, echoed Washakie's displeasure. Her behavior offended the cleric, who never revealed why she irritated him. In April 1879, Spalding wrote to a fellow bishop that

> Patten is a good honest fellow. I do not believe any conscious wrong doing in him. He is, however, rather weak & inefficient. His wife is bad in every sense though[?]. We insisted with Patten as the condition of nominating him that he . . . keep his wife & her relations off the reservation. He has I understand lately sent her away in fear of losing his position through her misdeeds. She has been a great detriment to our day & boarding school work.[47]

Despite Spalding's admonitions to Patten, the agent could not resist putting his wife to work on the reservation. Ellis Ballou, the Arapahoes' teacher, noted that Clara Patten was employed as the Shoshone Matron. Although policies forbade nepotism, Ballou wanted to obtain a similar position for his own wife.[48]

A week later Spalding expressed his feelings to another member of the Episcopal Indian Commission (identified only as "Doctor"). This letter also illustrates the lack of clarity concerning the relationship between the church and the government: "Coombs is doing splendidly, but Patten's wife is ruining him. If there sh[oul]d be a change in the agency, can we control the appointment of the agent? I can't learn from the Department what our reply as to nominating really [illegible]. Have we practically any thing to do with the appointments[?]"[49]

There was still nominal cooperation between the Indian Office and the church. On the same day Spalding queried the unnamed "Doctor," Commissioner Hayt solicited A. T. Twing, the Secretary of the Domestic Committee of the Episcopal Church, for candidates to replace Patten.[50] Twing replied a few days later that the Domestic Committee would "send you the names of persons whom they would like to have you appoint"[51] The Twing-Hayt correspondence sparked a flurry of behind-the-scenes negotiations to fill the expected vacancy at Wind River. The nominees included Captain G. F. Jocknick and R. R. Goddard of Colorado, Joseph W. Coombs, A. M. Lawver of Illinois, and Charles Hatton of Michigan. Patten, therefore, was on his way out after not quite two years in office, although the final decision to replace him came much later in the year.[52] Clara Patten's part in her husband's dismissal is not explicit—no one detailed the exact nature of her sins—but she clearly alienated too many people and certainly contributed to his downfall.

## PATTEN'S REMOVAL

In 1879, agency inspections provided the final blows to Patten's hold on his office. General John McNeil, Indian Inspector, followed by Abraham Earle, the chief clerk of the Board of Indian Commissioners, observed Wind River activities in October. McNeil pinpointed what he thought was the source of the agency's problems, claiming that the Shoshones' teacher, J. W. Coombs, "appears to me to be a disturbing element at the Agency. Like too many Agencies this is somewhat divided against itself, and Mr. coombs appears to be the fomenter of this case. He presumes on the countenance and support of his church an assumes authority [on] that account."[53]

Earle visited immediately following McNeil, but at a time when Patten was on the last freighting expedition of the season to Bryan. Earle, however, was not content to report conditions at the agency, he actually made them worse, perhaps inspired by Clara Patten. Ella Young, Clara Patten's replacement as the Matron for the Shoshone school—she also was Bishop Spalding's niece—wrote her uncle about the two inspectors. She thought that McNeil came away with favorable impressions of the school. Earle's visit, on the other hand, left a far different legacy:

[Earle] visited our school and criticized it most severely. He objected, most decidedly, to teaching the Creed and Commandments. He said, in the presence of the pupils, who understood every word he uttered, that we were teaching them to lie and something nobody believed, and didn't believe it ourselves. That the Commandments were done away with, and it was impossible for anyone to keep all the Commandments. He said that if we could not live in the school with the Indians all the time, day and night, we should not be taking Government money under a pretence of a boarding school, but should give it up at once, for all that we have done is useless. Our teaching the scholars to read, write and speak English is of no use, for they will learn all that when they see the need of it. . . . Mr. Patten was away when this gentleman, Mr. Earle arrived. . . . He stays with Mrs. P. and I think she has inspired him with her spirit. He came into the Sunday school today when it was about half through, and raised his objections again to our forms of Sunday School Service. If he had made such talk to us outside the school it would not have been so bad. His talk is very discouraging, and made us almost heart-sick.[54]

Commissioner Hoyt immediately apologized to Twing for Earle's behavior: "Mr. A.L. Earle is a clerk of the Board of Indian Comns. [*sic*] and is certainly old enough to know better than to make that sort of a harangue either in a day or Sabbath school. I will call the attention of the Board of Ind. Comns. to his bad taste, as disclosed in the remarks made, and will request them to keep him from visiting any agency schools. He is manifestly unfitted for such work."[55]

This communication, however, did nothing to change departmental decisions about Patten's status. Patten was fired and Charles Hatton, of Hillsdale, Michigan, was hired in his place. Like his predecessor, Hatton was an Episcopalian and thus favored by church officials. He accepted the position in late December 1879, took charge in early February 1880, and thus ended Patten's uncomfortable tenure.[56]

For the Shoshones, Patten's term was marked by the grudgingly accepted presence of the Arapahoes and by stepped-up efforts from the larger white society to dominate their lives and "teach" them the benefits of "civilization." On the other hand, the Arapahoes found a home during Patten's administration and, like the Shoshones, sought to continue their own traditions in the face of increasing white opposition. White members of the Wind River community also attempted to continue their traditions during Patten's leadership by trading with the tribes and gouging government. In other words, with the exception of the Arapahoes' new status at Wind River, not much changed between 1877 and early 1880.

There were, however, some subtle differences between the end of James Irwin's first term as agent and the end of James Patten's. Federal guidelines clearly became more influential in terms of agency management, restricting Native American traditions, and reversing Peace Policy reforms. Patten had possessed far less authority to act on his own counsel than had Irwin. Regular investigations of agencies had begun, which meant graft, corruption, or ineptitude were harder to camouflage. Finally, the church-state partnership was reaching the end of its life. Each of these developments expanded over the course of the next three administrations.

## CHARLES HATTON AND THE LAST DAYS
## OF THE PEACE POLICY, 1880

From the point of view of the Indian Commission of the Episcopal Church, Charles Hatton's nomination and confirmation as Indian Agent started on a few good notes and continued the illusion that the Peace Policy still functioned. According to Hatton's rector, the Reverend William Wirt Raymond, the new Shoshone and Bannock Agent was a good Episcopalian, a clothing retailer, and a member of the Hillsdale, Michigan, city council.[57] Although he lacked experience with native peoples, Hatton's retailing and local-area political background at least encompassed some of the attributes needed by an agent. Further, his religious preference met nominal Peace Policy requirements. The church's influence in Hatton's nomination, however, represented the next-to-last gasp of the Peace Policy initiatives at Wind River. The Indian Office filled other agency positions sans consultation with church officials.

In particular, the church lost its already weak grip on Indian education at Wind River. During the administrations of Irwin and Patten, education had never been an effective "civilizing" arm of either the Episcopal Church or the government, despite Bishop Spalding's attempts to rectify the situation. This legacy continued during the transition from Patten to Hatton. In the wake of the inspections of the agency in October 1879, Joseph W.

Coombs and Ella Young were fired, a move that thoroughly angered Spalding. Patten communicated the bishop's ire to Inspector McNeil (McNeil generally supported Patten's and Spalding's work at Wind River): "Bishop Spalding of Denver is giving me fits for closing the schools, and is hot after Mr. Earle, as by representations made to him by Coombs and Miss Young, the blame is laid to Mr. Earle & to Mrs. Patten for their discharge. He (the Bishop) orders me not to close the schools, and I have heard that he has written to Coombs not to leave and argues, that Mr. Coombs is an employe of the Church, as well as of the Gov't."[58]

Spalding's view was partially correct, since his diocese contributed 30 percent of Coombs's annual salary. Spalding would have been even more upset, however, had he known that Patten was contemplating a change in teachers before Earle dismissed Coombs and Young. Patten's plans began when the agency physician resigned in July 1879 because of a reduction in the pay schedule (from $1,200 per annum to $600). The agent had concocted an idea whereby two positions, namely the agency physician and the head teacher, might be combined into one position at the same pay rate that previously applied to the physician alone (i.e., $1,200). The three hundred dollars raised by Spalding, which helped pay for Coombs, never factored into Patten's thinking. This was approved in September.[59] However, the new physician-teacher, Dr. Edward T. Gibson, did not arrive until March 1880. Agent Hatton, not Patten, welcomed him to Wind River, and Hatton was quite ignorant of his predecessor's plan and its acceptance. He refused to pay Gibson the double salary, rightly following general procedures that an employee could not receive pay for two jobs. Gibson complained.[60] So did Bishop Spalding, but not over the salary dispute. In a long letter to President Hayes, Spalding protested that the government had not informed the church about this decision and that "the whole matter of education at the Agency [is] out of our hands."[61]

The demise of the educational thrust of the Peace Policy, however, was not the only casualty in Hatton's administration. Larger policy issues also fell by the wayside. The church-state relationship of the Peace Policy had been predicated on finding agency employees who would be good Christians and immune to the scandals and corruption that marred administration of Indian reservations. Thus the core of the policy was not aimed at involving churches in governmental affairs per se, but in limiting fraud, or eliminating theft of Indian goods, or promoting peace and harmony between agency employees, or navigating the dangerous waters of local politics and economics. These laudable goals disappeared relatively early in Hatton's reign, although the beginning of his term started innocently enough.

## HAULING AND HUNTING, 1879 AND 1880

The opening days of Hatton's tenure mirrored some of the experiences of Irwin and Patten before him. Hatton's troubles, like Patton's, started within three weeks of his arrival at the agency. And, similar to Irwin's situation nearly a decade earlier, Hatton's initial worries stemmed from his predecessor's administration. During the summer of 1879, Patten had sent the Indian Office overly generous estimates needed by the agency for seed stock (potatoes, wheat, oats, etc.) and building materials for construction of cellars and granaries. The Indian Office honored these requests, but, unfortunately, the goods were shipped late and in partial lots. In early September, the two tribes hauled what was available from the Bryan depot. Then the Shoshones refused to make another run to meet later deliveries, preferring to hunt instead. The Arapahoes, still trying to prove themselves worthy enough for their own reservation, made an October trip and returned with another piecemeal load. The remainder of the agency goods finally reached Bryan in mid-November, but the Arapahoes' ponies were too worn out to make another journey. Patten and two employees made one last try in December to retrieve the rest of the materials, but heavier than normal snows blocked the road over South Pass. Patten therefore stored the supplies near a ranch at Pacific Springs, approximately four miles southwest of the pass. This plan saved storage fees at the Bryan depot but required agency employees to guard the goods.[62]

As in the Gibson affair, Hatton had to deal with the consequences of Patton's actions. He also had to confront the realities of two corollary decisions made by Patten. First, in a futile attempt to persuade the Shoshones to go freighting instead of hunting, Patten had increased beef rations well above the maximum allowances in August and September. By the following March, Hatton discovered he had only enough beef left to supply the tribes through April.[63]

The second problem evolved from the overestimate of the amount of seeds needed for the 1880 farming season. Hatton discovered that there was no way to plow enough ground to plant all of the seeds ordered because the equipment needed for that task was still stored at Pacific Springs. Moreover, neither the agency's oxen nor the Indian ponies were in condition to haul the supplies. Hatton also believed that, even if the machinery and tools were available, the Shoshones and Arapahoes were not prepared to use them. He told Roland E. Trowbridge, the Commissioner of Indian Affairs, that "the working capacaty of these Indians . . . has been greatly overestimated."[64]

Regardless of the accuracy of Hatton's opinion about Indian "capacaty," little farming took place in 1880. The tribes made two trips each in the spring to get what was left of the supplies left at Pacific Springs, but the seed stock arrived too late to be of much use. The Indians grew small-scale vegetable gardens, but few planted potatoes, wheat, or other staples that summer. Although the Arapahoes plowed 75 additional acres, the Shoshone farm efforts remained at previous levels. Together, both groups worked 325 acres.[65]

As summer changed into fall, both tribes paid little attention to harvests and prepared for the upcoming hunts. In the meantime, another fiscal year started and Indian supplies moved from manufacturers to government warehouses and finally to the railroads. This set the stage for another round of late deliveries and crisis management but with a slightly different outcome. Earlier in the year, Hatton changed railheads from Bryan to Rawlins. This move saved about 150 railway miles and avoided the ferry crossings on the Green River. It also shortened the distance from the railroad to the agency by a few miles. On the other hand, the new, shorter road was rough. Each tribe's freighters hauled one load in late September to early October 1880, but another trip was necessary to get the remaining supplies. Washakie flatly refused to send his men again; he said they needed to hunt. The Arapahoes, however, gamely tried to do the task, but were snowed in at Crook's Gap, about halfway between the agency and the Rawlins depot. As a result, the latter tribe lost twenty-four horses, which threatened the effectiveness of their hunting. In this situation, working for pay like white men took time away from hunting and cost the Arapahoes the ability to haul away their kills. The Shoshones suffered as well—Hatton docked their rations and annuities because they went hunting instead of hauling.[66]

Hatton's decision infuriated Washakie. According to Ellis Ballou, on January 8, 1881, "Washakie came in from the hunt and when he learned that an order not to issue rations to the Shoshones had been issued he was terribly angry."[67] Hatton downplayed Washakie's wrath and reported this scene with the Shoshone leader to acting Commissioner E. M. Marble in mid-January, 1881:

> Washakie said He knew it was too late to go after Freight—feed all gone[,] roads bad—because He knew more than the Arapahoes, the Great Father refused to give them Rations. They went away with the bad heart. I inquired when they intended to return[;] they said, they could not tell. Since their departure different Ranchmen have notified me that the Shoshone Indians were slaughtering White mens Cattle[.] this will make trouble if it is not Stopped and it will be impossible for anyone to Stop them while they are hungry they will kill any Cattle that comes within reach.[68]

From Washakie's perspectives, Hatton's own words indicate that the agent dishonored the rules of being the "good Father"—he failed to provide his Indian "children" with food. In fact, he denied food when it was available. In addition to the rations that Hatton withheld from the tribe, many Wind River goods were left at Rawlins. N. W. Wells, the government transportation agent, reported that over 100,000 pounds of supplies were still at Rawlins in January, and that 8634 pounds of agricultural tools had been in the Bryan depot since the previous April 1880![69] Clearly, from the Shoshone viewpoint, the government and its principal representative, Hatton, maliciously violated the terms of the Fort Bridger Treaty. Although Hatton minimized the breach that his actions caused in his relationship with the Shoshones, his concerns about Shoshone beef kills were well-founded. The Shoshones turned to available food sources, albeit illegal ones, in the absence of sufficient government supplies.

The freighting incidents illustrate two serious problems facing Hatton in his management of Wind River affairs. First, the reservation's distance from suitable railheads and the government's timetable continually frustrated hopes of efficient and timely deliveries of rations and supplies. These transportation problems stymied all of the Wind River agents during the nineteenth century, but the Shoshones and Arapahoes held the agents personally accountable. To the Indians, the trustworthiness of the agents depended on how they handled these ongoing obstacles. Hatton's actions revealed his shortcomings as a suitable advocate or intermediary on behalf of the two tribes: he was not even present during the freighting fiasco of fall 1880! He had taken a leave of absence from Wind River from mid-October to mid-November to attend his daughter's wedding in Michigan, returning when the Arapahoes were already snowbound in Crook's Gap. Incredibly, he waited more than three weeks before suggesting a solution, one that he knew violated policy. He asked the Indian Office to hire commercial teamsters to retrieve the supplies, a request that the commissioner turned down because Indians were supposed to haul their own supplies. These decisions doomed the freight to storage until late spring (June) 1881, when Indian teams again hauled the loads from Rawlins and Bryan. In the meantime, agency employees were pulled from their other duties in order to guard the supplies, just as had been the case during the winter of 1879–80.[70]

## THE CRIMES BEGIN: OR WHOSE SCALES DO WE TRUST?

Although Hatton's absence from the reservation in 1880 did not cause the mishaps with the weather or the late deliveries from the government's supply warehouses, his lackadaisical activities clearly showed his disregard for the concerns of Wind River's Indian inhabitants. In fact, Hatton had profit in mind, not the welfare of his immediate constituents. During that same winter, he masterminded several schemes to defraud both the government and the tribes. The first idea involved the beef herd. According to Louis Ballou, the son of the Arapahoes' teacher, Ellis Ballou, a conspiracy was hatched by Hatton, M. R. Curtiss, and Eugene Amoretti to short-weight beef rations. Curtiss was the agency farmer whom Hatton had hired, and Amoretti, the Lander merchant, had won the beef contract for the 1880–81 fiscal year. Louis Ballou claimed the three men slaughtered two- and three-year-old steers averaging nine hundred pounds each, but reported on the issue returns that the animals weighed twelve hundred pounds. Furthermore, Ballou said the agency scales were frozen for most of the winter. When they thawed, Ballou and agency employees Nelson Yarnall and Peter Walls secretly checked the beef issue scheduled for

March 25 by weighing the cattle the night before. According to Ballou, the nighttime weights were significantly lower than those certified at the next day's issue.[71]

The alleged conspiracy between Hatton, Curtiss, and Amoretti reflected other irregularities at the agency, which involved a tangled web of employees, traders, merchants, and freighters. Hatton's employee force included holdovers from Patten's administration as well as several he brought with him from Michigan. Patten's hires included Leander C. Bliss (carpenter), Peter Walls (engineer), Luke White (clerk), and Nelson Yarnall (blacksmith). Hatton's additions were the farmer, M. R. Curtiss, and Hatton's new son-in-law, William B. Hastings, who worked a variety of positions—trainmaster (the white man who supervised the Indian freight teams), engineer, and agency clerk. He also hired Thomas McDermott as the agency storekeeper (that is, the supervisor of the agency's warehouse). Added to this mix were Ellis Ballou and his extended family—his daughter Mary, son Louis, and brother-in-law, Lester S. Clark. Ellis and Mary taught in the Arapahoe school. Clark and Louis Ballou usually aided the Indian teamsters; they also were the guards of the abandoned goods at Pacific Springs and at Crooks Gap. The outside "agitators" in this situation included the Noble brothers (W. N. and Worden P.), and traders James K. Moore and Thomas W. Vallentine.[72] Louis Ballou's charges, therefore, suggest that the employees, freighters, and traders were divided in their loyalties—Patten's men obviously distrusted those hired by Hatton, or at the very least, were trying to find ways to remove them from agency operations.

The bickering began in 1879 with a promise made by Inspector McNeil to Ellis Ballou. At that time, Ballou taught school in a makeshift canvas-covered frame building. McNeil guaranteed the teacher a properly constructed school for the next year. The funds for a wood frame schoolhouse were appropriated in 1880, but Hatton changed the design after the materials were already on-site. He also tried to divert the school's building materials to the construction of a kitchen addition on his house.[73] Ballou then complained that the funds and lumber for the new school were used to build "stables, Hen houses, privies, and other necessary institutions."[74] Much to Ballou's chagrin, the department ignored or overlooked his statement and approved Hatton's uses of the lumber.

## THE LESSONS LEARNED AT SCHOOL:
## OR, HOW TO COOK THE BOOKS

A few months later, Ballou had a more serious concern when Hatton discharged Ellis's daughter, Mary, from agency employment. However, Mary was working illegally in the first place, and at an unauthorized job in the second place! Her father's letter to acting commissioner Marble spun a fantastic story of the intricacies of nepotism and corruption that were deeply woven into the fabric of the agency's administration. According to Ballou, his political backers had promised his wife a job at Wind River in addition to his own. When Mrs. Ballou remained in Helena, Montana, to nurse a sick sister instead of moving to the agency, daughter Mary took the position. Rather than seek official approval of this change, both Patten and Hatton kept Mrs. Ballou's name on the books. The Arapahoe school had not been in session since October 1879, yet Mary continued to draw her mother's paycheck for over eighteen months. Instead of operating a school, the two agents used the skills of Ellis and Mary to sort through agency paperwork. It was far easier to keep the Ellises on the books as teachers than to get more clerk positions approved for the agency. Hatton fired Mary when the paperwork was finished.[75] However, Ballou had anticipated opening the Arapahoe school again in early 1881 and thus expected to use Mary as a teacher. It seemed to him that Hatton was deliberately interfering with his plans. Ballou's unhappiness over this situation prompted his next complaint.

On January 9, 1881, only three days after his letter to Marble, Ballou wrote C. M. Carter of Washington, D.C., about agency conditions. In particular, he noted that "the Indians found a wagon load of their annuities cached in a gulch a few miles from the Agency. They reported to the agent and wanted permission to hunt up the thieves but the Storekeeper [Thomas McDermott] had the matter 'hushed up.' Three of the employees went and found a portion of the goods. They think, as do others that their goods are being sold."[76]

Ballou went on to ask Carter to use influence to bring an inspector to Wind River. At the end of the month, however, Ballou and Hatton patched up their relationship to some extent, no doubt aided by the fact that Mary Ballou won official reinstatement as Matron. Hatton also explained to Ballou's satisfaction that some of the problems in reopening the Arapahoe school were the result of miscommunications between Hatton, Luke White (the official agency clerk), and the storekeeper, McDermott. According to Hatton, McDermott had borrowed equipment from the dilapidated school building on White's authority when Hatton was on leave in Michigan during the fall of 1880. Ballou admitted using this evidence, together with "false accusations" by other employees against Hatton, to blame the agent for the agency's problems.[77] The "false accusation" referred to the alleged fraud on the part of Amoretti and Curtiss over the beef rations and McDermott's coverup of stolen Indian goods.

Nevertheless, grumbling by the other disgruntled employees—Yarnall, Bliss, Walls, as well as Ballou—prompted the department to send John McNeil on another inspection. The inspector arrived at the agency on February 5, interviewed Shoshone and Arapahoe leaders in a council held on February 11, then basically cleared Hatton of any wrongdoing in his report of February 16. (Unfortunately, the details of the report are missing; McNeil mentions only the council with the Indians.)[78] Hatton, feeling vindicated, recorded in his monthly report for February 1881 that Bliss, Walls, and Yarnall all apologized to him after McNeil left the agency. They apparently told Hatton that he was not the target of their accusations. Rather, they were after McDermott and said that Thomas W. Vallintine and brothers Worden P. and W. N. Noble had concocted the entire "scheme." Vallentine had just received his Indian Trader's license in February 1881, but given the political nature of such benefits, lining up the appropriate support had been underway for some time. Hatton did not reveal the details of the scheme, however.[79]

The respite between Ballou and Hatton was short-lived. Their relationship deteriorated over the next few months to the extent that Ballou recorded an alternative version of McNeil's visit. He wrote that in the wake of the discovery of the stolen goods, several of the Indians threatened to take vengeance on an employee (probably McDermott, but Ballou did not identify the individual). Ballou said the Indians' threat goaded other employees to request an inspection. However, Ballou maintained that McNeil's investigation was a violation of due process, if not actually a case of tampering with witnesses. Ballou stated that "some of the Chiefs and other Indians, came from the Post to the Agency under the influence of liquor while the Inspector was there. The Inspector stopped with the Post Trader J.K. Moore, to which place the Chiefs were taken to be examined.

Mr. Moore sent to the camps after them; sent them presents, as did also other interested parties, among them the Beef Contractor [Amoretti]."[80]

Then Ballou explained that McNeil threatened to subpoena the employees who had levied the charges "if they were seen or heard to talk with an Indian during the examination."[81] The teacher also charged that "gross fraud has been practiced in the weighing of beef, and I have good reasons to believe is still carried on."[82] He made references to his earlier complaints, claiming that Hatton totally neglected education of Indian children and had made no attempt to erect a temporary school building, which he had been authorized to do. Finally, trying to cast suspicions on any who seemed to take Hatton's side in the dispute, Ballou disparaged McNeil's character, concluding that "McNeil did not do his duty; that he is a drinking man and that he boasted that the best of liquors are furnished by the beef contractor. That beef contractor furnishes liquors, oysters, cigars, &c. that the Agent boards with him & that all including Inspector McNeil had a good time while the pretended investigation was going on."[83]

Despite these statements and the testimony of Peter Walls and other employees, the only immediate casualties were Walls and J. K. Moore. Walls was fired in late March because Hatton considered him the "ringleader" of the "mutinous" faction of employees and Moore was forced out of business in May 1881.[84]

The reasons for Moore's suspension are unclear. Possibly, the fact that he sold liquor at his Fort Washakie saloon and its proximity to the Indian trading store spelled trouble to the Indian Office. However, Moore's traders' license and his association with the agency had followed a convoluted path since the days of Governor Hoyt's visit in the summer of 1878 when the Arapahoes complained about his prices. These series of events deepened the mysteries of agency politics during Patten's and Hatton's respective administrations. Moore lost his license following the 1879 inspection that toppled agent Patten. However, his replacement, Seth Cole, never opened and Moore stayed in business. The fact that he still had the Fort Washakie concession also made his agency store de facto if not de jure. He then won official reprieves and renewals of his license in July 1880 and January 1881, only to lose it once more in February 1881. Nevertheless, he continued his lucrative business until May 1881. Then, in November 1881, he received special permission to renew his operations again, but by June 1882 he had suspended his official relationship with the agency. (Three years later, in 1885, the department granted him still another license.) In addition to these vagaries or license forfeitures or renewals, Moore's associations with agency business had other interesting ties. During the summer of 1880, W. B. Hastings, Hatton's son-in-law, worked as Moore's bookkeeper. Albert D. Lane, who later operated a competing Indian trading store on the reservation, also served as one of Moore's clerks.[85]

At the same time that the government revoked Moore's license in February 1881, it granted permission to another trader, Thomas Vallintine, to start a second trading business. The Noble brothers bonded Vallintine's application and Worden Noble actually became a partner in the new trading venture, using it to expand his merchant empire.[86] Together with Thomas McDermott, the agency storekeeper, the Noble brothers, Vallintine, and Hatton formed the "ring" which was accused (by Yarnall, Bliss, Walls, and Ballou) of cheating the government and the Indians. Despite the testimony of the accusers, the "conspirators," along with Eugene Amoretti (the beef contractor), avoided serious recriminations and remained entrenched in their respective positions.[87]

## ATTENDING TO THE FAMILY BUSINESS

Hatton thus survived one potentially scandalous situation after barely a year in office, but before the rumors dissipated he was already in the midst of plans to embezzle government funds. This new plot began in November 1880 (about the same time as the short-weighting activities) when he returned to Wind River from his leave of absence to attend his daughter's wedding. William B. Hastings, Hatton's new son-in-law, accompanied him and joined the agency staff in late January or early February. His first job was trainmaster, replacing Lester Clark. In July, Hatton transferred Hastings to the position of engineer, although the young man possessed no qualifications for the job. Hatton also assigned Hastings to clerical duties and raised his pay from $700 to $900 per year.[88]

The Indian Office unknowingly approved the initial appointment, the transfer, and the raise because Hatton failed to inform his superiors that Hastings was a relative. This was a direct violation of the anti-nepotism order issued by the department in March 1880.[89] Wandering still farther into criminal territory, Hatton then granted Hastings a thirty-day leave of absence in August to attend the birth of his first child. The department did not authorize this leave. Moreover, Hastings stayed away from Wind River for nearly four months, during which Hatton continued to carry him on the agency payroll. At the same time, Hastings worked for the firm of H. E. Mallory and Brothers Live Stock Commission Merchants in Chicago. According to W. J. Henderson, an employee discharged from the agency by Hatton in December 1881, Hastings reportedly said "that he had a good thing that Mr. Hatton was to carry him on the Rolls while he (Hastings) worked for a firm in Chicago."[90]

The extent of the criminal malfeasance surfaced during a routine agency inspection in February 1882. Inspector W. J. Pollock explored a number of possible infractions that Hatton might have committed beyond the Hastings affair. (During his sworn testimony, Hatton maintained that Hastings was only gone the thirty days, despite evidence given by Henderson and Mallory and Brothers). These other alleged incidents included kickbacks, loans of equipment, the ongoing claims about short-weighting, and liquor violations. The kickback scheme involved replacement of Arapahoe horses killed during the winter freighting trek of 1880. Hatton played the part of the "good Father" by contracting with Trader Vallintine to purchase horses for the Arapahoes at the government's expense. Pollock believed that part of the forty dollars per-head cost was returned to Hatton, but could not find enough evidence to prove his suspicions. Hatton was also questioned about loaning (more correctly, renting or leasing) agency equipment to area farmers. Other testimony focused on concerns about the beef ration weights and whether employees supplied alcohol to Indians. Ellis and Louis Ballou had raised many of these same questions in 1880 and 1881, but Hatton denied all hints of impropriety. As in the inspection conducted by McNeil a year earlier, Pollock possessed no clear evidence of pervasive corruption in these other matters. The solid evidence of fraudulent nepotism and outright embezzlement in the employment of Hastings, however, was more than enough reason to suspend Hatton from his position.[91]

Hatton's administrative legacy thus added careless, if not criminal wrongdoing to the list of ills that infected the reservation home of the Shoshones and Arapahoes. To some extent, this provided some relief to the tribes in that the government concentrated more on ferreting out official misbehavior than on forcing additional "civilization" on Indians.

Washakie, for example, could block the success of the Indian Police force or refuse to haul freight during the critical hunting season and still garner support by friendly whites. Black Coal and the other Arapahoe leaders continued to show their desire to be "good Indians" within the framework of their own traditions. Nevertheless, the inept or even shady actions of Patton and Hatton left the reservation vulnerable to increased interference and manipulation by local farmers, merchants, and traders. Ultimately, this left tribal leaders without a white advocate who could be the "good Father" for their people. By March 1882, when James Irwin took up the reins of agency administration for the second time at Wind River, the pressures to become "civilized" increasingly circumscribed the Indian view of the way the world was supposed to be.

# Chapter Eight

# Administrations of James Irwin and Sanderson R. Martin

## 1882–1885

### THE ILLUSION OF TRANQUILITY, 1882

The abrupt departure of Hatton set the stage for the return of James Irwin. Irwin had served only a short stint as the agent for Red Cloud Agency after he left the Shoshone and Bannock Agency in 1877. By 1880 he was back in the Wind River Valley, operating a cattle ranch between the Wind River and the North Fork of the Little Wind River, a location clearly within the reservation boundaries.[1] By March, he was officially on-site as agent. His second tenure in the valley began much like his first, with his predecessor attempting to undermine his authority. Hatton tried to smear Irwin's reputation before the agency changed hands by accusing Irwin of duplicity with respect to Hatton's recent troubles: "James Irwin the party who has urged these parties to make these complaints [that led to Pollock's inspection] has allready tendered the position of Agency Farmer to one of his neighbors in Lander, who formerly held the same position when He was Agent but resigned to become a Government contractor. the Agent a Silent partner in the transaction (So I am informed)."[2]

Hatton referred to F. G. Burnett, who indeed had secured the agency beef contract in the mid-1870s following his resignation as the agency farmer. Burnett, however, was not part of Irwin's second administration. Nevertheless, Hatton's charges against Irwin contained hints of problems to come. Essentially, Irwin was a respected resident of the Wind River region, a justice of the peace and, at age sixty-five, perhaps more interested in maintaining amicable relations with his neighbors and employees than pushing the programs of the Indian Office. For example, in mid-June 1882, he requested permission to buy seed potatoes from three area residents—James Rogers, William Jones, and Ernest Hornecker.[3] The request was normal, but the vendors were not. Both Jones and Rogers, who were among the original homesteaders in the valley at the time of the reservation's creation, still resided illegally on Wind River lands. From 1871 through 1873, Irwin tried to relocate them; in 1882, he accepted them as neighbors.

Agency affairs proceeded under an aura of tranquility for the remainder of 1882, with little evidence of wrongdoing or mismanagement on the part of Irwin. Yet all was not mere routine. The Shoshone Agency doctor under Hatton, Dr. E. T. Gibson, complained that Irwin relieved both Gibson and the farmer, M. R. Curtis, as soon as he took charge of the agency. Gibson believed Irwin wanted to appoint Irwin's son-in-law, William Stephenson, to the position of physician. Gibson said that, officially, Irwin wanted both men to resign; when they refused, he discharged them for "neglect of duties."[4]

Moreover, violence marred the spring freighting trip. Irwin reported that William McCabe, the Shoshone trainmaster and former Lander sheriff, "shot and killed Callison, a rough character who beat McCabe last Fall at the same place [Rawlins]. The trouble grew out [of] Callison selling whiskey to McCabe's Indians."[5] Among other things, this incident reveals that controlling liquor sales to Wind River Indians was impossible because willing buyers could find willing sellers almost anywhere. Preventing alcohol sales and consumption both on and off the reservation would become a major component of agency administration during the rest of Irwin's term.

In other matters, such as requesting larger salaries and more employees, Irwin sang a familiar refrain. In July he bewailed his chances of obtaining "good, or tolerable Machanics, who are Sober, Moral men" for $700 per annum. He wanted to offer $800.[6] As a corollary, he noted that Shoshone Agency needed an assistant farmer because "nothing has been done for the last five years. Fenses [sic] I made in 1872 are rotted and poor, and fields grown up with weeds. Indians have to be taught to make fenses, plow, make ditches, plant[,] irrigate, etc[.], and when they are scattered with fields and patches twentyfive miles up and down the valley it will be readily seen that an assistant farmer is greatly needed."[7]

In his loose construction of regulations, Irwin suggested that if an assistant farmer could not be hired, then the Indian Office could list the position as "assistant blacksmith" to meet treaty stipulations. Irwin's idea illuminates, to some extent, his political acumen. Whereas Patten and Hatton surreptitiously carried Mary Ballou on the payroll in much the same manner as Irwin's suggestion, Irwin had the good sense to alert his superiors of his intentions. There is no evidence, however, that they gave him permission to carry out this plan.[8]

As to his relations with the Shoshones and the Arapahoes, Irwin apparently continued his past practices of advocating for their needs. For example, he relayed their complaints about losing J. K. Moore's trading post, which ceased operations in the late spring of 1882. Seventy-seven headmen from both tribes signed a petition asking for Moore's reinstatement, saying that "while we had two stores we could buy goods cheaper, and sell our products at better prices, than we can get now, with only one store."[9] The tribal leaders went on to state that, with only one official trading post, the people went off reservation to seek better deals. This, of course, exposed them to the whiskey trade.

In another act of advocacy, Irwin justified his overly generous beef issues, which during the summer had averaged significantly higher that the mandated fifty-two-week ratio set by the department. According to Irwin, he made up for short supplies of other food goods by greater distributions of beef, figuring that the absence of the Indians during the eight to twelve weeks of hunting season would bring the overall rations back into balance. He promised to "not over average or expend more beef during the fiscal year than the Department will consider proper."[10]

Finally, he sided with the Shoshones and Arapahoes in a freighting problem. Twenty-five teams of men and horses from both tribes made the final fall freighting trip during mid-October 1882. Unfortunately, like so many other times, not all the goods and foodstuffs were on hand at the railroad depot. The teamsters waited for several days until a six- to eight-inch snowfall endangered the remaining forage for their ponies. They returned to Wind River with only partial loads. Irwin took the stance that if he paid the men by the pound, as the Indian Office suggested, then they would earn only $7.50 each for their trouble. Instead, he wanted to pay them seventy-five cents per diem, which reduced their normal rates by 25 percent a day. This plan saved money, but still allowed the men to earn a large portion of their expected salary. Irwin came up with his plan by analyzing the time spent and wages paid on previous freighting expeditions. One hundred seventy-eight different Indian men hauled supplies during 1882 and generally earned $25 to $30 each for their efforts. Although the amount hauled determined the wage rate, the total pay worked out to approximately one dollar a day, based on the usual four-week, round-trip journey to Rawlins. From Irwin's perspective, paying per diem had several advantages. First, he would not have to calculate individual wages based on freight weights. This method of payment also equalized the benefits among the Indians and avoided potential conflicts over favoritism. Secondly, and perhaps more importantly, Irwin hoped to sidestep one of the headaches concerning the temporary nature of freighting. According to the department's regulations, each trip required both an approved nomination of prospective Indian employees and an authorized discharge of each man upon completion of the job. Irwin wanted discretionary power simply to dispense daily wages without sending in official nomination forms.[11] There was no indication whether Irwin's idea was accepted.

The only exceptional event during Irwin's 1882 administration was the burning of the agency office on December 10. The fire destroyed the log office and medicines but the employees saved the papers and books. A defective flue, newly installed, caused the blaze. Irwin sarcastically commented: "Our new safe comes out of the fire divested of all its beauty, door frame cracked across at both hinges, and contents cooked. It now stands in the debris, reminding us of the perishable nature of all things, and especially 'fire safes,' made only to sell."[12] In the aftermath, the warehouse office served double duty as the general agency office, further crowding an already overburdened facility.

Irwin's management suffered its first major blow when agency clerk Luke White experienced some type of psychological setback. Irwin wrote Commissioner Price that White "is not, as you may suppose from my writing Crazy, but laboring under, what might be called, Intelectual debility or febleness of mind."[13] Irwin thought the clerk might recover with assignment to outdoor duty, but by January 27, White's condition incapacitated him for further agency work. Irwin sought an immediate replacement.[14]

## SCHOOL BEGINS, AGAIN

Although this incident in itself had little bearing on Irwin's stay in office, it marked the beginning of a whole series of troubles that overtaxed the agent's abilities. Specifically, Irwin faced four obstacles: supervising the construction of a new school, eradicating the illegal whiskey sales to the Indians, making the Indians do "civilized" work, and stretching the annuity/rations budget. The school situation came first when the energetic Bishop Spalding succeeded in his efforts to hire a teacher-missionary for the reservation. The new teacher, the Reverend John Roberts, arrived on February 13, 1883. His presence made it imperative to start construction on the new agency boarding school. Furthermore, Roberts arrived long after the budget had been set. He magnanimously offered to teach sans salary for the balance of the fiscal year. Irwin quickly seized this opportunity to expand his staff (and his family income) and nominated his own wife as Matron for the new school, with a salary of $500 per year. In the interim, Roberts and Mrs. Irwin used the much-repaired old school building, operating a day school.[15] However, Irwin gave Roberts three of the employee houses to board himself, an assistant teacher, and several students. Inspector Samuel S. Benedict later criticized this move during his visit to the agency. He also thought hiring a matron, an assistant teacher, and a cook wasted $1,600 in salaries when a proper school building was not yet erected.[16]

Meanwhile, Irwin sketched plans for a one-story wood frame structure, with several rooms angling from a large central meeting area, but J. M. Haworth, an inspector of Indian schools for the Office of Indian Affairs, rejected Irwin's drawings. Instead, they settled on an adobe building, one and one-half stories, with local builder Edward W. Hancock submitting the only bid ($11,000 for the completed project).[17] Hancock's bid gave an inkling of the kind of work he intended to do: "Now when we take into consideration the kind and class of scholars the building is intended for I think a plain neat substantial job is just the thing for them. There is no use putting on mouldings for an Indian, he does not know the difference, and it[']s a useless expense for nothing."[18] Hancock won the contract and finished construction in April 1884, although under a new agent's supervision. His handiwork garnered little admiration from Sanderson M. Martin (Irwin's replacement), who noted that "the nearer the completion the worse the building looks for occupancy."[19] Hancock delivered what his bid offered—"a plain job." Martin used agency employees to finish sanding the walls and floors, outfitting shelves and fixtures, and building entrance steps and outhouses.[20]

During the remainder of his time at the agency, Irwin confronted one other aspect of Indian education that troubled the larger Wind River community. In their continuing efforts to display their "good hearts," Arapahoe band leaders had agreed to Ellis Ballou's idea to send some of their children to Carlisle Indian School in Pennsylvania. Four Arapahoe boys—William Shakespeare (son of Old Man Scarface), Raleigh (son of New Lodges), Grant (Iron's son and Friday's grandson), and Peter (Grasshopper's son)—returned in February 1883.[21] The problem was that the experience left them misfits, partially acculturated to white ways. As Irwin stated, "They have no inclination to return to Indian life, and, it would be very injudicious to have them do so."[22] The agent hoped to employ the boys in the agency boarding school where they could serve as examples of "civilized" behavior to the younger students.

Irwin's letter, however, reveals that he was aware that these difficulties of assimilation could only grow worse as more and more young Arapahoes and Shoshones gained schooling—how might these young people, educated in two cultures, integrate themselves into the life of the reservation community? From Irwin's perspective, they needed to be separated from the "heathen" influences of their families and tribal connections. Yet the off-reservation schools emphasized classical learning, which did not prepare the children for farm or ranch work and increased the confusion over acculturation to the "civilized" aspects of Wind River life. The tribal leaders added another element; they wanted their sons and daughters to learn white ways in order to mediate tribal needs and concerns. Irwin was the first agent at Wind River to discover the consequences of attempts to alter native traditions by education, and every agent following him ran into similar situations.

## WHISKEY AND THE ABSENCE OF "CIVILIZATION"

Restarting the schooling process, regardless of the delays and frustrations involved, provided only minor challenges to Irwin's abilities. Catching whiskey sellers and buyers proved far more elusive. In summer 1882, Irwin pressed charges against three Mexicans, "the leading men except one in the business," who had been detected selling whiskey near the reservation to several Indians.[23] This was, however, atypical law enforcement. Irwin actually made little effort to enforce the laws against the trade, nor could he convince the U.S. Marshal to take a strong stand. For example, in March 1883 Irwin noted that the marshal said insufficient funds blocked him from vigorous pursuit of whiskey-selling violators. Irwin also observed: "I am so closely watched that I can do or see very little myself in the way of detecting parties. Indian Police by reason of fear amount to nothing as whiskey detectives."[24]

A few months later, Irwin determined why the Indian Police made poor detectives. He wrote, "The difficulty that has heretofore existed arose from the fact that they were controlled by that portion of Indian element, that encouraged the sale and use of whiskey and other illegal practices, and by old Chief Washakie, who is zealous of his chieftanship, and will keep on the popular side, right or wrong."[25] According to Irwin, few Indians, including Washakie or the policemen, were willing to witness against either consumers or sellers. This native resistance to agency interference in their lives thwarted most attempts to enforce prohibition.

Samuel S. Benedict, who inspected agency affairs in October 1883, believed that a special detective, operating in disguise and aided by "trustworthy" Indians, was necessary in order to root out the liquor sellers. Benedict blamed the problem on the inhabitants of North Fork (on the southern boundary line). He reported that "there are four saloons who furnish whiskey to Middle men, some of these men being Mexicans with Indian wives, who sell it to the Indians. Some of the saloon men sell it direct to the Indians, but ply their illegal traffic with the assistance of these low degraded outlaws who live for the most part along the North Fork of the Popo Agie."[26]

The whiskey traffic represented part of Irwin's failure to enforce "civilization" on the native community at Wind River. As always, the Indian Office expected reservations and agents to transform traditional ways. Irwin took a different tact; he merely advocated for "his" Indians without demanding behavioral change. He found it much easier to curry Washakie's favor than to insist on real attempts to curb the liquor traffic, to farm, or to pursue other acceptable occupations.

In mid-March 1883, Irwin clearly indicated his reluctance to force rigid adherence to Indian Office requirements. Commissioner Price evidently reprimanded Irwin for issuing rations to Indians who had not worked at "civilized" activities. In his defense, Irwin said appropriations were unavailable to hire Indians at "regular labor" and he did not think hunting qualified for departmental wages. He neglected to say anything about farm work, which the two tribes were supposed to be doing. Instead, he suggested that

> until such time as a systematic plan for labor can be brought to bear uniformly upon them and a way, open and plain, laid out before them by which an Indian is left to his own election, as to whether he will work or not, then, and not till then, can the provisions of said act [containing the work requirement] be properly applied to the Indians belonging to this Agency, for, aside from working an injustice, or hardship upon them, it will have a tendency to, and will drive many of them back to their old time nomadic habits of acquiring a livelihood.[27]

In other words, Irwin considered wage labor as the only viable option to meet the "no work, no food" clause and discounted farming as a means to achieving the desired end.

As it stood, however, both tribes relied heavily on "old time nomadic habits." This made moot points of Irwin's objections. Hunting still earned more income than the combined wages from farming, freighting, or working as part-time laborers for the school or the agency. In both 1882 and 1883, government rations supplied the Shoshones and Arapahoes with 75 percent of their support, but income came primarily from hunting: Combined tribal earnings amounted to $20,000 in 1882 and $15,000 in 1883.[28] By comparison, hauling freight generated approximately $5,000 each year while farm production merely supplemented rations. In 1882, the tribes farmed only 50 acres, increasing to 370 acres in 1883. Even in 1883, the combined output of wheat, vegetables, corn, oats, and barley was less than 4000 bushels, hardly sufficient to feed the Indian population of 1730 and insufficient to market commercially.[29]

In other instances, Irwin's freighters manipulated the "no work, no food" system to their advantage. In May 1883 he sought approval for his decision to ration freighters during the last two quarters of 1882 and to continue that policy in the future, justifying his action by stating "When they are thrown upon the road . . . the Govt. should supply them with rations."[30] The Shoshones and Arapahoes pressured Irwin to this position, insisting that they should be fed, as well as paid, for this work. To the tribes, rations and annuities were treaty obligations and not dependent on the whims of yearly appropriations or policy changes. They felt the government was bound to issue food and supplies, as well as pay wages for hauling freight, cutting timber, or working at other agency odd jobs. This view obviously contradicted federal regulations.

The focus on rations became a critical issue in Irwin's management of agency affairs. Irwin no longer could rectify shortages by resorting to techniques he used in the 1870s, that is, by appeals to the government purse. Instead, agents were expected to control costs, exhibit frugality, and make Indians become self-supporting (albeit not by traditional economies). These implicit demands had explicit corollaries. If the Shoshones or Arapahoes insisted on more food, then they had to agree to cuts in their clothing accounts to pay for the extra rations.[31]

Irwin failed on all counts. He still spent money first, then sought permission and reimbursement. For example, in March he bought supplies without approval. In April, he paid the fee charged by the Sweetwater Stage Company for excess baggage incurred when the four Arapahoe boys returned from Carlisle. Again, he sought reimbursement after the fact.[32] The distribution of rations to the Indian teamsters in 1882 represented another variation of his normal approach to executive decision-making.

His tactics finally foundered in the face of a government-mandated reduction in the beef supply for the 1883–84 fiscal year. In reality, Congress returned the beef allowances to 1873 levels, negating the increases granted during the years of Plains warfare and Patton's "excess" distributions. However, the beef reductions came on top of significant decreases in other food allotments. Under the new contract, delivered in September 1883, a weekly ration consisted of 4 pounds of beef, 3 ounces of bacon, $3/5$ ounce of baking powder, $1^1/3$ ounces of beans, $2^1/4$ ounces of coffee, $1^6/10$ pounds of flour, and $2^3/4$ ounces of sugar.[33] In 1873, the beef allowance was $3^1/2$ pounds weekly, but each person received 4 pounds of flour. Bacon, baking powder, beans, rice, and coffee measured two pounds per ration.[34] In very real terms, this meant an overall reduction from over 2300 calories per person a day in 1873 to just under 1100 calories per person a day in 1883 (see Tables 1 and 2). Given the fact that most

Table 1. Nutritional Assessment of Rations, 1873

1873 Daily Allowances
Per Serving Nutritional Information

| Calories (kcal): | 2303.6 | % Calories from Fat | 42 |
|---|---|---|---|
| Total Fat (g): | 110.9 | % Calories from Carbohydrates | 36 |
| Saturated Fat (g): | 41.3 | % Calories from Protein | 20 |
| Monounsaturated Fat (g): | 50.4 | % Refuse | 3 |
| Polyunsaturated Fat (g): | 10.1 | Vitamin C (mg): | 0 |
| Cholesterol (mg): | 265 | Vitamin A (i.u.) | 0 |
| Carbohydrate (g): | 215.0 | Vitamin B6 (mg): | 1 |
| Dietary Fiber (g): | 33.3 | Vitamin B12 (mcg): | 0 |
| Protein (g): | 120.0 | Thiamin B1 (mg): | 2 |
| Sodium (mg): | 12,465 | Riboflavin B2 (mg): | 1 |
| Potassium (mg): | 3,021 | Folacin (mcg): | 51 |
| Calcium (mg): | 9,824 | Niacin (mg): | 2 |
| Iron (mg): | 35 | Caffeine (mg): | 7 |
| Zinc (mg): | 17.4 | Alcohol (g): | 0 |

Source: Table calculated using Master Cook.

active female adults need, on average, approximately 2000 calories per day to maintain body weight (males require 2700; small children need less than 1000), the rations of 1883 fell below subsistence levels. This grim comparison clearly illustrates the relative wealth of the Eastern Shoshones in 1873 as well as the absolute necessity for both tribes to find other food sources in 1883.

To some extent, official declines in Shoshone and Arapahoe populations precipitated the subsistence reductions. In 1880 and 1881, Agent Hatton reported 2063 Indians at Wind River. However, as of July 1, 1883, only 1730 Indians were on-site, although Irwin expected 200 to 250 more to return in the fall.[35] The census figures thus indicated an official 16 percent decrease in the population of Indians in residence. The beef contract was reduced accordingly, from 900,000 pounds gross weight to 750,000 pounds, again representing a 16 percent decrease.[36]

On the other hand, ongoing nomadism allowed Irwin and his predecessors to avoid strict accounting of ration distributions. Some of the

Table 2. Nutritional Assessment of Rations, 1883

1883 Daily Allowances
Per Serving Nutritional Information

| | | | |
|---|---|---|---|
| Calories (kcal): | 1095.8 | % Calories from Fat | 43 |
| Total Fat (g): | 51.5 | % Calories from Carbohydrates | 35 |
| Saturated Fat (g): | 20.3 | % Calories from Protein | 21 |
| Monounsaturated Fat (g): | 22.2 | % Refuse | 7 |
| Polyunsaturated Fat (g): | 2.8 | Vitamin C (mg): | 0 |
| Cholesterol (mg): | 165 | Vitamin A (i.u.) | 0 |
| Carbohydrate (g): | 95.6 | Vitamin B6 (mg): | 0 |
| Dietary Fiber (g): | 1.3 | Vitamin B12 (mcg): | 0 |
| Protein (g): | 57.9 | Thiamin B1 (mg): | 1 |
| Sodium (mg): | 526 | Riboflavin B2 (mg): | 0 |
| Potassium (mg): | 924 | Folacin (mcg): | 6 |
| Calcium (mg): | 228 | Niacin (mg): | 1 |
| Iron (mg): | 10.0 | Caffeine (mg): | 0 |
| Zinc (mg): | 9.7 | Alcohol (g): | 0 |

Source: Table calculated using Master Cook.

Shoshone bands stayed off-reservation for most of the year (the 200 to 250 that Irwin expected in the fall) and both tribes hunted two to three months during the fall and winter. Thus, they skipped their weekly rations during these times. Irwin made up the difference when all Indians were on the reservation by generally increasing distributions above the 1/52 ratio called for in departmental regulations. Under the new contract, each person received 216 pounds net per year, or a little over four pounds per week. A forty-week division, instead of the normal fifty-two, would result in a five-pound issue. In his letter to Commissioner Price on July 29, Irwin noted this possibility, suggesting that five pounds of beef per person per week could be issued if the Indians hunted for three months per year.[37]

Regardless of official appropriations and policies, past agency practices accustomed Shoshones and Arapahoes to more food. In early August, Washakie, Norkok, and Oatah of the Shoshones and Black Coal, Sharp Nose, and Washington of the Arapahoes petitioned the Indian Commissioner for more beef, stating that five pounds weekly per person was too small.[38] In lieu of a favorable reply, the Indians killed more game, such as antelope, deer, and elk, as well as buffalo. More importantly, they also turned to a ready supply of meat sources—white-owned cattle on Wyoming's open ranges.

In September, the *Cheyenne Daily Leader* complained about roving bands of Cheyennes, Sioux, Crows, Arapahoes, Bannocks, and Shoshones. These groups allegedly confronted cowboy outfits and sometimes prostituted Indian women in exchange for food. Other encounters turned violent—a Bannock was killed for butchering a cow. The article asked "what is done with the food and clothing which the government has appropriated for their use? If they were well fed at the agencies, would they rove about the country in a condition of beggary?"[39]

This, of course, was not the first public outcry against Indians hunting off-reservation and bothering white citizens. James Patten and Charles Hatton heard similar complaints. But as cattle rapidly replaced buffalo on the open ranges, especially after 1882, white complaints grew more frequent. (This issue will receive further attention in the next chapter.) In February 1883 the president of the Wyoming Stock Growers' Association, N. M. Davis, protested the Indian presence in the Powder River country.[40] Irwin answered this complaint by noting the Arapahoes had the right to hunt in that region, and besides, "both tribes see hundreds of their own cattle, with new brands in the white men's herds, and it is a great wonder they don't kill them wherever they see them."[41] Irwin may have overstated the theft of Indian cattle, but went on to blame the problem on stingy congressional funding.

Irwin addressed the hunting situation again in late September. He noted that the Shoshones usually confined their activities to the Big Horn Basin and were on good terms with the cattlemen in that vicinity. The Arapahoes, however, were a different story. If they stayed on the headwaters of the Powder River and its tributaries, generally no problems occurred. But if they traveled downstream, then

> they meet the Crows and plenty of bad white men and whisky. I observe that amongst the white cattle men who do most of the growling are foreigners who have no claim to a foot of Government land. They live in Europe and spend their gains there, while the Indian who inherits his title to the soil by descent of generations,

becomes the victim of their avarice. It is not the cattle the Indians kill as much as jealousy and the grass their numerous horses consume. . . . If we forbid their going and cannot supply them with sufficient provisions they will go off in detachments in spite of us, and more likely to do more harm than they would be [*sic*], if they move and stay together as a village, with their Chiefs and headmen.[42]

More than likely, Irwin astutely observed the reality of the situation. With short rations and little homegrown produce available, Wind River Indians continually made their own subsistence decisions and solutions. However, Irwin's own internal policies contributed to the exterior difficulties. Just as he exercised little control over the activities of "his Indians," he also maintained little discipline over his employees. In the short run, this caused his ouster; in the end, his management actually cheated the two tribes.

Inspector Samuel S. Benedict's routine visit to the newly named Shoshone Agency (formerly the Shoshone and Bannock Agency) in October 1883 revealed Irwin's flaws.[43] Benedict ferreted out the details of the agency during a three-week investigation. Interviews with a number of employees as well as with a few people who lived near the reservation borders confirmed Benedict's own observations. The interviews took place between October 13 and 19, the last week of Benedict's stay at Wind River. The informants included the following employees: storekeeper L. C. Bliss, physician William A. Olmstead, clerk Claude F. King, butcher Lester S. Clark, farmer Charles Silber, and carpenter James D. Russell. Benedict also talked with local sheep owner J. D. Woodruff, who ran his outfit on Owl Creek at the northern edge of the reservation, and with Speed Stagner, married to a mixed-blood Cheyenne woman and owner of five hundred cattle grazing in the northeast corner of the reserve.[44] The inspector's report spelled out the details:

It has not been my fortune to visit an Agency in a more demoralized condition, and I must confess, that I saw very little at Shoshone Agency that inspired me with much confidence in their civilization, under the present management. . . . Drinking whiskey and gambling seems to be almost the entire occupation of the Shoshone when not out on the hunt. . . . The Shoshones are inveterate gamblers. Any day cores of small circles of Indians can be seen every where about the Agency buildings & traders store gambling. On the second day after my arrival I made a visit to Trader Noble's store [W. P. Noble assumed control of the Indian trading post from his former partner, T. W. Vallentine, during spring 1883] and found it Jacked full of Indians gambling. Silver money and brass checks [the illegal in-store scrip] given them by trader being scattered all over the floor within their circles, if there was one there was fifty Indian[s] gambling in the store.[45]

Benedict went on to lay the blame for this flagrant display of "uncivilized" activity squarely on Irwin's shoulders:

Agent Irwin is a very kind hearted old gentleman, dislikes to tell an employee to do what he knows[;] he does not want to because it would hurt his feelings, and thus a great many things go undone, that ought to have been done. Absolutely he is not a proper person to manage white men, saying nothing about Indians. . . . The Agency about runs itself. . . . What these Indians most need is an Agent who never begs of an Indian to do so & so, and if he refuses no harm done, but a McLaughlin, a McGillicuddy or a Miles, who assume that they know what is best for the Indians and command them to do it, or suffer consequences.[46]

Benedict's comparisons referred to the autocratic agents James McLaughlin of Standing Rock Agency (home of the Hunkpapa Sioux leader Sitting Bull) and Vallentine T. McGillicuddy of Pine Ridge Agency (formerly known as Red Cloud Agency). Both men were just beginning to establish their reputations in 1883. Colonel Nelson A. Miles was the successful leader of army campaigns against Indians during the Red River War, 1874–75, and the Nez Percé battles of 1877.[47] In Benedict's eyes, Irwin's easy-handed ways and advocacy for Indians had resulted in chaos. Most of the agency buildings needed repair. The agricultural tools and implements were stored haphazardly in the mill building or in a fenced corral behind Irwin's house. He termed the mill "a museum, being a medley of Agricultural implements, repairs for wagons, . . . nails, hoes, rakes, mowing machines, reaping machines, grain drills, Harrows, grain cradles, . . . piled in promiscuously."[48] The makeshift corral housed 250 plows, 100 harrows, and 90 wagons in various states of destruction (repairs having been made by cannibalizing parts from new wagons).

What Benedict found was not entirely due to Irwin's neglect. Rather, the accumulation of farm equipment had begun under Patten and continued during Hatton's rule. Irwin had done nothing to break the chain of abuse or to organize the mess. In some respects, Benedict aimed his anger at Irwin, but actually lamented events that preceded Irwin's arrival. For instance, Benedict chronicled the loss of the Shoshones' stock cattle, which disappeared during Hatton's tenure:

> The twenty five thousand dollars worth of stock that was furnished the Shoshones is almost entirely out of their hands. They sold them about as fast as they received them. . . . Nearly every stock man in this country has bought Shoshone cattle. Many without doubt were stolen, but as they never vented [registered] the brand of those they sold the whole herd became a prey to white men if they were so inclined. . . . The Arapahoes have sold very few of their five hundred head of cows and heifers delivered to them three years ago, until the past season.[49]

Benedict noted that the Arapahoes generally lost their calves because they neglected to brand them. Furthermore, their cattle came from non-reservation herds located in various parts of the Wind River Valley and tended to wander back to the home ranges. During spring or fall roundups, local stockgrowers simply allowed any calves belonging to Indian cows to remain in white-owned herds, rather than cutting them out and returning them to the Arapahoes. Then they waited until the calves were yearlings and weaned from their mothers and claimed the yearlings as mavericks.[50] (On the open range system practiced in Wyoming, spring roundups depended on biology to determine the ownership of winter-born calves. That is, calves usually stayed with their mothers. During the roundup, cowboys branded a calf according to its mother's ownership. Motherless calves, called mavericks, generally were divided up proportionately among the owners who sponsored the roundup. After 1884, with the passage of the so-called Maverick Law, all mavericks were sold at auction and the proceeds benefited the powerful Wyoming Stock Growers Association.)[51]

Two other events sealed Irwin's fate and convinced Benedict to recommend his dismissal. One involved the delivery of the beef herd just before Benedict's arrival. The other concerned employee theft of Indian rations, goods, and articles. The first problem started in September when Irwin agreed to take early delivery of the beef cattle. He saw no harm in this as long as the contractor paid for herders until the official contract date of October 15. In fact, Irwin believed this would give extra time to fatten the cattle on Wind River grasses before initial slaughtering commenced.[52]

On the surface, this was a good plan. However, quite a number of things went wrong, not the least of which was bad timing and decision-making on Irwin's part. Benedict found out that the beef herd had been trailed from Oregon to the Powder River country the year preceding the delivery to Wind River. This meant they were still somewhat "wild" at the time of the September roundup and difficult to manage. The contractor, George Newman, arranged for the early delivery because his five cowboys and their twenty horses could not control the herd. Yet, at the time of the delivery to the reservation (about September 26), only Mathias McAdams, on Irwin's recommendation, was left in charge.

McAdams often had herded the beef cattle in the past and Irwin had employed him at various times to look after his own stock. But McAdams had less than sterling habits. According to Dr. Olmstead's testimony to Benedict, an inebriated McAdams had contracted syphilis from a twelve-year-old Shoshone girl, prostituted by her mother. McAdams was still married to Julia Bazil (daughter of a Shoshone headman) at this time. Whether compelled by remorse or by his well-known fondness for the bottle, McAdams killed himself on October 2 after a drinking bout. In the meantime, Irwin had left the agency to tend to his own ranch and no one even knew his whereabouts for several days. Without a herder's presence, the cattle scattered. On their own, Lester Clark and Charles Silber (the agency butcher and farmer, respectively) did their best to bring the herd together again. Irwin was still trying to collect the wandering cattle while Benedict was at the agency.[53]

The second mistake made by Irwin actually reflected the normal state of affairs at the agency. Irwin allowed his employees to take extra coffee, beef, sugar, and flour from the agency warehouse without paying for these items because he believed their salaries were too low and they needed extra compensation. Since the foodstuffs came from Indian supplies, Irwin's generosity actually cheated the Indians out of several hundred dollars yearly.[54] This was untenable in view of shortfalls in rations. Furthermore, Irwin allowed his employees unsupervised access to other agency wares. Benedict discovered that almost all of the employees wore Indian annuity clothes on the job and furnished their living quarters with stoves, cookware, chairs, and other items intended for Indian dwellings. Irwin extended his kindness at the expense of the Indians in other ways by hiring a cook, matron, and assistant teacher for the new boarding school, but before the building was completed. Finally, Irwin knew that his son-in-law, William Stephenson, traded a dilapidated wagon to a Shoshone for a cow and calf, wholly in violation of departmental regulations.[55]

Generally, then, Benedict believed Irwin's administration (or maladministration) reflected an overall lackadaisical state of affairs. Indians gambled, drank liquor, and hunted instead of learning to farm. Employees did as they pleased and used annuities, rations, and liquor without reprimand. No locks existed on the storehouse or warehouse; and the property returns did not match agency inventories. Three weeks later, Irwin refuted Benedict's facts. Claiming that more progress had been made at the reservation during his term than in the previous five years, he pointed out the fences erected, crops grown, and repairs made. Nevertheless, Irwin resigned on November 19, 1883.[56] Once more, the Shoshones and Arapahoes faced the necessity of breaking in a new agent to the ways of Wind River. Unfortunately, their power to bend administrations to their will ended with Irwin's resignation.

## SANDERSON R. MARTIN, 1884

Irwin's successor, Sanderson R. Martin, arrived in February 1884. On paper, to repeat a familiar verse, Martin seemed a good choice. He combined both personal business experience with knowledge of Indian agencies. Before the Civil War, he operated a successful Philadelphia trading house, catering primarily to southerners. Ruined by the outbreak of the war, he later joined the Department of Justice and served as a special investigator. Martin's tasks included examining Indian agency operations. When Commissioner Price sought Irwin's replacement, Martin won the job without making a formal application.[57]

Martin, like others before him, inherited a disorganized agency. Changing agents did not solve the problems at the Wind River reservation. Annuity goods still arrived late and were stored in random piles, and farm implements still littered the grounds and warehouses of the agency headquarters. More importantly, rations still remained in short supply. In fact, Martin's first communications to Commissioner Price concerned the lack of flour, bacon, and beef. Poor hunting during the winter made the situation worse. Martin learned that "the Indians have been very unsuccessful in their winter hunt, and will have but few robes or pelts to sell and if we do not feed them they must starve or steal."[58]

Although the Indian office grudgingly approved Martin's requests for additional flour, his supervisors questioned his calculations for beef and bacon. Noting that he had only 3400 pounds of bacon left to last four months, Martin redoubled his efforts to get his point across: "If I should divide this through four months the Indians would not get enough at any one time to grease their frying pans. . . . Beyond the smallness of quantity it now smells so loud to heaven that I hold my nose while it is cut up. One hot day and it will be in a condition that a coyote would run from it."[59]

For the next two years, Martin's letters to Washington generally repeated the litany of concerns over food shortages. He also mentioned three other familiar subjects—the increasing pressures from beyond the reservation borders by Wyoming's stockgrowers; the reservation boarding school; and the attempts made at persuading the Shoshones and Arapahoes to farm. White stockowners flexed their considerable political muscle coincidental to Martin's arrival at Wind River. In March 1884, the Wyoming Territorial Legislature passed a bill, popularly known as "The Maverick Law," which established new standards for roundups on the open land.[60]

Essentially, the law divided the territory into stock districts and gave the Wyoming Stock Growers Association the power to oversee all open-range roundups. Martin told association representatives that he would not allow trespassers on Wind River lands. However, he offered the services of William McCabe, his chief of police, as the foreman for the reservation portion of the roundup.[61] The association evidently turned down this gesture, for two Wind River area white stockmen, Jules Lamoreaux and R. H. Hall, were named the leaders of the Wind River district.[62]

In addition to the growing influence of the Wyoming Stock Growers Association, Wind River whites continued their incursions on the reservation. In early April, Martin named the stockowners who grazed their animals on the reservation. These included long-time residents William Jones, William Evans, James Rogers, and Nelson Yarnall, as well as ex-agent Irwin. Speed Stagner and J. D. Woodruff also increased their ranching operations. However, Martin turned up several other people not included in previous surveys. For example, he noted the presence of Charles Sorell (or Surrell) and William O'Neil, both married to Shoshone women. Others were Fremont County lawyer Philip Vidal, Robert Bragg (who was a partner of Lander merchant Eugene Amoretti), and partners Boyd and Stephenson (probably William Boyd and William Stephenson). Some of these men had paid Washakie for their grazing rights or were willing to pay, while others used the agency lands free of charge.[63]

## ONCE AGAIN: TO FARM OR NOT TO FARM?

As far as converting Shoshones and Arapahoes to farming, Martin experienced results similar to those posted by former Wind River agents. He reported in mid-April that the original three hundred acres plowed by Irwin a decade earlier had now "gone back to nature" and that few Indians farmed.[64] His assessment of this outcome echoed those of his predecessors, with minor variations: Indian ponies were too weak to plow and agency oxen were too old; the Indians themselves were "too starved" to work; and several bands of Indians remained off the reservation. Furthermore, funding reductions forced him to seek permission from the tribes to divert monies from their clothing accounts in order to buy seeds.[65]

At this stage of his tenure, however, Martin's management provoked little criticism. Indeed, Cyrus Beede, a special agent under the direction of the Indian Commissioner, found little fault during an April inspection of the agency and thought the agency was in better condition than Benedict had reported the previous October. For example, he uncovered no evidence of the drinking and gambling incidents described by Benedict. He also noted that the road to North Fork remained free of drunken Indians. However, Beede disliked the annuity and ration-issue methods employed at Wind River—"squaws" collected goods and food for multiple families and never actually made their "marks" to indicate receipt of the items (the agency clerk checked off each family as goods were issued).[66]

Beede made a few constructive suggestions. He asked that Charles Silber and John Steers, the farmer and his assistant, reverse their positions and that Martin hire Silber only during the actual farming season. In addition to this money-saving idea, Beede thought that enough annuities existed on-site to forgo the next delivery. He wanted the savings used to hire more temporary farmers during the summer to speed up the Indians' transition to farming and to buy additional rations. Finally, Beede recommended that Martin evict all unauthorized whites, except for Speed Stagner, "whose children are the bright-lights in the Agency School."[67]

Despite Beede's subtle emphasis on making the farm effort the top priority at Shoshone Agency, Martin gave more credence to rations, complaints from off-reservation whites, and the school. Frequently these concerns intertwined. For example, according to a report in the *Green River Gazette*, the Shoshones who camped along the Harris Fork of the Green River killed cattle and committed other depredations. In response, Martin sent a cavalry troop to Green River

> to capture and punish a small band of renegade Shoshone Indians who may possibly been interfering with cattle not their own. These Indians though belonging on this reservation have never accepted the position and made this their home—but have always refused to acknowlege Washakie as their chief and are governed by To-be-she [Tawunasia]. They are the Indians who fought the Bear Creek fight contrary to Washakie's orders. Washakie would be very glad to have them properly punished by the Government and says he has turned them off and never wants them back again.[68]

The troops indeed found a Shoshone camp on Green River, headed by Tawunasia (or Tobeshe) and Toweyaga and using cow brains to tan hides. However, Lieutenant G. W. Read, the officer leading the cavalry, saw no conclusive evidence that the Shoshones had killed the cow or taken its calf.[69] Although exonerated in this instance, off-reservation Indians drew other criticisms.

In late June 1884 William Hale, Wyoming's Territorial Governor, conveyed a petition from members of the Wyoming Stock Growers Association in the Big Horn Basin, to Interior Secretary H. M. Teller, protesting against Indian hunters in their region during the past winter.[70] About the same time, Fremont County Sheriff Benjamin F. Lowe wrote Commissioner Price that when the Indian freighters were on the road to Rawlins, "there is no excuse for one hundred or more male Indians of said tribes [accompanying the freighters] saying nothing of women and children who are at this time hunting south of the south line of their Reservation."[71] Martin refuted Lowe's claims, saying that only five Arapahoes and a few more Shoshones were hunting, but that they had legitimate right to do so.[72]

Nevertheless, the food situation frustrated Martin and made him powerless to exercise any control over the two tribes. An emergency beef purchase made in late June carried him into the next fiscal year, but the 1884–85 deliveries were late (as usual). By mid-July, the meat stores were depleted again and he could only issue flour.[73] Martin wrote that "meat is the natural food of the Indian and without it he is hard to control. It must be given him or he will take it where he can find it."[74] Ten days later he vented his anger more forcefully with a scarcely concealed warning:

> I am sorry to see that in all the necessaries of life my supply has been fearfully cut down. I have passed through four months of great anxiety owing to the very short rations I was forced to issue and the threatened outbreak [of Indians] which I was constantly hearing of from every side. . . . At the present time rumours are floating around of a treaty made by Washakie with the Arapahoe that they will not assist the soldiers while he takes the warpath. . . . I considered it only the idle talk of an old man who did not wish to lose his character as a "big brave." I am still of the same opinion, though I have satisfied myself that the talks with the Arapahoes did take place.[75]

As Martin suspected, no "outbreak" occurred, but his words suggest that at least the Shoshones were in a rancorous mood over the reductions in their rations. Martin's fears and the Indians' plight were very real. His annual report for 1884 graphically detailed the extent of the cutbacks. In 1882 the tribes killed 2400 buffaloes and received 1,200,000 pounds of beef. In 1883, the buffalo harvest dropped to 1500 and the beef allowance dropped to 750,000 pounds. During 1884, only 525,000 pounds of beef were scheduled, while buffalo kills declined to 500 animals. Martin believed that less than 200 buffaloes would be killed during the 1884–85 winter. Although deer and elk hunting netted 4500 animals in 1883 and 6000 in 1884, the tribes clearly suffered a declining subsistence base. In terms of total meat supply, the combination of buffalo, beef, deer, and elk in 1884 dropped about 20 percent from 1882. This assumes that buffaloes and cows weighed approximately 900 to 1000 pounds each, while the combination of deer and elk averaged 300 pounds. Tribal income from robes and furs also fell, from $20,000 to $12,000.[76]

## JOHN ROBERTS AND THE AGENCY SCHOOL

The problems with rations, with supervising Indian farms, and controlling the off-reservation behavior of both whites and Indians were intractable, but Martin's handling of the Wind River boarding school proved more successful. School enrollments increased under the leadership of the enthusiastic Reverend Roberts, especially after the new building opened. Martin indicated Roberts's dedication by noting that before the new building was completed, Roberts slept in a small log cabin "with the boys, having one for his bed fellow. A thing I would not have done even had it been necessary to have made the school a success."[77] At the start of the fall school season, between forty and fifty young Shoshones and Arapahoes enrolled in the school, triple the number that Roberts taught and housed in the old log school.[78] Martin was pleased especially with Washakie's cooperation: "We have at last got Washakie to see and acknowledge the necessity of having the children of his tribe educated. Today he brought in about a dozen or maybe fifteen. Six of them I believe are girls. The boys had their hair cut—a hard thing to get the Indians to Consent to. . . . I think within a week our school will number over fifty."[79]

Unfortunately, this rapid growth outstripped both the appropriations and the funding allocated to the school. Roberts and his one assistant had sole responsibility for supervising the school farm, cooking, cleaning, teaching, and performing other necessary duties connected with the boarding school. Supply problems also surfaced and Martin commingled agency and school rations to such extent that he tangled his bookkeeping. He scrambled to sort out his books, as well as hire a cook, an industrial teacher, and laborers, but these remedial measures took place over several months and after several trial-and-error approaches. Eventually, a combination of Indian mothers, returned Carlisle students, and white teachers

John Roberts and the first log mission school and church. Courtesy American Heritage Center, University of Wyoming.

headed the school staff. All the while, enrollments kept climbing. By December, eighty young Indians—the maximum number of pupils— attended the school.[80]

## PRODUCE FROM THE GROUND, NOT FROM THE "CHASE"

Martin's efforts met with the approval of Inspector Robert A. Gardiner, who observed the agency in early December. Gardiner's report mirrored that of Inspector Beede's eight months earlier. He believed Martin was "a man of Honesty, Integrity and good business capacity."[81] According to Gardiner, Martin had made good strides toward cleaning up and repairing the farm tools and more Indians now attempted to farm than ever before. The inspector listed seventy-seven Shoshones and twenty-six Arapahoes who produced small amounts of wheat, oats, and potatoes. These people generally represented the vast majority of tribal leaders for both groups, but the average harvest for each person fell far below subsistence levels. At best, the Indian farms were small vegetable gardens; only thirty acres were actually cultivated.[82]

With this minimum "progress" in mind, Gardiner indicated his thoughts on the future direction of the agency: "More attention however should be given by Agency Farmers to the Indians, as the day is not far distant when these indians will have to depend for support upon what they produce from the ground, and not from what they obtain from pursuing the chase, the Buffalo are about extinct and Elk and Deer are rapidly becoming less numerous."[83]

Perhaps in response to Gardiner's wishes, Martin received notice that he could hire two more farmers for the coming year.[84] The school gained additional aid as well when Sherman Coolidge took up teaching and pastoral duties under Roberts's tutelage. Coolidge was a full-blood Arapahoe who had been adopted as a boy by a white family. Two young women also assisted at the school, one of whom, Lilly Steers, was the sister of William Steers, the school's industrial teacher. Their father, John C. Steers, was an agency farmer.[85] Thus Martin entered 1885 with an enlarged employee force, most of whom Gardiner deemed "efficient," and with what seemed like relatively bright "prospects" for success.

The only damper to these hopes, at least on the surface, was the ongoing food and supply shortages. Instead of increasing the allowances, the department insisted on the tribes forgoing some of their clothing appro-priations and diverting the monies into the ration and supply accounts.[86] Then, after receiving the tribal elders' permission for this diversion, the department delayed authorization for Martin to purchase the necessary items, in this case farm and garden seeds. Furthermore, Martin discovered that the two additional agency farmers sent to Wind River had no experi-ence either in working with Indians or in irrigation. He also thought the department was remiss in not sending the proper plows as he had requested.[87]

## "GO TO WORK AND STOP BEGGING," 1885

These were ordinary difficulties, however, quite representative of past Wind River bureaucratic experiences. More serious problems existed beneath the surface, barely hinted at in Martin's correspondence to the commissioner. In May, the agent held a general council with the Arapahoes, who wanted action on their desire for their own reservation and agency. Over one hundred men attended the meeting, including Black Coal, Sharp Nose,

Eagles Dress, and Little Wolf, the head medicine man. Black Coal led off the discussion:

> I am now going to tell you the truth. I will not lie. I want to be a good Indian and all my people want to be good. I hear the President is a good man and that he intends to be kind to the Indians. We want a reservation of our own and an Agent for our own. They will work better if they had a reservation of their own. Twenty of the Headmen want to visit the President, so that he can tell them what he wants them to do. Other Indians are better provided for than they are. They want everything—same as the Sioux. The Arapahoes own all this country and they want all white men kept off. I dont want my Indians to be poor. We want all this country for Arapahoes and Shoshone. They stay here as though kept in a guardhouse. They want more to eat. Arapahoes and Shoshone are starving—papooses have nothing to eat. We want more cattle. . . . Tell this to the President.[88]

Sharp Nose, Eagles Dress, and Little Wolf addressed the agent in turn, each reiterating the points made by Black Coal, as well as adding a few more details. For example, Sharp Nose brought up the Horse Creek (Fort Laramie) Treaty of 1851, which gave the Powder River country to the tribe. He added that "the game is all gone and we want the President to put Cattle on the range so that we can shoot them."[89] Little Wolf named specific services he wanted—carpenter shop, school, churches, blacksmith, etc.— at any new agency. Martin squashed the Arapahoe speakers with a harsh rebuttal:

> You have to work or starve. Every year you will get less and less given to you. You have got to work the same as the white man if you dont you will all starve. I have given you wire to make your fence. I have given you plows, harness, harrows, . . . picks and rakes to prepare your ground. I have given you all kinds of garden seeds and I have given you plenty of oats to plant. The President has sent you a farmer to show you how to work. Now if you cant help your- selves you will have to starve. The President, by your request, put you here with the Shoshones. You did not want to live any longer

with the Sioux. The big council at Washington has said to the President that never again as long as the sun shines shall he make another treaty with an Indian. You can not go to Powder River—here you must stay and die—so must your children."[90]

He went on to say that the Arapahoe treaty did not promise food. Instead, the rations they received were gifts that would someday end. As to their demands for more cattle, Martin dismissed the idea, noting that they had either sold or killed what they had been given. He added, "You cared more for a ten dollar sore back horse than for a cow and calf—now you want them. You are too lazy to take care of them. Go to work and stop begging."[91]

The Arapahoes went to work, but with "sullen" dispositions and "bad hearts."[92] Nevertheless, Martin exulted over their accomplishments. According to the reports of the Arapahoes' farmer (who had resigned his position on May 19), over one hundred members of the tribe planted from one quarter to two acres, for a total of fifty-five acres. This was the first time, according to Martin, that the Arapahoes had been willing to farm. But, he noted, "It is slow work to educate a wild Indian to the use of farming implements. The Shoshones are a much better race of Indians and work with a will and judgement."[93] The latter peoples, he believed, had tilled over 150 acres, but their farmer had not yet made a detailed report.

Martin's words clearly indicated that tensions at Wind River were rising beyond his ability to soothe them. The Arapahoes' unhappiness spawned rumors of war. In response, the agent asked the department "Would it not be the part of wisdom as well as charity to spend a little more money in food than to have to spend an immense amount in war material and to sacrifice many lives—white as well as Indian[?]"[94] Of course, the agent rightly calculated Indian reactions to the food shortages, but overlooked his own tactless handling of the crisis.


## CREATIVE ACCOUNTING AND MARTIN'S DISMISSAL

Besides infuriating the Arapahoes, Martin's search for solutions to the supply problems irked more politically powerful people—his superiors. He devised a system to insure that goods would arrive at Rawlins on time.

His creation, however, relied on a very unorthodox accounting procedure. He overestimated agency needs for the 1885–86 fiscal year and applied the overage to the next fiscal year. This meant he received goods during spring 1886 (that is, the goods held in storage over the 1885–86 winter) that normally would not have been ordered until after July 1, 1886. As he explained, "It is necessary to have our annuity goods en route the summer preceeding the year in which they should be issued," in order to combat the travails of tardy transportation.[95]

Although this seemed plausible, Martin's Washington supervisors criticized him in August for not reducing his annual subsistence estimates. Again Martin defended his actions, explained the reasons for ordering goods and supplies a year in advance, and said he did not know how to rectify the situation. The goods and food scheduled for distribution during the coming fall had been paid from his 1884–85 estimates, not from the current 1885–86 fiscal year budget.[96] In other words, Martin had managed to stockpile some goods (but not food). This information should not have surprised the department. Gardiner's inspection report from the previous December mentioned specifically that the annuity items issued in October 1884 actually were from 1883 supplies, and the goods received during fall 1884 had been stored and not issued.[97]

In a related incident, the Indian Office accused Martin of killing too many steers for rations. He again said that weekly individual rations totaled only two and one-half pounds of beef, which required a weekly slaughter of ten animals. In his defense, he mentioned that Inspector E. D. Bannister, who was in residence at Wind River and examining agency affairs, also called for a higher beef issue. Moreover, he claimed the officers at Fort Washakie donated two steers to the tribes in hopes of appeasing the disgruntled Indians. Finally, he stated that the beef issue would decrease in a few weeks when many of the Indians began their fall hunt.[98]

Inspector Bannister indeed backed Martin on the beef squabble. He said, "There is very little game left in the country, and I fear that if they do not get the additional rations, that they may resort to the killing of cattle to prevent starvation."[99] On other matters, however, Martin's actions disturbed him. Particularly, he was unimpressed with the extent of the Shoshone and Arapahoe farming efforts and blamed Martin on several counts. First, he found that "both the Arapahoes and Shoshones complain that Agent Martin has not assisted them in their farming, also that he never visits them to even see how they are getting along, and that the Agency farmers never have given them instructions in farming."[100]

Bannister gleaned this information from councils held with the tribal leaders, as well as from Martin himself. Apparently, Martin assigned the extra farmers sent from Washington to oversee the Indian farms, but used the full-time farmers only for the agency's own stock and farm. Secondly, Martin told Bannister that the office sent farm equipment and machines for use on the agency farm, not for the benefit of the Indians. Most damning, the agent "further stated that he had charged the Indians for cutting their hay, he took one half of the Hay for the cutting, that he was not going to have his farmers cut their hay for nothing, that he wanted the hay for Agency purposes."[101]

Thus, Martin laid down a curious "work or starve" policy. When Indian farmers needed to harvest their hay, Martin took half their crops as payment for the use of the agency machines and the time spent by the agency farmers on the harvest. In other words, he penalized Indians for doing "civilized" work, despite the fact that the agency employees were hired solely to help the Indians in the first place! Furthermore, the two agency farmers held in reserve by Martin did precious little farming on the main agency field. Although four hundred acres were under fence, the farmers had planted only thirty acres of oats. Bannister concluded that "the attempt made at farming by Agent Martin to be a most miserable failure and I understand that in farming he wears the shoes of his predecessor."[102]

As far as the rest of Martin's managerial abilities were concerned, Bannister found few faults. Except for the two main agency farmers, he thought most of the employees were good workers. The books were straight; the only thing he questioned was what he deemed an exorbitant contract for lumber purchased from a local vendor, W. P. Townsend. Martin had done a reasonable job overseeing the repair or replacement of agency equipment (although Bannister felt the agent too readily condemned usable equipment merely because it was slightly dated or did not contain the lasted technological innovations). Bannister summed his estimate of Martin by writing:

> The moral character of Agent Martin is good as are his habits, and I do not question his capacity, but do seriously question his efficiency, faithfulness, & energy, and the interest taken by him in the welfare

of the Indians and the Interest of the Government. He is what might be termed a good Agent "on paper." He is entirely too gruff with the Indians and does not seemingly want to encourage or assist them. He seldom if ever visits their camps, they say never unless he happens to pass through on his way somewhere else.[103]

Bannister's report led to Martin's termination. Although he had escaped the criminal or gross mismanagement charges levied against his predecessors, Martin failed to carry out the principal aims of the Indian Office. That is, he did not convert Wind River's Indians to agriculture, nor did he reduce their dependency on traditional native economy and government support. In Martin's defense, he, like all agents, faced an almost insurmountable task of securing supplies on time and pleasing Indians, superiors, and local whites. His most grievous error, however, was in not working. He used his status to build a comfortable fiefdom for himself at the expense of the Shoshones and Arapahoes. Bannister's charge against Martin of "not visiting their camps" indicated a serious neglect of duty. President Grover Cleveland fired Martin on September 9, 1885, and named Thomas M. Jones, a professor of agriculture from Virginia, to the vacated position.[104]

Martin's departure did not end the legacy of agency mismanagement, white encroachment on Indian lands, or Shoshone and Arapahoe attempts to chart their own paths and means of existence in the changing environment of the late nineteenth century. In fact, these and other issues continued to weigh heavily on reservation life for the duration of the century and into the next era. In reality, however, Martin's administration marked a key change in life and living in the Wind River Valley. For the first time, Shoshone and Arapahoe freighters earned more money than did Shoshone and Arapahoe hunters—$5,841 and $4,250, respectively.[105] More importantly, these figures indicate the vast changes wrought in native economy in the few short years following the Arapahoes' settlement on the reservation. The total buffalo harvest for 1885 was a mere ten animals.[106] Ultimately, this meant that both tribes would undergo a wrenching transformation in their spiritual lives, in addition to the economic devastation brought about by the decimation of the Great Plains herds. Unfortunately for the Shoshones and the Arapahoes, their era of relative economic parity vis-à-vis their white neighbors died with the buffalo.

PART THREE

~

*A Transforming Community*

1878–1885

# Chapter Nine

# Wind River White Settlers

## 1878–1885

The community of peoples living in the Wind River Valley in 1885 looked very different from the one of fifteen years earlier. Whereas in 1870 the Eastern Shoshones still clung to their nomadic life, by 1885 most bands were settled into a general residency within the reservation borders. Moreover, the Northern Arapahoes occupied the eastern ranges of the reservation, a move that forced accommodations from both tribes. The agency had grown from a few buildings and employees in 1871 to a bastion of bureaucratic corruption and inefficiency by 1885. Its agents no longer mediated or advocated for Indian peoples as James Irwin did during the early 1870s. Instead, agents and employees became the vanguards of government assaults (including the Peace Policy mandates) on tribal traditions, or brigands out for their own enrichment.

Changes among white members of the Wind River community were equally significant and occasionally paralleled or responded to developments on the reservation. Essentially, three major transformations took place, each of which spawned repercussions within the reservation itself. First, during the early 1870s whites relocated northward from the mining towns near the original southern boundary of the reservation to the valleys along the post-1872 borders. This migration entailed building Camp Brown, to protect both settlers and Shoshones from Sioux attacks, within the reservation borders. Second, the development of Lander in 1875 marked the beginning of a more intense phase of white settlement. The third stage and most far-reaching metamorphosis of the white community began in 1879 as large-scale stock grazing operations hemmed in the reservation on the north and east and literally transformed the environment of the Upper Wind River Valley and the Big Horn and Powder River basins. At the same time, Fort Washakie evolved into a fully developed military reservation within the Shoshone's territory.

## CREATING WHITE SETTLEMENTS

The roots of these changes lay in the mining bust of 1869 to 1870. Whereas over two thousand people lived in Atlantic City, South Pass City, Miners Delight, Smith Gulch, and the other mine sites in 1869, a year later the population of those areas declined to less than eleven hundred.[1] Although a small contingent of diehard miners stayed on in each area, by 1872 most of the mines were closed and the majority of the town inhabitants had drifted elsewhere. The remaining hangers-on continued to work the mines, or perhaps served the stage line, which still ran through the region. Camp Stambaugh, which probably provided some economic benefit to the towns, closed in 1878 when the threat of "hostile" Indians no longer existed. By 1880 the population in the mine region had dwindled to 175 persons.[2] While a great many people simply left the region for good, others migrated northward, deserting the steep hills and narrow valleys of the Sweetwater Mining District for homesteads in the broader valleys of the various branches of the Little Wind and Popo Agie Rivers.

The ex-miners were not the first future farmers to invade the Wind River region. Even before the creation of the reservation, nine white men had already claimed acreage in the Little Wind River Valley near the site of the future agency headquarters. James Irwin tried, unsuccessfully for the most part, to evict these settlers in 1871. The Brunot Agreement of 1872 encouraged others to join them. By 1875, at least thirty more people farmed or grazed livestock on Little Wind River lands. Even though only a few of these new settlers had legal rights to be there, Irwin made no effort to dissuade them as long as they remained peaceable.[3] In addition to the forty or so whites who made dubious claims to the reservation lands along the Little Wind River, fifty others staked legal sites in the newly ceded area, which lay south of the North Fork of the Popo Agie River. But these numbers include just the real property owners. According to the 1875 Sweetwater County Tax Roll, at least 159 total taxpayers (real and personal) lived in these two main areas. Since many of the farmers or stock owners started families, a characteristic not true of miners, between four hundred and six hundred persons lived in proximity to the reservation.[4]

The pace of white settlement near the reservation quickened in the mid-1870s and led to the establishment of Lander in 1875. This second phase of white demographic expansion included not only small-scale farmers and homesteaders, but also merchants, businessmen, and other commercial innovators who hoped to profit from nearby Camp Brown and the Shoshone and Bannock Indian Agency. Without question, the reservation and Camp Brown played crucial roles in the creation of Lander and its rival town, North Fork.

Both Lander and North Fork were located on the stage and supply-road river crossings leading from Green River and Rawlins to the agency. Lander, or Pushroot as it was known initially, formed on the site of old Camp Brown on the banks of the Middle Fork of the Popo Agie River, while North Fork (later changed to Milford) was located on the North Fork of the Popo Agie. North Fork was perhaps the more strategic site, since it bordered the reservation, but Lander developers had the advantage of putting abandoned army buildings to use. By 1873, a small settlement of fifteen people was in place on the Middle Fork. Major Noyes Baldwin's trading store, which he opened during the summer of 1874, probably provided further stimulus to Lander's formation. However, neither Lander nor North Fork could exist legally until mid-1874 because the 1872 Brunot Agreement was not ratified until that time.[5]

There were other developments between 1874 and 1879 that spurred Lander's growth. In 1874 Benjamin F. Lowe, Irwin's old nemesis, claimed a forty-acre section near the site of old Camp Brown.[6] About the same time Peter P. Dickinson, who managed Baldwin's store at South Pass City, scouted the terrain on behalf of Baldwin and claimed an additional ten acres. Their two claims became the nucleus of the Lander Townsite Company. That same year Ben Decora and his wife opened a boarding house. In March 1875, the government granted post office status to the growing community with James Patten, former school teacher for the agency, serving as the first postmaster. Baldwin's small but evidently profitable enterprise attracted a much larger operation in 1877 when Eugene Amoretti opened a combination bank and retail store, branching out from his South Pass City banking and mercantile businesses. In 1879 he bought shares in Lowe and Dickinson's fledgling townsite company. The town officially came into being in 1884, when Amoretti, Dickinson, and Lowe filed plats for the Townsite of Lander.[7]

The population of Lander, North Fork, and the other areas ceded by the Shoshone in 1872 increased substantially after 1875. By 1880, 433 people lived within fifteen miles south of the reservation. These included 97 persons in North Fork, 50 more spread out on Baldwin Creek (between Lander and North Fork), 193 in Lander proper, and 93 others homesteading on the Big Popo Agie River northeast of Lander. Farther south, approximately half-way between Lander and the mining towns, 119 others lived along Red Canyon, Beaver Creek, Twin Creek, Willow Creek, Cottonwood Creek, and the Little Popo Agie River. Miners Delight and Camp Stambaugh still sheltered fifty-six people. Perhaps as many as fifty of the people listed on the census were Indians or mixed-bloods who essentially adopted white economic strategies.[8]

The white population living on the reservation in 1880 also increased, the majority of whom worked for the agency or Fort Washakie. However, sixty-six whites without official connections populated areas around Trout Creek, the North Fork of Little Wind River, the north side of the North Fork of the Popo Agie River, and the North Fork of the Big Popo Agie River. Some of these, such as John Myers, Joseph Trehero, Charles Surrell, Richard May, and Jesus Aragon, were married to Indian women, but most were simply illegal white residents. Thirty-four people lived in or near the agency grounds and Fort Washakie housed 194 soldiers, officers, and civilian employees. Thus, a total of nearly 900 white people lived in or near the southern regions of the reservation by 1880.[9] The combined Shoshone and Arapahoe population, however, still greatly exceeded the numbers of whites. In 1880 Agent Hatton reported that 1050 Shoshones and 913 Arapahoes were listed on the tribal censuses.[10]

Camp Brown, which officially changed names to honor Washakie on December 30, 1878, played an important role in the transformation of the reservation. Beginning in 1880, the War Department sought access to dependable sources of hay and wood for the military post without requiring permission from the agency or the Indians. In particular, officers eyed two tracts of land to the south and west of the post buildings. One contained 335 acres along Trout Creek, with good hay land, building stone, and both a tar pit and hot spring. The other tract, 358 acres, was quite hilly, but held good grass, water, and white pine.[11] According to the agent at the time,

Charles Hatton, Washakie opposed certain aspects of this reduction of Wind River Indian property. Specifically, Washakie said, "When I was at Bridger, Big Chief at Washington gave me this Land, told me it was mine, the Hot Springs are mine. Now Soldiers wants to take them from me. They cannot have the Springs."[12]

Washakie referred to a naturally occurring hot springs and tar pit located three and four miles from the agency, respectively. The site of the hot springs was a favorite bathing spot of Shoshones, soldiers, and local whites. At one point, Washakie tried to claim the tar pit for himself, but always insisted the hot springs stay open to all comers. (In 1890 Washakie told Agent John Fosher that he had found the "oil spring" in 1852. When he saw a white man nosing around the site in the early 1890s, Washakie tried to establish his own rights to the area. Washakie's attempt to obtain ownership of the tar pit failed. By 1898, it was considered military property.)[13] Hatton supported Washakie's objections to the military takeover of the hot springs and presented his own opposition to the loss of the hay field, observing that the tract contained "the most valuable Meadow Land in the whole Valley, in fact it is the only Hay Land in the Valley."[14] Nevertheless, Hatton suggested only minor modifications—to keep the hot springs on Indian land—to the military's plan. Perhaps Washakie's resistance stopped the proceedings; at any rate, no action was taken on the proposal.

The matter rested at this point until 1887, then the army attempted another coup on the hot springs. In essence military leaders asked for fourteen hundred acres for a military reservation, one which included the disputed hot springs and tar pit. One of the officers who considered the feasibility of the idea, Captain L. H. Rucker, noted that "in case of the Indian reservation being thrown open to settlement, the reservation [military] would not be large enough and should then include the Hot Spring and the Tar or Asphalt Spring, both of great value and not now on the military reservation."[15] Rucker referred to possibilities that portions of the reservation might open to white settlers in the wake of the Dawes Act, which had recently passed Congress (and was enacted on the day Rucker wrote his recommendations).[16] Undoubtedly, the captain was guarding the interests of the military, but he was not the only person interested in the springs at the time. A few months later, Agent Thomas Jones asked that he be allowed to fence off an acre around the springs in order to prevent further encroachments from Arapahoe farms. It is unknown if Jones's request received approval.[17]

Washakie and other Shoshone leaders eventually accepted the proposed military reservation, sans the hot springs and the tar pit. The new military reserve within the Indian reservation was approved by President Grover Cleveland on May 21, 1887.[18] The agreement, however, still depended on Indian largess: the tribes retained title to the land and held the right to revoke the order.[19] That right was tested in 1890 when the army again tried to enclose the hot springs, going so far as to station a guard at the site to restrict access. When an Indian was turned away, Washakie angrily denounced the action, declaring that the springs could not be controlled by "any person, company or organization, but [was] to remain, as it always has been, for the free use of the Indians and Whites."[20] The army backed off, but for the duration of the decade, the commanders occasionally presumed ownership rights to their "reservation," rather than acknowledge Indian title authority.[21]

## THE ECONOMICS OF PROXIMITY

The history of Fort Washakie's encroachment on the reservation perhaps serves as a backdrop for the major changes promulgated by the overall white population. The presence of the post strengthened the economic base of local whites. Assuming that homesteaders possessed enough capital to make a good start, then the lands they claimed offered good potential for commercial farming and stock raising. The ease of access to the reservation and post assured ready markets for local products despite the fact that most of the supplies for both the agency and the military installation came from national vendors, not from the local valley. Locals sporadically sold firewood, coal, beef, fruits, vegetables, and flour to the two government agencies, as well as to individual soldiers and Indians. Local carpenters and contractors had more success in erecting agency buildings.

The most lucrative local industry with respect to reservation proximity was raising livestock. In 1875, for example, the Sweetwater County Tax Assessor listed forty-six cattle owners in the Big Popo Agie and Little Wind River Valleys. These stockgrowers represented approximately one-fourth to one-third of the total white population in those two areas in 1875.

Excluding the four largest outfits, forty-two owners claimed 848 cattle, averaging about 20 animals each. However, the numbers of cattle were distributed unevenly. Seventeen owners claimed 9 or fewer animals; seventeen more owned between 10 and 38 cows. The other twelve (including those commanding the four largest herds) owned 40 or more cattle.[22]

Two-thirds of the twelve owners of the largest herds reflected reservation affiliations. Five of the eight taxpayers who owned herds numbering 40 to 85 cattle either lived on the reservation, were working or had worked for the agency, or were married into Shoshone families. They were James Patten—former agency teacher and later agent; William Stephenson—Irwin's son-in-law; James Rogers—one of the "trespassing" settlers; William Boyd—marriage to Shoshone; and Edmo LeClair—a Shoshone mixed-blood and one of the scouts during the 1876 military campaigns.[23]

The remaining stock owners had extremely large herds compared to the rest of their Wind River neighbors. Jules Lamoreaux (200 cattle) was a freighter and store owner during the mining boom and an 1874 homesteader in the Popo Agie Valley. He had the distinction of being married to the sister of Gall, one of the Oglala Sioux leaders at the Battle of the Little Big Horn. Unlike many mixed-blood children, however, the Lamoreaux offspring were later members of Lander's social and political elite.[24] The other three owners of large herds, William O'Neil, Charles Oldham, and James K. Moore, basically lived on the reservation.

O'Neil (or O'Neal) was married to a Shoshone woman; they had 100 cattle. Charles Oldham, the agency carpenter under James Irwin, was credited with 120 cattle. He probably sold most of these animals during the summer of 1875 since he won the agency beef contract for the 1875–76 fiscal year. In 1877 he purchased William Boyd's homestead, and later sold it in 1881 to another agency and civilian military employee, Charles Yarnell. By far the largest stockgrower in the area was James K. Moore, the agency and military post trader. He had 575 cattle, with 40 more in joint ownership with Captain Robert Torrey, the post commander.[25]

Between 1875 and 1878, the size of the herds using reservation ranges increased dramatically as ranchers, farmers, and freighters freely ranged their stock on those lands. For example, James Irwin's cattle numbered 350 in 1878, and his herder, Mathias McAdams, kept his own 150 cows (up from 20 in 1875) with Irwin's herd. J. K. Moore's herd, which generally stayed on the upper Wind River north of the reservation (but with no viable barrier to keep them from wandering over the border), grew to 1400 cattle. S. G. Davis, the dairyman for the army post, saw his stock increase from 15 to 150 head. Freighters W. P. Noble, Angus McDonald, and Henry DeWolf occasionally foraged up to 190 head of cattle or oxen on the reservation. According to the 1875 tax records, none of these men had holdings in either the Little Wind or Popo Agie Valleys. Finally, another individual with close ties to the reservation, the former agency farmer F. G. Burnett, also benefited from his agency association. In 1878 he won the beef contract for the Shoshones and Arapahoes and proceeded to graze 380 animals on reservation range at government expense.[26] Given the increases in stock during these years, these figures suggest that, for the most part, living in the vicinity of the reservation tended to enhance one's livelihood.[27]

Until 1880, however, most Wind River whites still led subsistence-oriented lives based on small-scale farming and stock raising. Although farming or ranching on or near the reservation was certainly advantageous, as was freighting or fulfilling government contracts, relatively few men and families possessed commercial ties to the reservation or the military post. The Wind River region itself remained a relatively isolated part of Wyoming Territory. Few roads traversed the area and the white population remained quite small. In fact, the official census of 1880 listed only 1,131 people who lived in the entire Sweetwater, Popo Agie, Wind, and Big Horn river systems. While this represents better than a 20 percent increase over 1875, Indians still outnumbered whites by almost a two-to-one margin.[28]

## ESTABLISHING CATTLE ON BUFFALO LANDS
## IN THE BIG HORN BASIN

But vast changes in the landscape were already underway at the time of the 1880 census. Beginning in 1879 and accelerating throughout the 1880s, the outside world broke through Wind River's isolation and changed the lives of area whites as well as those of the native peoples. In October 1879, Judge William Carter of Fort Bridger sent between 2700 and 3800 cattle (approximately half of his total holdings) to the Big Horn Basin, supposedly at the invitation of Chief Washakie. The herd apparently wintered quite well on a tributary of the Stinking Water (Shoshone) River.[29] Perhaps this news influenced others, for within five more years a number of owners

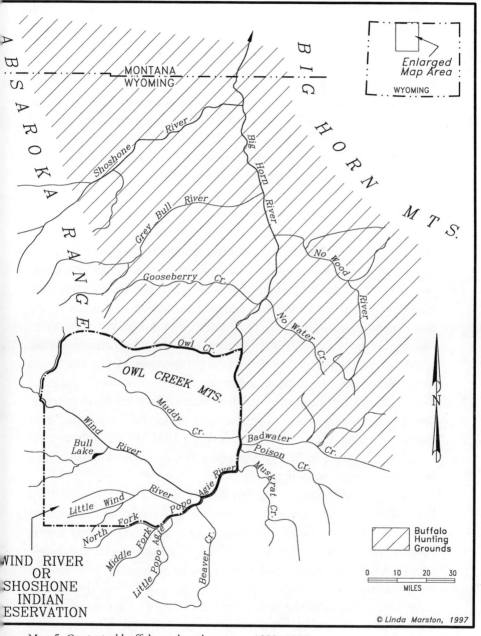

Map 5. Contested buffalo and cattle ranges, 1880–1900

trailed large herds into the Basin. For example, Otto Franc, a transplanted Austrian by way of New York and formerly engaged in wholesaling bananas, brought 750 cows from Montana to the Greybull River in 1880. That same year, Henry Belknap, originally from Massachussetts, and Henry Lovell, from Michigan, established ranches on the Stinking Water and the Big Horn Rivers, respectively. In 1881, George Baxter came from Oregon and founded a ranch on Grass Creek, while John Luman started operations on Paint Rock Creek.[30] According to Wyoming's eminent historian, T. A. Larson, "many others [scrambled] to acquire choice locations in the Big Horn Basin, so that the area was quite well stocked by 1884."[31]

At one level, this represented the newest push in Wyoming's burgeoning stock industry. During most of the 1870s, Wyoming's cattle-raising businessmen confined their herds to the ranges near Cheyenne and Laramie. The end of the Indian wars on the northern Plains, however, allowed expansion into the Powder River and Big Horn Basins. At a more significant level, the Wyoming stock industry itself was part of a larger western counterpart to the midwestern and eastern post–Civil War phenomenon of corporate capitalism and industrialization.[32] Unlike their "old timer" neighbors, the most recent entrants into the greater Wind River community did not owe their prosperity either to the reservation or to the military. Instead, they marketed their beef to the nation at large. As a result, their on-the-hoof capital far exceeded the capital of the wealthiest early settlers. In 1884, Jules Lamereaux was the richest Wind River pioneer, listing over $32,000 in taxable property. In comparison, Henry Belknap claimed over $44,000, Henry Lovell listed over $50,000, Otto Franc topped $112,000, and the giant Wyoming Cattle and Ranch Company paid taxes on property worth more than $205,000![33]

The rapid infusion of cattle into the Big Horn Basin between 1879 and 1885 had serious ecological consequences: Oregon- and Idaho-bred cattle replaced native buffalo. This process was facilitated to some degree by white buffalo hunters. Historian John K. Rollinson, a romantic chronicler of Wyoming's early cowboy days, noted that "in 1879–80 buffalo were very numerous. In 1881 and 1882 the herd had diminished somewhat, and by 1883–84, the hide hunters had cleaned the country of this marvelous game animal, once so numerous on the Western plains. As the cattle population increased their grass consumption, the buffalo decreased theirs."[34]

To a large extent, Rollinson's assessment is accurate regarding both the buffalo killed and the effect of encroaching cattle. The Big Horn buffalo herds, over which the Shoshones, Crows, and Arapahoes fought many battles, were not affected directly by white hide hunters who slaughtered vast numbers of buffalo on both the Northern and Southern Plains during the 1870s and 1880s. This decimation generally occurred near railroad lines. No railroads, however, reached the Big Horn Basin during that period. But when the Northern Pacific Railroad was completed through southern Montana in 1883, its hunters killed enough buffalo that the over-all size of the herds wandering into the Big Horn region contained fewer animals. Yet the greatest threat to buffalo, as Rollinson points out, came from grazing cattle, especially given the free-range technology employed by stockgrowers. The presence of over forty thousand cattle roaming the range clearly offered more than enough competition to drive buffalo from the Basin, regardless of the hunting effect.[35]

## THE CATTLE FACTOR IN INDIAN ECONOMICS

The changes wrought in the white residents of the greater Wind River community (including the Big Horn Basin) seriously affected their rela-tionships with their native neighbors. Three basic patterns are worth noting. First, those whites living far from the reservation, especially to the east in the Powder River country and to the south in the Sweetwater area, increasingly called for controls on Indians going off-reservation. Strident voices urged that Shoshones and Arapahoes be confined to their "quarters," so to speak, and no longer exercise their treaty-guaranteed hunting rights. By 1884, Wind River residents themselves joined the larger white com-munity of Wyoming to call for actions against off-reservation hunting. At the same time, reductions in ration appropriations and the concurrent depletion of buffalo meant that native hunters were forced to rely on hunting or face starvation. Their guns and arrows first aimed at traditional targets, such as deer and elk, but as the stockgrowers feared, free-range cattle began to supplement their declining food resources.

Second, Wind River whites who used reservation lands tended to nego-tiate independent agreements with Shoshone and Arapahoe leaders concerning Indian access to white stock. In other words, from the white perspective, stockgrowers bribed native leaders with "gifts" of cattle or sheep, or by payment of a "head" tax. From the Indian perspective, the agreements represented trade bargains similar to those struck in earlier years. By 1884, however, reservation agents tried to make such payments or bribes legitimate, first by collecting grazing fees from off-reservation owners whose stock foraged on reservation property, then by suggesting long-term lease arrangements.

Finally, the formation of Fremont County in 1884 led to several confrontations between county officials and agency management. Constitutional issues undergirded the dispute. It was not clear, for example, what jurisdiction or rights the Fremont sheriff had in enforcing the laws of Wyoming Territory on reservation property. More germane, since the sheriff was the individual with the power to enforce county tax assessments, questions rose over the power of Fremont County to levy taxes on white ranchers who grazed their stock on reservation property. Another legal issue involved enforcement of Wyoming game laws vis-à-vis Indian rights to hunt.

Complaints about Shoshones or Arapahoes hunting cows in lieu of buffaloes came slowly at first. In part, this reflected relatively plentiful game resources within reach of Wind River hunters. For example, in December 1881 Agent Charles Hatton reported that both tribes had good fall hunts—with Arapahoes collecting buffaloes and Shoshones harvesting beaver and deer.[36] A little over a year later, however, C. E. Wilson, the foreman of the Prest, Pratt, and Ferris Cattle Company, noted that there were too many Indians in the Tongue River, Clear Creek, and Powder River area (near present-day Sheridan, Wyoming) "for comfort or safety of Men and Property."[37] The stockgrower who received Wilson's news, J. H. Pratt, then notified U.S. Representative M. E. Post. Post, in turn, contacted Hiram Price, the Commissioner of Indian Affairs, and apprised him of the potential danger in the Big Horns. In the meantime, Pratt also wrote Lt. Gen. Phil Sheridan, who then informed his superiors that the Indians in question were Sioux, Crows, and Arapahoes, all with permission to hunt in the region.[38]

This flurry of letter writing basically outlines the mounting problems faced by most of the Plains tribes in the 1880s, including those from Wind River. As influential stockgrowers imported increasing herds of cattle on the former buffalo ranges, they became direct competitors with Indians for the resources found there. Stockgrowers had no more rights to the

Plains than did most Indians; the various acts granting timber claims, homesteads, mining rights, etc., basically limited white ownership of land to 1120 acres. In arid regions such as Wyoming, this acreage could support no more than thiry to forty cows at best.[39] Therefore, most stock owners grazed their herds on the unclaimed lands of the territories. That is, they fattened their cattle, sheep, or horses on government grass. The conflicts with Indians developed because many tribes had the right to hunt in unclaimed or unoccupied land near their reservations either as "long as the buffalo roamed," or, in the Shoshones' case, in perpetuity. Since most ranchers did not lease government lands, then, technically, the ranges remained open and unoccupied and available for multipurpose use. The stockgrowers generally overlooked this point. As Pratt complained to Post, "As long as the Indians are fed & clothed on their reservations it[']s better they should stay there."[40]

The domestication of the Plains occurred at the same time that the government began its reduction of aid to Indians. For example, in July 1882, Agent Irwin called a council of the two tribes to ask if they wanted a $5,000 funding decrease to come from their annuity clothes or from rations. The council attendants chose a full ration of food—they still had annuity goods left from the previous year.[41] This accounting procedure provided temporary relief, but Irwin recorded in his annual report that the appropriations for food were still inadequate and that the tribe was forced to hunt "two to three months each year" during winter.[42]

Predictably, the anti-hunting forces raised their voices the next winter. (This issue was introduced in the last chapter.) In mid-February 1883, N. M. Davis, the president of the politically powerful Wyoming Stock Growers Association, contacted Congressman Post about Crows, Cheyennes, Sioux, and Shoshones roaming the Powder River country again. Post did his part and asked Commissioner Price for relief on behalf of Davis's constituency.[43]

In April Irwin defended the Shoshones, claiming that at most only fifteen or twenty had crossed the Big Horns to go into the Powder River drainage (see the previous chapter for Irwin's support of the Arapahoes). The majority of the Shoshones, Irwin maintained, stayed along the Grey Bull and Stinking Water Rivers in the Big Horn Basin. He also pointed out that both tribes had a right to hunt under the 1868 treaty terms, and furthermore, he implied that a few members of the Wyoming Stock Growers Association had wrongfully placed their brands on large numbers of calves belonging either to the Shoshone or Arapahoe cattle. As proof that Wind River's Indians left white cattle alone, he said they returned from their winter hunts with over $12,000 in "robes and pelts."[44]

Later, during the summer, Irwin commented on the seriousness of the situation—noting that a Bannock had been killed on June 26 in the Green River area for "slaughtering a steer." For Irwin, this was evidence that the government was not providing enough food to prevent Indians from turning to other sources. He went on to say that, although the Shoshones and Arapahoes had a good hunting season, they still killed "a number of their own cattle, even cows."[45]

By early fall 1883, Indians going off-reservation to hunt became a topic of newspaper discussions. An article titled "Indians and Stockmen" from the September 7 issue of the *Cheyenne Daily Leader* described several encounters between cowboys and various Sioux, Cheyennes, Arapahoes, Bannocks, Crows, and Shoshones in which the whites appeased hungry Indians with gifts of food. In one instance, an Indian woman prostituted herself on behalf of her band in exchange for food. The article's author also mentioned the June killing of the Bannock and asked "While Indians are absent, what is done with the food and clothing which the government has appropriated for their use? If they were well fed at the agencies, would they go about the country in a condition of beggary?"[46]

Irwin may have seen this article, for he wrote a long apologetic for the Shoshones and Arapahoes two weeks later. Irwin claimed that Shoshones, for the most part, stayed in the Big Horn Basin, where they were "on good terms with the cattle-men."[47] On the other hand, he said that the Arapahoes might get into trouble if they consorted with the Crows or whiskey-selling white men on the lower reaches of the Powder River. His solution, if the government refused to provide enough food to keep the tribes on reservation, was to restrict hunting to traditional sites—such as the Big Horn Basin and the upper Powder River area (south of the Big Horn Mountains)—and for the tribes to stay away from white settlements. Irwin offered one other bit of analysis that apparently went unnoticed: he suggested that the real reason behind stockgrower complaints was the amount of grass consumed by the Indians' horses on the hunting trips. The loss that the ranchers feared most, therefore, was not occasional cattle kills, but competition for rangeland fodder.[48]

To the Wyoming Stock Growers Association, the prospect of Indians hunting anywhere in the territory was simply unacceptable. William Sturgis, secretary of the organization, wrote Governor William Hale in October that the Indians had no more business on the government's ranges than the stockgrowers did on Indian reservations. He maintained that both activities represented trespass (obviously, Sturgis ignored the fact that ranchers freely grazed their cattle on government land and on Indian reservations). Sturgis begged for "protection" from the hunters.[49] Hale obligingly conveyed the request to Commissioner Price and asked for military aid.[50]

Hale's letter to Price eventually filtered to Irwin. In response, the agent said that the Shoshones were going about their hunting peacefully in the Greybull Valley, and only a few Arapahoes were out on the headwaters of the Powder River. Furthermore, the Arapahoes were under the leadership of a "good man" and accompanied by three of the Arapahoe policemen.[51] Irwin also corresponded with Congressman Post, answering questions about the off-reservation hunting practices and attempting to pressure Post from a different angle—he quoted the ration allowances and asked Post "to supply them [the Indians] with enough to eat and not keep them starved and tempted."[52]

Up to this point, the voices calling for restraints on Indian rights emanated from beyond the geographical confines of the Wind River community. Beginning in 1884, Wind River whites increasingly joined the chorus. To some extent, the change in agency personnel in early 1884 may have precipitated some of the clamor. Two months into his administration, Sanderson Martin called for a count of all unauthorized white stock on the reservation. The list included the usual names of those who had been there from the early days of the agency, such as William Evans and James Rogers, but also contained new violators—J. D. Woodruff, with 6000 sheep; Robert Bragg, herding 2000 sheep for Lander banker and merchant Eugene Amoretti; Lander attorney Philip Vidal with 70 cattle and 60 horses; and John Lee, who owned 700 cattle in partnership with Indian Trader Worden P. Noble. Interestingly, James Irwin had switched from cattle to sheep; he now grazed 2000 animals on Wind River pastures. Other old-timers were also listed: William Jones with 150 cattle and a twenty-three-acre farm, Nelson Yarnell (Yarnall) with a seventy-five-acre farm, and a partnership formed by William Stephenson and William Boyd.

The roll contained a few whites married to Indian women: Speed Stagner (500 cattle); Frenchman Charles Surrell (200 cattle, 30 horses); and William O'Neil (600 cattle and eighty acres).[53]

## SAGEBRUSH REBELLION, OR
## HOW TO AVOID A GRAZING FEE

Martin hinted that, in addition to the head count, he wanted these people to pay for the privilege of keeping their stock on Wind River lands. In May, the hint became reality: he required twenty cents for each illegal cow, five cents for each sheep. This announcement was timed so that the stock owners could gather their herds during the spring roundup, get an accurate count, and either pay the requisite fee or drive their animals to other pasture.[54]

Martin's hint got encouraging responses from Woodruff, Lee, and Stephenson and Boyd,[55] but set off an immediate negative outcry from the ranchers to the north of the reservation. On April 15, the Big Horn Basin members of the Wyoming Stock Growers Association met at Meeteetse and petitioned the territorial governor (William Hale) to keep Indians out of the area. The signers included almost all of the recent immigrants and large-scale ranchers who had moved to the basin in the post-1879 period, namely Otto Franc; H. B. Chapman, foreman of the Belknap, Asheworth, and Johnston outfit; M. C. Traccey for Count DeDore; Peter McCulloch of the Carter operation; J. J. Flourney, foreman for H. C. Lovell; independent owners Angus McDonald, S. A. Wilson, the David brothers; and O. K. Garvey, George Wise, and W. D. Pickett.[56] These individuals and ranching operations paid taxes on over $300,000 of stock, real estate, and personal property, ranging from the relatively small but comfortable estate of W. D. Pickett ($625) to the massive ranch of Otto Franc ($112,250—second largest in Fremont County).[57]

Following their petition to the governor, the stockmen put their tax dollars to work and commissioned their newly elected sheriff of newly created Fremont County, Benjamin F. Lowe, to lay a personal protest at Martin's feet. Lowe, one of Irwin's old nemeses from the 1870s, told Martin that the stockgrowers refused to pay grazing fees unless both tribes were kept on the reservation "and not allowed to roam over the body of the county of Fremont killing and destroying the game in violation of the Law and passing through farms and enclosiers [*sic*] to the injury of the owners of Ranches and to the annoyance of all settlers."[58] Lowe made it clear that he represented only those who bordered the reservation and whose stock wandered on and off but did not habitually graze Wind River ranges. He said that if the grazing fee went into effect, it would be "detrimental" to the stockmen's interests because they paid Fremont County taxes as well.[59] In answer, Martin said that he only proposed the grazing fees for those who clearly and regularly used the reservation, not those whose herds occasionally wandered over the borders.[60]

Lowe's letter brought up another point of contention between whites and Indians. The sheriff charged that when the Indian men went on their freighting trips, their wives and children accompanied them, making for quite large parties "roaming" the area between the reservation and Rawlins. The implication was that tribal movements of that size invariably meant killing cattle as well as game. Lowe then stated that at the time of his letter, a large band was hunting south of the reservation.[61] Lowe probably exaggerated the size of the hunting party, for Martin claimed that five Arapahoes were out and implied only a few Shoshones were gone, but that all had permission to hunt.[62] Nevertheless, Wyoming Stock Growers Association member R. B. Connors wrote the association's secretary that a hunting party in the Rattlesnake Hills was moving toward the Connor Brothers' herd. The Rattlesnake Hills is a small mountain range approximately eighty miles southeast of Fort Washakie and seventy miles due north of Rawlins. The north side of the range is the headwaters area for the South Fork of the Powder River.[63] Whether the Connor Brothers lost any steers to Indians is unknown, but the dispute between the agency and Fremont County continued to cause problems.

In particular, Martin may have been accurate when he stated that the real reason behind Lowe's (and Fremont County stockgrowers') opposition to the grazing fee was based both on questions of legal jurisdiction and on taxes. The legal problem, as far as Martin could see, was that the Fremont County commissioners hoped to get the Wind River grazing fee lifted in order to persuade those owners who paid such fees to pay a similar tax to the county instead. The tax situation was such that Martin believed that many of the owners had avoided paying taxes to Sweetwater County when the Wind River area was still part of that legal body, but too distant to make tax codes and collections really feasible. But the organization of Fremont County more or less closed that tax dodge and Martin believed both the county officials and the potential taxpayers were jockeying for position. He feared that the ensuing scramble might jeopardize his own political authority: "If county officers are to be assumed to over run Indian reservations, assess taxes and distrain for the collection of the same then the authority of the Department will soon be usurped by the civic officers of the Territory and power and control pass out of the hands of the Agent."[64]

Neither the legal disputes nor the tax situation dissipated easily, in part because the Shoshones and Arapahoes did not recognize white authority over their own traditions. It had been customary for many of the ranchers to negotiate private contracts with Washakie, Black Coal, and other tribal leaders in order to secure permission to graze their herds on the reservation. Although no proof exists, those men whom Martin indicated met with Washakie's approval—William Jones, James Rogers, J. D. Woodruff, Speed Stagner, Charles Surrell, and Philip Vidal—probably reached this arrangement. (For example, in 1894 Captain Patrick H. Ray, the agent-in-charge, bluntly claimed that such "deals" had been operative for a number of years. According to Ray, Indians killed non-reservation beef and the owners saw this as the cost of doing business on the reservation.)[65] In December 1884, Woodruff, Lee, and Vidal complained that they paid the grazing fees as required by Martin, but then the chiefs refused "to grant them permission to remain unless they themselves are paid. The cattle men naturally think that paying once ought to be sufficient, and this money to the chiefs they must pay to insure the safety of their herd."[66]

Quite clearly, the Shoshone and Arapahoe leaders resented usurpation of their expected rights and tried to block the grazing fee plan unless the monies were paid to them directly and not channeled through the agency headquarters. At the same time, the county still insisted it had the right to levy and collect taxes from whites who used reservation grass and water. Martin continued to deny access to Fremont officials, but he was unsure of his authority to do so. Finally, there was the parallel situation of those growers who claimed that they were Wind River users and therefore not liable to Fremont taxes, but then refused to pay grazing fees because they said their animals only occasionally crossed the boundaries. In order to combat some of these problems, Martin proposed that the Indian Department lease blocks of land, rather than attempt per-head grazing fees. He believed this would produce more money for Indian lands than the piecemeal grazing fee collections.[67] Martin's idea was the first time such a plan had surfaced; it became de rigueur in the 1890s.

The issues of taxation, cattle killing, and tribal hunts off-reservation continued unabated during the remainder of the decade; indeed, through the end of the century. Essentially, the conflicts resulted from the growth of the white portion of the Wind River community relative to the native population. In the 1870s Shoshones and Bannocks, and, later, Shoshones and Arapahoes outnumbered their white neighbors. Although some local whites profited from commerce with the reservation (and with Camp Brown/Fort Washakie), most whites, like their Indian counterparts, maintained a subsistence existence and one of relative economic parity. As long as Indians hunted or traveled through unsettled regions, then most white members of the community grudgingly accepted ongoing native traditions (or even actively promulgated them by encouraging trading, gambling, or other "uncivilized" intercourse).

The decade of the 1880s, however, was marked by radical alterations in the white segment in both population and economic growth. Settlements in the Big Horn Basin, in Jackson Hole, along the upper reaches of the Green River Basin, and in other regions once deemed "unoccupied" left Shoshones and Arapahoes precious little acreage to maintain traditional hunting practices. Although the reservation remained an important asset to some whites—witnessed by increased non-Indian livestock roaming reservation ranges—the size of the white community itself offered alternative business and commercial opportunities. At the same time, the national market economy of the large-scale stockgrowers further reduced economic ties to the reservation and to Fort Washakie. Thus, many of the Fremont County whites no longer farmed or raised stock at the subsistence level. According to the 1890 federal census, Wind River area farms (including those in the Big Horn Basin) contained an average of 160 to 320 acres worth between $6 to $10 per acre (or from $960 to $3,200, for total average range).[68] Furthermore, between 1884 and 1890 livestock population in the county grew from approximately 40,000 animals in 1884 to 144,580 sheep and 91,546 cattle in 1890.[69] Thus the tribes' persistence in following tradition, rather than joining the white-defined market economy, brought about cultural conflict—either for killing cattle, for killing game out of season, or for simply traveling through lands homesteaded or claimed by white ranchers.[70]

By the mid-1880s whites no longer needed the Indian peoples to help sustain life in the valley. This was not true of the reservation land. For many area whites, indeed for many Wyomingites, Wind River offered over two million acres in potential agricultural resources and Indians hindered the development of this potential. Unfortunately for the Shoshones and Arapahoes, the changing attitudes and growing economic power of their white neighbors reflected national trends as well. In 1887 Congress, through passage of the Dawes Act, provided the means by which to deprive native peoples of their tribal lands, open up reservations to more white settlers, and ultimately impoverish Indians to a greater degree than ever before. The process of allotting lands in severalty, the root of the future impoverishment, began in the late 1880s, gathered steam during the 1890s, and culminated with the 1904 cession of two-thirds of the existing reservation. In the early 1880s, however, only a glimmer of that future appeared. Older goals still held sway: agents still hoped to Christianize and civilize the Indians, while Shoshones and Arapahoes sought to face the future on traditional terms. By 1885, however, it was clear that the Indian traditions had to give way in a changing world where cattle and sheep, not buffalo, reigned supreme.

# Chapter Ten

# Christian Missions at Wind River

## 1880–1885

The introduction of Christianity to the Wind River community began during the fur trade era as a by-product of Indian-white contact. It remained a by-product during the Peace Policy years despite official support for Christian missions and schools. Until 1883, no single denomination made a truly concerted and long-lasting effort to convert the Eastern Shoshones or the Northern Arapahoes. Furthermore, the varieties of Christian beliefs espoused by the white members of the Wind River region—Roman Catholicism, Mormonism, Episcopalianism, and other forms of Protestantism—led to polyglot interpretations of doctrines and practices.

No doubt, the first Christian messages to the Shoshones reflected the beliefs of individual mountain men who probably professed Roman Catholic or generic Protestant tenets. For example, Norkok, the Shoshone's primary interpreter and an important band leader, may have been exposed to some Roman Catholic rituals as a youngster, since he was the son of a Creole-French mulatto man and a Ute woman.[1] Even so, it is highly unlikely that any Protestant or Catholic clergy would have termed Norkok or any other child born to fur traders and Indian women as "Christian." Baptisms, regular church attendance, and other signs of "true conversions" generally were not part of the trapper-Indian unions. Any documented Christian legacy of the fur trade period is thin at best. This tenuousness extends to stories of Iroquois Catholics who visited the Flathead regions of Montana in the 1820s and who may have had limited influence among the more northerly Shoshone bands. Another early Christian voyager, the well-known Father Pierre-Jean de Smet, conducted a mass in the Green River area and may have attempted some mission work. Like the Iroquois, however, de Smet left few long-lasting marks on Shoshone hearts.[2]

## THE MORMON INFLUENCE

Beginning in 1850, Mormons had greater success in promulgating their brand of Christian witness. Members of the short-lived Fort Supply community, traders and merchants in Salt Lake, and the residents of towns that developed near the Mormon ferry crossings on the Green and Bear Rivers gradually influenced some Shoshones' belief systems. Because of this irregular interchange, Indian understandings of Mormon Christianity sometimes took interesting twists.

For example, in the 1870s many of the Basin and Wind River Shoshone bands created their own version of Mormonism in the aftermath of the Ghost Dance movement. This transformation of belief systems illustrates the ongoing process of cultural transmission that led to the formation of a distinctive community at Wind River. According to ethnomusicologist Judith Vander, the original Ghost Dance movement began with the visions in 1869 of a Northern Paiute, Wodziwob. He may have used the Round Dance mourning ceremonies as a basis for the new dance and evidently tried to introduce it to Paiutes on the Walker River Reservation, but failed to excite many converts.[3] However, some of his teachings migrated eastward. Anthropologist Joseph G. Jorgensen believes the Ghost Dance moved by 1870 into Bridger Basin, involving Ute bands from Colorado and Utah, Bannocks, and a few of the Wind River Shoshones.[4] Jorgensen states that this Ghost Dance promised to "rid the world of whites, restore Indian land and the resources thereon, and resurrect the dead Indians so that Indian life could be restored and practiced unhindered by whites."[5] The ceremony apparently flourished from 1870 to 1872, then lost favor when it failed to deliver the expected benefits. As it waned, several Shoshone bands discovered—or rediscovered—that Mormon beliefs contained similar elements to the Ghost Dance, especially those emphasizing kinship reunions. In particular, Mormons thought that the baptismal rituals assured such kinship reunions in an afterlife.[6] Shoshone participants in the Mormon ceremonies probably overlooked the distinction about the afterlife—as Ghost Dance adherents, they retained the understanding that uniting with dead kin and restoring native life would take place in the temporal world. This blending of Mormon and Ghost Dance rituals exerted a strong, albeit confusing, influence on many of Wind River's Shoshones during the 1870s.

In 1875, Agent Irwin commented in his annual report that a number of Shoshones left the reservation in early summer in order to be baptized.[7] James Patten noted similar journeys in 1879 and added the information that the Mormon bishops told the Shoshones they were supposed to renew the covenant—baptism—every year.[8] Jorgensen thinks Patten either misinterpreted or was misled about the activities of 1879. Instead of submitting to Mormon baptisms, Jorgensen believes, the Shoshones participated in renewed Ghost Dance ceremonies. Evidently, large numbers of White River and Uintah Utes, Bannocks, and Western Shoshones informed the Eastern Shoshones about the ritual during a visit to Wind River in the previous summer.[9]

Regardless of whether the trips in the 1870s were for the Ghost Dance or for baptism, in 1880 more Shoshones sought baptism at Salt Lake. This time, they asked the Mormons to send them a preacher.[10] Perhaps this request (which violated Peace Policy guidelines authorizing the Episcopal Church as the sole religious body for the reservation) stemmed from the turbulence of the 1878–80 period. During these two years, Arapahoes were forced onto Shoshone lands, rations were cut and work requirements enforced, and two prominent Shoshones died. The deaths, both in 1880, were those of Wanapitz and Bishop Washakie. Wanapitz, a mainstay in Washakie's council, was a signer of the 1868 and 1872 treaties. The latter was Washakie's eldest son.[11] It is quite likely that these series of events compelled many Shoshones to turn toward alternative spiritual solutions to their temporal problems. The Episcopal Church, linked as it was to agency administrations, was not an acceptable spiritual haven. On the other hand, Mormonism, with its theological similarities to the Ghost Dance, may have offered an attractive addition to more traditional forms of Shoshone religious life such as the Sun Dance. Mormonism offered material benefits as well—Mormon communities provided unfettered trading opportunities free from the restrictions of agency policies and politics.

Whatever the impetus for turning to the Mormon Church, Mormon leaders responded to the Shoshone request. In September 1880 they sent

Amos R. Wright, a forty-year old, Shoshone-speaking missionary to Wind River. Officials at the Shoshone reservation knew Wright. According to his biographer, Geneva Wright, Amos lived in Bennington, Idaho, and evangelized the Shoshones who camped near his farm on their summer excursions from Wind River.[12] Wright knew his presence at the agency was unwelcome: "The former agt Mr Patten upon being introduced to one of my brothers, at Evanston one day, told him that if ever he could get hold of me he would put me in Irons[.] I heard also from other sources that the present agt [Hatton] has made similar threats and considers our Missionary Work among the Indians as an Insurrection against the government, though I am not prepared to Vouch for the truth of this last report."[13]

Avoiding contact with other whites as much as possible, Wright traveled twelve days to Wind River, made contact with a Mormon Shoshone named Tornampe, then lodged in the main camp of the tribe at Fort Washakie. During the course of his stay among the Shoshones, who vigilantly shielded his whereabouts from Hatton and other Wind River employees, Wright baptized over two hundred men, women, and children. Among those baptized were Norkok, Washakie, and a half-brother to Norkok, John Sinclair.[14] Wright followed this first solo mission with other visits in 1884, 1885, and 1901–1902, staying five to six months each time.[15] These later travels involved other Mormon missionaries and plans called for a Wind River Shoshone mission church, but no permanent Mormon mission was founded among the Wind River native peoples until 1934.

## THE REVEREND JOHN ROBERTS
## AND EPISCOPAL EVANGELISM

Although the Mormons failed in their initial hopes to found a church on the reservation, beginning in 1883 the Episcopal Church successfully established and thereafter maintained a Christian missionary station at Wind River. To some extent, the Roman Catholic Church also inaugurated full-time missionary activity at Wind River in 1883, but did not begin uninterrupted services until July 1886.[16] Both denominations laid the groundwork for their programs through political maneuverings in 1882. In September 1882 the Right Reverend James O'Conner, the Roman Catholic Bishop of the Diocese of Nebraska and Wyoming, wrote a general letter of reference indicating that the Reverend D. W. Moriarty was assigned the "spiritual care" of the Indians at Wind River.[17] Moriarty, who already was in Lander, wrote Commissioner of Indian Affairs Hiram Price a week later, enclosed O'Conner's authorization, and requested official permission to evangelize and start a school among the two tribes.[18] At nearly the same time, Bishop John F. Spalding of the Episcopal Diocese of Colorado and Wyoming put his own plans into action. Spalding counted on the strong support of Agent James Irwin—the agent and his family were church members—to aid the resumption of Episcopal school and missionary activities. Furthermore, he had located a priest who was willing to undertake the task.[19]

The Reverend John Roberts, the priest whom Spalding had in mind, was a thirty-year old Welshman who actively sought missionary work with Native Americans. Spalding recruited the young man after Roberts had immigrated from Wales to New York City by way of the Bahamas. Roberts's first post under Spalding was in Greeley, Colorado. After that, Roberts worked a missionary stint among coal miners in Pueblo, Colorado, where he established Trinity Church in 1882. In early 1883, Spalding reassigned Roberts to the Shoshone Agency.[20]

Roberts picked an inauspicious time to travel to the reservation. He left Cheyenne by rail for Green River on February 1, 1883, and almost immediately experienced one of Wyoming's famous blizzards. Roberts eventually reached the reservation on February 13, following a harrowing eight-day mail run from Green River in weather plunging to fifty degrees below zero.[21]

Roberts, Irwin, and Spalding immediately started the Episcopal mission and tried to counteract the Roman Catholic "invasion." On March 1, Roberts wrote to Spalding, noting that he held services in one of the agency houses, visited some of the older Indians in their camps (most Shoshones were out hunting), and conferred with Irwin about the agency school. He also sounded the alarm about the Catholics: "The Roman Catholics are wide awake to the importance of the work here. They are very quiet about it, but I am told that they intend coming in force in the spring, and will build schools and accommodations for 200 children, if they can get permission to do so."[22]

Irwin, for his part, advanced the Episcopal cause almost as rapidly as Roberts. Irwin submitted plans for a new school building at the agency and noted that Roberts would fill the position of school superintendent. He, too, upon learning the Catholic goals from Moriarty, expressed concerns about Catholic encroachment and about the feasibility of maintaining missions and schools operated by different denominations.[23] Spalding echoed Irwin's worries and complained to Secretary of the Interior Henry M. Teller that the Catholics were "interfering with our School for the Indian children at the Shoshone Agency."[24]

Roberts opened classes on March 10, using one of the agency houses furnished to him by Irwin as a makeshift boarding school. A month later, Irwin refused to act on Moriarty's request for permission to open a Catholic mission until he received authority to do so from the Indian Office. Irwin then forged ahead and let bids in June for construction of the new government school.[25] This last information upset Bishop O'Conner because he assumed, rightly, that the government was aiding the Episcopalians. He informed Teller of his displeasure and reminded the secretary of an earlier communication between them that broached the subject of Catholic mission work at Wind River. According to O'Conner, Teller told him that the Peace Policy "had been abandoned by the Department, that I [O'Conner] was quite free to send priests and teachers to Indian Reservations, and, you [Teller] were good enough to add, that if they should be hindered in the exercise of their duties, at Washaki, I had only to acquaint you of the fact, and you would apply the remedy."[26] O'Conner continued by stating that the Sisters of Charity had agreed to set up a mission school. On their behalf, he asked that they have access to the new boarding school building soon to be under construction. He tried to convince Teller that the government should not feel obligated to the Episcopal Church merely because the latter denomination finally placed a priest on the reservation.[27] The federal records do not indicate if Teller replied to Bishop O'Conner's letter or applied any "remedy," but for the remainder of 1883 Roberts continued as the sole director of Christian missionary activities at Wind River.

Roberts's employment, despite the official abandonment of Peace Policy ideas, still linked the Episcopal Church to the federal government. His initial $800 salary for teaching (raised to $900 in 1885) came from the government, not the church. In fact, Roberts's primary employment throughout the remainder of the century depended on federal funding—either directly as the superintendent or teacher for the agency's Wind River Boarding

School, or as a private entrepreneur operating a contract boarding school for girls (Shoshone Mission School). Federal spending thus supported his missionary and priestly activities among Indian and white peoples both on and off the reservation.[28]

Roberts's activities beyond the confines of the reservation were made possible because Bishop Spalding increased his own efforts to have the "Wind River Mission" counter the perceived threat from Roman Catholicism. In his annual report to the 1884 Wyoming Episcopal Convocation, which met in late May of that year, Spalding proposed diocesan support for Trinity Church in Lander (organized with Roberts's help), because the town was "the centre of a fine farming region. The Roman Catholics have a church here. The people generally who do not belong to that body prefer and will help to build and support an Episcopal Church."[29] At the same time, he obtained a $1,500 donation toward construction of a church building at the agency (the Church of the Redeemer).[30] Two days after the church convention ended, Spalding dashed off a letter to Teller. He gloated over Roberts's initial management of the school and revealed the goals for the mission: "We have the means in hand to build a Chapel, and desire to make the work permanent and . . . as successful as the Missions to the Indians under Bishop Whipple and Bishop Hare."[31] The real thrust of his message, however, still aimed at blocking the Catholic presence at Wind River. Spalding noted that Irwin had done nothing to aid the proposed Catholic institution, but the bishop was fearful that the Catholics would seek intervention directly from the Department of the Interior and would therefore "divide the work and if possible . . . crowd us out and compel Mr. Roberts'[s] withdrawal."[32]

With the backing of Spalding and the agency administrations of James Irwin and Sanderson Martin, Roberts's small school and preaching enterprise expanded rapidly from its humble beginnings. For example, he started his tenure in March 1883 by conducting school and sharing sleeping space with thirteen children in the cramped quarters of his agency house. More people crowded into the makeshift school for the 1883–84 term: boarding school enrollments rose to eleven full-blood and five mixed-blood children. To add to the confusion, eight more youths attended as day students. The staff increased as well. Charlotte Hinkley was hired as the assistant teacher and Mrs. Sarah Ann Irwin, the agent's wife, served as the boarding school matron.[33] When the new building opened in April, Roberts retained the services of Lilly Steers, the daughter of agency farmer John Steers. She took over Hinkley's role as assistant teacher and Hinkley then worked as the school's cook. Arthur C. Jones joined the staff during the summer. He was a postulant for Holy Orders who decided to test his clerical call with a round of missionary duty. According to Mrs. Baird Cooper, an early historian of the reservation, Jones "gave up a good position in Laramie . . . to assist Mr. Roberts." Finally, Spalding also assigned the Reverend Sherman Coolidge, an Episcopal deacon and a full-blood Northern Arapahoe, to the mission and school. The church funded the salaries of Steers, Jones, and Coolidge, although the government paid Hinkley.[34]

Coolidge's participation in Wind River history is full of intriguing twists and turns. His Arapahoe family was part of Black Bear's band that suffered near annihilation at Shoshone and army hands in 1870. After becoming separated from their mother during the battle, white families adopted Coolidge and his sister; his adoptive father was an army officer. The Coolidges reared Sherman as an Episcopalian and he later attended Seabury Divinity School and lost all knowledge of his native language. Despite this barrier, Sherman Coolidge assumed primary missionary responsibilities to the Arapahoes in 1884. He preached in their camps and taught a class of Arapahoe students in the boarding school, some of whom were his relatives. Spalding priested Coolidge in 1885 and he continued to serve the reservation as a missionary, schoolteacher, and part-time storekeeper, working at other jobs as well until 1910.[35]

By mid-1885, it appeared that the Episcopal efforts at Wind River had achieved solid gains. The agency church building, the Church of the Redeemer, was nearing completion while Trinity Church at Lander would hold its first service in late December.[36] Roberts reported that twelve of his students could read English (from St. Matthew's Gospel) and that Coolidge's class of Arapahoes and Jones's Shoshone students were doing well. Furthermore, Roberts believed that there had been "at least three genuine conversions of young men to Christianity" from among the Arapahoes.[37] Several young Arapahoe men and women who had been educated at Carlisle Indian School in Pennsylvania worked at the school either as day laborers or as assistant industrial teachers—thus serving as role models for the younger children. In 1884 these included Cyrus White Horse, Sumner Black Coal, and Mollie Naatha. They were the children of Arapahoe chiefs White Horse, Black Coal, and Little Shield.[38]

Agency mission school, 1883–1884. Standing, left to right: The Right Reverend Spaulding, Arthur C. Jones, the Reverend John Roberts, and the Reverend Sherman Coolidge. The children are unidentified. Courtesy American Heritage Center, University of Wyoming.

As missionaries, Roberts, Coolidge, and their assistants had other duties beyond teaching academic subjects. Large parts of their responsibilities were aimed at inculcating various aspects of "civilization." To that end, students were taught "practical" knowledge—boys received training in farming, herding stock, and carpentry, while girls were taught to keep house, cook, and sew.[39] Roberts believed that these skills were necessary for Indian youths to survive in the changing world of the reservation. He had another motive as well. He learned that federal funds (or perhaps the distribution of such funds by agency administrations) were undependable. To avoid problems of food shortages, Roberts sought to make his schools as independent as possible. Therefore he planted vegetable gardens, acquired cattle, pigs, and chickens, and did whatever else he could to make his operations self-sufficient.[40] His work garnered high praise in

1886 from Special Agent Dickson, who recorded in his inspection report: "My only regret is that I cannot find any words that can possibly convey to your Office the real worth of this man. To know him is to trust him. . . . His mild, yet firm manner conquers all, and all the Indians with whom I talked, expressed themselves well of their Supt."[41] The school employees and students harvested their first good crop in 1886: 40 bushels of wheat, 5 bushels of corn, 125 bushels of oats, 700 bushels of potatoes, 400 bushels of turnips, and 65 bushels of various other vegetables and beans. They also collected 4000 cabbage heads and 200 squashes. Besides this agricultural produce, the school owned 90 cattle (mostly milk cows), 3 pigs, and 6 chickens.[42] Therefore, it was likely that Roberts was well on the way to meeting one of his goals.

Similar goals guided missionary interactions with Shoshone and Arapahoe adults. For example, in 1885 Coolidge said that he had convinced three Arapahoe men to start farming "and to continue until they have secured a home for themselves and their families."[43] Perhaps buoyed by this success, Coolidge sought closer contact with his Arapahoe constituency. He left his teaching post at the agency school and announced plans to build a home for himself in the Arapahoe settlement headed by his uncle, Sharp Nose. On the surface, this move solved two problems. First, the realignment of his missionary duties from teaching to full-time pastoral care meant that he had to vacate his quarters at the agency school. Second, since most of the Arapahoe villages, including that of his uncle, were thirty miles from the agency, his new work virtually required him to change residency.

At a deeper level, Coolidge's announcement represented ongoing competition for converts between the Episcopalians and the Roman Catholics. The Catholic mission, St. Stephens, opened in 1884 under the auspices of the Reverend John Jutz, a Jesuit priest. Jutz built a mission house, then returned to the East in 1885. Quite likely, Coolidge saw an opportunity to take advantage of Jutz's departure and attempt to delay or prevent further Catholic incursions among the Arapahoes. Nevertheless, St. Stephen's reopened in 1886.[44]

Coolidge's proposed homesite placed him in the middle of the three main Arapahoe settlements. Sharp Nose's camp was located between the camps of Chief White Horse and Chief Black Coal. All three leaders and their followers occupied the Little Wind River Valley approximately twenty to thirty miles east and downstream from the agency headquarters. White Horse's village, the nearest to the agency, was located near the confluence of the Little Wind River and Mill Creek. Sharp Nose's camp was farther east, near the confluence of the Little Wind and Popo Agie Rivers. St. Stephen's Mission and Black Coal's people were near the confluence of the Little Wind and Big Wind Rivers.[45] Coolidge's central position, therefore, could provide him with good opportunities to impress "civilized" ideas upon his relatives and the other Arapahoes.

## SHOSHONES, ARAPAHOES, AND THE EPISCOPAL CHURCH

Underneath these missionary "successes" as reported by Roberts, Coolidge, and Spalding lay another story. Arthur Jones left after one year of trying to convince Shoshones of the efficacy of Christianity. As Roberts gently put it: "Mr. Jones . . . has decided to leave the field. He has labored now for a year faithfully, but is disheartened at the apparent small result of his self-sacrificing efforts to do good." Ultimately, Jones decided that a different cut of collar suited him better. He moved to Laramie, where he became part of the management of the First National Bank of Laramie. He maintained his ties, however, with the Episcopal Church and served as treasurer of the Cathedral Chapter of the Diocese.[46] His replacement, the deacon Reverend William Jones, who arrived in August 1885, stayed only five months, departing in December of the same year. This Mr. Jones left the reservation because of poor health.

The "small result" among the Shoshones that disappointed A. C. Jones is worth analysis. Despite the overall growth of enrollment in the boarding school between 1883 and 1885, Roberts reported that he had had a great deal of difficulty attracting Shoshone sons and daughters. The majority of his first pupils were Arapahoe and white children—the latter belonging to agency employees. In fact, throughout 1883–85, Arapahoes generally composed two-thirds of the students. During 1884 to 1885, the first full year the new boarding school opened for business, there were forty-six Arapahoes, twenty-seven Shoshones, and five children of agency employees. Some of the Shoshones were the children of important headmen— Washakie enrolled several of his sons and daughters in 1884—but others were mixed-bloods.[47] For the most part, however, the Shoshones proved particularly resistant to education and, by inference, to Christian conversion.

This resistance was the source of Jones's disappointment. In addition, despite the greater numbers of Arapahoe pupils, Roberts's educational efforts reached very few of the reservation's school-age native peoples. At best only 30 percent of Shoshone and Arapahoe children crossed the school's threshold.[48]

If the Episcopal missionary attained minimal initial success as an educator among Wind River Indians, his spiritual evangelism showed even less progress. Between the time of his arrival in 1883 until 1888, Roberts baptized only one full-blood, an Arapahoe youth named Peter Grasshopper. Grasshopper, the son of a tribal headman, had been a student at the Carlisle.[49] Bishop Spalding thought two Arapahoe baptisms had taken place during his 1884 Wind River visit, but the second was Alice Stagner, the mixed-blood daughter of Speed Stagner, one of the white ranchers whose cattle grazed on Wind River lands. Stagner's wife was Cheyenne, not Arapahoe. In 1888 Roberts added one more mixed-blood Arapahoe to the baptismal roll.[50] The official record thus contradicts Roberts's enthusiastic statement about "three genuine conversions" among the Arapahoe young men that he reported in 1884.

Shoshones demonstrated even less willingness to embrace Roberts's teachings. They conspicuously avoided official commitment to the Episcopal fold until the mid-1890s. Even then, Roberts's recruits came from the ranks of his students.[51] Still fewer Indians, either Arapahoes or Shoshones, underwent the rite of confirmation, the symbol of adult commitment to Christianity as set forth in Episcopal doctrines. The first Arapahoe confirmands, five students of Sherman Coolidge, submitted to the ceremony in 1895. More Arapahoes were confirmed during the next five years, but no Shoshone was confirmed before the turn of the century.[52]

To some extent, Roberts's lack of knowledge of Shoshone and Arapahoe languages hampered his missionary work among Wind River peoples. His preaching, however, reached far beyond Indian ears. In fact, his greatest "successes" in the nineteenth century—as measured by membership rolls, baptisms, confirmations, and other church statistical data— occurred among white Wind River residents. White employees and family members formed the bulk of the official communicants of the Church of the Redeemer from 1883 to 1890.[53] Roberts also experienced good results among off-reservation whites. For example, in early 1884 he held evening services every Sunday in Lander for a congregation that could afford a monthly rental fee of $25 and was able to organize and build Trinity Episcopal Church in 1885. He also organized a Sunday School at South Pass City and made biweekly visits to the North Fork settlement. Furthermore, Roberts officiated regular services for the officers and soldiers stationed at Fort Washakie.[54] According to church records, nearly all his baptismal ministrations from 1884 through 1887 were officiated for white families or for mixed-blood children whose parents followed a "civilized" existence.[55]

In later years, Roberts responded to the call for evangelism among white settlements and helped to establish many different churches and missions throughout the Wind River area. Roberts's record for church planting was remarkable: between 1905 and 1912 he founded or helped organize St. Thomas in Dubois; Trinity Church in Thermopolis; St. Luke in Shoshoni; St. James in Riverton; St. Matthew in Hudson; St. Andrew in Atlantic City; and St. Paul in Milford (North Fork).[56] He also headed efforts to build a hospital and public library in Lander and to force Fremont County to provide a district school for white children on the reservation.[57] Furthermore, Roberts rode horseback to reach these diverse preaching stations, spanning a territory that covered nearly one hundred miles north-to-south and eighty miles east-to-west!

In the meantime, the Roman Catholic community of St. Stephens eventually opened for good in 1886, having made sputtering starts in both 1884 and 1885, and after spending over $15,000 trying to win the blessings of Black Coal and other Arapahoe leaders.[58] The Catholic mission thus presented a third form of Christianity to the native peoples of Wind River. However, as anthropologist Loretta Fowler so clearly points out, Arapahoes made only nominal commitments to Catholic tenets.[59] Therefore, while Episcopalians and Roman Catholics might have prided themselves in the establishment of their missions, the physical changes forced on reservation lands did not necessarily imply spiritual success. Shoshones and Arapahoes found their own solutions to the problems of living in the Wind River Valley in the post-1880 period. Conversion to Christianity was not one of the chosen solutions.

# Chapter Eleven

# Shoshone and Arapahoe Strategies

## 1879–1885

In the years following the Arapahoe relocation to Wind River, both groups of Indian peoples pursued policies that reflected native interpretations of living in the changing environment of the reservation. Their actions, however, were specific to each tribe. Thus, Shoshones continued to follow Shoshonean traditions in combating pressures of increased white population and demands of "civilization," while Arapahoes emphasized cooperation with whites in order to gain a homeland. The Arapahoes, like the Shoshones, worked toward their goals from within their own traditions and perspectives. Until 1885, both tribes experienced success and, to some extent, achieved a working tolerance for one another. However, during this period Shoshone and Arapahoe leaders never forged common goals to thwart or provide alternatives to the strengthening agenda of Wind River whites.

### WASHAKIE AND INDIAN POLICE

Despite the lack of unity between the two tribes, Wind River's Indian peoples still exerted strong influences on agency affairs. For example, leaders from both tribes continued to interpret reservation residence in terms of native, not white, standards. Agent James Patten first felt this strength when Washakie blocked plans to enroll Shoshones in the Indian Police in 1878. By mid-July 1879, the Shoshone chief's decision influenced Arapahoes to quit the force, effectively neutralizing governmental efforts to override traditional means of tribal control. As Washakie forcefully told Patten, "Shoshones are not white people."[1] Patten interpreted this statement to mean that the Shoshones did not need a police force.[2] That understanding certainly had merit. At a deeper level, however, Washakie probably would have stated that white-made laws or enforcement procedures had no claims on Shoshone (or Arapahoe) allegiance, nor would he want to allow such possibilities within tribal practices.

Washakie placed other demands on Patten. Following a council meeting of Shoshone leaders, held in June 1879, Patten reported that Washakie wanted Tendoy's band of "Western" Shoshones (actually one of the Northern Shoshone groups) evicted from the reservation. In Washakie's opinion, these were "bad" Indians, still committed to the nomadic life.[3] More than likely, Tendoy, along with Bannock bands clustered near Fort Hall, enticed at least a few members of Eastern Shoshone bands away from Washakie's control. Furthermore, a rekindled Ghost Dance movement, referred to by contemporary observer Albert Brackett as "some prophet predicting the speedy end of the world,"[4] surfaced in the Basin in the late 1870s. The Northern Shoshones and the Bannocks communicated the messianic ideas of the Ghost Dance to Tawunasia and his followers. Washakie hoped to head off any possible trouble from divisive religious movements by asserting his will in the Shoshone council and by inducing Patten to enforce his decision.[5]

## EMERGENCE OF SHOSHONE COUNCIL SYSTEM

In the eyes of whites, Washakie reigned supreme over other Shoshone leaders. To some extent, he held the same lofty place with respect to agency policies during the 1870s. The authority he exhibited to James Patten, however, began to wane in the 1880s. Possibly this reflected his age; at seventy-plus years, his voice perhaps no longer commanded the respect it once did. Cuts in ration allowances also undermined his power in two other ways. First, smaller appropriations made it harder for agents in the post-Patten years to meet Washakie's pleas for more food. Therefore, he lost the ability to manipulate Wind River whites to the same degree that he had in the 1870s. For example, his refusal to cooperate with freighting expeditions during the late fall of 1880 resulted in loss of rations to the tribe.[6] In past years, Washakie might have convinced James Irwin and James Patten of the logic for his decision—too late in the season, with poor grass, etc.—but Charles Hatton marched to different orders.

Second, lower food subsidies forced Shoshones to hunt for survival—both to offset ration shortages and to earn money to buy other needed goods. This meant that more Shoshone families relied on their own men, rather than Washakie, to ameliorate deteriorating reservation conditions. Furthermore, hunting, like warring, gave status to Shoshone males. Ultimately this implied that the band leaders acquired new strength at Shoshone council meetings.

Beginning in 1881, Washakie attempted more conciliatory measures to win agency support, instead of contradicting or confronting official policies. During the spring of 1881, Hatton boasted: "The greatest Improvement I saw [in farming] was made by Washakie, his Friends, and relatives who have built a fence about two miles long inclosing a Strip of Land on the South Side of the little Wind River, of an average width from the river of fifteen Rods. These same Indians have made an irrigating ditch by which every foot of land inclosed can be irrigated."[7] Hatton went on to say that Washakie also agreed to organize Shoshone freighters in the future. Evidently, the hunger pains brought about by lack of rations and decreasing game convinced the old leader that cooperation with governmental authorities was unavoidable in order to assure survival.[8]

Washakie advocated cooperation in other ways as well. Following the completion of the agency boarding school in 1884, the chief brought in his own sons and daughters in a show of good faith. As Agent Martin noted, "The boys had their hair cut—a hard thing to get the Indians to Consent to all were provided with clothing."[9] Thus, perhaps taking a cue from the example provided by the Arapahoes (discussed below), Washakie demonstrated that the Shoshones were "good" Indians, willing to become "civilized."

Other than Norkok, who either enrolled his adopted children in the agency school or saw them join the Arapahoes at Carlisle, few Shoshones placed their children into the hands of John Roberts or the other white teachers. Yet, Washakie and Norkok were not the only leaders who demonstrated Shoshone willingness to try white ways. Inspector Robert A. Gardiner reported that seventy-seven men were farming small plots in 1884. These included Washakie, Oatah (often listed as 2nd Chief), Bahhahgusha,

SHOSHONE COUNCIL SIGNERS, 1880–1890

— 1880

— 1885

— 1890

1884
Washakie
Oatah (1872 signer)
Bazil (1882 signer)
Toghyogge
Tonevook (1872 signer, now age 53)

Bishop
Tommookah (age 48)
Hovatse (age 38)
Utah (age 36)
Tonambe (1872 signer)

1885
Washakie
Oatah (1872 signer)
Terengotze (age 36)
Hiyagoudogo
Toppaa (age 44)
Battse

Peahgoosha (or Bahagushia? Age 43)
Ishuguash
Naniahdzauna (age 43)
Tehahrahgueeshi (or Sweating Horse, age 59)
Cunootsee (age 54)

1888
Washakie
Oatah
Tegundum (age 62)
Tigee (age 37)

Tibershee (possibly Tawunasia, age 52)
Weahwat (probably Weitche, age 62)
Anguitah (age 47)

Shown in order of signing
Age    = Probable age at time of signing
Signer = Signer of 1872 Brunot Cession

©B. Hudnall Stamm, 1998

Tagundum, Tigee, Tabunshea [Tawunasia], Wesaw, Battis, Weitch, Norkok, Toshia, John Sinclair, Tidzamp, Dick [Richard May?], Enos, Bazil, Utah [Ute], Naakie, Andrew Bazil, Tonevook, and Movo, among others. Of these men, both Bazils were important Sun Dance leaders. Norkok, Wesaw, and Sinclair were Shoshone-white mixed-bloods. Utah was a Lemhi, or Mountain Shoshone, while Enos, along with Washakie, represented the Flathead-Shoshone presence at Wind River. Others were band leaders such as Bahhahgusha, Tagundum, and Tawunasia. The Shoshone farmers presented a unified symbol to Gardiner and the government that the tribe was sincere in attempts to modify their economy.[10]

Shoshonean unity also emerged in the council sessions of the 1880s. These meetings generally debated the transfer of clothing or annuity funds to ration accounts. Normally the agent called the councils into session because Indian Office regulations required that the headmen or tribal leaders approve such monetary manipulations. At other times, Indian leaders met to protest ration reductions. For example, in 1883 Washakie, Norkok (as Shoshone interpreter), and Oatah acted on behalf of the Shoshones (Black Coal, Sharp Nose, and Washington represented the Arapahoes) to protest their beef rations.[11] This was the last time so few Shoshones acted on behalf of the tribe. In actual councils, unlike the petition of 1883, Shoshones were represented by a crosssection of band leaders, spiritual elders, and rising young headmen. Thus, the signers of an 1884 council included Washakie (age approximately seventy-five), Oatah, Bazil, Togyogge, Tonevook (age thirty-nine), Bishop (twenty-two), Timookah (forty-eight), Toppa (forty-three), Hovatse (thirty-eight), Utah (thirty-six), and Tonambe.[12] In 1885, a council consisted of Washakie, Oatah, Terengotze (age thirty-six), Tagoitah, Hiyogoudogo, Toppaa (forty-four), Battse (or Battis), Peahgoosha (probably a variation of Bahugooshu, forty-three), Ishuguash (twenty-nine), Mamahdzanna, Tyborocedo, Tehahrahgweshi (also known as Sweating Horse, fifty-nine), and Cunootse.[13] Norkok (fifty-seven in 1884) interpreted both councils.

Existing records make identification of all these men difficult, but what remains suggests that the council signers represented many of the tribal elders or mature males, as well as some of the younger men who were gaining status. Interestingly, Tawunasia, Washakie's rival, often missed these council proceedings, or was purposely ignored, but he signed an 1888 agreement.[14] The overall implication from these various council meetings is that as the material wealth of the Shoshones declined Washakie no longer acted as the primary mediator between the tribe and whites. Instead, decisions affecting the welfare of the Shoshones required community action by representatives from all the factions and bands. On the other hand, Washakie still dominated the tribe as far as whites were concerned: his mark (X) graced every council petition or decision until the late 1890s.

## INDIAN SCHOOLS AND ARAPAHOE STRATEGIES

Meanwhile, the Arapahoes pressed their own concerns. In January 1879 they asked for their own separate herd of stock cattle, having convinced Patten that "there is no question as to the propensity of giving said tribe stock—their every action shows they are earnest in their desire to become civilized."[15] To Patten, Indian ownership of cattle meant acquiescence to "civilized pursuits." However, Arapahoes probably had other aims; they continually sought parity with the Shoshones and the latter tribe owned cattle. The Arapahoes also tried to shape their children's education. According to Ellis Ballou, the Arapahoes' teacher, enrollments quickly swelled from six boys in early January 1879 to forty boys and girls by mid-May. Ballou wrote that "week after week" the parents pleaded for places in the makeshift canvas-covered frame school.[16] Arapahoe leaders took such an active interest in their children for at least two reasons. First, school rations insured that the students ate well, allowing their families to cope better with reduced supplies from the government. Second, the Arapahoes wanted to put the best face possible on their efforts to cooperate with white authorities so they might win a separate agency apart from the Shoshones.

This strategy proved partially successful. By December 1879, Black Coal had influenced Ballou and Patten to the extent that the teacher and agent suggested an eastern trip for some of the "scholars" and a few of the headmen, with the purpose of observing schools "and other things of interest throughout the states."[17] This proposed trip contained at least two agendas, each meshing nicely with the other. First, Black Coal undoubtedly hoped to use the tour to push his tribe's requests for a separate reservation.[18]

Second, Ballou hoped to gain recognition for his teaching prowess and money for his school. In a letter to Commissioner Hayt, Ballou outlined his

ideas. He wanted his students to perform songs and dances. Afterward, Black Coal would orate on the Peace Policy, War Policy, and the Indian Policy. Ballou proposed splitting receipts from performances between the Indian Office and the school. Overall, Ballou envisioned a prototypical "Wild West" character for the tour: "[Black Coal] is accompanied by a number of young braves, and fair, though dusky maidens. The troupe will sing in their native tongue some of their wild songs; will perform the celebrated 'Sun Dance' and also the 'Big War Dance' ending with the startling 'War Whoop.'"[19] The song-and-dance routines, however, never left the reservation.

Instead, the change in reservation administrator during the winter of 1879–80 (from James Patten to Charles Hatton) sidetracked the plans of both Ballou and Black Coal. Ballou seemed satisfied by promises allegedly made by Inspector McNeil that the government would build a separate school for the Arapahoes—to Ballou, this implicitly acknowledged his accomplishments. Meanwhile, Black Coal apparently bided his time to see if the new agent paid greater attention to the needs of the Arapahoes. By late fall 1880, however, neither man was happy with Hatton. Funds appropriated for the Arapahoe school built other structures at the agency, while conditions steadily worsened for both tribes—beef and flour rations had been in short supply since March.[20]

This turn of events may have prompted the Arapahoes' next move. In November 1880, Black Coal used Ballou's influence to gain admittance for several of the Arapahoe children to the Carlisle Indian School in Pennsylvania. The Arapahoes then expected to meet with officials in Washington after a period of "five moons" to air their grievances.[21] Sacrificing their children to Carlisle carried tremendous symbolic meaning for the Arapahoes. The children—the sons and daughters of Arapahoe chiefs and headmen—took with them "peace pipes" to present to the President of the United States and other highly placed federal officials. As Fowler suggests, the pipes represented "peaceful intent, truthfulness, and mutual obligation."[22] In June 1881, in a letter channeled through Hatton to

OPPOSITE: Shoshone Council, ca 1885. Washakie is posed standing. Left to right: George Wesaw, George Washakie, Sopahahamma, Tigee, Tibish Tigee (son of Tigee), Dick Washakie, Biagoosa (or Bahhagoosha) hidden, Matavish, Bonzi, Panzook, Jim Washakie, and Zagiva (or Zagovatsie) lying down. Courtesy American Heritage Center, University of Wyoming.

Commissioner Price, Sharp Nose reiterated Arapahoe expectations of that "mutual obligation": "Sharp Nose wishes me to tell the Great Father that his heart is good, to know that his pipe was delivered to this Friend the Great Father in Washington. Mr[.] Ballou when He took our Boys away to School, said He would talk with You, and in five moons, we go to Washington and See our boys, we would like to go when the weather is good before the Snow falls."[23]

When five moons passed with no response, the Arapahoes laid siege to Hatton's office until the agent finally arranged the long-desired meeting.[24] A delegation of five Arapahoe chiefs, accompanied by Hatton, finally departed for Washington in late January 1882. The leaders accomplished little more than transmitting Arapahoe needs to federal officials. They did not return to Wind River empty-handed, however; they picked up Lincoln Little Wolf, whom they found quite ill at Carlisle.[25] Unfortunately for the Arapahoes, Lincoln was the first of many Wind River native children who either died at Carlisle or other boarding schools, or returned home to die. White education thus proved deadly to Wind River's children—influenza, tuberculosis, and other potentially deadly diseases attacked students throughout the duration of the century just as destructively as white hunters decimated the northern Plains buffalo herd.[26]

Perhaps disappointed in their efforts to gain their own agency, Arapahoes worked in other ways to show their cooperation with federal officials and thereby win concessions for the tribe in return. Whereas Washakie and the Shoshones had rejected service as Indian policemen, by 1880 the Arapahoes signed on for such duty. In May 1882 James Irwin hired White Horse, Wallowing Bull, Six Feathers, and Yellow Bear. Several of these men were chiefs or headmen and together they represented the three main Arapahoe settlements.[27] Although this state of affairs made it possible for Irwin to disseminate information to the Arapahoes, and perhaps to exert some control over native behaviors, it also gave the tribe access to information at agency headquarters.

This communication became increasingly important as complaints mounted in the mid-1880s about off-reservation hunting and cattle killing. Irwin relied on the evidence given him by the chiefs and headmen to refute charges made against the Arapahoes for molesting white-owned cattle herds. For example, in November 1883, he noted that a "good man" led the Arapahoe hunting party in the headwaters region of the Powder River. Moreover, the Indian Police accompanied the hunters.[28]

Through 1885, however, the main political goal for Arapahoe leaders clearly focused on winning a separate reservation. During the 1870s and early 1880s, the chiefs and headmen manipulated friendships with white army officers and cooperation with agency civilization programs to press their concerns.[29] In 1884, they tried a new tack and drew on the knowledge gained by one of the returned Carlisle students, the son of Chief White Horse, to draft a letter outlining their needs. Charles White Horse, signing himself "Indian school boy," indicated the tribal plans: "We want to go to Tongue River and stay all the time because We would like it another Agency at Tongue River."[30] He went on to say that Shoshones were "bad people," mixed up with the whiskey trade, and a harmful influence on the Arapahoes, who were "good" (and therefore cooperating with the government). He probably was accurate about a portion of the Shoshones.

Agent after agent complained about the sales and consequences of alcohol on or near reservation borders. Generally, these reports referred to Mexicans or mixed-blood Shoshones as the primary culprits. Arapahoes evidently avoided the whiskey trade near the reservation during this period.[31]

## RESERVATION DREAMS DENIED

Unfortunately, even the requests of a "civilized" Arapahoe were denied. The council chiefs and leaders made one more effort, in 1885, to plead for a new reservation. Black Coal, Sharp Nose, Eagles Dress, and Little Wolf asked for another trip to Washington to discuss the needs of the people—a separate agency, carpenters, school, churches, blacksmith, and other rights guaranteed to their reservation neighbors, the Shoshones. Agent Martin bluntly and harshly informed them that no more treaties or meetings with federal officials would be allowed. "You have to work or starve," he said in a speech quoted earlier. "You can not go to Powder River—here you must stay and die—so must your children. . . . Go to work and stop begging."[32]

After this meeting, Martin reported that the Arapahoes were "sullen" and "their hearts were bad."[33] No wonder—the May 1885 council defeat radically altered the meaning of Arapahoe existence at Wind River. From 1878 to 1885, the Arapahoes sought their own agency, shared in the decreasing resources of the reservation with the Shoshones, and cooperated somewhat with agency policies. Beginning in 1885, sharing with Shoshones took on new symbolism: Arapahoes focused on proving their legal rights to Wind River lands, while Shoshones worked to deny their claim.

## THE YEAR THE BUFFALO DIED

For both peoples, however, 1885 signified even greater changes beyond their internal conflicts: the buffalo were eradicated from the Plains. The world faced by the Shoshones and Arapahoes at the end of 1885 thus looked far different from the one seen in 1878. Their hunting-based economy rapidly spun into a deep depression from which it would never emerge. In 1884 the tribes earned $12,000 from their hunting and trapping activities; this dropped to $4,250 in 1885 and declined still further in 1886, to $2,000.[34] The year 1885 marked the first time they earned more money freighting ($5,841)[35] than hunting, but the combined total did not equal the hunting output alone for the previous year. Increasing hunger and malnutrition characterized the precipitous decline in the economy; the periodic councils requiring headmen to transfer funds from annuities to rations offers a strong witness to native conditions. The censuses confirm the seriousness and extent of the hunger. By 1885, both tribes were in the second year of a long-term decline in their populations that would not reverse until the early years of the twentieth century.[36]

At the same time, white numbers in the Wind River region were rising, as were cattle and sheep. The death of the buffalo thus marked a drastic shift in the equilibrium among the community of peoples gathered in the Wind River Valley. Native inhabitants slipped into long-term poverty; white residents profited by their neighbors' losses. For the remainder of the century, those conditions intensified.

# Epilogue

## *The Nadir*
## 1885–1900

On December 11, 1896, the Reverend John Roberts wrote to Bishop Ethelbert Talbot about allotments and farming at the Shoshone Indian Agency in Wyoming: "Most of the Indians are settled on homesteads of their own. . . . We have a very able and successful Agent, [and] in two years he has made hard working farmers out of these two tribes of wild nomads."[1] Roberts's letter suggests that the Eastern Shoshones and Northern Arapahoes were well on their way toward "civilization" as defined by whites and that the hard times and cultural resistance of the 1880s were but a distant memory. The "successful" agent, Richard H. Wilson, was less enthusiastic. His 1896 annual report stated that "the main work of the agency this year consisted in inducing the Indians to undertake the pursuit of agriculture. . . . They are, however, so extremely ignorant of even the simplest operation of farming that the process has been very difficult."[2]

The two contrasting observations lead one to ask: which man told the truth? Or, perhaps, did either man know the truth? Taken together, Roberts and Wilson paint a picture of people who were hard workers, but poor farmers. This composite image points toward a more accurate assessment of conditions in the Wind River Valley in the mid-1890s, but still lacks clarity and overlooks the continuing transformations within the community as a whole.

Shoshones and Arapahoes indeed worked hard, as Roberts surmised, and, as Wilson noticed, they had trouble farming. Most importantly, they were poor—and their poverty was due in large part to the systematic deprivation forced on them by the larger white community surrounding the reservation and supported by government policies. In other words, the years following the death of the buffalo treated the native peoples quite harshly, while whites enjoyed a measure of continuing growth and prosperity.

Although a thorough analysis of the transitions of the last fifteen years of the nineteenth century lies beyond the scope of this work, at least three developments took place. These include (1) increased native mortality, near-starvation, and further erosions of traditional hunting-gathering economies that were not offset by concomitant reliance on "civilized" sources of revenue; (2) ongoing clarification of the political relationship between the Shoshones and the Arapahoes with respect to occupancy of the reservation; and (3) the adaptations of native spirituality in response to the transformations within the community at large. Each of these changes among the Indians of Wind River paralleled and sometimes overlapped similar shifts in the white community.

## DESEASE, POPULATION LOSS, AND
## ECONOMIC DECLINE, 1885–1900

Beginning in 1884, the Shoshones and Arapahoes suffered increased mortality from a variety of sources—malnutrition, poor sanitary conditions resulting from enforced confinement in reservation villages, and waves of epidemic or near-epidemic diseases. These calamities most often affected the elderly and the young, especially newborns. Sometimes the deaths in one year outnumbered the births, while in other years, such as in 1897, epidemic diseases ransacked both tribes and decimated the population. Measles, diphtheria, and la grippe (or influenza) periodically swept through the reservation, occasionally infecting only a few families, at other times spreading to larger segments of the population. Influenza spread in the 1889–91 period, diphtheria broke out in 1892, and measles killed 152 people in 1897.[3] Although Wind River whites also suffered outbreaks of killing disease, the tribal peoples shouldered a greater burden: chronic malnutrition undermined tribal resiliency to microbial attacks. The net result was that by 1900 only 841 Shoshones and 801 Arapahoes were alive. This represents a net loss of life of 199 people, or 10.8 percent of the total population of the two tribes, from the 1885 figures. The full impact of population loss is even clearer when calculated from the year of the

Arapahoes' arrival in the valley. In 1878, James Patten recorded 1250 Shoshones and 938 Arapahoes. Thus in stark, blunt terms—deteriorating reservation life contributed to net population losses of over 32 percent of Shoshones and 14.6 percent of Northern Arapahoes between 1878 and 1900! In comparison, Shoshones gained net population between 1874 and 1878, although the gains came primarily from a lower death rate, not from increased births.[4]

Tribal mortality rates climbed in inverse proportion to tribal economies. The war on off-reservation hunting escalated in the last decade of the 1800s, altering traditional subsistence patterns and forcing greater participation in "civilized" monetary systems. The amounts that tribal members earned, however, did not yield enough purchasing power to offset food and trade values lost in the conversion from full-time hunting. In 1891, for example, the tribes earned a mere $1,650 from their crops and freighting activities, far below the levels of income achieved by hide sales a decade earlier.[5] Moreover, the weekly per capita ration of beef and flour fell to one pound each and agents increasingly attempted to enforce the "work or starve" federal policy. Despite even those miserly standards, in 1890 inspector Peter Moran thought most Indians received less than half of the official amounts.[6] As it turned out, Shoshones and Arapahoes both worked and starved. In 1894 the beef ration decreased still further, to a mere three-quarters of a pound weekly. This means that the government provided only 227 calories daily to Shoshone and Arapahoes in return for their commitment to "civilized" work. Quite literally, the tribes were paid "starvation wages."[7]

In order to combat their shared depression, men from both tribes attempted either small-scale farming or sought part-time paid labor. These "civilized pursuits" entitled them to rations, but did not replace traditional economies—Indian "farmers" derived little economic or food value from agriculture. Ration reductions still necessitated sporadic hunting, gathering, and trading activities—regardless of whether they engaged in wage labor or farming (or both).

Other obstacles accompanied the transition to farm and wage work. For example, farming meant putting hopes in a good harvest—at best a tenuous proposition when individual Indians lacked sufficient agricultural knowledge, proper tools, and irrigation. Furthermore, the rationing procedure generally required one- to four-day absences to make the round trip to the agency slaughter pens—agents did not make deliveries to homes or villages. Arapahoe leaders won relief from this arduous trek in 1892. They convinced the government to establish a subagency near their main villages at the confluence of the Little Wind and Popo Agie Rivers.[8] However, for Shoshones and Arapahoes who lived far from the distribution centers, issue day necessitated regular departures from the fields, which might have affected overall farm productivity. Finally, few Indians grew vegetables or other foodstuffs. Instead, they concentrated on cultivation of wheat, oats, and hay—commercial crops they could sell either to Fort Washakie or to the agency. In essence, they farmed to earn money to buy food, not to grow food.

Wage labor had its own pitfalls—most jobs were temporary and provided meager incomes. Men earned money by freighting, digging irrigation canals (the federal government began appropriating small sums for this purpose), hauling wood for Fort Washakie, or working for the agency or the Episcopal and Catholic schools. A few women cooked for the boarding schools or provided meals to agency or school employees. Regardless of the position, however, wages were low. For example, in 1885 freighters earned approximately 2.25 cents per pound, or about $25 to $30 per trip. This rate, however, dropped dramatically in the early 1890s to .2 cent per pound and slowly climbed to 1.25 cents per pound by 1900. A steady, year-round position with the agency police paid $10 per month. Interpreters earned $300 yearly, while assistant industrial teachers or school cooks might earn $400. Ditch-digging paid approximately $1 per day.[9]

Therefore, it is highly unlikely that yearly wages topped $200 for most families. In fact, for most of the 1890s, per capita income derived from "civilized pursuits" (including farm-based revenues) totaled no more than $11 or $12! A poor year, such as 1892, might bring in half that income. Even the banner year of 1899 averaged just a little over $17 per person![10] Thus, most Indian families existed on less than $100 per year. Although no comparable figures are available for Wind River area whites, the agency's white employees commanded salaries from $600 to $1,500 per person per year and agents constantly complained that these amounts were too little to attract qualified people for the positions and were not comparable to wages paid off-reservation.[11]

The lack of cash income and insufficient rations virtually required Indians to continue hunting, fishing, and trading in order to counter the specter of starving children and elders. Off-reservation hunting perhaps retained its preeminence in the native economy, but horse trading and other types of intertribal commerce offered additional sources of income. For example, native-owned horse herds on the reservation increased from 3600 animals in 1890 to 13,000 in 1900.[12] Throughout the decade, agents noted that various bands of Utes, Cheyennes, Bannocks, and Sioux participated in the Wind River horse trade, although the extent of the trading is unclear.[13]

Despite these efforts to ward off starvation, hunger and malnutrition stalked reservation residents. Many Indians thus turned to other food resources—namely their own herds of stock cattle. This conclusion, however, requires detailed explanation. In 1890, the tribes owned 550 head of cattle. These increased to 1000 by 1900.[14] On the surface, this represents a significant growth in stock; approximately 6.5 percent annualized gain for the decade. However, since most of the cattle were heifers, a much larger herd should have resulted after a decade of management—perhaps as much as 17 percent per year (over 2600 cattle).[15] Instead, Shoshones and Arapahoes ate their stock, rather than concentrating on building up the herd size.

## RESERVATION POLITICS, 1885–1900

Although staving off starvation probably occupied the minds of most Shoshone and Arapahoe leaders, they also faced new political realities. From 1885 to 1887, the headmen of both tribes still grudgingly cooperated with one another, but the passage of the General Allotment Act in February 1887 changed the nature of their relationship.

Specifically, the allotment policy, or Dawes Act as it is better known, called for dividing tribal lands into individual parcels, or allotments, to be assigned to each adult Indian or head of a household. The deed would be held in trust by the Interior Department for twenty-five years to assure that the individual allottees could learn to farm before assuming complete control and to discourage potential white "landgrabbers" who might attempt to defraud the Indians. Afterward, the allottees would receive a clear title to their property.[16] This affected the Shoshones and Arapahoes in two ways. First, allotments would guarantee Arapahoes ownership rights to Wind River lands, an idea that Shoshones absolutely opposed and refuted. Beyond this long-standing dispute between the two peoples, western whites expected that "surplus" tribal lands would be sold or opened for white settlers.

Implementing the Dawes Act at Wind River required tedious and complex negotiations, which highlighted Shoshone-Arapahoe tensions and exposed rifts in Indian-white relationships. When land cession negotiations took place in the 1890s over Wind River territory, Arapahoes successfully staked their claim to an equal share in the proceeds. Again, this countered Shoshonean ideas, which centered on selling the Arapahoe-settled portion of the reserve to the government, or dividing the lands in half and being compensated by the United States for the Arapahoe side. Between 1887 and 1891, Shoshones and Arapahoes squabbled over legal rights, with each side complaining to the agent, to the Secretary of the Interior, or to the President of the United States.

The land-cession negotiations of 1891 finally established the precedent for a Shoshone-Arapahoe partnership by making both tribes equal owners of the reservation, at least de facto if not de jure. Under the terms of this agreement, the Shoshones and Arapahoes authorized the sale of 1.2 million acres on the north and east sides of the Wind River, but reserved 900,000 acres for themselves.[17] During the bargaining they fended off an attempt by the chair of the treaty commission, John D. Woodruff (a Fremont County stockowner and merchant), to acquire a strip of land on the southern part of the reservation between Mill Creek and the North Fork of the Popo Agie. The tribes agreed to the sale for three reasons: (1) to assure adequate food supplies; (2) to combat white-owned stock from running amok on Indian lands (whites could wrangle among themselves for control and access on the ceded lands while the reduced reservation could be better defended from white-owned cattle); and (3) to comply with the tremendous demands imposed by agency officials and local whites to sell the lands. Monies from the sale were supposed to establish cattle herds, new schools, and interest-bearing accounts. The Department of the Interior could spend the proceeds from the accounts on behalf of the two tribes. The U.S. Senate, however, never ratified the document. Woodruff's written comments about the agreement may have undermined the ratification process. He signed, but stated his opposition to the terms and his dissatisfaction with the denial of a land cession from the southern parts of the reservation.[18]

In 1893, another cession commission attempted to obtain a more drastic settlement. This time the government insisted on the sale of the southern tract and an overall reservation reduction of 1.8 million acres. In the end, the tribes rejected the offer (the Arapahoes, in particular, vociferously voiced objections).[19] In both the 1891 and 1893 councils, the tribes considered selling reservation lands because of chronic food shortages and the realization that their annuity agreements would run out at century's end.

The government finally concluded a sale in 1896, when both tribes agreed to the disposal of a ten-mile square area surrounding the hot springs at the northeast corner of the reservation (the site of present-day Thermopolis). Washakie attempted to force the government to treat with each tribe separately, but backed down from this arrangement when James McLaughlin, the federal negotiator, refused to acknowledge separate rights. The council achieved a compromise when Sharp Nose, on behalf of the Arapahoes, agreed to the basic terms desired by Washakie. Washakie wanted cash payments, while the Arapahoes and a few Shoshones wanted compensation in cattle. Sharp Nose arranged for the agent to buy cattle with the cash, thus solving the dilemma.[20] This agreement severed over sixty thousand acres (for $60,000) from Indian control, but also gave Arapahoes legal and political legitimacy at Wind River that blocked future Shoshone challenges to their residency. Eventually, in 1937, the Shoshones won a legal claim against the United States that compensated the tribe for the lands settled by the Arapahoes. This ruling recognized that the Shoshones were the original owners of Wind River lands and that the government wrongfully abrogated Shoshone rights.[21]

In 1904 the government finally accomplished the purchase of so-called surplus lands when both tribes signed away over 1.3 million acres. This cession, ratified in 1905, led to the founding of the town of Riverton in what had been the eastern portion of the reservation.[22] It also meant several hundred white settlers could move on to prime irrigable lands. The first large-scale irrigation projects, in fact, benefited the new white owners and allowed them to exhibit the productivity of Wind River lands. In other words, once Indians lost control of the best agricultural region, the government was willing to back massive water development projects needed for white economic development. Government officials ignored the possibility that Shoshones and Arapahoes needed a similar infusion of technology and money during the 1880s and 1890s. They never received it.

The passage of the Dawes Act held other consequences for Wind River peoples in addition to making land sales and treaty cessions possible. Most Shoshones and Arapahoes believed that tribal lands existed for the good of the band or tribal community. Thus, allotment in severalty challenged the core structure of community-held property. Traditionally oriented peoples of both tribes, therefore, generally resisted allotments throughout the 1890s. When forced to take claims, they tried to readjust survey boundaries according to traditional principles. As far as possible, both Shoshones and Arapahoes staked claims in band or family groups, and thus thwarted the more heinous features of individually owned parcels. Furthermore, chiefs and headmen distributed the produce from their farms and vegetable gardens to needy band and tribal members.

Despite governmental demands that Indians take up allotments, the allotment process in the late 1880s and throughout the 1890s never received official sanction. Confusion reigned in recording surveys and plats. Two different allotting agents marked the various boundaries during this time, but in 1898 discrepancies and disputes over their procedures, accuracy, and honesty finally squelched the allotment assignments. By 1900, Agent Herman G. Nickerson reported that only a few allotments were found "suitable" and he advised against further allotting work until competent surveys were made.[23] Nickerson may have had other interests in mind. As a long-time Lander resident, insurance agent, rancher, and general businessman, he wanted a treaty cession and probably hoped to forestall further Indian allotments on land that was likely to be sold.

On the other hand, several allotments survived the legal tangles of the 1880s and 1890s. Mixed-blood Shoshones and white men married to Shoshone women took full advantage of their blood or marriage ties and quickly claimed the best grazing and irrigable farmlands on the Shoshone side of the reservation. Many of these people, such as Edmore LeClaire, had unbroken ties to their full-blood relatives and were accepted as completely integrated Shoshones. Others of Shoshone descent, however, were fully "civilized," and often grew up in white-based cultures, economies, and educational systems. Among these was Isabelle Kinnear, whose full-blood mother had been married to mountain man Jim Baker. Isabelle, in turn, married civil engineer Napolean Bonaparte Kinnear. Isabelle claimed Wind River land in October 1888.[24]

By 1889 the Kinnears worked an allotment about fifteen miles northeast of the agency and dug an irrigation canal to the Wind River. In the mid-1890s their children, Isabelle's sister (married to Jesus Aragon), Isabelle's mother, and other family members staked out adjoining allotments. Altogether, the family controlled nearly one thousand acres of prime irrigated hay and wheat fields. Eventually their claims became the foundation for the present-day town of Kinnear.[25] Similar ventures characterized allotments taken by the children of Jules Lamereaux (also spelled Lamoureaux), whose wife was a full-blood Sioux. Despite their dubious ties to Wind River peoples, at least three Lamereaux males were able to claim reservation lands.[26]

A comparison of the extant censuses for the Shoshone tribe reveals the influx of mixed-bloods onto tribal and allotment rolls. Harrises, Lanigans, Robinsons, Herefords, Lamereaux, Guerras, Stagners, Boyds, O'Neils, and other names indicating possible mixed-blood backgrounds loom from the pages of the 1891 census. None of these had been counted as Shoshones in the 1885 census.[27] This does not mean that these tribal latecomers lacked proper credentials. John McAdams, for example, the son of James Irwin's former herder, Mathias McAdams, became a regular Sun Dance participant. Norkok and Bazil, to name two other Shoshone mixed-bloods, were important band leaders. John and White Sinclair (or St. Claire), half-brothers to Norkok, were other individuals who always maintained a Shoshonean identity. Nevertheless, at least some of the mixed-blood allottees took advantage of their kinship affiliations and acted from purely individual motives.[28]

These new allottees influenced the larger body of Shoshones in several ways. First, some of them were successful farmers and hired other tribal members to help with plowing, planting, and harvesting. Thus, they occasionally injected much needed cash into the Shoshone economy. Also, although this is speculative, these "rich" Shoshones may have represented the agricultural "successes" reported by various agents with respect to the "civilizing" intent of agency programs. Second, some of the younger mixed-bloods who possessed sufficient education and/or other "civilized" skills took jobs with the agency. For example, Robert Hereford Jr. worked as a herder during the 1890s, while Charles Meyers served as the interpreter following Norkok's death in 1896. These positions offered possibilities for channeling information (in both directions) between the agent and the Shoshones.[29]

Third, the mixed-blood allottees moved into the political arena, although for the most part they did so after Washakie's death in 1900. As long as he lived, he remained the dominant symbol of Shoshonean authority. Most Shoshones, including the mixed-bloods, supported or at least tolerated his decisions. Some mixed-bloods (whose individual identities are unknown), however, played active roles in the behind-the-scenes maneuvering in both the 1891 and 1893 cession councils. J.D. Woodruff called them "privileged characters" because of their dual status on and off the reservation. According to Woodruff, these men sought a voice in the treaty proceedings in order to expand their own grazing operations. No doubt he saw them as potential competitors to his own ranch operations and to other Fremont County whites.[30]

Finally, mixed-blood children made up about one-third of the students at the government boarding school during the 1890s.[31] This put them in position to model individual achievement—as one inspector noted, Speed Stagner's children were the "bright lights" of the school. Thus, such children unwittingly exemplified "civilized" behavior. Whether Shoshones saw this positively or negatively is unknown. (One can imagine a Shoshone parent suggesting that a mixed-blood child's use of English or achievement of better marks actually polluted, rather than improved, Shoshonean culture.) The fact that nearly one hundred school-age students avoided school throughout their childhood implies that education was of dubious value to Shoshone (and many Arapahoe) parents. Yet, the mixed-blood children represented very real links to the white world that might prove useful to the tribe at some future time.

## RESERVATION RELIGION, 1885–1900

All of the transformations discussed above—disease, population declines, land cessions, politics, and allotments—challenged Shoshone and Arapahoe understandings of their spiritual world. Given the close links between the buffalo economy and native religious traditions, the loss of that economy subjected faith to rigorous trials. Neither tribe, however, deserted its own interpretations of the cosmology for Christian beliefs. This does not mean, however, that all off-reservation spiritual innovations fell on deaf Shoshone and Arapahoe ears. In fact, they clearly heard when a voice cried out in the Nevada desert and called the tribes to repentance and a new dance. Wovokah, a Paiute, spoke his message of reincarnation of dead friends and relatives, of the return of the buffalo and times of plenty, and the disappearance of whites. He entreated his followers to spread the "good news." In 1889, the Round Dance (or the Ghost Dance, as whites knew the movement) worked its way from Nevada by way of Fort Hall to the Shoshone Agency.[32]

As could be predicted from past associations with the Ghost Dance of the 1870s, Tawunasia and his followers were principle leaders in the Round/Ghost Dance among the Shoshones. Other proponents included Tassitsie and Moohabi (a mixed-blood band leader).[33] Sage, Sitting Bull (an Arapahoe who later exported the ceremony to his relatives in Oklahoma), and Bill Friday carried the news of the dance to the Arapahoes.[34] Shoshone participation declined by 1891, however, when the movement's promise failed to materialize. Furthermore, Washakie opposed the ceremony because of Tawunasia's leadership role in the ritual. Ever the mediator, Washakie feared that Tawunasia's involvement might lead to a confrontation similar to the one that resulted in the death of the Hunkpapa Sioux medicine man Sitting Bull. (Sitting Bull, the spiritual leader of the famous Little Big Horn battle in 1876, promoted the Ghost Dance among his people. Agent James McLaughlin of Standing Rock Reservation, South Dakota, ordered Sitting Bull's arrest in 1890 in hopes of calming rising tensions among Sioux Ghost Dance believers and the U.S. Army. Instead, confusion over the arrest resulted in Sitting Bull's killing at the hands of Sioux police).[35] Black Coal also opposed the dance, probably for the same reasons, but Sharp Nose continued the ceremony for several years. By 1893, the majority of followers from both tribes abandoned the original intent of the movement (although a few true believers still sang the songs well into the 1980s). At this point, the ritual lingered as a social function called the Round Dance, which included opportunities for sexual encounters for young men and women.[36]

Another native-born ceremony emerged in the 1880s as an alternative to buffalo-based spirituality. Peyote religion and rituals migrated to the Wind River in 1888 when Wahwannabiddie and White St. Claire returned from a visit with the Comanches, who had taught them the new ceremony. Most Shoshones, however, did not become peyote practitioners immediately (probably in deference to the Ghost Dance).[37] In 1895 or 1896, some Arapahoes adopted peyote rituals when William Shakespeare, a young man educated at the Indian boarding school in Genoa, Nebraska, was cured of his sinus and thyroid troubles by the use of peyote. His healing took place on a quest to undergo the ritual among the Southern Arapahoes in Oklahoma (many of peyote's first devotees were various southwestern peoples).[38] Thereafter, Charley Washakie, one of the chief's sons, adopted peyote and spread its use among the Shoshones. Tassitsie and his son, Moses Tassitsie, then made another trip to the Comanches to learn more, which resulted in peyote religion becoming an important medicine or healing practice.[39]

Traditional spiritual leaders among the Shoshones and Arapahoes responded to these new religious accretions in different ways. For example, rather than repudiating the new ceremonies, Arapahoe ritual elders countered them by coopting the rituals. According to Fowler, the tribe's religious leaders tolerated the Ghost Dance and peyote as long as the people still paid obeisance to the obligations of the Sacred Pipe ceremony, the primary sacred tradition of the Arapahoe people.[40]

Meanwhile, the Shoshone Sun Dance retained its vitality and importance because the ceremonial leaders shifted its emphasis. Whereas in the pre-reservation era and into the 1870s, Shoshones performed the Sun Dance to gain hunting or war power, in the post-buffalo world they focused more on tribal health and individual healing.[41] Healing had always been part of the gift of puha for various individuals; now this aspect loomed larger. At the same time, Shoshones may have presented the ritual to white onlookers as a native interpretation of Christianity—during the 1890s, agency administrations tried to eliminate purely native religious traditions and to support the work of the Episcopal and Roman Catholic missions.

In addition to the continuing emphasis on native traditions by most Shoshones and Arapahoes, Christianity gained some adherents as the tribes searched for new ways to interpret and alter the reservation world. By 1900, Sherman Coolidge and the St. Stephen's clergy and nuns counted sixty Arapahoes as church members. As Fowler points out, however, many of these "converts" continued to practice native religions as well as attend Christian services. The Shoshones remained as reticent as ever; only twelve had joined Roberts's congregation.[42] In fact, Roberts (or at least his bishop, Ethelbert Talbot) missed an opportunity to expand the Episcopal presence.

In 1897, Washakie suffered a serious illness. Native remedies, including an extended stay at the Thermopolis Hot Springs, brought little relief. Eventually he sought help from Roberts; this included undergoing baptism in 1897. His reasons for being baptized are unknown, but he had once recovered from another serious malady following his Mormon baptism in 1880. Regardless of his reasons, Washakie's baptismal ceremony rewarded him with another recovery. This triumph led to several more baptisms among Shoshones at the Episcopal mission during the next year. However, Bishop Talbot glossed over the significance of the event: "It was strange that to a superstitious people this remarkable recovery should have seemed entirely due to the magic effect of baptism. . . . It was difficult to make them understand that the real virtue of baptism was spiritual and not physical."[43] Shoshones, of course, hardly noted differences between physical and spiritual. Talbot, and probably Roberts, did not try to sell the healing aspects of Christianity and thus let a useful evangelistic tool go to rust. The Episcopal Church, as a mainline Christian denomination, ignored the healing aspects of faith during the nineteenth century. Pentecostal belief, which teaches biblical healing, emerged in the early 1900s but it was highly unlikely that Roberts, Talbot, or other contemporary Episcopal clergy would have sanctioned such "radical" theology.[44]

Quite clearly, the decade of the 1890s was one of massive disruptions to Shoshones and Arapahoes. Their economies lay in shambles, their lands were under siege, and new theologies and ceremonies altered their religious views. At the same time, the wisdom deposited in their elders' memories died before apprentices could receive thorough tutelage. For example, Black Coal died in 1893; Plenty-Poles, the last of the ritual elders or priests of the Arapahoes, died in 1894; and Sharp Nose died in 1901. The Arapahoes adapted to these losses by reinterpreting ceremonial leadership requirements (but still used traditional lodge ceremonies) in order to provide men with opportunities for continuing political and religious mobility. Nevertheless, the transition to new political and religious leaders was a difficult process.[45]

The Shoshones also suffered great political and religious turmoil, with more fissures developing than those displayed by the Arapahoes. Lacking the age-set, age-grade structure that characterized Arapahoes and provided

Washakie, 1897 or 1898, about two years before his death. Courtesy American Heritage Center, University of Wyoming.

them with ongoing leadership development, the Shoshones depended on the individual bands to raise up leaders from one generation to the next. The deaths of long-term band leaders—such as Bazil (1886), Norkok (1896), Oatah (ca. 1890), Wesaw (ca. 1890), and Tawunasia (ca. 1893)— posed potential pitfalls to the tribe, because younger men often lacked experience in council negotiations with whites. In fact, mixed-blood Shoshones first signed council documents at the close of the century, which suggests that the tribe sought new avenues in dealing with their economic and political crises.[46] As long as Washakie lived, however, the Shoshones remained relatively unified under his authority.

This unity disintegrated in early 1900 with Washakie's death on February 20. This event fractured and demoralized a large segment of the tribe. In July 1900, nearly half of the adult males signed a petition that poured out their sorrow and confusion in Washakie's absence:

> Our Great Father: We your children The Shoshones, Would be pleased if you would appoint some one of our number to be our Chief or in some way give us a head. As you must know that our old Chief Washakie is dead, and we are now left with out a head to look too. It is now with us like a man with many tongues all talking at once and every one of his tongues pulling every which way. We are feeling bad that things should be in such shape among us. So we leave it to you to say who shall be our chief, or you name any number say nine or eleven but we want you to say and we will abide by what you say.[47]

Within a few years band factionalism splintered into violence that worsened under the pressures of the 1904 land cession council. George Terry, a mixed-blood who was instrumental in the 1904 agreement, was murdered and John Roberts reported that his own life was threatened.[48]

It is important to note, however, that similar episodes of political disunity characterized the Shoshonean past. In fact, from 1840 to 1890 Washakie experienced periodic disavowals of his leadership. Yet through all those turbulent years he was the one person around whom the tribe rallied or from whom they split. After his death, no one of similar stature emerged to take his place. Washakie's death thus prepared the way for the Shoshones to depart from a two-generation-old political structure.

Despite the presence of strong band leaders, he had functioned as the titular head of the tribe for at least sixty years. His passing severed both the real and the symbolic connection to a single leader.[49] During the early 1900s, the Shoshones (and Arapahoes) formed business councils that assumed primary leadership functions. To some extent, this reflected a return to band leadership by selected headmen, but these new council positions were elected and not dependent on older mechanisms of recognizing leaders.

Therefore, the Indian members of Wind River entered the twentieth century with their traditions battered, yet still important in the lives of the people. Religious rituals and ceremonies embraced new ideas, but still represented native world-views. Band and kinship obligations still factored in political elections. On the other hand, Shoshones and Arapahoes were relegated to second-class citizenship in the larger community: clearly, Wind River whites dominated the political and economic landscape of the valley.

By 1900, the Wind River Reservation and its Indian residents were well on the way toward the periphery of social and economic power. This deterioration mirrored the experiences of many other Indian communities, and for many of the same reasons. For example, the agricultural woes of the Northern Utes, Hupas, and Tohono O'odham seemed to stem from the same inadequacies as those suffered by Eastern Shoshones and Northern Arapahoes. According to historian David Rich Lewis, government policies failed to provide sufficient instructors to train and supervise Indian farmers over the widespread and arid areas of Utah, California, and Arizona. Much the same occurred at Wind River. Other difficulties included the lack of access to water at timely intervals, the vagaries of participating in market economies (especially the unpredictable agricultural markets), leasing land to non-Indian ranchers or farmers, and grappling with the idea of producing for the market as opposed to centuries of seeking subsistence. The cultural conflict caused by attempting to replace subsistence values with those of capitalism uncannily points to the experience of the Navajos. As Richard White notes, the Navajos rebounded from their nineteenth-century defeat to create a relatively stable, diversified, subsistence-based herding economy sustained by sheep, goats, and horses. The reforms of the New Deal in the 1930s replaced this self-sufficiency with wage-based poverty, a process begun at Wind River in the 1880s. The Anishinaabeg at White Earth Reservation fell victim to the same process during the 1900 to 1920 period.[50]

The Wind River experience also paralleled that of the Choctaws, Pawnees, Navajos, Anishinaabeg, Northern Utes, Hupas, and Tohono O'odham in other ways. Some individuals flourished even as the majority around them declined, either by adapting to white modes of operation or by redefining their "Indianess" in ways that allowed them some measure of success in the larger American society. In most of these communities, Indian peoples continued to search for solutions to their twentieth-century dilemmas just as they had sought solutions to earlier environmental, religious, or economic obstacles—by looking to their material and spiritual world. Thus, despite the shift in economic power in the Wind River region, the Shoshones and Arapahoes persistently injected traditional religious and economic meanings into hunting, herding livestock, trading horses, and perhaps even into farming. In the midst of starvation, high mortality, and broken treaty promises, Shoshones and Arapahoes still trusted native ways, not white "civilization," to keep body and soul together. In 1900, therefore, the Wind River community evoked memories of pre-reservation years—with separate human streams sometimes flowing together, but generally competing for the political, economic, and spiritual resources of the land and waters of the Wind River Valley.

# Notes

AMC      American Heritage Center
CIA      Commissioner of Indian Affairs
EA       Episcopal Archives
LR       (followed by 953–58) Letters Received by Office of Indian Affairs. Numbers refer to microfilm reel.
LR-RG75  Letters Received by Office of Indian Affairs, 1881–1907, in Record Group 75, National Archives. Letters are filed by file number followed by year.
MIC      Microfilm; a catalog system at Episcopal Archives
RCIA     Annual Report to the Commissioner of Indian Affairs
RG       Record Group
SCF      Special Case File
WSA      Wyoming State Archives

## PREFACE

1. The U.S. Congress authorized the creation of Wyoming Territory on July 25, 1868; Fort Bridger was included in the new territory.

2. Francis Paul Prucha, *The Great Father*, vol. 1, 485–500.

3. Brian W. Dippie, *The Vanishing American*, 79–160; and David Rich Lewis, *Neither Wolf nor Dog*, chap. 1.

4. Mark A. Knoll, *A History of Christianity in the United States and Canada*, chaps. 7, 9.

5. Melissa L. Meyer, *The White Earth Tragedy*.

6. Richard White, *The Roots of Dependency*; Loretta Fowler, *Shared Symbols, Contested Meanings* and *Arapahoe Politics*.

7. Catherine Price, *The Oglala People, 1841–1879*; Thomas Kavanagh, *Comanche Political History*; and Lewis, *Neither Wolf nor Dog*, chaps. 2–3.

## INTRODUCTION: SHOSHONE HISTORY TO 1825

1. Standard works are Robert Lowie, "Notes on Shoshonean Ethnography"; Demitri B. Shimkin, "Shoshone-Comanche Origins and Migrations"; Åke Hultkrantz, "Shoshoni Indians on the Plains"; and Robert F. and Yolanda Murphy, "Shoshone-Bannock Subsistence and Society."

2. Richard N. Holmer, "Prehistory of the Northern Shoshone," 52–57.

3. Julie E. Francis, "An Overview of Wyoming Rock Art," in George C. Frison, *Prehistoric Hunters of the High Plains* 2d ed., 420–23. Also, Lawrence Lowendorf, personal communication, February 17, 1997.

4. Thomas W. Kavanagh, *Comanche Political History*, 41–42.

5. Ibid.

6. Hultkrantz, "Shoshones in the Rocky Mountain Area," 196–97, 200–201, 204–9; *Belief and Worship in Native North America*, 22; and *Native Religions*, 42–62.

7. Kavanagh, *Comanche Political History*, 52.

8. Ibid.; Lowie, "The Northern Shoshone," 223–36; Albert G. Brackett, "The Shoshonis, or Snake Indians, Their Religion, Superstitions, and Manners," 330–32.

9. Kavanagh, *Comanche Political History*, 31.

10. George Tinker, "God, Gods, Goddesses and Mystery in Native American Religious Traditions."

11. Hultkrantz, "Configurations of Religious Beliefs," 200.

12. Ibid.; Lowie, "The Northern Shoshone," 223; Hultkrantz, *Native Religions*, 51–53.

13. Frank Raymond Secoy, *Changing Military Patterns on the Great Plains*, 28–31; Thomas Hoevet Johnson, "The Enos Family and Wind River Shoshone Society," 15–25; Colin G. Calloway, "Snake Frontiers": 83–92; Åke Hultkrantz, "Shoshones in the Rocky Mountain Area," 173–214; D. B. Shimkin, "Wind River Ethnogeography," 245–89 and "Shoshone-Comanche Origins and Migration's," 21; and Kavanagh, *Comanche Political History*, 56–66.

14. Secoy, *Changing Military Patterns*, 28–38; Frank Gilbert Roe, *The Indian and the Horse*, chaps. 4–5; Johnson, "Enos Family," 25; Calloway, "Snake Frontiers," 86.

15. Frederick E. Hoxie, *Parading through History* (paperback ed., 1997), 39–40.

16. Calloway, "Snake Frontiers," 86–89.

17. Kavanagh, *Comanche Political History*, 140–48.

18. Richard Glover, *David Thompson's Narrative*, 240–42; Johnson, "Enos Family," 26–27, 31; Calloway, "Snake Frontiers," 88–90; John C. Ewers, *The Blackfeet*, 21–23, 28–31; Murphy and Murphy, "Shoshone-Bannock Subsistence," 296; and Kavanagh, *Comanche Political History*, 110–112.

19. Hoxie, *Parading through History*, 51–52.

20. Calloway, "Snake Frontiers," 90–92; and De Voto, *The Journals of Lewis and Clark*, 209.

21. Reuben G. Thwaites, *Journals of the Lewis and Clark Expedition*, 2: 366–67.

22. Holmer, "Prehistory of the Northern Shoshone," 52–57.

23. Brigham D. Madsen, *The Lemhi*; Julian H. Steward, "Basin-Plateau Aboriginal Sociopolitical Groups," 186–87; and Murphy and Murphy, "Shoshone-Bannock Subsistence," 322–23, 329–31.

24. Shimkin, "Wind River Ethnogeography," 247; Hultkrantz, "Shoshones in the Rocky Mountain Area," 204–205; Calloway, "Snake Frontiers," 92; and Johnson, "Enos Family," 31.

25. Shimkin, "Wind River Ethnogeography," 246; Hultkrantz, "Shoshones in the Rocky Mountain Area," 182.

26. Shimkin, "The Wind River Shoshone Sun Dance," 409–10.

27. Ibid.; Hultkrantz, *Belief and Worship*, 241–42.

28. Kavanagh, *Comanche Political History*, 112, 115, 119, 142–43.

29. Ibid., 52–53, 146–48, 178.

30. Hultkrantz, "Yellow Hand," 296–98; Shimkin, "Wind River Shoshone Sun Dance," 410–13; Murphy and Murphy, "Shoshone-Bannock Subsistence and Society," 316; and Donald Fowler, "Notes on Chief Washakie," 37; and Osborne Russell, *Journal of a Trapper*, 145–46.

31. Hultkrantz, "Shoshones in the Rocky Mountain Area," 196–97, 200–201, 204–9; *Belief and Worship*, 22; and *Native Religions*, 42–62.

32. Hultkrantz, "Configurations of Religious Belief," 204.

33. Wilson, *White Indian Boy*, 20, 23, 25; Shimkin, "Wind River Shoshone Sun Dance," 411–14; and Hultkrantz, *Belief and Worship*, 241.

34. W. Raymond Wood, "History of the Fur Trade on the Northern Plains," 2–4.

35. Leroy R. Hafen, "Introduction," *Mountain Men and the Fur Trade of the Far West*, 1:55–165; Johnson, "Enos Family," 45, 54–62; Shimkin, "Wind River Ethnogeography," 254–55, and "Dynamics of Recent Wind River Shoshone History," 451n.

36. Howard L. Harrod, *Becoming and Remaining a People*, 20

## CHAPTER ONE: SHOSHONE COUNTRY, 1825–1863

1. Marshall Sahlins, *Stone Age Economics*, chap. 1; and Shimkin, "Wind River Ethnogeography," 265–78.

2. Russell, *Journal of a Trapper*, 16–17, 34, 40, 62, 86–89; Murphy and Murphy, "Shoshone-Bannock Subsistence," 296.

3. Frank Gilbert Roe, *The North American Buffalo*, 262–65, 267–69, 272.

4. Murphy and Murphy, "Shoshone-Bannock Subsistence," 303.

5. Russell, *Journal of a Trapper*, 113–15; and Nolie Mumey, "James Baker," in *Mountain Men and the Fur Trade*, 3:42.

6. Mixed-blood descendants such as Norkok, Moonhabi [Moonhave], Wesaw, Bazil, and Tosah became band leaders. See Shimkin, "Recent Wind River Shoshone History," 451; and Robert Beebe David, *Finn Burnett, Frontiersman*, 307. The children and grandchildren of mountain men John (Jack) Robertson, Jim Bridger, William Baker, Robert Hereford, Charles Lajeunesse, and Mathias McAdams tended to remain

in the middle position between Shoshone and white society. Nevertheless, they played important roles in the Wind River community. See Johnson, "Enos Family," 87–96; Leroy R. Hafen, "John Robertson ('Jack Robinson')," in *Mountain Men and the Fur Trade*, 7:247–54.

7. Cornelius M. Ismert, "James Bridger," in *Mountain Men and Fur Traders of the Far West*, 261; Robert S. Ellison, *Fort Bridger: A Brief History*, 7–11; and John D. Unruh Jr., *The Plains Across*, 199, 202.

8. W. A. Ferris, *Life in the Rocky Mountains*, 70–73, 309–10,

9. Marvin C. Ross, *The West of Alfred Jacob Miller*, 35, 199.

10. Kavanagh, *Comanche Political History*, 204–205; Russell, *Journal of a Trapper*, 13, 115; Hultkrantz, "Yellow Hand": 297–300;

11. Ferris, *Life in the Rocky Mountains*, 309–10; Russell, *Journal of a Trapper*, 115; Field, *Prairie and Mountain Sketches*, 140–41.

12. Russell, *Journal of a Trapper*, 115.

13. Ibid.

14. Ibid.

15. Ross, *Alfred Jacob Miller*, 31; Dale L. Morgan, "Washakie and the Shoshoni," pt. 3, 174; George W. Armstrong to Brigham Young, December 31, 1855, ibid., 177.

16. Field, *Mountain and Prairie Sketches*, 141.

17. John Wilson to Thomas Ewing, Secretary of the Interior, August 22, 1849, in Morgan, "Washakie and the Shoshoni," pt. 1, 146.

18. Field, *Mountain and Prairie Sketches*, 141–42.

19. W. T. Hamilton, *My Sixty Years on the Plains*, 135–37.

20. Grace Raymond Hebard, *Washakie*, 47–48n.

21. Richard H. Wilson, "The Indian Treaty of 1896," 541.

22. Hebard, *Washakie*, 51–53.

23. Fowler, "Notes on Chief Washakie," 36.

24. Ismert, "James Bridger," 254; Fowler, "Notes on Chief Washakie," 36.

25. Fowler, "Notes on Chief Washakie," 36.

26. D. B. Shimkin, "Childhood and Development among the Wind River Shoshone," 305–308.

27. Ewers, *The Blackfeet*, 55

28. Fowler, "Notes on Chief Washakie," 38–40; and Ewers, *The Blackfeet*, 124–27.

29. Ismert, "James Bridger," 262; Shimkin, "Childhood and Development among the Wind River Shoshone," 305–308.

30. Russell, *Journal of a Trapper*, 146; Fowler, "Notes on Chief Washakie," 36.

31. Ibid.; and Fowler, "Notes on Chief Washakie," 36–37.

32. Wilson to Ewing, August 22, 1849, in Dale L. Morgan, "Washakie and the Shoshoni," pt. 1, 146.

33. Unruh, *Plains Across*, 178–81.

34. Wilson to Ewing, August 22, 1849, in Morgan, "Washakie and the Shoshoni," pt. 1, 149.

35. Hoxie, *Parading through History*, 86.

36. Jacob H. Holeman to Brigham Young, August 11, September 21, 1851, in Morgan, "Washakie and the Shoshoni," pt. 1, 163, 167–68; and Fowler, "Notes on Chief Washakie," 37. See Morgan, "Washakie and the Shoshoni," pt. 1, 144; and Brigham Young, Proclamation, July 21, 1851, in Morgan, "Washakie and the Shoshoni," pt. 1, 160. See also Loretta Fowler, *Arapahoe Politics*, 28–34; and D. D. Mitchell, Superintendent, to Luke Lea, Commissioner of Indian Affairs (hereafter CIA), November 11, 1851, *RCIA for 1851*. A concise record of the boundary agreements is listed in Charles C. Royce, *Indian Land Cessions in the United States*, 786–87.

37. Fowler, "Notes on Chief Washakie," 37; and Holeman to Luke Lea, September 21, 1851, in Morgan, "Washakie and the Shoshoni," pt. 1, 167.

38. Holeman to Lea, September 21, 1851, in Morgan, "Washakie and the Shoshoni," pt. 1, 168–69. Conflicts between Washakie's followers and the Utes involved long-standing mutual horse raids. Furthermore, the Mormon settlements seriously affected Ute economy, causing territorial dislocations that put Ute and Shoshone bands in closer proximity. See Joseph G. Jorgensen, *The Sun Dance Religion*, 32–38.

39. Young to Lea, September 29, 1852, in Morgan, "Washakie and the Shoshoni," pt. 2, 78.

40. Ibid., 78–79.

41. Holeman to Lea, April 29, 1852, ibid., 69.

42. Mumey, "James Baker," 42, 44; Hafen, "John Robertson," 252; and Unruh, *Plains Across*, 225.

43. Unruh, *Plains Across*, 237–38.

44. John M. Hockaday to George Manypenny, June 17, 1854, in Morgan, "Washakie and the Shoshoni," pt. 3, 160.

45. Ellison, *Fort Bridger*, 13–14; Unruh, *Plains Across*, 243–44.; and Young to Lea, September 29, 1852, in Morgan, "Washakie and the Shoshoni," pt. 2, 78.

46. James S. Brown, *Life of a Pioneer*, 318.

47. Morgan, "Washakie and the Shoshoni," pt. 3, 161n, 162n; and Virginia Cole Trenholm and Maurine Carley, *The Shoshonis: The Sentinels of the Rockies*, 148–49.

48. Young to Manypenney, June 30, 1855, in Morgan, "Washakie and the Shoshoni," pt. 3, 166.

49. Brown, *Life of a Pioneer*, 357.

50. Ibid., 350–64.

51. *RCIA for 1855*, 196, 200, 247; Trenholm and Carley, *The Shoshonis*, 137; Morgan, "Washakie and the Shoshoni," pt. 3, 174–75. Tracing the name variations for Tibaboendwartsa is an adventure in itself: Fibobountowatsee, Tavenduwets, Tibebutowats, Tababooindowestay.

52. See Morgan, "Washakie and the Shoshoni," pt. 3, 174.

53. Armstrong to Young, December 31, 1855, in Morgan, "Washakie and the Shoshoni," pt. 3, 177; Fred R. Gowans and Eugene E. Campbell, *Fort Supply: Brigham Young's Green River Experiment*, 42–44.

54. Quoted in Morgan, "Washakie and the Shoshoni," pt. 3, 185; and Shoshone Census 1885. Brown also provides the earliest written estimate on Washakie's age.

He was surprised that Washakie was so young—thirty-five to forty years old. This suggests a birth date of 1816 to 1821, which contradicts Washakie's own testimony. The 1885 Shoshone census lists John Bazil, Bazil, *and* Brazil, as well as Andrew Bresil, or Brazil or Bazil depending on the source. Andrew was Bazil's son.

55. See William A. Hickman, Isaac Bullock, and Lewis Robinson to Young, August 19, 1856, in Morgan, "Washakie and the Shoshoni," pt. 3, 186.

56. Trenholm and Carley, *The Shoshonis*, 157.

57. Wilson, *White Indian Boy*, 15–105.

58. Royce, *Indian Land Cessions*, 786–87 and plate CLXXIII. See also Hoxie, *Parading through History*, 87.

59. Armstrong to Young, December 31, 1855, in Morgan, "Washakie and the Shoshoni," pt. 3, 177; and Wilson, *White Indian Boy*, 79–80, 83–96.

60. *Report of F. W. Lander*, 49, 69.

61. Jacob Forney to Charles E. Mix, acting CIA, May 21 and September 6, 1858, in Morgan, "Washakie and the Shoshoni," pt. 4, 73, 79–80; and F. W. Lander to CIA, February 11, 1860, in Morgan, "Washakie and the Shoshoni," pt. 5, 200.

62. Wilson, *White Indian Boy*, 29.

63. Lander to Commissioner, December 11, 1860, in Morgan, "Washakie and the Shoshoni," pt. 5, 201.

64. Marion McMillan Huseas, *Sweetwater Gold: Wyoming's Gold Rush, 1867–1871*, 6

65. Ibid.

66. Ibid., 6–7; James D. Doty, special agent for the post office, to George W. McLellan, Assistant Postmaster General, December 14, 1861, in Morgan, "Washakie and the Shoshoni," pt. 5, 216; and Trenholm and Carley, *The Shoshonis*, 192.

67. *RCIA for 1859*, 733.

68. William H. Rogers to William H. Russell (Russell, Majors, & Waddell were operators of the Pony Express.), April 18, 1861, in Morgan, "Washakie and the Shoshoni," pt. 5, 209.

69. Ibid.: 210.

70. Benjamin Davies to William P. Dole, CIA, June 30, 1861, in Morgan, pt. 5: 211.

71. Henry Martin to Dole, October 1, 1861, in Morgan, pt. 5: 215.

72. Young to Lea, September 29, 1852, in Morgan, "Washakie and the Shoshoni," pt. 2, 78–79; and Young to Manypenney, June 30, 1855, in Morgan, "Washakie and the Shoshoni," pt. 3, 166.

73. Dole to James Duane Doty, Luther Mann Jr., and Henry Martin, July 22, 1862, in Morgan, "Washakie and the Shoshoni," pt. 6, 80–81.

74. James Duane Doty to Dole, August 5, 1862, in Morgan, pt 6: 83; Luther Mann, Jr., to Doty, September 20, 1862, in ibid.: 91, 92. The best analysis of the Basin conflicts is Brigham D. Madsen, *The Shoshoni Frontier and the Bear River Massacre*, chaps. 6–9.

75. Doty to Dole, November 26, 1862, in Morgan, pt. 7: 193.

76. Madsen, *The Shoshoni Frontier,* chs. 10–11: Doty to Dole, February 16, 1863, in Morgan, pt. 7: 197–98; Mann to Dole, June 1863, in Morgan, pt. 7: 200; and Doty to Dole, 20 June 1863, in ibid., 201–2, 203.

77. Hultkrantz places Norkok at the fight, although he does not cite his source. See Hultkrantz, *Shoshones in the Rocky Mountain Area,* 208; *RCIA for 1869,* 274–75; and "Neikok, the Shoshone Interpreter," 561–62.

78. Sanderson R. Martin to CIA, May 2, 1884, File 8982-1884, LR-RG75; *RCIA for 1869, House Executive Documents,* 41st Congress, 2d sess., 1869, ser. 1414, 717; Shimkin, "Wind River Ethnogeography," 247; Trenholm and Carley, *The Shoshonis,* 137; and Morgan, "Washakie and the Shoshoni," pt. 3:174–75; and *RCIA for 1878,* 150.

79. Doty and Mann to Dole, July 3, 1863, in *RCIA for 1878,* 204–7.

80 Royce, *Indian Land Cessions,* 786–87.

CHAPTER TWO: SHOSHONE COUNTRY, 1863–1872

1. Roe, *North American Buffalo,* 457–58, 567n, 658n.

2. Hoxie, *Parading through History,* 88–89.

3. Hultkrantz, *Shoshones in the Rocky Mountain Area,* 205–6.

4. Ibid., 204.; and *RCIA for 1865,* 311.

5. *RCIA for 1865,* 327.

6. Hultkrantz, *Shoshones in the Rocky Mountain Area,* 191–95.

7. Smoak, "Band Chiefs and Head Chiefs," 5.

8. Ibid., 197–98; and Wilson, *White Indian Boy,* 28–29.

9. Hultkrantz, *Shoshones in the Rocky Mountain Area,* 197–98; *RCIA for 1864,* 319; and *RCIA for 1865,* 311.

10. Hultkrantz, *Shoshones in the Rocky Mountain Area,* 199–201.

11. Roe, *North American Buffalo,* 629–49; Murphy and Murphy, "Shoshone-Bannock Subsistence and Society," 312–13.

12. Shimkin, "Wind River Shoshone Ethnogeography," 247.

13. Ibid.; Hultkrantz, *Shoshones in the Rocky Mountain Area,* 207–8; and Patterson to Parker, September 18, 1869, in *RCIA for 1869,* 717.

14. Shimkin, "Wind River Shoshone Ethnogeography," 254–55; Murphy and Murphy, "Shoshone-Bannock Subsistence and Society," 307–11; *RCIA for 1865,* 311; and *RCIA for 1866,* 126.

15. *RCIA for 1858,* 564; *RCIA for 1859,* 733; *RCIA for 1865,* 327; *RCIA for 1867,* 174; and Morgan, "Washakie and the Shoshoni," pt. 8, 88–89 n. 194.

16. Mann to O. H. Irish, Superintendent of Indian Affairs, October 5, 1864, and Irish to Dole, October 13, 1864, in Morgan, "Washakie and the Shoshoni," pt. 9, 198–203.

17. Huseas, *Sweetwater Gold,* 11–12.

18. "Pioneer Profiles: Major Noyes Baldwin," 2.

19. Huseas, *Sweetwater Gold*, 10–11, 145–47. See James K. Moore Jr., "Post Trader and Indian Trader Tokens," 131–34; Elizabeth Johnson Reynolds Burt, "An Army Wife's Forty Years in the Service," 111; and Mann to F. G. Head, Superintendent of Indian Affairs, July 29, 1867, in Morgan, "Washakie and the Shoshoni," pt. 10, 57.

20. "The Genesis of a Town," 8. Other sources suggest that Baldwin's store in Lander opened in 1876. See Huseas, *Sweetwater Gold*, 85–86; "Pioneer Profiles: Major Noyes Baldwin," 2.

21. "Pioneer Profiles: Worden P. Noble," 2.

22. Huseas, *Sweetwater Gold*, 69.

23. Fowler, *Arapahoe Politics*, 14–16, 39–45; George Bird Grinnell, *The Fighting Cheyennes*, 124–262; and Thomas B. Marquis, *The Cheyennes of Montana*, 245-59.

24. James C. Olson, *Red Cloud and the Sioux Problem*, 37–40.

25. Mann to Head, July 29, 1867, in Morgan, "Washakie and the Shoshoni," pt. 10, 58.

26. Robert M. Utley, *The Indian Frontier of the American West*, chap. 4.

27. Indian Peace Commission Report, January 7, 1868, in Morgan, "Washakie and the Shoshoni," pt. 10, 65n.

28. Articles of a Treaty with the Shoshone (Eastern Band) and Bannack Tribes of Indians, July 3, 1868, in Morgan, "Washakie and the Shoshone," pt. 10, 67–72. Congress ratified the treaty on February 26, 1869.

29. Shimkin, "Wind River Shoshone Ethnogeography," 267–69.

30. Ibid., 279.

31. Mann to Head, September 12, 1868, in Morgan, "Washakie and the Shoshoni," pt. 10, 74.

32. Huseas, *Sweetwater Gold*, 67–68.

33. Ibid., 69–70; John A. Campbell to Ely S. Parker, CIA, June 10, 1869, LR-953.

34. Campbell to Parker, June 10, 1869, LR-953.

35. Ibid.; Huseas, *Sweetwater Gold*, 71.

36. Huseas, *Sweetwater Gold*, 71–72.

37. Ibid., 72–74.

38. Fowler, *Arapahoe Politics*, 46.

39. Ibid., 47; Huseas, *Sweetwater Gold*, 72–73; and Campbell to Parker, November 20, 1869, LR-953.

40. Fowler, *Arapahoe Politics*, 48; Huseas, *Sweetwater Gold*, 76.

41. Huseas, *Sweetwater Gold*, 79.

42. Prucha, *Great Father*, 468.

43. Ibid., 485–88.

44. Robert H. Keller Jr., "Episcopal Reformers and Affairs at Red Cloud Agency, 1870–1876," 116; Campbell to W. F. Cady, acting CIA, September 21, 1869; Shoshone-Bannock Agency Quarterly Report, November 22, 1869; George T. Metcalf, Chief Clerk of the Department of the Interior to CIA, July 20, 1870, LR-953.

45. Keller, "Episcopal Reformers," 116–17.

46. James Irwin to Parker, May 16, 1871, LR-953.

47. Campbell to Secretary of the Interior, February 21, 1870, ibid.

48. Campbell to Parker, May 26, 1870, ibid.

49. Ibid.

50. Lieutenant G. M. Fleming to Campbell, June 14, 1870, ibid.

51. Campbell to Parker, July 12, 1870, ibid.

52. J. W. Wham to Parker, August 21, 1870, ibid.

53. Ibid. (four different letters on same date.)

54. Wham to Parker, November 14, 19, 20, 1870; Wham to Campbell, November 12, 14, 1870, ibid.

55. Wham to Parker, November 29, 30; December 5, 1870, ibid.

56. Wham to Parker, December 1, 1870, ibid.; *South Pass News,* January 18, 1871.

57. Huseas, *Sweetwater Gold,* 24–25, 27–28, 85, 95, 113, 148–50; *South Pass News,* January 18, 1871.

58. *South Pass News,* December 14, 1870.

59. Wham to Parker, December 19, 1870, LR-953.

60. Wham to Parker, December 17, 1870, ibid.

61. Wham to Parker, December 24, 1870; J. E. Hodges to Parker, January, 9, February 3, 20, 21, 1871, ibid.

62 Hodges to Parker, February 20, 1871, ibid.


## CHAPTER THREE: JAMES IRWIN VS. WIND RIVER WHITES, 1871–1873

1. See Felix R. Brunot, "Report of Testimony, Statements and Investigation," in Brunot to Delano, October 26, 1872, LR-954.

2. Executive Committee Minutes of the Indian Commission, November 1871 to January 1879, Episcopal Archives.

3. Henry Dyer to Columbus Delano, February 23, 1871, Interior Department Papers.

4. F. A. Walker, CIA, to the Rev. Henry Dyer, Secretary of the American Church Missionary Society, December 26, 1871, Episcopal Archives; and Missionary Bishops' Annual Reports, MIC-60, Rolls 2, 15, 48–49, Episcopal Archives.

5. Robert H. Keller Jr., "Episcopal Reformers and Affairs at Red Cloud Agency," 118; and James C. Olson, *Red Cloud and the Sioux Problem,* 132–43.

6. Henry Dyer to Columbus Delano, Secretary of the Interior, February 23, 1871, Interior Department Papers; Keller, *American Protestantism,* 93; and Francis Paul Prucha, *Great Father,* 1:525.

7. Joseph W. Cook, *Diary and Letters of the Reverend Joseph W. Cook,* 20; Recommendation letters to Department of Interior, October 5, 1870; January 25, 1871, Interior Department Papers.

8. Keller, "Episcopal Reformers and Affairs at Red Cloud Agency," 118.

9. "Pioneer Profiles: Dr. James Irwin," 2; *Wyoming State Journal,* July 27, 1950; and James I. Patten, WPA 240, WSA.

10. Patten, WPA 240, WSA; Huseas, *Sweetwater Gold*, 24; Marie H. Erwin, *Wyoming Historical Blue Book*, 447.

11. Decreasing gold production coincided with increased Sioux attacks on the miners. The combination of pressures drastically depopulated the mining region. Irwin may have seen the reservation in terms of his own fiscal survival, at least initially.

12. Wham to Parker, November 20, 1870; Irwin to Parker, June 26, 1871, LR-953.

13. Irwin to Parker, May 17, June 5, 26, 1871; Irwin to H. R. Clum, acting CIA, September 1, 1871, ibid.

14. Wham to Parker, May 3, 26, 1871, ibid.

15. Irwin to Parker, June 5, July 1, 15, 1871; Irwin to Clum, September 16, 1871, ibid.

16. See R. L. Smith to Parker, December 15, 27, 29, 1870, April 24, 1871, and May 3, 1871; Hodges to Parker, February 21, 1871, ibid.; *South Pass News*, February 8, 1871.

17. C. F. Fleming, Chief Clerk for Auditor in Treasury Department, to Parker, March 18, 1871, LR-953.

18. Grenville H. Dodge to Commissioner of Indian Affairs, September 15, 1871; Irwin to H. R. Clum, Acting CIA, September 23, 1871, ibid.

19. Irwin to Clum, December 11, 1871, ibid.

20. Ibid.

21. Brunot to Delano, October 26, 1872, LR-954.

22. Irwin to Parker, June 5, 1871, LR-953.

23. Brunot to Delano, October 26, 1872, LR-954.

24. Irwin to Parker, June 5, 1871, LR-953.

25. 1880 Wyoming Census; Erwin, *Wyoming Blue Book*, 415; Nellie L. Wales Collection, Houghton and Cotter Ledger Book, AHC; and Brunot to Delano, October 26, 1872, LR-954.

26. David, *Finn Burnett*, 244, 260; Irwin to Parker, July 15, 1871; Irwin to Clum, September 11, 1871, LR-953.

27. Irwin to William T. Jones (a Wyoming Supreme Court justice), April 3, 1872, LR-954.

28. James I. Patten to CIA, September 23, 1872, LR-954; and Irwin's letter to the Board of Indian Commissioners and his statement to Brunot in Brunot to Delano, October 26, 1872, LR-954.

29. Irwin to Anthony, April 6, 1872, ibid.

30. *South Pass News*, May 24, 1871.

31. Ibid., December 14, 1870; and Wham to Parker, December 8, 1870, LR-953.

32. Wham informed Commissioner Parker that he understood people were pressing for a detachment of the Popo Agie Valley. See Wham to Parker, December 24, 1870; Hodges to Parker, February 3, 1871, LR-953.

33. Irwin to Captain R. A. Torrey, November 21, 1871, LR-954.

34. Irwin to Board of Indian Commissioners, n.d.; and Brunot to Delano, October 26, 1872, LR-954.

35. Ibid.

36. Irwin to Clum, December 11, 1872, LR-953.

37. Lowe to Clum, November 9, 1871, LR-954; quote taken from Irwin to Walker, April 4, 1872, ibid.

38. Irwin to Anthony, Conoway, Felter, Johnson, Davison, and Kutch (separate letters), April 6, 1872; May 21, 1872. Ibid.

39. Irwin to Walker, April 12, 1872; Brunot to Delano, October 26, 1872, ibid.; 1870 Census of Wyoming. Felter also affected reservation life in longer-lasting ways. He and his wife had adopted a young Arapahoe girl who had been captured by the Seventh Cavalry in 1870. The girl's brother also was taken, but was reared in an officer's family. The boy, Sherman Coolidge, received a college and theological education, eventually became an Episcopal priest, and moved to the Wind River reservation in the mid-1880s to assist in the Episcopal school and mission. Meanwhile, the young girl, Julia Felter, grew up in Evanston with the Felter family. Julia married two white men: John Burns, with whom she had two sons; then Anton Weilaudt, two daughters. Following her second divorce, Julia Felter—she took back her adoptive name—moved to the reservation, where she and her children became enrolled and allotted Shoshones since the Arapahoes had refused her enrollment request. Julia then married a mixed-blood Shoshone, John Hereford, and stayed on the reservation. Eventually, Julia was able to enroll all her children as Arapahoes in 1909. One of the daughters, Nell, born in 1888, married a white Bostonian, William T. Scott, and the two built a home on the reservation in 1927. Nell Scott was the first woman elected to the Arapahoe Tribal Council—in June 1937—but she also worked quite closely with mixed-blood Shoshones to establish a Catholic congregation at Fort Washakie. See Minnie Groscurth Hammond Collection, "Some Memories of a Native Wyomingite from 1868 to 1937," WPA 773, p. 10, AHC; Johnson, "Enos Family," 235; and Fowler, *Arapahoe Politics*, 184.

40. Jones to Walker, April 23, 1872, LR-954.

41. Brunot to Delano, October 26, 1872, ibid.; and Prucha, *American Indian Policy in Crisis*, 212–16.

42. 1870 Census of Wyoming; Irwin to Walker, February 20, 1872, LR-953; and David, *Finn Burnett*, 241.

43. Brunot to Delano, October 18, 26, 1872, LR-954.

44. Brunot to Delano, October 26, 1872, ibid.

45. Torrey to Brunot, September 28, 1872, ibid.

46. Brunot to Delano, October 26, 1872, ibid.

47. James K. Moore Papers, Roll H-2c, WSA; and Irwin to Brunot quoted in Brunot to Delano, October 26, 1872, LR-954.

48 See Henry A. Coffeen to Hoke Smith, Secretary of the Interior, July 11, 1893, File 26732-1893, LR-RG75.

CHAPTER FOUR: SHOSHONES, BANNOCKS,
AND THE BRUNOT TREATY, 1871–1872

1. Wham to Parker, May 26, 1871, LR-953.

2. Captain Robert A. Torrey, commander at Camp Brown, to the Assistant Adjutant General, June 26, 1871; Irwin to Parker, June 28, 1871; General C. C. Augur to Torrey, July 5, 1871, LR-953.

3. Irwin to Parker, July 1, 30, 1871; Lt. Gen. P. H. Sheridan to CIA, August 5, 1871; and Irwin to Clum, August 16, 17, 18, September 1, 1871, LR-953.

4. Irwin to Clum, September 4, 11, 1871, ibid.

5. Irwin to Clum, October 14, 1871, ibid.

6. Irwin to Clum, October 20, 1871, ibid.

7. Richard White, "The Father Image."

8. Irwin to Clum, September 11, 1871, LR-953.

9. Irwin to Clum, September 13, 1871, ibid.

10. Irwin to Clum, September 13, 1871, LR-953.

11. Washakie to Brunot, September 1872, in Brunot to Delano, October 26, 1872, LR-954.

12. Brigham D. Madsen, *The Bannock of Idaho*, 163–64.

13. Ibid., 18; Hultkrantz, "Shoshones in the Rocky Mountain Area," 191–95; and Madsen, *Bannock of Idaho*, 21–22.

14. Ibid., 27.

15. Ibid., 140–63; and Brigham D. Madsen, *Chief Pocatello*, 11, 71.

16. Madsen, *The Bannock of Idaho*, 172.

17. Irwin to Walker, April 27, 1872, LR-954.

18. Madsen, *Chief Pocatello*, 69–71.

19. Ibid., 77–82, 105–6.

20. Madsen, *The Bannock of Idaho*, 176–80; and Wham to Parker, December 8, 10, 14, 1870, LR-953.

21. Irwin to Walker, February 16, May 24, 1872, Delano to Walker, March 2, 1872 LR-954.

22. Ibid.

23. Irwin to Walker, May 31, August 26, October 4, 1872, LR-954.

24. Campbell to Parker, August 5, 1869, LR-953.

25. Campbell to the Secretary of the Interior, February 21, 1870; and Wham to Parker, December 19, 1870, LR-953.

26. See Morton Keller, *Affairs of State*, chap. 4; Robert A. Trennert, "Educating Indian Girls," 271–90; and Anthony M. Platt, *The Child Savers*.

27. Brunot to Delano, October 18, 1872, LR-954.

28. Charles Lewis Slattery, *Felix Reveille Brunot*, 187–93.

29. Slattery, *Felix Reveille Brunot*, 193; and David, *Finn Burnett*, 291–93.

30. *South Pass News*, September 7, 1871; and Brunot to Delano, October 18, 1872, LR-954.

31. Brunot, Report of Council with the Shoshone Indians (1st day), September 26, 1872, LR-954.

32. Ibid.

33. Ibid.

34. Ibid.

35. Irwin to Walker, May 24, 1872, ibid.

36. Lt. G. M. Fleming to Campbell, June 14, 1870, LR-953.

37. Brunot, Report of Council (1st day), LR-954.

38. Ibid. The Crows, in fact, had ceded their Wyoming lands on May 7, 1868. See Royce, *Indian Land Cessions,* 848–49.

39. Brunot, Report of Council (1st day), LR-954.

40. Ibid.

41. Ibid.

42. Irwin to Parker, June 5, 1871, LR-953.

43. Patten to Board of Indian Commissioners, September 25, 1872, LR-954.

44. Brunot, Report of Council (1st day), LR-954.

45. Brunot to Delano, October 18, 1872, ibid.

46. Brunot, Report of Council (2nd day), September 27, 1872, LR-954.

47. Ibid.

48. Ibid.

49. Ibid.

50. Brunot to Delano, October 18, 1872, LR-954.

51. Brunot, Report on Council (3rd day), September 28, 1872, LR-954.

52. Ibid.

53. Ibid.

54. Ibid.

55. Ibid.

56. Joseph Carey to J. Q. Smith, Commissioner of Indian Affairs, March 1, 1875, LR-955; Irwin to Smith, July 15, 26, 1875, ibid.; and Hampton B. Denman to Smith, August 23, 1876, LR-955.

57. Brunot, Report on Council (3rd day), List of Shoshone signers, September 28, 1872, LR-954.


CHAPTER FIVE: TO FARM OR NOT TO FARM:
SHOSHONE ECONOMY, 1872–1877


1. James, "Brigham Young—Chief Washakie Indian Farm Negotiations," 249–50.

2. Irwin to Parker, June 3, 5, 1871, LR-953; and David, *Finn Burnett,* 256–57.

3. Irwin to Clum, September 11, 1871, LR-953; and David, *Finn Burnett,* 260.

4. Irwin to Walker, February 16, 1872, LR-954.

5. Irwin to Walker, April 23, May 18, 1872, ibid.

6. Irwin to Walker, May 14, 1872, ibid.

7. David, *Finn Burnett*, 261–62.

8. F. G. Burnett to Mrs. Robert Horne, January 10, 1933, Mrs. Robert Horne Collection, AHC.

9. Irwin to Walker, May 24, 31, 1872, LR-954.

10. Irwin to Walker, July 26, August 18, 1872, ibid.

11. Irwin to Walker, November 8, 1872; and Irwin to Clum, January 23, 1873, ibid.

12. The ration allotments are extrapolated from various sources. Irwin mentioned a daily eight-ounce beef ration (and the beef herd numbered about four hundred head, which would yield 180,000 to 200,000 pounds net weight). David cites Burnett's memories of food portions; the 1873–1874 fiscal year flour contract called for 300,000 pounds. The calculations reflect the approximate per-person portions using a base population of one thousand people. See Irwin to Clum, February 26, October 1, 1873; William J. Baker to Edward P. Smith, Commissioner of Indian Affairs, June 28, 1873, LR-954; and David, *Finn Burnett*, 279. The Shoshone population was 1024 in 1873. See *RCIA for 1873*, Statistical Abstracts. Although Burnett remembered coffee and sugar as additional rations as early as 1871, these items apparently were added later—the Shoshone requested them in May 1873. See Irwin to Smith, May 15, 1873, LR-954.

13. Irwin to Smith, May 15, 1873, LR-954.

14. Ibid.

15. Irwin to Smith, June 2, 1873, LR-954.

16. *RCIA for 1873*, 245.

17. *RCIA for 1866*, 122; *RCIA for 1867*; and Irwin to Smith, May 15, June 2, 1873, LR-954.

18. *RCIA for 1873*, Statistical Abstracts. Determining values for products is inexact. The 1873 annual report lists the values of the furs sold as well as the quantities of agricultural products, but does not list the latter's value. However, a complete estimate for the government's annuity and subsistence budgets for the Shoshones for the 1878 fiscal year came to $22,000 for food, and $9,000 for clothing and other items. See Irwin to Smith, March 5, 1877, LR-955. In 1878 fur production was $2,200, while Shoshones grew over 5000 bushels of various agricultural products (mostly oats, barley, and vegetables). The fur sales and farm produce made up only one-fourth of the Shoshonean subsistence, with the government providing the remainder. See *RCIA for 1878*, 310–11. Finally, Tilford Kutch sought $192.00 for 3200 pounds of potatoes consumed by the Shoshones in 1870, which equals six cents per pound (or approximately $3.25 per bushel—probably much too high a figure for the normal market levels of that time). This meant that the 1873 Shoshonean output probably was worth from $5,000 to $10,000. See Wham to Parker, November 29, 1870, LR-953. It is assumed that farming and hunting provided about the same proportions of Shoshonean income in 1873 as they did in 1878.

19. *RCIA for 1874*, 270.

20. See Irwin to Clum, February 26, March 17, April 12, 1873; and Irwin to Smith, May 1, 1873, LR-954.

21. David M. Delo, "Post Trader, Indian Trader," part 1, 4–7; and James K. Moore Papers, Reel H-2c, WSA.

22. J. K. Moore Jr., to Russell Thorp, February 6, 1959, James K. Moore Biographical File, AHC.

23. J. K. Moore Jr., "Post Trader and Indian Trader Tokens," 131–34.

24. Ibid.: 134.

25. Irwin to Walker, April 23, October 9, 1872, LR-954.

26. Irwin to Clum, April 12, 1873, ibid.

27. David, *Finn Burnett*, 290–91, 298; Moore, "Post Trader and Indian Trader Tokens," 132; Irwin to Smith, August 5, 21, 1873, LR-954; and Catherine Price, *The Oglala People*, 119.

28. Burnett to Grace Raymond Hebard, Fincelius Gray, AHC; and *RCIA for 1874*, 271.

29. Burnett to Hebard, December 21, 1921, October 29, 1929, Burnett Biographical File; and David, *Finn Burnett*, 300–301.

30. Burnett to Maggie (Margaret Burnett Simpson), n.d., Burnett Biographical File, AHC; and David, *Finn Burnett*, 299, 335–36.

31. Irwin to Smith, August 15, 21, 1873, LR-954.

32. Irwin to Smith, September 24, 1873, ibid.

33. Irwin to Smith, January 20, 1874, ibid.

34. Irwin to Smith, October 1, 16, 1873, LR-954; Johnson, "Enos Family," 90, 129; William A. Carter to Hebard, April 27, 1929, William A. Carter Sr. Biographical File, AHC; and Irwin to Smith, January 7, 1874, LR-954.

35. Irwin to Smith, February 7, 1874, LR-954. The fiscal problems stemmed from congressional appropriation delays, perhaps reflecting the problems from the Panic of 1873. Funding for fiscal year 1873–74 was approved on February 14, 1873, but Congress did not act for fiscal year 1874–75 until June 22, 1874. With only nine days before the beginning of the new year, departmental budgeting and orderly contract negotiations were disrupted. See *Indian Department Appropriation Act, Statutes at Large*, 17, chap. 138 (1874), 455; and *Indian Department Appropriation Act, Statutes at Large*, 18, chap. 389 (1874), 166.

36. Irwin to Smith, March 3, 1874 (two letters), LR-954.

37. Irwin to Smith, March 3, 14, 1874, ibid.

38. *Indian Department Appropriation Act, Statutes at Large*, (1874) 166; and *Act of Confirmation, Statutes at Large* (1874), 291–92.

39. Irwin to Smith, September 18, 1874, LR-954; *RICA for 1874*, 270

40. Irwin to Smith, January 31, May 5, 1874, LR-954.

41. Irwin to Smith, May 5, 1874; and B. R. Bowen, Acting Secretary of the Interior, to CIA, July 21, 1874, LR-954.

42. Irwin to Smith, July 6, 31, 1874, ibid.; and *RICA for 1874*, 125.

43. Irwin to Smith, February 15, 1875, LR-955.

44. Joseph M. Carey to Smith, March 1, 1875, LR-955; and W. R. Steele to Smith, September 12, 1874, LR-954.

45. Irwin to Smith, January 2, 1875, LR-955; George N. Williams, U.S. Attorney General to Delano, February 5, 22, 1875; and Irwin to Smith, July 12, 1875, LR-955.

46. There are discrepancies about the cattle payments. Irwin's annual report of September 23, 1874, indicated that the cattle arrived late. See *RCIA for 1874*, 270. However, in May 1875 he questioned Commissioner Smith about the first two installments that still were due at the agency. By July, Irwin was still waiting for the delivery. Anticipating problems with fall shipments, he recommended that the first three payments be made the following spring, that is, in 1876. In fact, $10,000 in cattle (307 cows and 10 bulls), representing two payments, finally arrived on August 15, 1876. See Irwin to Smith, May 5, July 15, 1875; and Hampton B. Denman, surveyor and cattle vendor, to Smith, August 23, 1876, LR-955. The statistical tables for the annual reports of 1874 through 1877 add to the confusion. They depict annual increases in cattle owned by the Shoshones, beginning with 200 head in 1874, then 700 for 1875, 1227 in 1876, and 1400 in 1877. See *RCIA for 1874*, 124; *RCIA for 1875*, 132; *RCIA for 1876*, 234; and *RCIA for 1877*, 317. The agents' written reports both confirm and contradict the tables. In Irwin's report of September 24, 1875, the agent believed $10,000 in cattle was due (i.e., for 1875 and 1876), which implies that the 1874 payment was made. See *RCIA for 1875*, 376. In 1876, Irwin reported 800 head, while the tables show 1227. Furthermore, Irwin wrote that only two payments had been made, probably referring to the 317 head delivered by Denman. See *RCIA for 1876*, 153, 234. By 1877, the tables list 1400 head of cattle, which agrees with the report of the new Shoshone agent, James I. Patten, dated September 1, 1877. Patten stated that two more installments were still due, implying that three payments had been made. See *RCIA for 1877*, 209, 317. The mystery apparently arose over a misunderstanding by both Irwin and the Shoshones about cattle payments. The Shoshones complained in April 1878 that the 130 cattle received in 1874 (note that this contradicts the statistical table listing 200 head) were not part of the Brunot agreement, but rather were a special appropriation. They still believed that they had three payments left, not two. See Patten to Ezra A. Hayt, CIA, April 11, 1878, LR-956. Irwin evidently acted on the same assumption as the Shoshones. I have not found any documentation to verify the Shoshone/Irwin position. The best guess I can make at the actual sequence of events is that the first installment (of either 130 or 200 head) was made in 1874. This was followed by a second installment, but consisting of two payments, in 1876 (the Denman delivery of 317 head). The final installment, consisting of two payments, came in November 1878. Fincelius G. Burnett, formerly the agency farmer, drove in 503 cattle, probably obtained from Oregon. See Patten to Hayt, December 1, 1878, LR-956.

47. Irwin to Smith, December 16, 1874, LR-954; and *RCIA for 1875*, 375–76.

48. *RCIA for 1875*, 376.

49. Irwin to Smith, April 26, June 19, 1875, LR-955.

50. *Indian Department Appropriation Act, Statutes at Large* (1873), 455; and (1874), 165–66.

51. *RCIA for 1875*, 375.

52. Irwin to Smith, September 1, 1875, LR-955; and *Indian Department Appropriation Act, Statutes at Large* (1875), 440.

53. *RCIA for 1875*, 376.

54. *RCIA for 1873*, Statistical Abstracts; *RCIA for 1875*, 133; and *RCIA for 1876*, 235.

55. Irwin to Smith, July 8, 1876, LR-955; Grinnell, *The Fighting Cheyennes*, 328–44; John G. Bourke, *On the Border with Crook*, 302, 306, 311–16; and Trenholm and Carley, *The Shoshonis*, 247–53.

56. Bourke, *On the Border with Crook*, 319, 334, 338, 354–57.

57. Irwin to Smith, July 24, 1876; and Denman to Smith, August 23, 1876, LR-955.

58. Irwin to Smith, November 6, 1876, LR-955; and *RCIA for 1877*, 209–10. The incidental funds were $5,000 per year from 1874 to 1876, but dropped to $1500 for the 1876–77 year and to $1,000 a year later. See *Indian Department Appropriations Act, Statutes at Large*, (1874), 172; (1875), 446; (1876), 198; and (1877), 293.

59. Bourke, *Mackenzie's Last Fight with the Cheyennes*, 3–28; Trenholm and Carley, *The Shoshonis*, 260; Fowler, *Arapahoe Politics*, 61; Grinnell, *Fighting Cheyennes*, 359–82.

60. Shimkin, "Dynamics of Recent Wind River Shoshone History," 454.

61. Irwin to Smith, March 5 and April 12, 1877, LR-955; and Patten to Smith, June 18, 20, 1877, ibid.

62. Patten to Smith, July 5, 25, 1877, ibid.

63. *RCIA for 1877*, 208.

64. Washakie, et. al, to President (USA), February 16, 1877, Appointment Papers.

65 Irwin to Smith, February 22, 1877, LR-955.

## CHAPTER SIX: PREACHERS, TEACHERS, AND NORTHERN ARAPAHOES, 1870–1878

1. James S. Brisbin to Eli Parker, September 5, 1870, Appointment Papers.

2. Missionary Bishop's Annual Reports, 1871, 95–96, MIC 60, 1835–1909, Roll 2 (1868–1872), Episcopal Archives.

3. Missionary Bishop's Annual Reports, 1872, 151, Roll 2, EA.

4. Ibid.

5. James Irving Patten Manuscript, Patten Papers, Film H-95, 25, Wyoming State Archives. Patten says fourteen received baptism, but only eleven are listed in the parish records. See Church of the Redeemer, Parish Register, vol. 1 (1873–1902), Fort Washakie, Wyoming (hereafter Redeemer Parish Register).

6. Patten Papers, Film H-95, 23.

7. Ibid., 25.

8. "Bishop Randall and the Indians," *Spirit of Missions* 38: 756–57.

9. Hultkrantz, *Native Religions of North America*, 42–45.

10. D. B. Shimkin, "The Wind River Shoshone Sun Dance," 409–11.

11. There are myriad writings on Anglican/Episcopal beliefs and spirituality. The following, although not contemporary to Randall, trace some of the historical influences that have shaped Episcopal thought and practice: James A. Pike and Norman Pittenger, *The Faith of the Church;* Richard A. Norris, *Understanding the Faith of the Church;* and William J. Wolf, ed., *Anglican Spirituality.*

12. *Indian Department Appropriations Act, Statutes at Large* 17, 439; and 18, 165–66.

13. Patten, "The Last Great Buffalo Hunt," *Big Horn County Rustler,* March 26, 1920.

14. Ibid.

15. Ibid.

16. Hultkrantz, *Belief and Worship,* 30–35.

17. Albert G. Brackett, "The Shoshonis, or Snake Indians, Their Religion, Superstitions, and Manners," 330–32.

18. Irwin to Smith, May 6, 1875, LR-955.

19. *Journal of the Convocation,* 18–21; and *Journal of the Second Convocation,* 19.

20. *Journal of the Third Convocation,* 14.

21. Report of the Indian Commission, *Spirit of Missions* 42: 660–63.

22. *Journal of the Fourth Convocation,* 24.

23. Report from Bishop Spalding, *Spirit of Missions* 41: 17.

24. Ibid., 17–18; Shimkin, "Childhood and Development," 293

25. *Journal of the Fourth Annual Convocation,* 24.

26. Hultkrantz, *Native Religions,* 38.

27. "Temporary" transformed into "permanent" because the United States violated the 1868 Fort Bridger Treaty, which gave Shoshones refusal rights on possible joint occupancy of the reservation. The federal government, however, treated the Arapahoes as de facto co-occupants, ignoring Shoshone complaints. Thus the former peoples cosigned land cession agreements in 1896 and 1904. The Shoshones eventually received compensation in 1939 from the federal government for the Arapahoe presence. The Arapahoes now are equal partners with the Shoshones in the reservation.

28. Fowler, *Arapahoe Politics,* 48.

29. Ibid., 49.

30. Ibid., 52–53, 55–56.

31. Ibid., 57; and Royce, *Indian Land Cessions,* 888–89.

32. Fowler, *Arapahoe Politics,* 58–62, quote on 62.

33. Black Coal, quoted in ibid., 65.

34. Ibid., 66.

35. E. O. Fuller, comp., *Report: Wind River Reservation,* 77.

36. Quoted in Fowler, *Arapahoe Politics,* 66.

37. Patten to Ezra Hayt, February 21, 1878, LR-956.

38. Ibid.

39. Irwin to Patten, December 6, 1877, enclosed with LR-956.

40. Lieutenant H. R. Lemly to Adjutant General, November 29, 1877, LR-955; Patten to Hayt, January 17, 1878, LR-956; and Fowler, *Arapahoe Politics*, 67.

41. Lemly to Adjutant General, November 29, 1877, LR-955; and Patten to Hayt, January 17, 1878, LR-956.

42. Patten to Hayt, January 17, 1878, LR-956.

43. Ibid.; Lemly to Adjutant General, November 29, 1877, LR-955. In the meantime, however, the annuities had finally reached Fort Fetterman. See Patten to Hayt, December 26, 1877, LR-956.

44. Patten to Hayt, January 17, 1878, LR-956.

45. Patten to Hayt, January 14, 1878, ibid.

46. Patten to Hayt, March 13, 18, 1878, ibid.; and March 18, 1878, Records of the Medical History of the Post at Fort Washakie, April 1873 to June 1887 (microfilm), James K. Moore Collection, AHC.

47. March 22, April 6, 1878, Medical History of Fort Washakie.

48. Patten to Hayt, April 8, 1878, LR-956.

49. Ibid.

50. Ibid.

51. Ibid.

52. Patten to Hayt, April 24, 1878, LR-956.

53. Patten to Hayt, July 24, 1878, ibid.; and July 22, September 4, 9, 1878, Medical History of Fort Washakie.

54. Patten to Hayt, July 24, 1878, LR-956.

55 Fowler, *Arapahoe Politics*, 7–10, 85.

## CHAPTER SEVEN: ADMINISTRATIONS OF JAMES IRVING PATTEN AND CHARLES HATTON, 1877–1882

1. Patten to J. Q. Smith, Commissioner of Indian Affairs, June 2, 1877, LR-955.

2. Sweetwater County 1875 Tax Rolls; and 1880 Wyoming Territorial Census.

3. *Big Horn County Rustler*, March 17, 1927; *Wyoming State Journal*, December 20, 1934; Pearl Oto B. Moses to Grace Raymond Hebard, October 4, 1926, in James I. Patten Biographical File, AHC; Parish Records, St. Matthew's Cathedral, Laramie, Wyo.; and 1870 Wyoming Territorial Census.

4. Prucha, *Great Father*, 1:526–27.

5. Henry E. Fritz, "The Board of Indian Commissioners and Ethnocentric Reform, 1878–1893," 59.

6. Patten to Captain J. Mix, June 12, 1877; Mix to Patten, June 13, 1877; and Patten to Smith, June 15, 1877, LR-955.

7. Patten to Smith, June 18, 20, 1877; Irwin to Smith, June 20, 1877; Patten to Captain Nash, June 22, 1877; Captain Nash to Commissioner of Indian Affairs, June 24, 1877; and Patten to Smith, July 5, 25, 1877; LR-955.

8. Charles Walker (John W. Anthony) to Patten, July 30, 1877; Patten to Walker, July 31, 1877; and Patten to Smith, July 31, 1877, LR-955.

9. Anthony to Secretary of the Interior, January 22, 1878, Interior Appointment Papers; and Anthony to Bishop Whipple, Episcopal Bishop of Minnesota; February 2, 1878, LR-956.

10. E. C. Watkins to Ezra A. Hayt, Commissioner of Indian Affairs, November 9, 1878, LR-956. Watkins was one of five special agents for the Indian Office who conducted regular investigations of agencies as a means of checking corruption.

11. Patten to Smith, October 11, 1877, LR-956.

12. See Irwin to Smith, September 1, 1876, ibid.

13. Patten to Smith, October 11, 1877, ibid.

14. Ibid.

15. Patten to Smith, July 5, 25, October 8, 11, 1877, ibid.

16. Lt. Gen. P. H. Sheridan to the Lieutenant General of the Army, June 2, 1877; and H. Crosby, Chief Clerk of the Secretary of War, to Secretary of the Interior, June 29, 1877; Secretary of War to Secretary of the Interior, October 30, 1877; and Patten to Smith, October 13, November 21, 1877, LR-956.

17. Spalding to Patten, March 14, 1878; Spalding to Hayt, March 14, 1878; Robert C. Rogers, Secretary of the Board of Indian Commissioners of the Episcopal Church, to Hayt, March 28, June 13, 1878; Spalding to Hayt, June 10, 1878, LR-956. Also, see Rogers to Commissioner of Indian Affairs, November 22, 1877; Rogers to Spalding, March 21, May 15, 1878; Rogers to Joseph W. Coombs, June 12, 19, 1878; Rogers to Patten, June 27, 1878, Episcopal Indian Commission, RG 44, Episcopal Archives; and Executive Committee Minutes, April 9, September 10, 1878, Episcopal Archives; and *Journal of the Fifth Convocation*, 22.

18. Spalding to Hayt, March 14, 1878, LR-956.

19. John W. Hoyt to Schurz, July 17, 1878; and Schurz to Commissioner of Indian Affairs, August 6, 1878, LR-956.

20. E. Ballou to William E. Leeds, Acting Commissioner of Indian Affairs, September 1, 1878; Ballou to Hayt, September 26, 1878, LR-956; Report of Bishop Spalding for 1879, Missionary Bishops' Annual Reports, MIC-60, Roll 3 (1873–1886), Episcopal Archives; and Ballou to E. M. Marble, Acting Commissioner of Indian Affairs, January 6, 1881, File 733-1881, LR-RG75.

21. Patten to Hayt, May 10, 1878, LR-956.

22. Patten to Hayt, May 8, 23, 1878, ibid.

23. Patten to Hayt, May 13, 1878; and Hoyt to Schurz, July 2, 1878, ibid.

24. Patten to Hayt, June 5, July 12, 1878, ibid.

25. *RCIA for 1878*, 151.

26. Ibid., 152; Patten to Hayt, May 8, June 12, 1878; and Schurz to Commissioner of Indian Affairs, March 30, 1878, LR-956; *Interior Department Appropriation Act, Statutes at Large*, 1877, 285–86, 293; and *Interior Department Appropriation Act, Statutes at Large*, 1878, 79, 85.

27. Patten to Hayt, April 1, 1878, LR-956.

28. Patten to Hayt, May 8, June 12, July 1, 12, 1878, ibid.

29. Ibid.

30. Patten to Hayt, February 12, 1878, LR-956.

31. Patten to Hayt, (two letters on 17th), December 10, 17, 1878; and Moore to Patten, December 14, 1878, ibid.

32. *RCIA for 1878*, 154.

33. Hoyt to Schurz, July 17, 1878, LR-956.

34. Ibid.

35. Ibid.; and Patten to Hayt, February 28, 1878, LR-956. *RCIA for 1878*, 153.

36. Patten to Hayt, May 15, 1878; and Captain E. M. Hayes, Camp Brown, to Adjutant General, June 23, 1878, LR-956.

37. E. C. Watkins to Hayt, November 9, 1878, ibid.

38. Ibid.

39. Ibid.

40. Patten to Hayt, July 11, 1879, LR-957; and *Eleventh Annual Report of the Board of Indian Commissioners*, 61–64.

41. J. Van A. Carter to Schurz, May 8, 1879, LR-957.

42. Patten to Hayt, May 6, 1878, ibid.

43. Patten to Hayt, June 24; July 7, 8, 30; September 9, 17; November 25, 1879, ibid.; and *Eleventh Annual Report*, 61–64.

44. Fowler, *Arapahoe Politics*, 85.

45. Patten to Hayt, September 17, 1879, LR-957; and *Eleventh Annual Report*, 61–64.

46. Seth F. Cole to Senator Alvin Saunders, February 10, 1879. Moore's dismissal as trader apparently resulted from Arapahoe complaints about being cheated and from Anthony's accusations that Moore sold whiskey to Indians. Cole, however, never opened a store and rumors flew about his own trustworthiness. Thus, while Moore's license was suspended, he still continued his business. The license was restored by 1880. For a sample of the voluminous correspondence on Moore's licensing disputes, see Moore to Joseph M. Carey, December 12; Moore to Hoyt, December 12; Patten to Moore, December 12; Carey to Schurz, December 20; Hoyt to Hayt, December 20; Saunders to Hayt, December 23, 1878, LR-956; Patten to Hayt, February 5; and Moore to Hayt, February 6, 1879, LR-957.

47. Spalding to the Right Reverend Henry Hobart Hare, Bishop of Niobrara, April 2, 1879, Letters received by the Episcopal Indian Commission, Episcopal Archives [hereafter LR—Episcopal Indian Commission].

48. Ballou to Hayt, May 5, 1879, LR-957.

49. Spalding to Doctor [Rogers?], April 8, 1879, LR-Episcopal Indian Commission, RG 51, Episcopal Archives.

50. Hayt to Twing, April 8, 1879, ibid.

51. Twing to Hayt, April 12, 1879, Correspondence of the Secretary-General Agent of the Domestic Committee, Domestic and Foreign Missionary Society of the Protestant Episcopal Church, RG 44, Box 6, Episcopal Archives (hereafter Sec-Gen Agent Correspondence).

52. See Sec-Gen Agent Correspondence and LR—Episcopal Indian Commission.

53. John McNeil to Hayt, October 29, 1879, LR-957.

54. Ella Young to Spalding, October 26, 1879, in A. T. Twing to Hayt, November 17, 1879, Sec-Gen Agent Correspondence.

55. Hayt to Twing, November 18, 1879, LR—Episcopal Indian Commission, RG 51, Box 31 of Episcopal Archives.

56. Twing to Charles Hatton, October 24, 1879, Sec-Gen Agent Correspondence; Hatton to Hayt, December 20, 29, 1879, LR-957; and Hatton to Hayt, February 5, 1880, LR-958.

57. The Reverend William Wirt Raymond, rector of St. Peter's Church, Hillsdale, Michigan, to Twing, April 10, 1879, LR—Episcopal Indian Commission.

58. Patten to McNeil, November 28, 1879, Inspection Reports.

59. Patten to Hayt, July 3, August 4, 1879; and A. Bell, acting CIA, to Hayt, September 1, 1879, LR-957.

60. See Edward T. Gibson to Dr. Kellogg, Supervising Surgeon of the U.S. Indian Service, March 8, 1880; and Hatton to R. E. Trowbridge, CIA, April 3, 1880, LR-958.

61. Spalding to President Hayes, April 2, 1880, LR-958. This letter also refers to the problems caused by "the notorious evil influences proceeding from the late agent's wife and members of her family."

62. Patten to Hayt, July 29, 31; September 9, 17, 21; October 7, 9, 18, 23; November 18, 25; December 6, 16, 22, 29, 1879, LR-957.

63. Patten to Hayt, September 17, 1879, LR-957; and Hatton to R. E. Trowbridge, CIA, March 9, 1880, LR-958.

64. Hatton to Trowbridge, March 11, 1880, LR-958.

65. *RCIA for 1880*, 177, 272.

66. Hatton to E. M. Marble, acting CIA, November 2, 15, 22, 1880; Luke White, acting agent at Wind River, to Marble, November 7, 1880, LR-958; and Hatton to Marble, January 15, 1881, File 1337-1881, LR-RG75.

67. Ballou to C. M. Carter, of Washington, D.C., January 9, 1881, File 1277-1881, LR-RG75.

68. Hatton to Marble, January 15, 1881, File 1337-1881, LR-RG75.

69. N. W. Wells to Trowbridge, January 8, 1881, File 565-1881, LR-RG75.

70. Hatton to CIA, September 2, October 14, November 15, 1880, Hatton to Marble, December 21, 1880, LR-958; Hatton to CIA, February 7, 1881, File 2887-1881; and March 28, 1881, File 5728-1881, LR-RG75.Hatton to Hiram Price, CIA, May 16, 1881, File 8697-1881; May 31, 1881, File 9704-1881; and June 30, 1881, File 12085-1881, LR-RG75.

71. Louis Ballou's Deposition before Isaac R. Alden, U.S. Commissioner for the Judicial District of Montana, Lewis and Clark County, November 11, 1881; and L. Ballou to Price, November 20, 1881, both in File 20884-1881, LR-RG75; and Ellis Ballou to CIA, March 16, 1881, File 4786-1881, LR-RG75.

72. Hatton to CIA, February 7, 1881, File 2887-1881; E. Ballou, L. C. Bliss, Peter Walls, and Nelson Yarnall to CIA, February 21, 1881, File 5008-1881; Ballou to CIA,

February 28, 1881, File 4310-1881; and W. J. Henderson, discharged agency employee, to CIA, December 31, 1881, File 619-1882, LR-RG75.

73. Hatton to Trowbridge, July 26; September 7, 1880, LR-958.

74. Ballou to Marble, October 2, 1880; and Hatton to Trowbridge, September 7, 1880, LR-958.

75. Ballou to Marble, January 6, 1881, File 733-1881, LR-RG75; and Ballou to Captain R. H. Pratt, Carlisle Indian School, Pennsylvania, November 23, 1880, LR-958.

76. Ballou to C. M. Carter, January 9, 1881, File 1277-1881, LR-RG75.

77. Hatton to Marble, January 29, 1881, File 2379-1881, and January 31, 1881, File 2551-1881, LR-RG75.

78. McNeil to Schurz, February 5, 1881, File 3051-1881, February 16, 1881, File 3728-1881, LR-RG75.

79. Hatton to CIA, February 28, 1881, File 4310-1881, LR-RG75.

80. Ballou to CIA, April 27, 1881, Interior Appointment Papers.

81. Ibid.

82. Ibid.

83. Ibid.

84. Hatton to Thomas M. Nichols, CIA, March 31, 1881, File 5909-1881; and Hatton to Price, May 31, 1881, File 9704-1881, LR-RG75.

85. James K. Moore Papers, WSA; Hatton to Price, February 7, 1881, File 2885-1881; Hatton to Price, May 31, 1881, File 9704-1881; Hatton to Price, November 14, 1881, File 20525-1881; and Shoshone and Arapahoe Council to Secretary of Interior, June 2, 1882, File 17196-1882, LR-RG75.

86. Hatton to Marble, December 21, 1880, LR-958; and John McNeil to Schurz, February 16, 1881, File 3728-1881; and Hatton to CIA, February 21, 1881, File 3843-1881, LR-RG75.

87. Hatton to CIA, February 28, 1881, File 4310-1881, LR-RG75.

88. Hatton to Price, August 29, 1881, File 15624-1881; W. J. Henderson to CIA, December 31, 1881, File 619-1882, LR-RG75; and W.J. Pollock, Indian Inspector, Examination of Charles Hatton, February 13, 1882, Inspection Reports.

89. Pollock, Examination of Charles Hatton, February 13, 1882, Inspection Reports.

90. Henderson, Affidavit taken by Justice of the Peace George T. Stringfellow, Sweetwater County, Wyo., February 3, 1882, File 3112-1882; H. E. Mallory and H. C. Mallory to Samuel J. Kirkwood, Secretary of Interior, n.d., File 5451-1882, LR-RG75; and Pollock, Examination of Charles Hatton, February 13, 1882, Inspection Reports.

91. Pollack, Inspection Reports.

CHAPTER EIGHT: ADMINISTRATIONS OF JAMES IRWIN
AND SANDERSON R. MARTIN 1882–1885

1. 1880 Wyoming Census (Agricultural Schedule).

2. Hatton to Price, March 15, 1882, File 5595-1882, LR-RG75.

3. Irwin to Price, June 13, 1882, File 11122-1882, LR-RG75.

4. E. T. Gibson to CIA, July 15, 1882, File 13140-1882, ibid.

5. Irwin to Price, June 21, 1882, File 11716-1882, ibid.

6. Irwin to Price, July 10, 1882, File 12820-1882, ibid.

7. Ibid.

8. Ibid.

9. Shoshones and Arapahoe Council to Secretary of the Interior, June 2, 1882, File 17196-1882, LR-RG75.

10. Irwin to CIA, August 12, 1882, File 15325-1882, ibid.

11. Irwin to CIA, December 7, 1882, File 22478-1882, ibid. See Irwin to CIA, November 10, 1882, File 21133-1882, ibid.

12. Irwin to CIA, December 11, 1882, File 22420-1882; and December 13, 1882, File 22929-1882, ibid.

13. Irwin to Price, January 5, 1883, File 811-1883, ibid.

14. Irwin to CIA, January 27, 1883, File 2691-1883, ibid.

15. Irwin to CIA, March 6, 1883, File 5119-1883, ibid.

16. Ibid.; and Samuel S. Benedict to H. M. Teller, Secretary of the Interior, October 24, 1883, Inspection Reports.

17. Irwin to CIA, 5 March 1883, File 4948-1883, April 10, 1883, File 7171-1883, June 16, 1883, File 11361-1883; J. M. Haworth to Price, March 24, 1883, File 5791-1883; and E. W Hancock to Irwin, June 7, 1883, File 11361-1883, LR-RG75.

18. Hancock to Irwin, June 7, 1883, File 11361-1883, ibid.

19. Sanderson M. Martin to CIA, March 19, 1884, File 6060-1884, LR-RG75.

20. Martin to CIA, April 9, 1884, File 7564-1884; and May 20, 1884, File 10334-1884, LR-RG75.

21. Irwin to CIA, March 6, 1883, File 5119-1883, ibid.; Fowler, *Arapahoe Politics,* 74; R. H. Pratt, Superintendent of Carlisle School, to CIA, February 10, 1883, File 2707-1883, LR-RG75; and Dr. O. G. Given to Pratt, February 10, 1883, File 2707-1883, LR-RG75.

22. Irwin to CIA, March 6, 1883, File 5119-1883, LR-RG75.

23. Irwin to Price, September 1, 1882, File 16378-1882, ibid.

24. Irwin to CIA, March 9, 1883, File 5198-1883, ibid.

25. Irwin to CIA, July 16, 1883, File 13384-1883, ibid.

26. Benedict to Teller, October 24, 1883, Inspection Reports.

27. Irwin to CIA, March 15, 1883, File 5878-1883, LR-RG75.

28. *RCIA for 1882,* 364–65; and *RCIA for 1883,* 282–83.

29. Changes in Employees, Shoshone and Bannock Agency, October 10, 1882, File 19348-1882; and Irwin to CIA, November 10, 1882, File 21133-1882, LR-RG75; *RCIA for 1882,* 364; and *RCIA for 1883,* 300–1, 313.

30. Irwin to CIA, May 26, 1883, File 9946-1883, LR-RG75.

31. Early reservation-era tribal council meetings often debated the rations versus clothing topic. See Irwin to CIA, March 26, 1883, File 6164-1883, ibid.

32. Irwin to CIA, March 6, 1883, File 4948-1883; and April 26, 1883, File 8030-1883, ibid.

33. Irwin to M. E. Post, Wyoming member of U.S. House, November 21, 1883, File 21841-1883, ibid.

34. David, *Finn Burnett*, 279; Irwin to Clum, February 26, 1873, October 1, 1873; and Baker to Smith, June 28, 1873, LR-954.

35. Irwin to CIA, July 29, 1883, File 14384-1883, LR-RG75. Hatton gave contradictory evidence. His written report stated a total population of 1963 in 1880, but the statistical report recorded 2063. See *RCIA for 1880*, 176, 254. For 1881 he reported 2048 (but the statistical abstract still listed 2063). See *RCIA for 1881*, 183, 288.

36. Irwin to CIA, July 29, 1883, File 14384-1883, LR-RG75.

37. Ibid.

38. Shoshone and Arapahoe Petition, August 3, 1883, File 14983-1883, ibid.

39. *Cheyenne Daily Leader*, September 7, 1883.

40. N. M. Davis to M. E. Post, February 14, 1883, File 4069-1883, LR-RG75.

41. Irwin to CIA, April 17, 1883, File 7704-1883, ibid.

42. Irwin to CIA, September 22, 1883, File 18116-1883, ibid.

43. Irwin suggested the name change in August, noting that the Shoshone and Bannock Agency supervised no Bannocks (since 1872 located at Fort Hall in Idaho) and that the agency post office and two-thirds of the official correspondence already reflected the Shoshone Agency title. Irwin to CIA, August 3, 1883, File 14474-1883, LR-RG75.

44. Benedict to Teller, October 24, 1883, Inspection Reports.

45. Ibid.

46. Ibid.

47. Utley, *The Indian Frontier*, 186, 232, 237

48. Benedict to Teller, October 24, 1883, Inspection Reports.

49. Ibid.

50. Ibid.

51. James Winton Eaton, "The Wyoming Stock Growers Association," 165–81.

52. Irwin to CIA, September 6, 1883, File 16876-1883; and George F. Newman (cattle contractor) to CIA, September 21, 1883, File 17517-1883, LR-RG75.

53. See Benedict to Teller, October 24, 1883, Inspection Reports; and Irwin to CIA, October 17, 1883, File 19566-1883, LR-RG75. Mathias and Julia's son, James McAdams, was one of the first Shoshone children to attend Carlisle school. James was in Pennsylvania when his father died. For the McAdams genealogy, see Johnson, "The Enos Family," 329.

54. Benedict to Teller, October 24, 1883, Inspection Reports.

55. Ibid.

56. Irwin to CIA, November 19, 1883, File 21924 and 21925-1883, LR-RG75.

57. Sanderson R. Martin to CIA, February 22, 1884, File 4115-1884, September 14, 1885, File 22092-1885; October 6, 1885, File 27072-1885; and Galen Eastman, Agent at Navajo Agency, to CIA, May 18, 1882, File 8724-1882, LR-RG75

58. Quote from Martin to CIA, February 22, 1884, File 41151884, ibid. See also Martin to CIA, February 24, 1884, File 3833-1884, ibid.

59. Martin to CIA, March 14, 1884, File 5796-1884, ibid. Correspondence concerning food supplies can be found in Martin to CIA, February 27, 1884, File 4529-1884; March 7, 1884, File 5260-1884; March 9, 1884, File 4679-1884; March 10, 1884, File 5430-1884; and March 14, 1894, File 5795-1884, all in LR-RG75.

60. T. A. Larson, *Wyoming: A History,* 120.

61. Martin to CIA, March 29, 1884, File 6544-1884, LR-RG75.

62. 1884 Round-up Schedule, Wyoming Stock Growers Collection, AHC.

63. Martin to CIA, April 11, 1884, File 7718-1884, LR-RG75.

64. Martin to CIA, April 15, 1884, File 7882-1884, ibid.

65. File 7882-1884; Martin to CIA, April 5, 1884, File 7812-1884; May 2, 1884, File 8982-1884; and May 7, 1884, File 8751-1884, ibid.

66. Cyrus Beede to Price, April 19, 1884, File 8250-1884, ibid.

67. Ibid.

68. Martin to CIA, May 2, 1884, File 8982-1884, LR-RG75. The *Green River Gazette* is mentioned in J. D. Taylor to Assistant Adjutant General, Division of the Missouri, May 10, 1884, File 9801-1884, ibid.

69. Lieutenant G. W. Read to Assistant Adjutant, Department of the Platte, May 9, 1884, File 9801-1884; and Read to Post Adjutant of Ft. Washakie, May 20, 1884, File 11891-1884, ibid.

70. William Hale to Teller, June 25, 1884, File 12295-1884, ibid.

71. Lowe to CIA, June 27, 1884, File 12420-1884, ibid. Sheriff Lowe, of course, had a long history of trying to influence agency affairs.

72. Martin to CIA, July 29, 1884, File 14675-1884, ibid.

73. Martin to CIA, June 27, 1884, File 12456-1884; and July 12, 1884, File 13655-1884, ibid.

74. Martin to CIA, July 12, 1884, File 13655-1884, ibid.

75. Martin to CIA, July 22, 1884, File 14304-1884, ibid.

76. *RCIA for 1884,* 184.

77. Martin to CIA, May 20, 1884, File 10334-1884, LR-RG75.

78. Ibid.; and *RCIA for 1884,* 185, 280.

79. Martin to CIA, August 15, 1884, File 15786-1884, LR-RG75.

80. Ibid.; Martin to CIA, September 4, 1884, File 17301-1884; October 29, 1884, File 21218-1884; November 26, 1884, File 23149-1884; and December 11, 1884, File 24127, all in LR-RG75.

81. Robert A. Gardiner, Inspector, to Secretary of the Interior, December 11, 1884, Roll 48, Inspection Reports.

82. Ibid. Shoshone harvests averaged four bushels of wheat, three bushels of oats, and two and one-half bushels of potatoes per farmer. Arapahoe production was not listed.

83. Ibid.

84. Martin to CIA, December 16, 1884, File 24953-1884, LR-RG75.

85. Gardiner to Secretary of Interior, December 11, 1884, Inspection Reports; "First Annual Report of the Missionary Juridiction of Wyoming Territory," *Spirit of Missions* 49: 587; and Martin to CIA, January 20, 1885, File 1851-1885, LR-RG75.

86. Martin to CIA, January 5, 1885, File 774-1885; and January 31, 1885, File 2697-1885, LR-RG75.

87. Martin to CIA, March 23, 1885, File 6448-1885, ibid.

88. Martin to CIA, May 20, 1885, File 11848-1885, ibid.

89. Ibid.

90. Ibid.

91. Ibid.

92. Martin to CIA, July 17, 1885, File 17169-1885, LR-RG75.

93. Martin to CIA, June 4, 1885, File 12947-1885, ibid.

94. Martin to CIA, July 17, 1885, File 17169-1885, ibid.

95. Martin to CIA, June 9, 1885, File 13416-1885, ibid.

96. Martin to CIA, August 19, 1885, ibid.

97. Gardiner to Secretary of the Interior, December 11, 1884, Inspection Reports.

98. Martin to CIA, August 19, 1885, File 19800-1885, LR-RG75.

99. E. D. Bannister to Secretary of the Interior, August 17, 1885, Roll 48, Inspection Reports.

100. Ibid.

101. Ibid.

102. Ibid.

103. Ibid.

104. Grover Cleveland to Martin, September 9, 1885; W. M. Lockwood, Chief Clerk of Interior Department, to CIA, September 10, 1885, File 20994-1885, LR-RG75; and Martin to CIA, September 14, 1885, File 22092-1885, ibid.

105. *RCIA for 1885*, 368, 392.

106. Ibid.


CHAPTER NINE: WIND RIVER WHITE SETTLERS, 1878–1885

1. Huseas, *Sweetwater Gold*, 15, 160–61; 1870 U.S. Census, Sweetwater County.

2. Huseas, *Sweetwater Gold*, 160; Claude F. King, "A Narrative from Shoshone Agency," 31; and 1880 U.S. Census, Sweetwater County.

3. Irwin to Smith, February 15, 1875, LR-955.

4. 1875 Sweetwater County Tax Roll.

5. Irwin to Smith, February 15, 1875, LR-955; and "The Genesis of a Town," 7–8.

6. Camp Brown relocated from the Middle Fork of the Popo Agie in the spring and early summer of 1871 to the Little Wind River.

7. "The Genesis of a Town," 9; and "Pioneer Profiles: The Amoretti Family," 2.

8. 1880 Census, Sweetwater County.

9. Ibid.

10. *RCIA for 1880*, 176.

11. W. S. Stanton, Captain of Engineers, to Assistant Adjutant General, Department of the Platte, November 22, 1880, File 3842, Special Case File 44 (hereafter SCF 44).

12. Hatton to CIA, February 21, 1881, SCF 44.

13. John Fosher to CIA, February 24, 1890, File 6485-1890; Herman G. Nickerson, agent, to CIA, December 19, 1898, File 58119-1898; and Fosher to CIA, Oct 14, 1890, File 32572-1887, all in LR-RG75

14. Hatton to CIA, February 21, 1881, File 3842, SCF 44.

15. Hatton to CIA, February 21, 1881, File 3842, SCF 44.

16. Francis Paul Prucha, *Great Father*, abridged ed., 226.

17. Jones to CIA, April 5, 1887, File 9444-1887, LR-RG75.

18. *RCIA for 1887*, 801.

19. Ibid.

20. Fosher to CIA, Oct 14, 1890, File 32572-1890, LR-RG75.

21. Major E. R. Kellogg explained to Fosher that the guard was posted to keep "improper white persons from camping in the vicinity, especially 'fancy women.'" The guard had no authority to turn away Indians. Also, the military had surveyed a triangle of land that included the springs; Fosher assumed the Indians believed this meant the military appropriated the area. See Fosher to CIA, January 7, 1891, File 1620-1891, LR-RG75. As for assuming too much authority, the post commanders continually let bids for wood or coal, giving permission to their vendors to use reservation resources, but without gaining prior approval from Indians or their agent to do so. See Patrick H. Ray, agent, to CIA, May 17, 1894, File 22260-1894, LR-RG75.

22. Extrapolated from the 1875 Sweetwater County Tax Assessment Roll. There were 159 persons from the Big Popo Agie and Little Wind River Valleys listed on the tax rolls.

23. 1875 Sweetwater County Tax Roll; David M. Delo, "Settlers Come to the Valley," 13–15; Tom Bell, "Edmore LeClair, From Indian Scout to Solid Citizen," 4–7; Sheila Hart, "Edmore LeClaire, Son of a Mountain Man," 8–11; Jean Mathisen, "Tracks and Traces," 19; and Johnson, "Enos Family," 93.

24. "Pioneer Profiles: The Lamoreaux Family," 2.

25. Irwin to Smith, July 26, 1875, LR-957; Johnson, "Enos Family," 91, 177–78; Delo "Settlers Come to the Valley," 15; and 1875 Sweetwater County Tax Roll.

26. 1875 Sweetwater County Tax Roll; and Patten to Hayt, February 12, 1878, LR-956.

27. No assessment rolls are still extant for either Sweetwater County or Fremont County from 1876 to 1890, so attempts to measure a "reservation effect" on the local white community for that period are difficult.

28. 1880 Census, Sweetwater County; and *RCIA for 1880*, 176.

29. John K. Rollinson, *Wyoming Cattle Trails*, 156–57.

30. Ibid., 157–58, 190–95; and T. A. Larson, *History of Wyoming*, 2d ed., 166–67. For a thorough list of cattlemen in the Basin, see Lawrence M. Wood, *Wyoming's Big Horn Basin*, chaps. 6–8.

31. Ibid., 167.

32. Alan Trachtenberg, *The Incorporation of America*, chap. 1.

33. 1884 Treasurer's Tax Receipt Book, Fremont County. Taxable property included stock, real estate, and some personal items such as vehicles. Unfortunately, since no tax assessment rolls from Fremont County have survived for the years 1884–1890, the exact proportions of taxable property cannot be determined.

34. Rollinson, *Wyoming Cattle Trails,* 195.

35. Larson, *History of Wyoming,* 159, 167. Approximation of cattle populations are extrapolated from the 1884 Tax Receipt Book, Fremont County (based on $17 per head evaluation—the mean assessment for all of Wyoming in 1885).

36. Hatton to Marble, December 31, 1881, File 679-1881, LR-RG75.

37. C. E. Wilson to J. H. Pratt, January 2, 1882, File 1042-1882, ibid.

38. See J. H. Pratt to M. E. Post, January 10, 11, 1882; Pratt to Lt. Gen. P. H. Sheridan, January 11, 1882; Sheridan to Adjutant General of the Army, January 12, 1882; and Post to Price, January 18, 1882, all in File 1042-1882, LR-RG75.

39. Larson, *Wyoming: A History* (1984), 117–18.

40. Pratt to Post, January 10, 1882, File 1042-1882, LR-RG75.

41. Irwin to CIA, July 17, 1882, File 13364-1882, LR-RG75.

42. *RCIA for 1882,* 499.

43. N. M. Davis to Post, February 14, 1883; Post to Price, February 28, 1883, File 4069-1883, LR-RG75.

44. Irwin to CIA, April 17, 1883, File 7704-1883, LR-RG75.

45. Irwin to CIA, July 29, 1883, File 14384-1883, ibid.

46. "Indians and Stockmen," *Cheyenne Daily Leader,* September 7, 1883.

47. Irwin to CIA, September 22, 1883, File 18116-1883, LR-RG75.

48. Ibid.

49. William Sturgis to William Hale, October 29, 1883, File 20708-1883, LR-RG75.

50. Ibid.

51. Irwin to CIA, November 22, 1883, File 21841-1883, LR-RG75.

52. Irwin to Post, November 21, 1883, ibid.

53. Martin to CIA, April 11, 1884, File 7718-1884, LR-RG75.

54. Martin to CIA, May 29, 1884, File 10709-1884, ibid.

55. Martin to CIA, April 11, 1884, File 7718-1884 ibid.

56. Petition enclosed in Hale to Teller, June 25, 1884, File 12295-1884, ibid.

57. 1884 Freemont Tax Book.

58. Lowe to CIA, June 27, 1884, File 12420-1884, LR-RG75.

59. Ibid.

60. Martin to CIA, July 29, 1884, File 14675-1884, LR-RG75.

61. Lowe to CIA, June 27, 1884, File 12420-1884, ibid. It is doubtful Indian freighters were on their way to Rawlins this early. They normally hauled the annuities in the fall because of the time lag between appropriations, bids, and transportation of the supplies to the railhead depots.

62. Martin to CIA, July 29, 1884, File 14675-1884, LR-RG75.

63. R. B. Connor to Sturgis, July 13, 1884, Wyoming Stock Growers Collection, AHC.

64. Martin to CIA, July 29, 1884, File 14675-1884, LR-RG75.

65. See P. H. Ray to CIA, May 31, 1894, File 21673-1894, LR-RG75.

66. Martin to CIA, December 16, 1884, File 24953-1884, ibid.

67. Martin to CIA, December 15, 1884, File 24592-1884, ibid

68. 1890 U.S. Census, Report on the Statistics of Agriculture.

69. Ibid.

70. Fosher to CIA, Nov 19, 1889, File 33905-1889; P. H. Ray to CIA, Dec 16, 1893, File 47294-1893; and Ray to CIA, May 29, 1894, File 21119-1894, all in LR-RG75.


CHAPTER TEN: CHRISTIAN MISSIONS AT WIND RIVER, 1880–1885

1. "Neikok, the Shoshone Interpreter," 562.

2. Hultkrantz, *Belief and Worship*, 214–15.

3. Judith Vander, *Shoshone Ghost Dance Religion*, 5–8.

4. Jorgensen derived his information from M. J. Sheldon, a Uintah reservation employee. The Uintah Agency lay in the northeastern mountainous region of Utah. See Joseph G. Jorgensen, *The Sun Dance Religion*, 39. See also Hultkrantz, *Belief and Worship*, 265–66. Hultkrantz believes the 1870 Ghost Dance ceremonies were linked strongly to an older Basin tradition called the Prophet Dance, 269–71.

5. Jorgensen, *Sun Dance Religion*, 6.

6. Ibid.

7. *RCIA for 1875*, 376.

8. *RCIA for 1879*, 168.

9. Jorgensen, *The Sun Dance Religion*, 77. Patten wrote at least three letters in 1878 describing Ute visits to Wind River to trade horses for buffalo robes. See Patten to Hayt, May 10, 13,23, 1878, LR-956. See also *RCIA for 1878*, 150.

10. *RCIA for 1880*, 177; and Geneva Ensign Wright, "Wind River Mission," 28.

11. *RCIA for 1880*, 177.

12. Bennington refers to present-day Bloomington, a small town just north of Bear Lake.

13. Amos R. Wright to John Taylor, President of the Church of Jesus Christ of Latter Day Saints, November 18, 1880, quoted in Wright, "Wind River Mission," 29–30.

14. Ibid., 32–33.

15. Ibid., 34.

16. *RCIA for 1886*, 261.

17. James O'Conner, September 3, 1882, File 17163-1882, Special Case File 143 (hereafter SCF 143).

18. D. W. Moriarty to Price, September 12, 1882, SCF 143.

19. "Ninth Annual Report," *Spirit of Missions* 47: 447.

20. Elinor R. Markley and Beatrice Crofts, with Sharon Kahin, ed., "Walk Softly, This is God's Country," 6 (hereafter Markley-Crofts). Markley was Roberts's daughter; Crofts is his granddaughter.

21. Roberts to Spalding, February 14, 1883, reprinted in "Our Missionary to the Shoshones," *Spirit of Missions* 48: 172. Markley-Crofts incorrectly gives the date as February 10, 1883. See Markley-Crofts, 9. This storm began on January 30, 1883. The physician at Ft. Washakie recorded temperatures ranging from –25° to four straight days of –53°, –56°, –57°, and –56°, followed by two more days of –42° and –35°. See A. F. C. Greene, transcript of "Medical History of Camp Brown, vol. 2, April 4, 1873 to June 30, 1887, p. 27, in William L. Marion Biographical File, AHC. On the way to the agency, Roberts officiated the burial service for a stage driver who lost his life during the early days of the storm. The normal travel time by stage from Green River to Wind River took thirty-six hours. See Markley-Crofts, 9–10.

22. Roberts to Spalding, March 1, 1883, "Our Missionary to the Shoshones": 173.

23. Irwin to CIA, March 5, 1883, File 4948-1883, LR-RG75; March 6, 1883, File 5119-1883, LR-RG75; and Irwin to CIA, March 9, 1883, File 5414-1883, SCF 143.

24. Spalding to Teller, March 12, 1883, File 5817-1883, SCF 143.

25. Irwin to CIA, April 11, 1883, File 7206-1883, SCF 143; and April 13, 1883, File 8644-1883, SCF 143.

26. O'Conner to Teller, June 6, 1883, File 11098-1883, LR-RG75.

27. Ibid.

28. Martin to CIA, April 24, 1885, File 9564-1885, LR-RG75; Roberts to CIA, August 2, 1893, File 29558-1893, LR-RG75; and Markley-Crofts, 35.

29. *Journal of the Primary Convocation in the Missionary Jurisdiction of Wyoming*, 11.

30. Ibid.

31. Spalding to Teller, May 24, 1884, File 22621-1884, SCF 143.

32. Ibid.

33. "Report from John Roberts," *Spirit of Missions* 49: 125; and Beede to Price, April 19, 1884, File 8250-1884, LR-RG75.

34. Sanderson R. Martin to CIA, May 20, 1884, File 10334-1884, LR-RG75; "First Annual Report of the Missionary Jurisdiction of Wyoming Territory," *Spirit of Missions* 49: 586–87; Mrs. Baird C. Cooper, *The Wind River Reservation, Wyoming*, 8; Beede to Price, April 19, 1884, File 8250-1884, LR-RG75; and *Journal of the Primary Convocation of Wyoming*, 12.

35. Markley-Crofts, 71–72; Fowler, *Arapahoe Politics*, 184–85, 335 n. 13; Grace Coolidge, with intro. by George L. Cornell, *Teepee Neighbors;* and "Report from John Roberts," *Spirit of Missions* 50: 363.

36. Roberts," *Spirit of Missions* 50: 363; and Markley-Crofts, 54.

37. "Roberts," *Spirit of Missions* 50: 363; quote from "First Annual Report of the Missionary Jurisdiction of Wyoming Territory," *Spirit of Missions* 49: 586.

38. Gardiner to Secretary of Interior, December 11, 1884, Inspection Reports; and Fowler, *Arapahoe Politics*, 74.

39. Letter from John Roberts, August 13, 1885, reprinted in *Spirit of Missions* 50: 531; and Charles H. Dickson, special agent to John D. C. Atkins, CIA, February 15, 1886, File 3650-1886, LR-RG75.

40. Martin to CIA, March 6, 1885, File 5263-1885, LR-RG75.

41. Dickson to Atkins, February 15, 1886, File 3650-1886, LR-RG75.

42. School Statistics for Wind River Boarding School, Annual Report, n.d., File 23236-1886, ibid.

43. "Report from Sherman Coolidge," *Spirit of Missions* 50: 425.

44. Ibid.; "Report from John Roberts," *Spirit of Missions* 50: 467; *RCIA for 1885*, 213; and *RCIA for 1886*, 261. In 1887, Coolidge was involved in a conspiracy to undermine St. Stephen's Mission. See the correspondence for 1887 in SCF 143.

45. Martin to CIA, January 20, 1885, File 1851-1885, LR-RG75; and Fowler, *Arapahoe Politics*, 82–84.

46. "Report from John Roberts," *Spirit of Missions* 50: 467; A. C. Jones to the Right Reverend Nathaniel S. Thomas, July 21, 1909, A. C. Jones File, Episcopal Church Collection, AHC; and Notes on the History of the Church, Episcopal Church Collection, AHC.

47. Thomas Jones, Shoshone agent, to CIA, March 31, 1886, File 10195-1886; and Roberts to CIA, August 26, 1890, File 271131890, both in LR-RG75.

48. The statistical summaries of the annual reports for 1883 through 1886 record school-aged population of 320, 407, 250, and 391 children, respectively. See *RCIA for 1883*, 256; *RCIA for 1884*, 280; *RCIA for 1885*, 354; and *RCIA for 1886*, 410. Average enrollments for the same period were 1883:13; 1884:16; 1885:71; and 1886:75.

49. Church of the Redeemer Parish Register, vol. 1.

50. "First Annual Report," *Spirit of Missions* 49: 586. See Redeemer Parish Register; and *Journal of the Primary Convocation*, 11.

51. Ibid.

52. Redeemer Parish Register. See also "Report from Sherman Coolidge," *Spirit of Missions* 61: 118.

53. See Redeemer Parish Register.

54. Letters from John Roberts, *Spirit of Missions* 49: 126, 281.

55. Redeemer Parish Records; and Trinity Parish Records, vol. 1.

56. Markley-Crofts, 52–53.

57. Ibid.

58. Thomas M. Jones, agent, to CIA, August 27, 1887, File 23334-1887, SCF 143; and Fowler, *Arapahoe Politics*, 86.

59. Fowler, *Arapahoe Politics*, 125–26.

CHAPTER ELEVEN: SHOSHONE AND
ARAPAHOE STRATEGIES, 1879–1885

1. *RCIA for 1879*, 168. See also Patten to Hayt, July 11, 1879, LR-957.

2. *RCIA for 1879*, 167.

3. Patten to Hayt, June 24, 1879, LR-957.

4. Brackett, "The Shoshonis," 332. Jorgensen believes this was the Ghost Dance movement. See Jorgensen, *Sun Dance Religion*, 77.

5. This conclusion is quite speculative; Patten recorded nothing about the council proceedings. However, Tawunasia led one of the Shoshone factions that consistently adhered to pre-reservation nomadic patterns. A Tendoy/Tawunasia combination certainly had the power to undermine Washakie's standing with both white and Shoshone communities.

6. See Hatton to Marble, November 2, 1880; White to Marble, November 7, 1880, LR-958; and Hatton to Marble, January 15, 1881, File 1337-1881, LR-RG75; Major J. W. Mason to Assistant Adjutant General of the Platte, January 16, 1881, File 2140-1881, LR-RG75.

7. Hatton to CIA, April 30, 1881, File 7754-1881, LR-RG75.

8. Ibid.

9. Martin to CIA, August 15, 1884, File 15786-1884, LR-RG75.

10. See Shimkin, "Recent Wind River Ethnography," 451; Johnson, "Enos Family," 87–96; and Fuller, *Wind River Report*, 115.

11. Washakie, Norkok, Oatah, Black Coal, Sharp Nose, and Washington to CIA, August 3, 1883, File 14983-1883, LR-RG75.

12. Martin to CIA, April 5, 1884, File 7812-1884, ibid. The ages are calculated from the 1891 Shoshone census. 1885 Indian Census Rolls (Shoshoni and Arapahoe Indians).

13. Martin to CIA, January 31, 1885, File 2697-1885, LR-RG75.

14. Jones to CIA, January 21, 1888, File 2561-1888, ibid.

15. Patten to Hayt, January 29, 1879, LR-957.

16. *RCIA for 1879*, 169; Ballou to Hayt, May 5, 1879, LR-957; and Ballou to Schurz, July 18, 1879, LR-957.

17. Ballou to Patten, December 13, 1879, LR-957. Quote from Patten to Hayt, December 16, 1879, LR-957.

18. No documents explicitly give Black Coal's thoughts about the proposed tour, but see Fowler's discussion of Arapahoe goals at this time. Fowler, *Arapahoe Politics*, 70, 73–74.

19. Ballou to Hayt, December 17, 1879, LR-958.

20. Hatton to Trowbridge, March 9, June 8, August 15, September 7, 1880; Ballou to Marble, October 2, 1880; Ballou to Pratt, November 23, 1880, all LR-958.

21. Ballou to Marble, November 25, 1880, LR-958.

22. Fowler, *Arapahoe Politics*, 74.

23. Sharp Nose to Price, June 8, 1881, File 10587-1881, LR-RG75.

24. Hatton to Price, November 24, 1881, File 20956-1881; December 23, 1881, File 22700-1881; December 30, 1881, File 340-1882; Hatton to Senator Thomas W. Ferry, November 24, 1881, File 21457-1881; R. H. Pratt to CIA, November 21, 1881, File 20437-1881, all LR-RG75.

25. Hatton to Price, January 26, 1882, File 2255-1882; and March 7, 1882, File 5081-1882, both LR-RG75.

26. John Roberts compiled the Wind River death list for all Shoshone and Arapahoe children who attended off-reservation schools between 1881 and 1894. See

Roberts to W. N. Hailman, Superintendent of Indian Schools, December 5, 1894, File 4057-1894, LR-RG75.

27. Irwin to CIA, May 9, 1882, File 10994-1882, LR-RG75; and Fowler, *Arapahoe Politics*, 85.

28. Irwin to CIA, November 22, 1883, File 21841-1883, LR-RG75.

29. Fowler, *Arapahoe Politics*, 69–86.

30. Ch[arles] W[hite] Horse to President Washington, August 12, 1884, File 16088-1884, LR-RG75.

31. Fowler interprets Charles White Horse's statement to mean the mixed-blood Shoshones. See Fowler, *Arapahoe Politics*, 73. Arapahoes and alcohol apparently mixed more freely during freighting or hunting trips, while Shoshones made their purchases without regard to location. See Benedict to Teller, November 19, 1883, File 21752-1883, LR-RG75; and Major Alfred M. Smith, commanding at Fort Washakie, to Assistant Adjutant General of the Platte, October 27, 1885, File 27072-1885, LR-RG75, for references to Shoshones and whiskey.

32. Martin to CIA, May 20, 1885, File 11654-1885, LR-RG75.

33. Martin to CIA, July 17, 1885, File 17169-1885, LR-RG75.

34. *RCIA for 1884*, 319; *RCIA for 1885*, 392; and *RCIA for 1886*, 448.

35. *RCIA for 1885*, 368.

36. See *RCIA for 1884*, 301; and *RCIA for 1885*, 369.


EPILOGUE: THE NADIR, 1885–1900


1. John Roberts to Ethelbert Talbot, December 11, 1896, File 12802-1897, LR-RG75.

2. *RCIA for 1895*, 335.

3. Fosher to CIA, August 24, 1892, in Agent's Annual Statistical Reports to Commissioner of Indian Affairs, DFC; J. F. Ludin to CIA, August 25, 1897, ibid.; *RCIA for 1884*, 301; *RCIA for 1890*, 465; *RCIA for 1892*, 801; and *RCIA for 1896*, 535.

4. *RCIA for 1874*, 105; *RCIA for 1875*, 121; *RCIA for 1876*, 223; *RCIA for 1877*, 305. *RCIA for 1878*, 296; and *RCIA for 1900*, 657.

5. See *RCIA for 1891*, vol. 2, 107.

6. Peter Moran, inspector, abstract from the special report of December 23, 1890, File 39786-1890, LR-RG75.

7. Ray to CIA, May 29, 1894, File 21119-1894, LR-RG75. Caloric content is derived from *Master Cook II*.

8. Fowler, *Arapahoe Politics*, 102.

9. Freight wages are extrapolated from *RCIA for 1885*, 368; *RCIA for 1890*, 479; *RCIA for 1891*, 107; and *RCIA for 1892*, 817. For other types of positions and pay scales, see *RCIA for 1892*, 1830; and Ray to CIA, May 31, 1894, File 21672-1894, LR-RG75.

10. Total official income for 1892 was $10,070 for 1719 people, while 1648 persons earned an official total of $31,696 in 1899. There are discrepancies in these

reports. For example, Agent Fosher's annual report suggests the tribes earned over $12,000 hauling freight in 1892, but he lists only $850 for the same task in the statistics section cited above. Even when Fosher's higher figures are used, tribal incomes in 1892 totaled only $21,495, or approximately $12.50 per capita. *RCIA for 1892*, 800, 817; *RCIA for 1899*, 580, 597; and *RCIA for 1892*, 521.

11. See, for example, *RCIA for 1892*, 831.

12. *RCIA for 1890*, 479; and *RCIA for 1900*, 677.

13. Agents had to give permission for intertribal visits by the Shoshones, Arapahoes, Sioux, Bannocks, and Utes, but generally did not note the specific details of trade or the values involved. For example, Black Coal and five Arapahoes visited Pine Ridge (Oglala Sioux) in 1892, while in 1893 Utes and Sioux came to Wind River. Fosher to CIA, March 23, 1892, File 11591-1892; Ray to CIA, August 20, 1893, File 31028-1893; and Captain Charles G. Penney, acting agent at Pine Ridge, to CIA, November 20, 1893, File 43756-1893, all in LR-RG75.

14. *RCIA for 1890*, 479; and *RCIA for 1900*, 677.

15. From 1890 to 1896, the Indian stock herd fluctuated from 500 to 600 cattle. There was one anomalous year in 1893 when over 2500 cattle were reported. The possibility of a 17 percent annual increase is based on the change from 1896 to 1900 (500 to 1000 cattle). See *RCIA for 1890*, 479; *RCIA for 1891*, vol. 2, 107; *RCIA for 1892*, 817; *RCIA for 1893*, 723; *RCIA for 1894*, 599; *RCIA for 1896*, 551; and *RCIA for 1900*, 677.

16. Prucha, *Great Father* (1986), 224–28.

17. The official record of the treaty negotiations is found in J. D. Woodruff to Thomas J. Morgan, CIA, 15, October 20, 1892, Irregularly Shaped Papers, LR-RG75.

18. Ibid.

19. Shoshone Commission and Council Proceedings, January 26, 1893 to February 14, 1893; and Shoshone Commission Report, February 22, 1893, File 10860-1893, SCF 147.

20. James McLaughlin, U.S. Indian Inspector, to Secretary of Interior, April 23, 1896, File 16453-1896, LR-RG75.

21. *U.S. Court of Claims Reports*, vol. 82, 23; and vol. 85, 331.

22. Fowler discusses the 1904 treaty council in detail. See Fowler, *Arapahoe Politics*, 93–96.

23. *RCIA for 1900*, 414. A reorganized allotment process began in earnest in 1904.

24. Mrs. Isabelle Kinnear to T. J. Morgan, December 25, 1890, File 60-1891, LR-RG75.

25. Ray to CIA, March 25, 1895, File 12219-1895; and John W. Clark, allotting agent, to CIA, April 1, 1895, File 14655-1895, both in LR-RG75.

26. William Lamoureaux to CIA, December 9, 1889, File 9665-1890, LR-RG75.

27. 1885 Shoshone Census; and 1891 Shoshone Census.

28. Johnson, "Enos Family," offers a good analysis of mixed-blood Shoshone influence on tribal culture, economy, and politics. See also Fowler, *Arapahoe Politics*, 144–47.

29. *RCIA for 1899*, 612.

30. Woodruff to Morgan, August 10, 1891, File 29818-1891, LR-RG75.

31. Statement of Arrival and Departures of Pupils at Wind River Boarding School, September 30, 1895, File 41003-1895, LR-RG75.

32. Shimkin, "Recent Wind River Shoshone History," 456; Jorgensen, *The Sun Dance Religion*, 83; and Hultkrantz, *Belief and Worship in Native North America*, 266–71.

33. Shimkin, "Recent Wind River Shoshone Ethnography," 457.

34. Fowler, *Arapahoe Politics*, 122.

35. Utley, *The Indian Frontier*, 255.

36. Shimkin, "Recent Wind River Shoshone Ethnography," 460. For a view on the persistence of Ghost Dance belief, see Vander, *Song-Prints*, 10–27.

37. Shimkin, "Recent Wind River Shoshone Ethnography," 457.

38. Fowler, *Arapahoe Politics*, 124–25.

39. Shimkin, "Recent Wind River Shoshone Ethnography," 457.

40. Fowler, *Arapahoe Politics*, 125.

41. Shimkin, "Recent Wind River Shoshone Ethnography," 460.

42. *RCIA for 1900*, 657; and Fowler, *Arapahoe Politics*, 125.

43. Ethelbert Talbot, "Old Chief Washakie," 29–30, unpub. ms, Francis Donaldson Collection, AHC.

44. Noll, *A History of Christianity*, 386.

45. Fowler, *Arapahoe Politics*, 118–20.

46. Shoshone Council to Secretary of the Interior, December 23, 1899, File 1492-1900, LR-RG75. This was Washakie's last council.

47. Shoshone Council to CIA, July 19, 1900, File 36291-1900, LR-RG75.

48. Fowler, *Arapahoe Politics*, 104; and Roberts to F. E. Leupp, CIA, February 6, 1907, John Roberts Collection, AHC.

49. Sharp Nose's death in 1901 stimulated a similar response on the part of the Arapahoes. See Fowler, *Arapahoe Politics*, 99–100, 291.

50. Lewis, *Neither Wolf nor Dog*, 170–75; White, *Roots of Dependency*, 309–11; and Meyers, *White Earth Tragedy*, chap. 5.

# Bibliography

MANUSCRIPTS AND ARCHIVES

American Church Missionary Society. Minutes of the Committee on Indian Agents, 1870–1871. Record Group 41. Archives of the Episcopal Church, Austin, Tex.

Burnett, Fincelius Gray. Collection. American Heritage Center. University of Wyoming. Laramie, Wyo.

Burt, Elizabeth Johnson Reynolds. Papers. Library of Congress. Washington, D.C.

Carter, Judge William Alexander. Collection. American Heritage Center. University of Wyoming. Laramie, Wyo.

Domestic and Foreign Missionary Society. Correspondence of the General Secretary and Treasurer, 1885–1919. Record Group 52. Archives of the Episcopal Church. Austin, Tex.

Domestic and Foreign Missionary Society. Correspondence of the Secretary-General Agent and Assistant Treasurer. Letter Press Books. Record Group 44. Archives of the Episcopal Church. Austin, Tex.

Domestic and Foreign Missionary Society. Correspondence of the Secretary-General Agent of the Domestic Committee. Letter Books and Letter Press Books (Letters Sent). Record Group 44. Archives of the Episcopal Church. Austin, Tex.

Domestic and Foreign Missionary Society. Domestic Committee. Minutes of the Indian Commission of the Protestant Episcopal Church, 1871–1877. Record Group 41. Archives of the Episcopal Church. Austin, Tex.

Domestic and Foreign Missionary Society. Letters Received by the Sub-Committee on Indians/Indian Commission. Record Group 51. Archives of the Episcopal Church. Austin, Tex.

Donaldson, Francis. Collection. American Heritage Center. University of Wyoming. Laramie, Wyo.

Episcopal Church. Collection. American Heritage Center. University of Wyoming. Laramie, Wyo.

Episcopal Church of the Redeemer. Parish Registers, vol. 1, 1883–1903. Fort Washakie, Wyo.

Hammond, Minnie Groscurth. Collection. American Heritage Center. University of Wyoming. Laramie, Wyo.

Hebard, Grace Raymond. Collection. American Heritage Center. University of Wyoming. Laramie, Wyo.

Horne, Mrs. Robert. Collection. American Heritage Center. University of Wyoming. Laramie, Wyo.

Indian Commission. Correspondence of the Secretary, 1874–1879. Letter Press Books. Record Group 44. Archives of the Episcopal Church. Austin, Tex.

Indian Commission. Executive Committee Minutes, November 1871–January 1879. Record Group 41. Archives of the Episcopal Church. Austin, Tex.

Missionary Bishops' Annual Reports. MIC–60. Rolls 2–5 (1873–1909). Archives of the Episcopal Church. Austin, Tex.

Moore, James K. Collection. American Heritage Center. University of Wyoming. Laramie, Wyo.

Moore, James K. Papers and Collections. Archives, Museums and Historical Department, Historical Research Publications Division. Cheyenne, Wyo.

Patten, James I. Papers and Collections. Archives, Museums and Historical Department, Historical Research Publications Division. Cheyenne, Wyo.

Roberts, John. Collection. American Heritage Center. University of Wyoming. Laramie, Wyo.

Trinity Episcopal Church. Parish Record, vol. 1, 1883–1905. Lander, Wyo.

Wales, Nellie L. Collection. American Heritage Center. University of Wyoming. Laramie, Wyo.

Wyoming Stock Growers. Collection. American Heritage Center. University of Wyoming. Laramie, Wyo.

## UNPUBLISHED GOVERNMENT DOCUMENTS

Fremont County. Treasurer's Tax Receipt Book, 1884, 1886. Lander, Wyo.

Sweetwater County. Tax Assessment Roll, 1875. Sweetwater County Museum. Green River, Wyo.

U.S. Department of Commerce. Bureau of the Census. Ninth Census of the United States, 1870. Wyoming Territory. Schedule 1 (Population), Reel 1748. National Archives. Washington, D.C.

U.S. Department of Commerce. Bureau of the Census. Report on the Statistics of Agriculture in the United States, 1890. Reel 38. National Archives. Washington, D.C.

U.S. Department of Commerce. Bureau of the Census. Tenth Census of the United States, 1880. Sweetwater County, Wyoming Territory. Schedule 1 (Population), Reel T9-1454. National Archives. Washington, D.C.

U.S. Department of Commerce. Bureau of the Census. Tenth Census of the United States, 1880. Wyoming Territory. Schedule 2 (Agriculture). Duke University. Durham, N.C.

U.S. Department of Interior. Bureau of Indian Affairs. Indian Census Rolls, 1885–1940. M595, Reel 498 (Shoshone and Bannock Indian Agency, 1885, 1890–1893, 1895–1899). National Archives. Washington, D.C.

U.S. Department of Interior. Bureau of Indian Affairs. Letters Received by the Office of Indian Affairs, 1824–1880. Wyoming Superintendency, 1869–1880. M234, Reels 953 (1869–1871); 954 (1872–1874); 955 (1875–1877); 956 (1878); 957 (1879); 958 (1880). National Archives. Washington, D.C.

U.S. Department of Interior. Bureau of Indian Affairs. Letters Received by the Office of Indian Affairs, 1881–1907. Irregularly Shaped Papers. Record Group 75. National Archives. Washington, D.C.

U.S. Department of Interior. Bureau of Indian Affairs. Letters Received by the Office of Indian Affairs, 1881–1907. Record Group 75. National Archives. Washington, D.C.

U.S. Department of Interior. Bureau of Indian Affairs. Reports of Inspection of the Field Jurisdictions of the Office of Indian Affairs, 1873–1900. M1070, Reels 58 (Wyoming Superintendency, 1873–1880), 48 (Shoshoni Agency, 1882–1888). National Archives. Washington, D.C.

U.S. Department of Interior. Bureau of Indian Affairs. Special Case File 44 (Fort Washakie Military Reserve). Record Group 75. National Archives. Washington, D.C.

U.S. Department of Interior. Bureau of Indian Affairs. Special Case File 143 (Shoshone Missions and Churches). Record Group 75. National Archives. Washington, D.C.

U.S. Department of Interior. Bureau of Indian Affairs. Special Case File 147 (Land and Allotments). Record Group 75. National Archives. Washington, D.C.

U.S. Department of Interior. Bureau of Indian Affairs. Special Case File 190 (Wind River Irrigation). Record Group 75. National Archives. Washington, D.C.

U.S. Department of Interior. Bureau of Indian Affairs. Special Case File 191 (Shoshone Leases). Record Group 75. National Archives. Washington, D.C.

U.S. Department of Interior. Interior Department Appointment Papers. Wyoming, Shoshone Indian Agent, 1870–1930. M830, Roll 6. National Archives. Washington, D.C.

## PUBLISHED GOVERNMENT DOCUMENTS

*Act of Confirmation. Statutes at Large*, vol. 18, 1874.

*Annual Report of the Commissioner of Indian Affairs for 1851. House Executive Documents.* 32nd Cong., 1st sess., 1851, ser. 636.

*Annual Report of the Commissioner of Indian Affairs for 1855.* Washington: Government Printing Office, 1856.

*Annual Report of the Commissioner of Indian Affairs for 1858. House Executive Documents.* 35th Cong., 2d sess., 1858, ser. 997.

*Annual Report of the Commissioner of Indian Affairs for 1859. Senate Executive Documents.* 36th Cong., 1st sess., 1859, ser. 1023.

*Annual Report of the Commissioner of Indian Affairs for 1864. House Executive Document.* 38th Cong., 2d sess., 1864, ser. 1220.

*Annual Report of the Commissioner of Indian Affairs for 1865. House Executive Document.* 39th Cong., 1st sess., 1865, ser. 1248.

*Annual Report of the Commissioner of Indian Affairs for 1866.* Washington: Government Printing Office, 1867.

*Annual Report of the Commissioner of Indian Affairs for 1867. House Executive Documents.* 40th Cong., 2d sess., 1867, ser. 1326.

*Annual Report of the Commissioner of Indian Affairs for 1869. House Executive Documents.* 41st Cong., 2d sess., 1869, ser. 1414.

*Annual Report of the Commissioner of Indian Affairs for 1873.* Washington: Government Printing Office, 1874.

*Annual Report of the Commissioner of Indian Affairs for 1874.* Washington: Government Printing Office, 1875.

*Annual Report of the Commissioner of Indian Affairs for 1875.* Washington: Government Printing Office, 1876.

*Annual Report of the Commissioner of Indian Affairs for 1876.* Washington: Government Printing Office, 1877.

*Annual Report of the Commissioner of Indian Affairs for 1877.* Washington: Government Printing Office, 1878.

*Annual Report of the Commissioner of Indian Affairs for 1878.* Washington: Government Printing Office, 1879.

*Annual Report of the Commissioner of Indian Affairs for 1879.* Washington: Government Printing Office, 1880.

*Annual Report of the Commissioner of Indian Affairs for 1880.* Washington: Government Printing Office, 1881.

*Annual Report of the Commissioner of Indian Affairs for 1881.* Washington: Government Printing Office, 1882.

*Annual Report of the Commissioner of Indian Affairs for 1882.* Washington: Government Printing Office, 1883.

A*nnual Report of the Commissioner of Indian Affairs for 1883.* Washington: Government Printing Office, 1884.

*Annual Report of the Commissioner of Indian Affairs for 1884.* Washington: Government Printing Office, 1885.

*Annual Report of the Commissioner of Indian Affairs for 1885.* Washington: Government Printing Office, 1886.

*Annual Report of the Commissioner of Indian Affairs for 1886.* Washington: Government Printing Office, 1887.

*Annual Report of the Commissioner of Indian Affairs for 1887.* Washington: Government Printing Office, 1888.

*Annual Report of the Commissioner of Indian Affairs for 1888.* Washington: Government Printing Office, 1889.

*Annual Report of the Commissioner of Indian Affairs for 1889.* Washington: Government Printing Office, 1890.

*Annual Report of the Commissioner of Indian Affairs for 1890.* Washington: Government Printing Office, 1891.

*Annual Report of the Commissioner of Indian Affairs for 1891.* 2 vols. Washington: Government Printing Office, 1892.

*Annual Report of the Commissioner of Indian Affairs for 1892.* Washington: Government Printing Office, 1893.

*Annual Report of the Commissioner of Indian Affairs for 1893.* Washington: Government Printing Office, 1894.

*Annual Report of the Commissioner of Indian Affairs for 1894.* Washington: Government Printing Office, 1895.

*Annual Report of the Commissioner of Indian Affairs for 1896.* Washington: Government Printing Office, 1897.

*Annual Report of the Commissioner of Indian Affairs for 1899.* Washington: Government Printing Office, 1900.

*Annual Report of the Commissioner of Indian Affairs for 1900.* Washington: Government Printing Office, 1901.

*Eleventh Annual Report of the Board of Indian Commissioners for the Year 1879.* Washington: Government Printing Office, 1879.

*Indian Department Appropriation Act. Statutes at Large.* vol. 17, 1873.

*Indian Department Appropriation Act. Statutes at Large.* vol. 17., 1874.

*Indian Department Appropriation Act. Statutes at Large.* vol. 18, 1874.

*Indian Department Appropriation Act. Statutes at Large.* vol. 18, 1875.

*Indian Department Appropriation Act. Statutes at Large.* vol. 19, 1876.

*Indian Department Appropriation Act. Statutes at Large.* vol. 19, 1877.

*Indian Department Appropriation Act. Statutes at Large.* vol. 20, 1878.

*Report of F. W. Lander. Senate Executive Documents.* 35th Cong., 2d sess., 1858, ser. 984.

## PUBLISHED CHURCH DOCUMENTS

*Journal of the Annual Session of the Convocation of the Clergy and Laity of the Missionary Jurisdiction of Colorado, New Mexico, and Wyoming.* Chicago: Knight and Leonard, Printers, 1874.

*Journal of the Eighth Annual Convocation of the Clergy and Laity of the Missionary District of Colorado and Wyoming.* Denver: Rocky Mountain News Printing Co., 1881.

*Journal of the Eleventh Annual Convocation of the Protestant Episcopal Church in the Missionary District of Colorado.* Longmont: Ledger Pub. Co., 1884.

*Journal of the Fifth Annual Convocation of the Clergy and Laity of the Missionary District of Colorado and Wyoming.* Denver: E. Price and Co., 1878.

Journal of the First Annual Convocation of the Missionary Jurisdiction of Boise. Boise: Statesman Printing Co., 1899.

*Journal of the Fourth Annual Convocation of the Clergy and Laity of the Missionary District of Colorado and Wyoming.* Erie, Pa.: Ashby and Vincent, Printers, 1877.

*Journal of the Ninth Annual Convocation of the Clergy and Laity of the Missionary District of Colorado and Wyoming.* Denver: Rocky Mountain News Printing Co., 1882.

*Journal of the Primary Convocation of the Protestant Episcopal Church in the Missionary Jurisdiction of Wyoming.* Chicago: Living Church Co., 1884.

*Journal of the Second Annual Convocation of the Clergy and Laity of the Missionary District of Colorado and Wyoming.* Erie, Pa.: Ashby and Vincent, Printers, 1875.

*Journal of the Second Convocation of the Protestant Episcopal Church in the Missionary Jurisdiction of Wyoming.* Cheyenne: Bristol and Knabe, Printers and Bookbinders, 1885.

*Journal of the Seventh Annual Convocation of the Clergy and Laity of the Missionary District of Colorado and Wyoming.* Denver: Rocky Mountain News Printing Co., 1880.

Journal of the Sixth Annual Convocation of the Clergy and Laity of the Missionary District of Colorado and Wyoming. Denver: Daily Times Steam Printing House and Book Manufactory, 1879.

*Journal of the Tenth Annual Convocation of the Clergy and Laity of the Missionary District of Colorado and Wyoming.* Denver: Rocky Mountain News Printing Co., 1883.

*Journal of the Third Annual Convocation of the Clergy and Laity of the Missionary District of Colorado and Wyoming.* Erie, Pa.: Ashby and Vincent, Printers, 1876.

*Proceedings of the First Annual Convocation of the Missionary Jurisdiction of Wyoming and Idaho.* Laramie: Boomerang Co. Job Print, 1891.

## NEWSPAPERS

*Big Horn County Rustler,* March 26, 1920.

*Cheyenne Daily Leader,* September 7, 1883.

*Frontier Index* (Laramie), April 21, May 26, 1868.

*South Pass News* (South Pass City, Wyo.), September 13; December 14, 21 1870; January 18, 25; February 8; March 1, 29; May 3, 10, 24; September 7, 1871.

*Wyoming State Journal* (Lander), July 27, 1950.

## UNPUBLISHED THESES, DISSERTATIONS, AND MANUSCRIPTS

Eaton, James Winton. "The Wyoming Stock Growers Association: An Application of Davis' and North's Theory of Institutional Change." Ph.D. diss., University of Missouri–Columbia.

Fowler, Donald D. "Cultural Ecology and Culture History of the Eastern Shoshoni Indians." Ph.D. diss., University of Pittsburgh, 1965.

Johnson, Thomas Hoevet. "The Enos Family and Wind River Shoshone Society: A Historical Analysis." Ph.D. diss., University of Illinois at Urbana—Champaign, 1975.

Markley, Elinor R., Beatrice Crofts, and Sharon Kahin, eds. "Walk Softly, This is God's Country: Sixty Six Years on an Indian Reservation." MS obtained from Sharon Kahin.

Wilson, Paul Burns. "Farming and Ranching on the Wind River Indian Reservation." Ph.D. diss., Lincoln: University of Nebraska, 1972.


## BOOKS

Atherton, Lewis. *The Cattle Kings.* Bloomington: University of Indiana Press, 1961.

Bourke, John G. *Mackenzie's Last Fight with the Cheyennes: A Winter Campaign in Wyoming and Montana.* New York: n.p., 1890.

———. *On the Border with Crook.* 2d ed. New York: Charles Scribner's Sons, 1902.

Brown, James S. *Life of a Pioneer.* Salt Lake City: George Q. Cannon and Sons, 1900.

Cook, Reverend Joseph W. *Diary and Letters of the Reverend Joseph W. Cook, Missionary to Cheyenne.* Laramie, Wyo.: Laramie Republican Co., 1919.

Coolidge, Grace. With introduction by George L. Cornell. *Teepee Neighbors.* Boston: The Four Seas Co., 1917. Reprint, Norman: University of Oklahoma Press, 1984.

Cooper, Mrs. Baird C. *The Wind River Reservation, Wyoming.* Hartford: Church Missions Pub. Co., 1914.

David, Robert Beebe. *Finn Burnett: Frontiersman.* Glendale, Calif.: Arthur H. Clark Co., 1937.

De Voto, Bernard, ed. *The Journals of Lewis and Clark.* Boston: Houghton Mifflin Co., 1953.

Dippie, Brian W. *The Vanishing American: White Attitudes and U.S. Indian Policy.* Lawrence: University Press of Kansas, 1982.

Ellison, Robert S. *Fort Bridger: A Brief History.* Cheyenne: Wyoming State Archives, Museums and Historical Dept., 1981.

Erwin, Marie H. *Wyoming Historical Blue Book: A Legal and Political History of Wyoming, 1868–1943.* Denver: Bradford–Robinson Printing Co., 1946.

Ewers, John C. *The Blackfeet: Raiders on the Northwestern Plains.* Norman: University of Oklahoma Press, 1958.

Ferris, Warren Angus. *Life in the Rocky Mountains.* Edited by Paul C. Phillips. Denver: F. A. Rosenstock, Old West Pub. Co., 1940.

Field, Matthew C. *Prairie and Mountain Sketches.* Norman: University of Oklahoma Press, 1957.

Fowler, Loretta. *Arapahoe Politics, 1851–1978: Symbols in Crises of Authority.* Lincoln: University of Nebraska Press, 1982.

———. *Shared Symbols, Contested Meanings: Gros Ventre Culture and History, 1778–1884.* Ithaca, N.Y.: Cornell University Press, 1987.

Frison, George C. *Prehistoric Hunters of the High Plains.* New York: Academic Press, 1978.

———. *Prehistoric Hunters of the High Plains,* 2d ed. San Diego: Academic Press, 1991.

Fuller, E. O., comp. *Report: Wind River Reservation, Wyoming.* N.p., n.d.

Glover, Richard, ed. *David Thompson's Narrative, 1784–1812.* Toronto: The Champlain Society, 1962.

Gowans, Fred R., and Eugene E. Campbell. *Fort Supply: Brigham Young's Green River Experiment.* Provo, Utah: Brigham Young University Press, 1976.

Grinnell, George Bird. *The Fighting Cheyennes.* Norman: University of Oklahoma Press, 1956.

Hafen, LeRoy R., ed. *Mountain Men and Fur Traders of the Far West.* Lincoln: University of Nebraska Press, 1982.

———. *The Mountain Men and the Fur Trade of the Far West.* 10 vols. Glendale, Calif.: Arthur H. Clark, Co., 1965–1972.

Hamilton, William Thomas. *My Sixty Years on the Plains, Trapping, Trading, and Indian Fighting.* Introduction by Donald J. Berthong. Norman: University of Oklahoma Press, 1960.

Harrod, Howard L. *Becoming and Remaining a People: Native American Religions on the Northern Plains.* Tucson: University of Arizona Press, 1995.

Hebard, Grace Raymond. *Washakie: An Account of Indian Resistance of the Covered Wagon and Union Pacific Railroad Invasions of Their Territory.* Cleveland: Arthur H. Clark Co., 1930.

Hoffman, Ronald, and Frederick E. Hoxie, eds. *Native Americans and the Early Republic.* Charlottesville: University Press of Virgina, forthcoming.

Hoxie, Frederick E. *Parading through History: The Making of the Crow Nation in America, 1805–1935.* New York: Cambridge University Press, 1997.

Hultkrantz, Åke. *Belief and Worship in Native North America.* Edited, with an introduction, by Christopher Vecsey. Syracuse, N.Y.: Syracuse University Press, 1981.

———. *Native Religions of North America: The Power of Visions and Fertility.* San Francisco: Harper and Row, Publishers, 1987.

———. *The Religions of the American Indians.* Translated by Monica Setterwall. Berkeley: University of California Press, 1967.

———. *The Study of American Indian Religions.* Edited by Christopher Vecsey. New York: Crossroads Publishing Co., 1983.

Huseas, Marion McMillan. *Sweetwater Gold: Wyoming's Gold Rush, 1867–1871.* Cheyenne: Cheyenne Corral of Westerners International, 1991.

Hyde, George E. *Red Cloud's Folk: A History of the Oglala Sioux Indians.* Norman: University of Oklahoma Press, 1975.

Jorgensen, Joseph G. *The Sun Dance Religion: Power for the Powerless.* Chicago: University of Chicago Press, 1972.

Josephy, Alvin M., Jr. *The Patriot Chiefs: A Chronicle of American Indian Leadership.* New York: Viking Press, 1961.

Kavanagh, Thomas W. *Comanche Political History: An Ethnohistorical Perspective, 1706–1875.* Lincoln : University of Nebraska Press, 1996.

Keller, Morton. *Affairs of State: Public Life in Late Nineteenth Century America.* Cambridge: Harvard University Press, 1977.

Keller, Robert H. *American Protestantism and United States Indian Policy, 1869–82.* Lincoln: University of Nebraska Press, 1983.

Knoll, Mark A. *A History of Christianity in the United States and Canada.* Grand Rapids, Mich.: William B. Eerdman's Pub. Co., 1992.

Larson, T. A. *History of Wyoming.* 2d. ed. Lincoln: University of Nebraska Press, 1978.

———. *Wyoming: A History.* Abridged ed. New York: W. W. Norton and Co., 1984.

Lewis, David Rich. *Neither Wolf nor Dog: American Indians, Environment, and Agrarian Change.* New York: Oxford University Press, 1994.

Madsen, Brigham D. *The Bannock of Idaho.* Caldwell, Idaho: Caxton Printers, Ltd., 1958.

———. *Chief Pocatello: The "White Plume."* Salt Lake City: University of Utah Press, 1986.

———. *The Lemhi: Sacajawea's People.* Caldwell, Idaho: Caxton Printers, Ltd., 1979.

———. *The Shoshoni Frontier and the Bear River Massacre.* Salt Lake City: University of Utah Press, 1985.

Malouf, Carling I., and Åke Hultkrantz. *Shoshone Indians.* New York: Garland Publishing Co., 1974.

Marquis, Thomas B. *The Cheyennes of Montana.* Algonac, Mich.: Reference Publications, Inc., 1978.

Norris, Richard A. *Understanding the Faith of the Church.* San Francisco: Harper and Row, 1979.

Olden, Sarah, Emilia. *Shoshone Folk Lore: As Discovered from the Rev. John Roberts, a Hidden Hero, on the Wind River Indian Reservation in Wyoming.* Milwaukee: Morehouse Publishing Co., 1923.

Oliphant, J. Orin, ed. *William Emsley Jackson's Diary of a Cattle Drive from La Grande, Oregon, to Cheyenne, Wyoming, in 1876.* Fairfield, Wash.: Ye Galleon Press, 1983.

Olson, James C. *Red Cloud and the Sioux Problem.* Lincoln: University of Nebraska Press, 1965.

Pike, James A., and Norman Pittenger. *The Faith of the Church.* Greenwich, Conn.: Seabury Press, 1957.

Platt, Anthony M. *The Child Savers: The Invention of Delinquency.* Chicago: University of Chicago Press, 1969.

Price, Catherine. *The Oglala People, 1841–1879: A Political History*. Lincoln: University of Nebraska Press, 1996.

Prucha, Francis Paul. *American Indian Policy in Crisis: Christian Reformers and the Indian, 1865–1900*. Norman: University of Oklahoma Press, 1976.

——. *The Great Father: The United States Government and the American Indians*. 2 vols. Lincoln: University of Nebraska Press, 1984.

——. *The Great Father: The United States Government and the American Indians*. Abridged ed. Lincoln: University of Nebraska Press, 1986.

Rich, E. E., ed. *Peter Skene Ogden's Snake Country Journals, 1824–1826*. London: Hudson Bay Record Society, 1950.

Roe, Frank Gilbert. *The Indian and the Horse*. Norman: University of Oklahoma Press, 1955.

——. *The North American Buffalo: A Critical Study of the Species in Its Wild State*. Toronto: University of Toronto Press, 1951.

Rollinson, John K. *Wyoming Cattle Trails*. Caldwell, Idaho: Caxton Printers, 1948.

Ross, Marvin C., ed. *The West of Alfred Jacob Miller*. Norman: University of Oklahoma Press, 1967.

Royce, Charles C. *Indian Land Cessions in the United States*. Washington: Government Printing Office, 1900. Reprint. New York: Arno Press, Inc., 1971.

Russell, Osborne. *Journal of a Trapper: Or Nine Years in the Rocky Mountains, 1834–1843*. Boise: Syms-York Co., 1921.

Sahlins, Marshall D. *Stone Age Economics*. Chicago: Aldine-Atherton, Inc., 1972.

——. *Tribesmen*. Englewood Cliffs, N.J.: Prentice-Hall, Inc., 1968.

Secoy, Frank Raymond. *Changing Military Patterns on the Great Plains (Seventeenth through Early Nineteenth Century)*. Monographs of the American Ethnological Society. Locust Valley, N.Y.: J. J. Augustin, 1953.

Shoshone Episcopal Mission. *From Trout Creek to Gravy High: The Boarding School Experience at Wind River*. Exhibit Catalogue, Warm Valley Historical Project, 1992–1993.

Slattery, Charles Lewis. *Felix Reveille Brunot, 1820–1898: A Civilian in the War for the Union, President of the First Board of Indian Commissioners*. New York: Longmans, Green, and Co., 1901.

Smith, Jane F., and Robert M. Kvasnicka, eds. *Indian-White Relations: A Persistent Paradox*. Washington, D.C.: Howard University Press, 1976.

Thwaites, Reuben G., ed. *Original Journals of the Lewis and Clark Expedition*, vols. 2, 4. New York: Dodd, Mead, & Co., 1904.

Trachtenberg, Alan. *The Incorporation of America: Culture and Society in the Gilded Age*. New York: Hill and Wang, 1982.

Trenholm, Virginia Cole and Maurine Carley. *The Shoshonis: Sentinels of the Rockies*. Norman: University of Oklahoma Press, 1964.

Unruh, John D., Jr. *The Plains Across: The Overland Emigrants and the Trans-Mississippi West, 1840–60*. Urbana: University of Illinois Press, Illini Books, 1982.

Utley, Robert M. *The Indian Frontier of the American West, 1846–1890.* Albuquerque: University of New Mexico Press, 1984.

Vander, Judith. *Shoshone Ghost Dance Religion: Poetry Songs and Great Basin Context.* Urbana: University of Illinois Press, 1997.

———. *Song-Prints: The Musical Experience of Five Shoshone Women.* Urbana: University of Illinois Press, 1988 (Illini Books, 1996).

Voget, Fred W. *The Shoshoni-Crow Sun Dance.* Norman: University of Oklahoma Press, 1984.

Walker, Tacetta B. *Stories of Early Days in the Wyoming: The Big Horn Basin.* Casper, Wyo.: Prairie Publishing Co., 1936.

White, Richard. *The Roots of Dependency: Subsistence, Environment, and Social Change among the Choctaws, Pawnees, and Navajos.* Lincoln: University of Nebraska Press, 1983.

Wilson, Elijah N. *The White Indian Boy: The Story of Uncle Nick among the Shoshones.* New York: World Book Co., 1926.

Wolf, William J., ed. *Anglican Spirituality.* Wilton, Conn.: Morehouse-Barlow, Co., 1982.

Woods, Lawrence M. *Wyoming's Big Horn Basin to 1901: A Late Frontier.* Spokane: Arthur H. Clark Co., 1997.

## ARTICLES AND BOOK CHAPTERS

Allen, Charley. "Sam Sing—Laundryman Extraordinary." *Wind River Mountaineer* 1 (January 1985): 7–8.

Bell, Tom. "Edmore LeClair, From Indian Scout to Solid Citizen." *Wind River Mountaineer* 5 (January-March 1989): 4–7.

"Bishop Randall and the Indians." *Spirit of Missions* 38 (December 1873): 756–57.

Brackett, Albert G. "The Shoshonis, or Snake Indians, Their Religion, Superstitions, and Manners." *Annual Report of the Smithsonian Institution* (1879): 328–33.

Calloway, Colin G. "Snake Frontiers: The Eastern Shoshones in the Eighteenth Century." *Annals of Wyoming* 63 (Summer 1991): 82–92.

Delo, David M. "Post Trader, Indian Trader." *Wind River Mountaineer* 2 (October-December 1986): 4–7; 3 (January-March 1987): 4–13.

———. "Settlers Come to the Valley." *Wind River Mountaineer* 3 (July–September 1987): 13–15.

Doyle, Susan Badger. "Indian Perspectives of the Bozeman Trail, 1864–1868." *Montana The Magazine of Western History* 40 (Winter 1990): 56–67.

"Extracts from the Report of the Indian Commission." *Spirit of Missions* 42 (December 1876): 660–63.

"First Annual Report of the Missionary Jurisdiction of Wyoming Territory." *Spirit of Missions* 49 (November–December 1884): 586–89.

Fowler, Don D. "Notes on the Early Life of Chief Washakie." *Annals of Wyoming* 36 (April 1964): 34–42.

Fritz, Henry E. "The Board of Indian Commissioners and Ethnocentric Reform, 1878–1873." In *Indian-White Relations: A Persistent Paradox*, edited by Jane F. Smith and Robert M. Kvasnicka.

"The Genesis of a Town." *Wind River Mountaineer* 8 (April-September 1992): 5–9.

Hart, Sheila. "Edmore LeClaire, Son of a Mountain Man." *Wind River Mountaineer* 5 (January–March 1988): 8–11, reprint from *Lander Evening Post*, February 1, 2, 1929.

Hafen, Leroy R. Introduction to *The Mountain Men and the Fur Trade*, vol. 1, edited by Leroy R. Hafen.

———. "John Robertson ('Jack Robinson')." In *The Mountain Men and the Fur Trade*, vol. 7, edited by Leroy R. Hafen.

Holmer, Richard N. "Prehistory of the Northern Shoshone." *Rendezvous: Idaho State University Journal of Arts and Letters* 26 (1990): 41–59.

Hultkrantz, Åke. "Configurations of Religious Belief among the Wind River Shoshoni." *Ethnos* 11 (1956), 194–215.

———. "The Peril of Visions: Changes of Vision Patterns among the Wind River Shoshoni." *History of Religions* 26 (August 1986), 34–46.

———. "The Shoshones in the Rocky Mountain Area." In *Shoshone Indians*, edited by Carling I. Malouf and Åke Hultkrantz.

———. "Shoshoni Indians on the Plains: An Appraisal of the Documentary Evidence." *Zeitschrift für Ethnologie* 93 (1968): 49–72.

———. "Yellow Hand, Chief and Medicine-man among the Eastern Shoshoni." *Proceedings of the 38th International Congress of Americanists* 2 (1968): 293–301.

Ismert, Cornelius M. "James Bridger." In *Mountain Men and Fur Traders of the Far West*, edited by Leroy R. Hafen.

James, Rhett S., ed. "Brigham Young—Chief Washakie Indian Farm Negotiations." *Annals of Wyoming* 39 (October 1967): 245–56.

Keller, Robert H., Jr. "Episcopal Reformers and Affairs at Red Cloud Agency, 1870–1876." *Nebraska History* 68 (Fall 1987), 116–26.

King, Claude F. "A Narrative from Shoshone Agency [27 April 1883]." *Wind River Mountaineer* 3 (April–June 1987): 31.

Lowie, Robert H. "Dances and Societies of the Plains Shoshone." *Anthropological Papers of the American Museum of Natural History* 11 (pt. 10, 1915): 802–35.

———. "Notes on Shoshonean Ethnography." *Anthropological Papers of the American Museum of Natural History* 20 (pt. 3, 1924): 185–312.

———. "The Northern Shoshone." *Anthropological Papers of the American Museum of Natural History* 2 (pt. 2, 1909): 165–306.

———. "Plains Indian Age–Societies: Historical and Comparative Summary." *Anthropological Papers of the American Museum of Natural History* 11 (pt. 13, 1916): 877–984.

Mathisen, Jean. "Tracks and Traces." *Wind River Mountaineer* 1 (April–June 1985): 19–20.

Moore, J. K., Jr. "Post Trader and Indian Trader Tokens." *Annals of Wyoming* 27 (October 1955): 130–35.

Morgan, Dale L., ed. "Washakie and the Shoshoni: A Selection of Documents from the Records of the Utah Superintendency of Indian Affairs (pt. 1). *Annals of Wyoming* 25 (July 1953): 141–88.

———. "Washakie and the Shoshoni," pt. 2. *Annals of Wyoming* 26 (January 1954): 65–80.

———. "Washakie and the Shoshoni," pt. 3. *Annals of Wyoming* 26 (July 1954): 141–90.

———. "Washakie and the Shoshoni," pt. 4. *Annals of Wyoming* 27 (April 1955): 61–88.

———. "Washakie and the Shoshoni," pt. 5. *Annals of Wyoming* 27 (October 1955): 198–220.

———. "Washakie and the Shoshoni," pt. 6. *Annals of Wyoming* 28 (April 1956): 80–93.

———. "Washakie and the Shoshoni," pt. 7. *Annals of Wyoming* 28 (October 1956): 193–207.

———. "Washakie and the Shoshoni," pt. 8. *Annals of Wyoming* 29 (April 1957): 86–102.

———. "Washakie and the Shoshoni," pt. 9. *Annals of Wyoming* 29 (October 1957): 195–227.

———. "Washakie and the Shoshoni," pt. 10. *Annals of Wyoming* 30 (April 1958): 53–89.

Mumey, Nolie. "James Baker." In *The Mountain Men and the Fur Trade*, vol. 3, edited by Leroy R. Hafen.

Murphy, Robert F. and Yolanda Murphy. "Shoshone-Bannock Subsistence and Society." *Anthropological Records* 16, no.7 (1960): 304–14.

"Neikok, the Shoshone Interpreter." *Annals of Wyoming* 8 (October 1931): 561–62.

"Ninth Annual Report of the Missionary Bishop of Colorado and Wyoming." *Spirit of Missions* 47 (November–December 1882): 444–48.

"Our Missionary to the Shoshones." *Spirit of Missions* 48 (March 1883): 172–73.

"Personal Mention." *Wind River Mountaineer* 1 (January 1985): 4–5.

"Pioneer Profiles: The Amoretti Family." *Wind River Mountaineer* 2 (January-March 1986): 2.

"Pioneer Profiles: Dr. James Irwin." *Wind River Mountaineer* 5 (July-September 1989): 2, 24.

"Pioneer Profiles: The Lamoreaux Family." *Wind River Mountaineer* 1 (April-June 1985): 2.

"Pioneer Profiles: Major Noyes Baldwin." *Wind River Mountaineer* 1 (July-September 1985): 2.

"Pioneer Profiles: Worden P. Noble." *Wind River Mountaineer* 3 (April-June 1987): 2.

"Report from Bishop Spalding." *Spirit of Missions* 41 (January 1876): 8–18.

"Report from John Roberts." *Spirit of Missions* 49 (March 1884): 125–26.

"Report from John Roberts." *Spirit of Missions* 49 (June 1884): 281.

"Report from John Roberts." *Spirit of Missions* 50 (July 1885): 363–364.

"Report from John Roberts." *Spirit of Missions* 50 (September 1885): 467.

"Report from Sherman Coolidge." *Spirit of Missions* 50 (August 1885): 425.

"Report from Sherman Coolidge." *Spirit of Missions* 61 (March 1896): 118.

Roberts, John. "Letter (13 August 1885)." *Spirit of Missions* 50 (October 1855): 531.

Schilz, Thomas F. "Robes, Rum, and Rifles: Indian Middlemen in the Northern Plains Fur Trade." *Montana The Magazine of Western History* 40 (Winter 1990): 2–13.

Schrems, Suzanne H. "Teaching School on the Western Frontier." *Montana The Magazine of Western History* 37 (Summer 1987): 54–63.

Shimkin, D. B. "Childhood and Development among the Wind River Shoshone." *Anthropological Records* 5, no.5 (1947): 289–325.

———. "Comanche Shoshone Words of Acculturation." *Journal of the Steward Anthropological Society* 11 (1980): 195–248.

———. "Dynamics of Recent Wind River Shoshone Ethnography." *American Anthropologist* n.s. 44 (1942), 451–62.

———. "Shoshone-Comanche Origins and Migrations." *Proceedings of the Sixth Pacific Science Congress* 5 (1940): 17–25.

———. "Uto-Aztecan Kinship Terms." *American Anthropologist* 43 (1941): 223–45.

———. "Wind River Shoshone Ethnogeography." *Anthropological Records* 5, no. 4 (1947): 245–88.

———. "The Wind River Shoshone Sun Dance." *Smithsonian Institution: Bureau of American Ethnology Bulletin* 151 (1953): 397–484.

St. Clair, H. H., II, and R. H. Lowie. "Shoshone and Comanche Folk Tales." *Journal of American Folk-Lore* 22 (July-September 1909): 265–82.

Steward, Julian H. "Basin-Plateau Aboriginal Sociopolitical Groups." *Smithsonian Institution Bureau of American Ethnology Bulletin* 120 (1938).

Swagerty, William R. "Marriage and Settlement Patterns of Rocky Mountain Trappers and Traders." *Western Historical Quarterly* 21 (April 1980): 159–80.

Trennert, Robert A. "Educating Indian Girls at Nonreservation Boarding Schools, 1878–1920." *Western Historical Quarterly* 13 (July 1982): 271–90.

Williams, P. L. "Personal Recollections of Washakie, Chief of the Shoshones." *Utah Historical Quarterly* 1 (October 1928): 100–106.

Wilson, Richard H. "The Indian Treaty of 1896." *Annals of Wyoming* 8 (October 1931): 539–45.

Wood, W. Raymond. "An Introduction to the History of the Fur Trade on the Northern Plains." *North Dakota History* 61 (Summer 1994): 2–6.

Wright, Geneva Ensign. "Wind River Mission." *Ensign* 12 (August 1982): 28–34.

### LECTURES AND PERSONAL COMMUNICATIONS

Lowendorf, Lawrence. Personal communication, February 17, 1997.

Tinker, George. "God, Gods, Goddesses and Mystery in Native American Religious Traditions." Religious Studies Speakers Series, Spring 1993 (May 4, 1993). University of Wyoming. Laramie, Wyo.

Smoak, Gregory E. "Band Chiefs and Head Chiefs: The Limits of Shoshonean Political Power." Presented at the Western History Association annual meeting, October 1997. St. Paul, Minn.

White, Richard. "The Father Image in White/Indian Relationships." Presented at U.S. Capitol Historical Society, February 1992. Washington, D.C.


### COMPUTER SOFTWARE

Master Cook II. Austin, Tex.: Arion Software, Inc., 1993.

# Index